SECOND EDITION

TEACHER'S HANDBOOK

Contextualized Language Instruction

Judith L. Shrum
Virginia Polytechnic

Eileen W. Glisan
Indiana University of Pennsylvania

 **Heinle & Heinle**
Thomson Learning™

Australia • Canada • Denmark • Japan • Mexico • New Zealand • Philippines •
Puerto Rico • Singapore • South Africa • Spain • United Kingdom • United States

The publication of *Teacher's Handbook,* Second Edition, was directed by the Heinle & Heinle College Foreign Language Publishing Team:

Wendy Nelson, Editorial Director
Stephen Frail, Marketing Development Director
Esther Marshall, Senior Production Services Coordinator
Helen Richardson, Developmental Editor

Also participating in the publication of this program were:

Publisher: Vincent P. Duggan
Production Editor: Lisa Cutler
Associate Marketing Development Director: Kristen Murphy-LoJacono
Manufacturing Coordinator: Judith Caldwell
Composition: Christine E. Wilson, IBC
Cover Designer: Carole Rollins
Printer: R.R. Donnelley

Library of Congress Cataloging-in-Publication Data

Shrum, Judith L.
    Teacher's Handbook : contextualized language instruction / Judith L. Shrum, Eileen W. Glisan.
    p.   cm.
    Includes bibliographical references and index.
    ISBN 0-8384-0879-6 (pbk.)
    1. language and languages—Study and teaching Handbooks, manuals, etc. I. Glisan, Eileen W.
    II. Title.
    P51.S48 2000
    418'.007—dc21   99-31821
                                                           CIP

For permission to use material from this text, contact us:
    web   www.thomsonrights.com
    fax   1-800-730-2215
    phone   1-800-730-2214

Printed in the United States of America

ISBN: 0-8384-08796

1 2 3 4 5   02 01 00 99

CONTENTS

CREDITS

We wish to thank the authors, publishers, and holders of copyright for their permission to reprint the following:

Courtesy of ACTFL: pp. 68, 173, 174, 180, 192, 193, 194, 229, 275, 280

Courtesy of *ACTFL Foreign Language Annals:* pp. 115, 116, 126, 327–329, 338–339, 349

Courtesy of Dr. Bonnie Adair-Hauck: p. 10

Reprinted by permission of Addison Wesley Longman: pp. 228, 230, 244

Courtesy of Dr. James E. Alatis: p. 261

Courtesy of Dr. Janis Antonek: p. 241

"Cajun Telephone Stomp Song from Cajun Conja", courtesy of Michael

Doucit/Rhino Records and Orange Sunrise/Dosay Publishing: p. 167

Courtesy of The Center on Learning, Assessment & School Structure: pp. 302, 303

Courtesy of The Council for Exceptional Children: p. 273

Courtesy of Professor Rick Donato: pp. 56–57, 157

Courtesy of Fairfax County Public Schools: pp. 254–255, 267–268

Courtesy of Foreign Language Instruction in the Elementary School by Helena

Anderson-Curtain and Carol Ann Pesola by Addison Wesley Longman (1994): pp. 82–83

Courtesy of Dr. Judith Liskin-Gasparro: p. 301

Courtesy of McGraw-Hill, Inc.: pp. 52–55, 236-238

Courtesy of *The Modern Language Journal:* pp. 109, 127, 277

Courtesy of Northeast Conference on the Teaching Foreign Languages: p. 80

Courtesy of NSFLEP: pp. 30, 32, 49, 107, 122

Used with permission of NTC/Contemporary Publishing Group, Inc.: pp. 85, 257, 336

Courtesy of Dr. June K. Phillips: p. 296

Courtesy of the Pittsburgh Public Schools (1992): pp. 183, 184, 185

Courtesy of Southern Conference on Language Teaching: pp. 234, 235

Courtesy of Dr. Marjorie Tussig: pp. 232–234

ACKNOWLEDGMENTS

Following the gratifying response to the first edition of *Teacher's Handbook,* we hope this second edition is as useful to those who have influenced us: our students, our colleagues, our publisher, and our families. We never have been able to do a second edition by simply "redlining" the parts to be changed from the first, and certainly, the changes in our profession between the two editions of this work required extensive re-thinking and adjustment. Nevertheless, we are still influenced by Dr. Robert Small and the teachers and students whose work became part of the case studies presented here. Some of these experiences are our own, while others are those we have observed during more than a half-century of combined teaching and research in language education. We hope that the case studies adequately reflect the valiant efforts of good teachers.

Again, in this edition we are grateful to Bonnie Adair-Hauck (University of Pittsburgh), Richard Donato (University of Pittsburgh), and Philomena Cumo (World Language Consultant, Pittsburgh, Pennsylvania) for their detailed application of story-based approaches to language teaching. We humbly thank Dr. Judith Liskin-Gasparro (University of Iowa), Dr. Robert Terry (University of Richmond), Leona LeBlanc (Florida State University) and Dr. Richard Donato (University of Pittsburgh) who, as reviewers, gave the text more than a simple check, often providing insights and suggestions beyond our expectations.

Our colleagues at our respective universities, teachers and students with whom we have worked, also provided the inspiration, the classroom laboratory, some of the materials, and the reasons for reflection, both as we wrote the book and as we tested concepts. We hope they will see themselves in the teach and reflect sections, in the case studies, and on the web page.

We are grateful to our editors at Heinle and Heinle Publishers. First, Wendy Nelson helped launch the new edition with the support of Vince Duggan. Beatrix Mellauner provided the impetus for our early revision efforts, and Helen Richardson helped us carry it through, also completing the web site for the book. Helen's supervision, with gentle prodding and humor, was much appreciated. Esther Marshall and Lisa Cutler supervised a strong production staff who turned the book out in less time than expected. Marianne Phinney's contribution in technological matters could not be matched. We are also pleased with the fine copy edit provided by Susan Lake.

Finally, we wish to thank our families for the role they played in maintaining our mental stability, giving up family time, and providing encouragement. Among those we wish to thank for such generous gifts are Elaine Shrum, Roy, Nina and Alexander Glisan.

Judith Shrum
*Virginia Polytechnic Institute
and State University*

Eileen W. Glisan
*Indiana University
of Pennsylvania*

PREFACE

meaning = "the thing one intends to convey, especially by language"
context = "the circumstances surrounding an act or event"
(Merriam Webster, 1995)

Teacher's Handbook was designed with the philosophy that the purpose of language use is to convey meaning in a variety of contexts. The central theme of the text is the contextualization of language instruction. Language that is introduced and taught in meaningful contexts enables the learner to acquire competency in using language for real-world communicative purposes. Integrated language instruction allows learners to approach the learning task by combining the skills of listening, speaking, reading, and writing in communication and by accessing their knowledge of culture and their background knowledge. The *Standards for Foreign Language Learning* (National Standards in Foreign Language Education Project, 1996) have brought to the forefront a renewed focus on context and content as we ask the question: What should students know and be able to do with another language? Each chapter of *Teacher's Handbook* assists language professionals as they develop a contextualized approach to language teaching that is based on meaningful language use, real-world communication, interaction among language learners, and learning of new information. The teaching examples and case studies in *Teacher's Handbook* offer a broad perspective of diverse teaching circumstances in elementary, middle/intermediate/junior high schools, high schools, and beyond. Further, the teaching examples are offered for various languages to show that the principles underlying contextualized instruction are constant for the many age groups represented and the languages taught.

It is common to hear language professionals and practicing teachers talk about the "basics" of instruction. This view of teaching, we believe, is problematic for several reasons. First, defining the basics is often arbitrary, based on professional experience and personal style of and preference for teaching. Second, if we knew what made up the basics of teaching, research would stop; there would no longer be a need to investigate how students learn languages in classrooms. Finally, what is considered basic in teaching and learning languages may differ drastically from one theoretical approach to another (see Chapter 1). For example, those who subscribe to an input processing perspective might consider the basics to be listening comprehension. For those who follow an interactionist approach, the basics might be considered group work and information-exchange tasks. For those who consider language learning to consist of knowing rules and vocabulary, the basics may be defined as vocabulary lists and pattern drills. The philosophy of *Teacher's Handbook* is that the language profession needs an openness to new ideas, research findings, and an ever expanding and emerging repertoire of practices that evolve as we discover more about teaching and learning foreign languages in today's classrooms.

What's New in the Second Edition?

While the basic pedagogical support within the structure of *Teacher's Handbook* has been maintained in the second edition, there are seven principal changes:

1. The theoretical base of each chapter has been updated to include more recent research and ways to use these findings to help shape classroom instruction. One example is the fuller treatment provided of sociocultural theory as it applies to language learning and instruction.

2. *The Standards for Foreign Language Learning* (National Standards in Foreign Language Education Project 1996) have been incorporated as a thread that links the theory and teaching applications presented throughout the text. After the initial presentation of these standards in Chapter 2, each subsequent chapter addresses key aspects of the standards that relate to the particular theme being explored.

3. Where appropriate, case studies have been revised or replaced with new, more engaging ones.

4. "Call-out boxes" have been added in the text to highlight key concepts and terms and to help the reader make connections to concepts explored in previous chapters. There are two types of call-out boxes: (a) the *key icon* signals an important concept or term, and (b) the *question mark icon* signals a question that will elicit knowledge and insights acquired in previous chapters.

5. The Appendix has been expanded and moved to **http://thandbook.heinle.com** to include examples of actual products developed by teachers to help them relate their professional work to their communities and to their school systems. For example, *Celebrate Diversity: A Handbook for Classroom Teachers of Limtied English Proficient Students*, by Pamela Neate, is an orientation packet for parents developed by a Roanoke County (Virgina) teacher. The packet explains how the ESL classroom helps build community in the U.S. while preserving students' native languages and cultural values.

6. New to the second edition of *Teacher's Handbook* is a Web site designed to be an invaluable teacher resource. Go to **http://thandbook.heinle.com** to download one of the 70 appendices, post questions to the bulletin board, view a video case study, or link to other professional resources.

7. Several new themes have been introduced: interactional competence theory; teaching heritage language learners; the importance of motivation and anxiety in language learning; authentic assessment (including the use of portfolios); block scheduling; and the evaluation and selection of textbook programs.

What Strengths of the First Edition Have Been Maintained?

Teacher's Handbook is designed especially for the teacher who is about to start her/his career in teaching foreign languages at the K-12 levels. It is also suited for more experienced teachers who are searching for an update in current theory and practice as well as for those who are returning to the classroom after an absence from teaching.

Teacher's Handbook enables foreign language teachers to use current theories about learning and teaching as a basis for reflection and practice. Teachers are active decision makers who use opportunities to apply theory through observing classroom interaction, designing and teaching their own lessons, and making appropriate decisions in a wide variety of situations that confront them daily. As developing foreign language teachers reflect upon their teaching and make decisions, they use many information sources: competence in the second language and culture; knowledge of how the curriculum is designed and implemented; application of subject knowledge to actual teaching; application of research findings to classroom teaching; understanding of the power that technology can have in a fully articulated language program; clinical experience; and knowledge of the means by which teaching effectiveness is examined within the school context (Lange, 1990; Schrier, 1993). Accordingly, *Teacher's Handbook* presents theoretical findings concerning key aspects of language teaching, together with observational episodes, micro-teaching situations, and case studies in order to assist beginning teachers as they develop their teaching approaches and experienced teachers as they update their theoretical knowledge and teaching practices.

Teacher's Handbook assists teachers as they begin their journey toward accomplished teaching by basing their learning, teaching, and reflecting on the five propositions established by the National Board for Professional Teaching Standards:

- Teachers are committed to students and their learning.
- Teachers know the subjects they teach and how to teach those subjects to students.
- Teachers are responsible for managing and monitoring student learning.
- Teachers think systematically about their practice and learn from experience.
- Teachers are members of learning communities.

(National Board for Professional Teaching Standards, 1994, pp. 6–8)

The philosophy of *Teacher's Handbook* reflects Freeman's *interpretist* view of teaching that is founded in the daily operation of thinking and acting in context; i.e., "knowing what to do" (Freeman, 1996, p. 98). Teachers learn to interpret their worlds (e.g., their subject matter, their classroom context, and the people in it) and to use these interpretations to act and react appropriately and effectively. Knowing how to teach does not simply involve knowing how to do things in the classroom, but rather it involves a cognitive dimension that connects thought with activity. This contextual know-how is acquired over time and its interpretations bring about effective classroom practice (Freeman, 1996, p. 99). Accordingly, novice and experienced teachers using *Teacher's Handbook* will find structured and open-ended opportunities to observe classroom teaching and to plan and conduct micro-teaching lessons, all in light of the theory and information discussed in each chapter. A variety of case studies for K-16 describe the reality of actual teachers and learners, sometimes in support of current research findings, sometimes adding puzzling contradictions to current research, but always enriching the interpretive experience of teaching. Related activities provide interesting opportunities to investigate and discuss effective classroom practice. Indeed, novice and experienced teachers can strengthen their individual approaches to teaching by observing, investigating, discussing ideas, teaching, and relating these activities to one another.

The flexible nature of *Teacher's Handbook* offers the possibility for a number of uses: as a primary methodology textbook used with other supplementary information and materials provided by the instructor; as a reference book; as an introduction to professional foreign/second language teacher education; and as a practical follow-up to courses in the historical and theoretical knowledge base of foreign/second language acquisition. Methodology instructors will be able to link specific activities to the sequence of their syllabus or related textbook by using the index that lists topics along with their corresponding micro-teaching activities and case studies.

Organization of *Teacher's Handbook*

Teacher's Handbook consists of twelve chapters: the first chapters present topics of a more general nature, and later chapters proceed to more specific technique-oriented issues. Chapter 1 explores the role of contextualized input, output, and interaction in the language learning process including a presentation of key theoretical frameworks that focus on the importance of meaning and learner engagement in acquiring language. In Chapter 1, the Observe and Reflect section will help teachers think about language learning and teaching as natural processes occurring in a nonschool environment. Chapter 2 examines an integrative approach to language instruction in which language is presented and taught in meaningful contexts, consistent with the *Standards for Foreign Language Learning* (SFLL). An overview of the standards framework in this chapter will be followed by specific ways to match activities and materials to the standards in subsequent chapters. In Chapter 3, teachers will learn how to organize content and plan for integrated instruction by means of long- and short-range planning that addresses standards-based goals. Suggestions are offered for using authentic input and content to organize instruction and to engage students in the learning process.

Special attention is given in Chapters 4 and 5 to foreign/second language learners in elementary and middle/intermediate/junior high schools. The unique cognitive and maturational characteristics of learners at these two levels respond best to particular approaches and strategies. An approach utilized with older adolescents, for example, may be inappropriate for young children. However, as will be highlighted throughout the chapters, many techniques can be adapted for use across instructional levels. The information in Chapters 4 and 5 is introduced in terms of the interaction between learning and children's developmental stages, the possible effects of maturity on language learning, and implications for teaching. Teachers will explore the cognitive and maturational differences between the elementary and middle school child and the adolescent learner and develop lessons appropriate to these cognitive levels. Ways of connecting learning across disciplines and grade levels are explored as the Connections goal area is addressed in Chapter 4. In Chapter 5, the Cultures goal area is explored in terms of the products-practices-perspectives framework.

Chapters 6–9 offer many opportunities for teachers to integrate the teaching of grammar, listening, reading, speaking, and writing, and to address the standards, all within real language contexts and various levels of instruction. Chapter 6 presents ideas for developing listening and reading skills through the use of authentic input and building of strategies, especially as they relate to the Interpretive mode of the Communication goal area. In

Chapter 7, teachers explore an approach for contextualizing grammar instruction through the use of story-based and guided participatory teaching using the PACE Model. In Chapter 8, teachers explore strategies for teaching speaking through meaningful contexts and opportunities for classroom interaction and the Interpersonal mode of the Communications goal area. Chapter 9 presents ideas for integrating writing into language instruction through techniques reflecting the Interpersonal and Presentational modes of the Communication goal area, such as writing across the curriculum, process-oriented writing, journal writing, and peer editing

Chapter 10 presents ideas for how teachers might handle factors concerning student diversity that affect classroom language learning, such as learning styles, multiple intelligences, and learning disabilities. Addressing the Communities goal area, teachers will explore strategies for helping students who are from a variety of cultural, ethnic, and racial backgrounds, and those who have been labeled as being "at risk" or "gifted," to use language to connect with target-language communities. In Chapter 11, teachers explore various alternatives for evaluating learner progress, including authentic assessment, portfolios, and other contextualized test formats and techniques that go beyond paper-and-pencil tests. Finally, Chapter 12 illustrates the role of technology in integrating language and standards within a communicative, contextualized teaching approach.

Chapter Organization

Each chapter of *Teacher's Handbook* is organized into three sections:

1. *Conceptual Orientation.* This section grounds teaching practices in a valid body of research and theoretical knowledge. It briefly describes the theoretical principles underlying the language learning observation, teaching tasks, and case studies presented later in the chapter. The section is a summary of what is known about topics in language teaching and includes references to the original research sources for additional in-depth study or review.

2. *Observe and Reflect/Teach and Reflect.* The Observe and Reflect (Chapter 1) and Teach and Reflect (all subsequent chapters) sections highlight practical elements of learning how to teach. Chapter 1 contains two guided observations and subsequent chapters contain two teaching episodes. Each observation or micro-teaching situation integrates the theoretical orientation to give novice teachers an opportunity to implement pedagogically sound teaching techniques within the environment of a methods class. These micro-teaching situations can also be useful for experienced teachers attempting to learn new techniques. Discussion questions following each teaching or observation situation will help teachers integrate certain teaching techniques into personal teaching approaches.

3. *Discuss and Reflect.* This section provides two case studies presenting *non-fictitious* situations actually experienced by foreign language teachers at various levels of instruction. The case studies offer teachers the opportunity to link the theoretically grounded practices explored in the first two sections of each chapter with the reality of teaching circumstances found in schools. Every day foreign language teachers face challenges like those presented in the case studies, challenges that may arise out of

mismatches among teaching goals, learner preparedness, and academic tasks, or out of institutional goals that are inconsistent with teaching goals. The Discuss and Reflect section includes two types of cases: those that present teaching situations that support the theoretical bases featured in the chapter and those that present problematic teaching situations that are inconsistent with the theory and rationale of the chapter. The cases present the information necessary to enable teachers to read the case and the referenced materials and to prepare a resolution of the case for class discussion. Often the cases include many details about teachers and/or teaching situations so that readers might decide which details contribute the most to resolving the case.

Case Study Pedagogy. The case study approach was recommended by the Task Force on Teaching as a Profession in their report entitled *A Nation Prepared: Teachers for the 21st Century* (Carnegie Corporation, 1986). The case study "focuses attention on a single entity, usually as it exists in its naturally occurring environment," and provides the basis for three levels of analysis and reflection (Johnson, 1992, p. 75). First, readers are given maximum guidance as they reflect upon the situations and attempt to analyze them. In the first several chapters of *Teacher's Handbook* , teachers are given a list of alternatives that represent plausible solutions to the problem or challenge presented in the teaching situation. The class discussion of each alternative assists readers in developing their own approaches to the case. In some chapters, addtional information is presented, as in Chapter 3, where comparisons of block scheduling designs are given as part of the reflective practice of novice teachers facing a variety of scheduling arrangements. In addition to the two case studies for each chapter, the web site contains a case study relating to the use of writing assistant technology.

Second, *Teacher's Handbook* users are encouraged to collaborate with their peers and the instructor as they discuss the alternatives and/or the development of their own approaches to the situations. Sharing ideas within the classroom greatly facilitates the problem-solving process and empowers teachers in the decision-making process. Teachers are also encouraged to consult other referenced works for additional information that will assist them in formulating sound approaches to the case development. *Teacher's Handbook* users may choose from among the suggested references or consult others recommended by their instructor.

Third, as readers become increasingly familiar with case study exploration, they are asked to assume greater responsibility for developing their own solutions to the problems and challenges presented in the cases on the basis of the information provided in the chapter, the class discussions, and the previously acquired knowledge and experience. *Teacher's Handbook* is designed to be used as a practical reference, a reflective planning notebook. Space is provided for notes and suggestions are offered for writing plans and thoughts as a springboard for discussion. These features personalize *Teacher's Handbook* for each user and encourage reflection in writing. Thus, the entire process leads teachers to develop their own problem-solving abilities while preparing them to reflect on their own teaching and classroom situations.

Additional Resources

The *Teacher's Handbook* Web site at **http://thandbook.heinle.com** contains a collection of useful materials and sources of information that foreign language teachers use and consult regularly:

- the *ACTFL Proficiency Guidelines*
- a list of sources for materials and information
- a list of professional organizations and agencies
- a list of professional publications
- a set of performance standards for foreign language teachers
- an instructional evaluation form used in school districts
- a contract or letter of expectation for use by learner teachers and cooperating teachers or between peer coaches and/or mentors
- other supporting material for *Teacher's Handbook* chapters

References

Carnegie Corporation. (1986). *A nation prepared: Teachers for the 21st century.* New York: Carnegie Corporation.

Freeman, D. (1996). Redefining the relationship between research and what teachers know. In K. M. Bailey & D. Nunan (Eds.), *Voices from the language classroom: Qualitative research in second language education* (pp. 88-115). Cambridge: Cambridge University Press.

Johnson, D. M. (1992). *Approaches to research in second language learning.* White Plains, NY: Longman.

Lange, D. (1990). A blueprint for a teacher development program. In J. Richards & D. Nunan (Eds.), *Second language teacher education* (pp. 245-268). Cambridge: Cambridge University Press.

Merriam Webster, Inc. (1995). *Webster's new American dictionary.* New York: Smithmark Publishers.

National Board for Professional Teaching Standards. (1994). *What teachers should know and be able to do.* Washington, DC: NBPTS.

National Standards in Foreign Language Education Project. (1996). *Standards for foreign language learning: Preparing for the 21st century.* Yonkers, NY: National Standards in Foreign Language Education Project.

Schrier, L. L. (1993). Prospects for the professionalization of foreign language teaching. In G. Guntermann (Ed.), *Developing language teachers for a changing world,* The ACTFL Foreign Language Education Series (pp. 105-123). Lincolnwood, IL: National Textbook.

CHAPTER *1*

Understanding the Role of Contextualized Input, Output, and Interaction in Language Learning

**thandbook.
heinle.com**

C hapter 1 presents a summary of several major theories that attempt to account for the role of contextualized input, output, and interaction in the language learning process. A framework based on sociocultural theory is posited in an effort to acknowledge that language learning processes are as much social as they are cognitive. Since only the key ideas concerning these theories are provided here, you may want to consult the references included at the end of the chapter in order to explore them in further detail.

In this chapter you will learn about:

- competence vs. performance
- communicative competence
- Krashen's Input Hypothesis
- input processing
- Variable Competence Model
- Long's Interaction Hypothesis
- negotiation of meaning

- interlanguage theory
- Swain's Output Hypothesis
- sociocultural theory
- Vygotsky's Zone of Proximal Development
- mediation
- interactional competence
- affect and motivation

Observe and Reflect: Observing a Child Interacting in Her/His Own Language; Observing a Beginning Language Class
- **Case Study 1: Creating Real Conversational Models**
- **Case Study 2: Conducting a Cooperative Learning Task**

Conceptual Orientation

In recent years, research in second language acquisition (SLA)[1] has provided the field of language teaching with new insights into the nature of language learning (Ellis, 1997; Hall,

---

1. See the entire Volume 81(3) of *The Modern Language Journal*, Fall 1997, for a series of articles on SLA.

1997, 1999; Schulz, 1991; VanPatten & Cadierno, 1993). Ellis suggests that SLA researchers can make their work relevant to language pedagogy by (1) making the research accessible and understandable to teachers; (2) using the research to construct theories that can then be applied to teaching; (3) conducting research with real learners in real classrooms; and (4) engaging teachers in researching their own classrooms (Ellis, 1977, pp. 33–36). By studying SLA research, teachers are able to examine critically the principles upon which they base foreign language instruction. In your reading of the research, you will often encounter the term *foreign language learning* to refer to formal classroom instruction outside of the geographical region where it is commonly spoken, and s*econd language acquisition* used to refer to acquiring another language within one of the regions where the language is commonly spoken. However, in our discussion, we will use the term *language learning* to refer to the process of learning a language other than the native language in either a natural or classroom setting. The term *target language* is used to refer to the language of instruction in the classroom.

Communicative Competence

What does it mean to "know" a language?[2] In the 1960s Chomsky (1965) distinguished between "competence," the intuitive knowledge of rules of grammar and syntax and of how the linguistic system of a language operates, and "performance," the individual's ability to produce language. In this view, language production results from the creative use of a learned set of linguistic rules. During the 1970s, Chomsky's definition was expanded by several linguists and researchers to a broader notion of "communicative competence," or the ability to function in a communicative setting by using not only grammatical knowledge but also gestures and intonation, strategies for making oneself understood, and risk-taking in attempting communication (Campbell & Wales, 1970; Hymes, 1972; Savignon, 1972). Canale and Swain (1980) further proposed that communicative competence includes (1) grammatical competence: the use of appropriate grammar, vocabulary, and pronunciation; (2) sociolinguistic competence: the use of style, register, and intonation in appropriate contexts and settings; (3) discourse competence: the ability to combine language elements to show cohesion in form and coherence of thought; and (4) strategic competence: the use of verbal and nonverbal communication strategies, such as gestures and circumlocution, to compensate for unknown language.

Role of Input in Language Learning

As early as Chomsky's (1965) research, the role of input in the language acquisition process was acknowledged. Chomsky (1965) maintained that children are born with a special ability to process language through an innate "language acquisition device" (LAD). This device is thought to contain the principles that are universal to all languages. When the child attends to language input (i.e., notices certain features of the language s/he hears), the LAD is activated and the child is able to match the innate rules to the language structures in the environment.[3] The research clearly indicates that both first and second

---

2. Chapter 2 presents a historical account of approaches to language instruction.

3. In more recent research, the innate set of universal principles is referred to as *Universal Grammar* (White, 1989).

language learners need large amounts of contextualized, meaningful input in order to acquire language. Children acquire their first language by hearing it spoken by family, friends, and others in a variety of communicative events and by interacting with others in activities such as games and storytelling. Second language learners who have opportunities to actively understand natural language, as in face-to-face conversation, acquire language more quickly and more successfully than learners exposed exclusively to exercises that focus on structure alone (Lightbown, 1985). Over the last two decades, much work has been done in examining how input contributes to language learning. Several major theories dealing with the role of input are presented below.

❐ Krashen's Input Hypothesis

Perhaps the most widely known and controversial theory is Krashen's (1982) "Monitor Model," which posits five hypotheses:

1. *the acquisition-learning hypothesis:* Acquisition (a subconscious "picking up" of rules characteristic of the L1 acquisition process), not learning (a conscious focus on knowing and applying rules), leads to spontaneous, unplanned communication.

2. *the monitor hypothesis:* The conscious knowledge of rules prompts the action of an "editor" or "monitor" that checks, edits, and polishes language output and is used only when the language user has sufficient time, attends to linguistic form, and knows the rule being applied.

3. *the natural order hypothesis:* Learners acquire the rules of a language in a predictable sequence, in a way that is independent of the order in which rules may have been taught. Studies have shown that learners experience similar stages in development of linguistic structures in spite of their first languages (see, for example, VanPatten, 1993). Other research has shown, however, that learners can learn rules taught in a prescribed order (see White, Spada, Lightbown, & Ranta, 1991), although the way this learned knowledge might lead to acquisition remains to be clarified.

4. *the input hypothesis:* Acquisition occurs only when learners receive optimal comprehensible input that is interesting, a little beyond their current level of competence ($i + 1$), and not grammatically sequenced, but understandable through their background knowledge, their use of context, and other extralinguistic cues such as gestures and intonation.

5. *the affective filter hypothesis:* Language learning must take place in an environment where learners are "off the defensive" and the affective filter (anxiety) is low in order for the input to be noticed and gain access to the learners' thinking (Krashen, 1982, p. 127).

Krashen's theories have been influential in terms of the strong implications for classroom instruction. Among these implications are that the primary function of the classroom is to provide comprehensible input in a low-anxiety environment in which learners are not required to speak until they are ready to do so, and optimal input is comprehensible, at the level of $i + 1$, interesting, relevant, and not grammatically sequenced; error correction should be minimal in the classroom since it is not useful when the goal is acquisition (Krashen, 1982).

Krashen's claims have been strongly criticized by various researchers on the grounds that (1) his theories have not been empirically tested in language learning environments; (2) concepts such as "comprehensible input" and the "learning-acquisition" distinction are not clearly defined or testable; and (3) his model presents far too simplistic a view of the acquisition process (Lee & VanPatten, 1995; McLaughlin, 1987; Munsell & Carr, 1981). Furthermore, use of the "acquisition-rich environment" diminishes the role of the learner in the foreign language classroom by highlighting the role of the teacher as the source of comprehensible input and by failing to recognize the function of learner-to-learner talk (Platt & Brooks, 1994). Few would deny that Krashen's model created a great deal of thought and discussion in the profession regarding the role of input in language learning. Nevertheless, many of his claims paint an unclear picture of the role of classroom instruction in language learning and remain to be empirically tested.

❏ Input Processing

Some researchers, in extending Krashen's ideas regarding input, have suggested that when input is simplified and tailored to the level of the learner, learners are better able to make connections between form and meaning and thus convert input to *intake* (a filtered, processed version of the input). This intake is then incorporated by the learner in developing a linguistic system that is subsequently used to produce output in the language. VanPatten and Cadierno (1993) argued that beginning language learners need structured input activities that enable them to focus on meaning while attending to form before they are expected to use the language to produce output. In their view, instruction may be more beneficial when it focuses on how learners perceive and process input rather than when it focuses on having learners practice linguistic structures by means of output. VanPatten (1993, pp. 438–439) suggests the following guidelines in developing structured input activities: (1) present one thing at a time; (2) keep meaning in focus; (3) move from sentences to connected discourse; (4) use both oral and written input; (5) have the learner "do something" with the input; and (6) keep the learner's processing strategies in mind.[4]

❏ The Variable Competence Model

A number of researchers questioned Krashen's claims that second language learners utilize primarily "acquired, subconscious" knowledge rather than "learned, conscious" knowledge in real communication and that these two types of knowledge are stored separately and are unrelated. The Variable Competence Model, as developed by Bialystok (1982), Ellis (1997), and Tarone (1983), for example, suggests that learners comprehend and produce language by using both subconscious, automatic linguistic knowledge and conscious, analytic linguistic knowledge. When engaged in a conversation task, for example, the learner may activate either automatic, unanalyzed knowledge or non-automatic, analytic knowledge as necessary, given the particular type of discourse being carried out. Learners may use "primary processes," drawing on automatic rules, when engaging in unplanned, spontaneous discourse and "secondary processes," drawing on non-automatic rules, when engaging in consciously pre-planned discourse. In a spontaneous situation, learners might speak without referring consciously to language rules. For example, beginning learners

---

4. See Lee and VanPatten (1995, pp. 106–107) for a sample sequence of structured input activities.

can ask someone her/his name in Spanish without consciously thinking through the use of reflexive verbs. On the other hand, in pre-planned speaking events, learners might draw upon formal language rules as they prepare their discourse. Explaining to a doctor how you sprained your ankle could require the conscious use of reflexive verbs and past tenses. Of course, in any given language-use situation, non-automatic processes and automatic processes may operate in concert.

 primary processes = automatic rules used in unplanned discourse

 secondary processes = non-automatic rules used in planned discourse

According to Ellis (1994), the integrated use of these two types of processes accounts for the individual variation in the language of a second language learner as different types of knowledge and procedures are activated in different communicative contexts. For example, in certain situations, learners might use a given structure with apparent mastery, while in other situations they might demonstrate an incomplete understanding of the same structure. In addition, the evidence convincingly indicates that the ability to verbalize a language rule does not signify that the language learner can use it in communication (Lightbown, 1985).

 Learners use a mix of conscious and subconscious processes to produce language.

Role of Modified Input, Interaction, and Output

Some key research has examined the ways in which input can be made comprehensible to the learner and the ways in which language production, or output, can facilitate language learning.

❏ Long's Interaction Hypothesis

According to Long (1983), input can be made "comprehensible" in three ways:

- by simplifying the input, i.e., using familiar structures and vocabulary;
- by using linguistic and extralinguistic features, i.e., familiar structures, background knowledge, gestures; and
- by modifying the interactional structure of the conversation.

This third element is the basis of Long's (1981) Interaction Hypothesis, which takes into account both input and learner production in promoting acquisition. Long (1983) maintains that speakers make changes in their language as they interact or "negotiate meaning" with each other. Negotiation of meaning has been characterized as "exchanges between learners and their interlocuters as they attempt to resolve communication breakdown and to work toward mutual comprehension" (Pica, Holliday, Lewis, & Morgenthaler, 1989, p. 65). Speakers negotiate meaning to avoid conversational trouble or to revise language when trouble occurs. Through negotiation of meaning, interactions are changed and redirected, leading to greater comprehensibility. What exactly does it mean to negotiate meaning? Just as in a business negotiation, two parties must participate by challenging, asking questions, and changing their positions. Merely conceding is not full negotiation. In the classroom this means that both parties in a teacher-student and student-student interaction must seek clarification, check comprehension, and request confirmation that they have understood or are being understood by the other. This process is often difficult to achieve in the classroom, given the traditional roles between teachers and students. Since students are often hesitant to question or counter-question the teacher, negotiation of meaning may not occur often. Although teachers often work to provide comprehensible input through a variety of techniques (visuals, simplified input, mime, etc.), this process does not necessarily imply or lead to the negotiation of meaning. For this type of interaction to occur, both interlocutors must have equal rights in asking for clarification and adjusting what they say.[5] Thus Long's theory implies that learners cannot simply listen to input, but that they must be active conversational participants who interact and negotiate the type of input they receive in order to acquire language.

As described in the previous section, interaction also plays a role as the cognitive processes of learners interact with the input to which they pay attention. Input can become implicit, or automatic language, when learners notice specific features of it, compare these features to those of their own output, and integrate the features into their own developing language system (Gass & Selinker, 1994; White, 1987).

 Modification in conversation makes input comprehensible.

❏ Interlanguage Theory

Interlanguage is the "language of the learner," a system in development and not yet a totally accurate approximation of native speaker language. Selinker (1974) defines interlanguage as an individual linguistic system created by second language learners as a result of five cognitive processes: (1) interference from the native language; (2) effect of instruction (approach, rules provided by the teacher, classroom activities, etc.); (3) overgeneralization of target language rules (application of rules to contexts where they do not apply);

---

5. Thanks to Dr. Rick Donato, University of Pittsburgh, for the insights here concerning negotiation of meaning. Furthermore, if students learn explicitly through instruction or implicitly through a teacher model and understand that their signals of noncomprehension are welcomed and are good for language learning, then classrooms can provide the context for negotiation of meaning. If learners are merely passive receivers of comprehensible input, or the beneficiaries of teacher reformulations, then we cannot claim that the classroom is providing opportunities for students to negotiate meaning.

(4) strategies involved in second language learning, such as role memorization, use of formal rules, and guessing in context; and (5) strategies involved in second language communication, such as circumlocution, use of gestures, appeal for assistance from a conversational partner. Current theories of L2 acquisition maintain that learners modify their own interlanguage only when they integrate into their long-term memories the input to which they attend, that is, construct new hypotheses in order to incorporate the noticed features into the interlanguage system (Ellis, 1997; Gass, 1988).

❐ Swain's Output Hypothesis

Evidence suggests that output, or production of language, may contribute to language acquisition (Swain, 1985, 1995). Swain (1995) suggests that "pushed output" (i.e., output that is accurate and sociolinguistically appropriate) may be necessary for learners to achieve higher levels of linguistic and sociolinguistic competence. According to Swain (1995), pushed output facilitates acquisition, as it (1) helps learners to discover that there is a gap between what they want to say and what they are able to say, (2) provides a way for learners to try out new rules and modify them accordingly, and (3) helps learners to actively reflect on what they know about the target language system. According to Ellis (1997), the use of linguistic knowledge becomes automatic only when learners make use of interlanguage knowledge under real conditions of communication. In other words, learners "need to see for themselves what has gone wrong, in the operating conditions under which they went wrong" (Johnson, 1988, p. 93).

Role of Sociocultural Theory

The ability to acquire and develop a new language through input, output, and interaction is one of the goals of classroom language instruction. Much of the research explored in the previous sections focuses on how L2 input is negotiated by learners and made more comprehensible. Although these studies acknowledge the importance of collaborative interaction in the learning process, their focus on negotiation of L2 input offers an incomplete picture of learners' interaction in an L2 classroom setting (Antón & DiCamilla, 1998). The interactionist view has been challenged by researchers examining the nature of sociocultural theory. According to sociocultural theory, our linguistic, cognitive, and social development as members of a community is socioculturally constructed (Vygotsky, 1978; Wertsch, 1991; Wertsch & Bivens, 1992). As Wertsch states, our development "is inherently linked to the cultural, institutional and historical settings in which it occurs" (1994, p. 203). In this view, learning and development are as much social processes as cognitive processes, and occasions for instruction and learning are situated in the discursive interactions between experts and novices (Appel & Lantolf, 1994; Brooks, 1990; Lantolf, 1994; Rogoff, 1990; Wells, 1998).

❑ Vygotsky's Zone of Proximal Development

The work of Vygotsky, a social psychologist, highlights the role of social interaction in learning and development. Vygotsky's views on learning and development in children differ markedly from those of Piaget, for whom learning and mental development are independent processes. According to Piaget (1979), learning does not affect the course of development since maturation precedes learning. In this framework, the learner must be cognitively and developmentally ready to handle certain learning tasks. In Vygotsky's (1978) view, however, learning precedes and contributes to maturation, and the learner's language performance with others exceeds what the learner is able to do with the language without assistance. The learner brings two levels of development to the learning task: an actual developmental level, representing what the learner can do, and a potential developmental level, representing what the learner should be able to do in the future. Through interaction with others, the learner progresses from the "actual developmental level" to the "potential developmental level." Between the two levels is the learner's Zone of Proximal Development (ZPD), which Vygotsky defined as "the distance between the actual developmental level as determined by independent problem solving and the level of potential development as determined through problem solving under adult guidance or in collaboration with more capable peers" (Vygotsky, 1978, p. 86). In this process, the potential development level of the learner becomes the next actual developmental level as a result of the learner's interaction with others and the expansion of cognitive abilities.

Figure 1.1 illustrates the continuous cycle of assistance in the Zone of Proximal Development, as it occurs in the task of co-constructing a puzzle with a novice. In Session 1, or the first attempt at building a puzzle, the novice recognizes the straight edges of the perimeter and is able to put those pieces of the puzzle together alone, without assistance from the expert. When performing this task, the novice is demonstrating her/his actual developmental level. With assistance from the expert, the novice puts together pieces of the puzzle that are within the puzzle but still close to the perimeter. When performing this set of tasks, the novice is working at her/his potential developmental level; s/he is able to perform the task, but only with expert assistance. Soon the novice will be able to perform this set of tasks without assistance, hence the term *potential developmental level.* Session 2 represents some future point in time (perhaps moments, weeks, or months later) when the novice can put more of the puzzle together on her/his own and needs assistance for only some of the puzzle. In other words, the potential developmental level of Session 1 became the *actual developmental level* of Session 2, illustrating the iterative nature of performance and assistance. In both sessions, the ZPD is depicted in the areas marked by assisted performance. Note that the ZPD gets smaller in Session 2, which is a sign of development and learning and indicates that the novice can now complete more tasks alone. In order to discover the ZPD of the novice, the expert or more capable peer enters into dialogic negotiation with the novice and offers help that is graduated (tailored to the level of the novice) and contingent (given only when needed and then withdrawn when the novice is able to function independently) (Aljaafreh & Lantolf, 1994). The following is an example of a dialogue that might occur between an expert and a novice as they complete the task depicted in Figure 1.1, Session 1:

EXPERT: Let's use the picture on the box to help us put the puzzle together. Why don't we find the straight-edge pieces first?

NOVICE: OK. I can make the outside with the straight pieces by myself [unassisted performance].

EXPERT: Great, now we have the frame. Let's try to find the pieces that have the same color. Can you find the blue and white pieces?

NOVICE: Here are some, but I don't know how they go together.

EXPERT: That's OK. We'll do it together. Can we find pieces that have similar shapes?

NOVICE: Does this one go in this way?

EXPERT: Here . . . maybe if you turn it around, it'll fit. There, you got it! [assisted performance]
. . . Let's try the other pieces that look the same. . . .

The language of the expert or more knowledgeable peers serves as directives and moves the learner through her or his ZPD to the point where the learner is able to perform a task alone (Aljaafreh & Lantolf, 1994; Vygotsky, 1978). The interaction between the expert and novice in a problem-solving task is called *scaffolding* (Duffy & Roehler, 1986; Wood, Bruner, & Ross, 1976). In scaffolding, the expert takes control of those portions of a task that are beyond the learner's current level of competence, thus allowing the learner to focus on the elements within her/his range of ability. The expert provides the novice with scaffolded help by enlisting the learner's interest in the task; simplifying the task; keeping the learner motivated and in pursuit of the goal; highlighting certain relevant features and pointing out discrepancies between what has been produced and the ideal solution; reducing stress and frustration during problem solving; and modeling an idealized form of the act to be performed by completing the act or by explicating the learner's partial solution (Wood, Bruner, & Ross, 1976, p. 98). The Vygotskyan concept of the ZPD suggests that language learning occurs when the learner receives appropriate types of assistance from the expert (i.e., teacher). Appendix 1.2 lists the types of language-promoting assistance that reflect scaffolded help (Scarcella & Oxford, 1992). Vygotsky's theory implies that, while learners need a great deal of contextualized input, acquisition may be contingent on cooperative, meaningful interaction.

 Today's potential developmental level becomes tomorrow's actual developmental level.

Figure 1.1 The Continuous Cycle of Assistance in the Zone of Proximal Development: Task of Co-Constructing a Puzzle

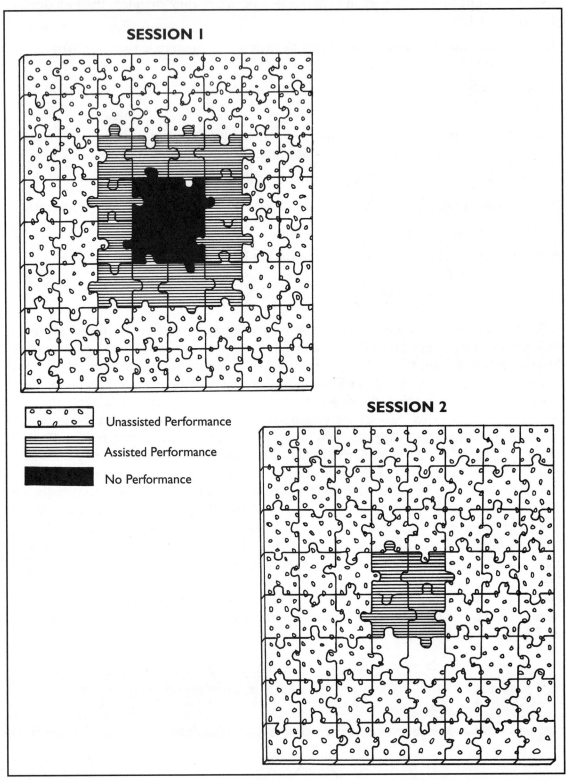

Source: Adair-Hauck, 1995.

❒ Mediation

Within a sociocultural perspective, learners use tools such as language and social interaction as a means of mediating between themselves and the world, i.e., as a way of making sense of the world around them. Mediation can take the form of the textbook, visuals, classroom discourse patterns, opportunities for interaction in the second language, direct instruction, or teacher assistance (Donato & McCormick, 1994, p. 456). Language is a symbolic tool that enables humans to organize and control mental processes such as voluntary attention, problem solving, planning, and learning (Lantolf, 1994). Collaboration with others is the conduit through which language can be acquired (Ellis, 1997, p. 242). Eventually learners are able to perform a new skill, that is, produce language without assistance. An example of the use of mediation is found in Donato (1994), who found that learners of L2 French negotiated linguistic forms with one another in small-group work, while no one individual in the group initially had knowledge of the forms being studied. Thus learners can successfully acquire language through the scaffolding provided by other learners, not only by experts (Donato, 1994).

Sociocultural theory also maintains that learning is facilitated by the learner's use of internal or external dialoguing (Ellis, 1997). According to Vygotsky (1986), one of the mediation tools used by children is speech for the self, or *private speech*, a type of thinking aloud that helps to clarify a task to be done or a problem to be solved. For example, Vygotsky cites the following example of private speech used by a child to overcome a cognitive difficulty: "Where's the pencil? I need a blue pencil. Never mind, I'll draw with the red one and wet it with water; it will become dark and look like blue" (Vygotsky, 1986, p. 29). Private speech is the convergence of thought and language, which acts as "an instrument of thought in the proper sense . . . as it aids the individual in seeking and planning the solution of a problem" (Vygotsky, 1986, p. 31). Adults use private speech or "whispering to the self" in second language learning as they attempt to make sense of a task or reveal that they suddenly understand or have mastered a source of difficulty with some aspect of the task (Antón & DiCamilla, 1998; Brooks, Donato, & McGlone, 1997; Frawley and Lantolf, 1985; McCafferty, 1994).[6]

Lantolf (1997) proposes that one of the functions of private speech is *language play*, the means by which learners experiment with those grammatical, phonological, and lexical features of the language being acquired. Children, for example, compare their old and new knowledge of the language by modifying language structures through strategies such as completions and substitutions, by imitating what others say, and by repeating their own utterances (Kuczaj, 1983, pp. 3–4). Children imitate parts of new utterances that are either within or slightly beyond their current level of linguistic competence (Kuczaj, 1983). For Vygotsky, language play creates a zone of proximal development in which the child "always behaves beyond his average age, above his daily behavior" (Vygotsky, 1978, p. 102).

Some studies suggest that adult language learners use mental rehearsal, a form of language play, through activities such as mental correction of errors, silent repetition, mental practice of grammatical rules, and taking notes (de Guerrero, 1994; Reiss, 1985). Although there has been little research in the area of language play by adult learners, some evidence suggests that those who engage in this activity are more successful language learners

---

6. Refer to Chapter 8 for a discussion of how learners use various types of "talk" during pair-work activities in order to understand the tasks more fully and ultimately to complete them more successfully.

(Ramsey, 1980) and that the value of language play in the acquisition process may decrease as the learner's proficiency in the language increases (Lantolf, 1997; Parr & Krashen, 1986). An interesting finding in Lantolf's (1997) study of the use of language play by university students studying Spanish was that learners tended to engage in language play most frequently after activities such as conversation and less so after less meaningful tasks such as grammar study and pattern drills. For foreign language instruction, language play may be activated through meaningful activities and may facilitate the language learning process.

Mediation can also occur through nonverbal means such as the use of instructional tools. One such tool is the portfolio, that students can construct to mediate reflection, to clarify and set goals, to select effective strategies to enhance performance, and to provide concrete evidence of strategy use (Donato & McCormick, 1994).

 Private speech or mental rehearsal helps to solve linguistic problems.

Interactional Competence

As seen in the previous section, sociocultural theory focuses on the social nature of language learning and development and the role of learners' interaction in the classroom setting. Within this framework, Mehan (1979) stresses the importance of "interactional competence," which includes the ability to manage discussions in relevant ways. Hall points out the significance of interactive practices, "recurring episodes of purposeful, goal-directed talk," in the establishment and maintenance of a community (Hall, 1995, p. 38). Competent participation in these practices requires the development of interactional competence. "Real" conversational models include the following characteristics, as adapted from Hall (1995):

- Opening utterances establish the topic and frame the rhetorical structure (e.g., "So, how was your vacation?").
- *Ellipsis* (not repeating information that is already known) makes clear the distinction between new and old information. As the conversational exchange continues, already established information is generally not repeated (e.g., in response to a question such as "When do you leave for class today?" one might give a short answer, "Ten o'clock," rather than the complete sentence "I leave for class today at ten o'clock.").
- Related lexical items occur in topic-specific discourse and are linked together because of their common referent. The meaning of new words is figured out by using the surrounding topically oriented words to help narrow the possible meaning choices (Clark, 1992; Halliday, 1994) (e.g., in a discussion about hunting, related lexical items might include these expressions: to go hunting, to shoot, gun, trap, deer, bears, turkeys, tracks, animal protectionists).
- Expressive reactions are made (e.g., "Oh my! I don't believe it!"), as are questions that advance the topic (e.g., "What do you mean by that?"), explanations or extensions, or a transition to a new topic (e.g., "By the way, I wanted to ask you . . . ").

In her 1995 study, Hall examined the nature of topic development and management of communication in classroom interactive practices that claimed to focus on speaking in a high school first-year Spanish classroom. She recorded classroom conversational exchanges between teacher and students and analyzed them for the characteristics of opening utterances, use of ellipses, and use of related lexical items. She found that the typical conversational exchanges that the teacher considered to be communicative showed little evidence of a real conversational topic, opening utterance, related lexical items, ellipses, or reactions. A major implication of Hall's (1995) study is that learners need interactive environments in the classroom if they are to develop the ability to interact effectively outside the classroom with other speakers of the target language. See Case Study 1 for examples of real-life utterances.

The Role of Affect and Motivation

Other variables that may influence the degree of success in learning another language are those pertaining to affect, such as motivation, anxiety, personality, and attitude. The Affective Filter Hypothesis, as first proposed by Dulay and Burt (1977), relates these affective factors to the second language acquisition process. As seen earlier, Krashen (1982) maintains that acquisition can occur only in the presence of certain affective conditions: i.e., the learner is motivated, self-confident, and has a low level of anxiety.

Motivation has been defined as "the direction of attentional effort, the proportion of total attentional effort directed to the task (intensity), and the extent to which attentional effort toward the task is maintained over time (persistence)" (Kanfer & Ackerman, 1989, p. 661). According to Gardner (1985), motivation is the most influential factor in learning a new language. However, it is also one of the most complex issues in SLA research. There are many sources of what motivates an individual to succeed in language learning, and it is difficult to match specific motivational factors to success. Gardner (1985) identifies two kinds of motivation: (1) *instrumental* (learning a language to get a better job or to fulfill an academic requirement) and (2) *integrative* (learning a language to fit in with people who speak the language natively). The research points to the likelihood that instrumental and integrative motivation are interrelated, that is, that they may operate in concert or that one may lead to the other (Gardner & MacIntyre, 1993). Gardner's paradigm was expanded by Oxford and Shearin (1994) to acknowledge the role of other motivational factors including relevance of course goals to the learner, personal beliefs about success or failure, the ability of the learner to provide self-reward and self-evaluation, the nature of the teacher's feedback and assistance to the learner, and instructional features of the course; other studies have suggested similar factors (Crookes & Schmidt, 1991; Ely, 1986; Tremblay & Gardner, 1995). Furthermore, Dörnyei maintains that language learners are often motivated by the classroom experience itself: (1) course-specific factors such as the degree to which the teaching method, materials, and learning tasks are interesting and engaging; (2) teacher-specific factors such as the teacher's personality, teaching style, and relationship to students; and (3) group-specific factors such as the dynamics of the learning group (Dörnyei, 1994, p. 277).

Wen's (1997) study illustrated that expectations of the learning task and of one's own ability play a significant role in motivation and learning: when learners think that learning experiences will lead to certain meaningful results, they exert more effort. Motivation has an effect on how and when students use language learning strategies and the degree to which they take responsibility for their own progress (Oxford & Nyikos, 1989).[7] Reiss (1985) and Gillette (1990), for example, found an absence of language play in the case of learners whose goal in language study was to fulfill a language requirement. Motivation encourages greater effort from language learners and usually leads to greater success in terms of language proficiency (Gardner, 1985) and maintenance of language skills over time (Tucker, Hamayan, & Genesee, 1976).

Personality or cognitive styles also affect language learning; these factors include the willingness to take risks, openness to social interactions, and attitude toward the target language and target language users, (Wong-Fillmore, 1985; Young, 1990). Motivation and attitudes are often related to anxiety or apprehension or fear about the language learning experience. In some cases, language activities such as speaking in front of a group can create performance anxiety, especially in the case of learners who do not enjoy interacting with others spontaneously or learners whose oral-aural skills are weaker than their visual skills (Scarcella & Oxford, 1992). Anxiety often stems from the traditional social structure of the classroom, in which the powerful teacher-centered atmosphere may inhibit interaction, or from the feeling that the learning experience is irrelevant or a waste of time (Scarcella & Oxford, 1992).

The research in motivation presented here indicates that teachers can heighten the motivation of their students by (1) identifying why learners are studying a language; (2) helping shape the learners' beliefs about success and failure in L2 learning; (3) illustrating the rewards of L2 learning; (4) providing a positive classroom atmosphere where language anxiety is kept to a minimum; and (5) encouraging learners to set their own personal goals for learning and to develop their own intrinsic reward system (Oxford & Shearin, 1994, pp. 24–25).[8] Strategies for reducing students' anxiety about language learning include providing opportunities for pair/group interaction, engaging learners in expressing their anxieties in diaries or dialogue journals, and helping learners outline performance expectations (Oxford, 1990).

 Motivation is a key factor in facilitating language learning.

Implications of the Research for Classroom Teaching

The research findings described above point to several implications concerning classroom language instruction. *Teacher's Handbook* supports a sociocultural view of language instruction, whereby learners have ample opportunities to interact meaningfully with others. Language learning may be facilitated by providing the following elements in the classroom:

• comprehensible input in the target language;

---

7. See Chapter 10 for a discussion of learning strategies.

8. See Dörnyei (1994) for a list of thirty strategies for motivating L2 learners according to language level, learner level, course content and activities, teacher-specific factors, and group-specific factors.

- an interactive environment that models and presents a variety of social, linguistic, and cognitive tools for structuring and interpreting participation in talk;
- opportunities for learners to negotiate meaning in the target language, with assistance from the teacher and one another;
- opportunities for learners to interact communicatively with one another in the target language;
- conversations and tasks that are purposeful and meaningful to the learner;
- a non-threatening environment that encourages self-expression.

Observe and Reflect

The following two activities will enable you to examine elements of language learning that occur in classrooms and in other settings.

Episode One

Observing a Child Interacting in Her/His Native Language

Observe a small child between the ages of two and a half and three years old who is interacting with one person or more (parent, older siblings, etc.) in her/his native language. Observe for at least one hour, paying particular attention to the child's use of language. Use the observation guide provided below to focus your attention during the observation. Afterward, reflect on the observation by answering the questions in the guide.

Episode Two

Observing a Beginning Language Class

Now observe a beginning language learning classroom in an elementary or secondary school. Use the same questions presented in the observation guide below as you observe the students interacting in the foreign language. Then answer the questions in the guide.

Observation Guide

The Language of Interaction

Novice = child or classroom learner

Expert = caretaker, older individual, teacher

1. Why are the expert and novice speaking? What is the topic of conversation?

2. When does the novice participate in the conversation? to answer questions? to ask questions? to provide additional information? How would you characterize the nature of the novice's talk?

3. When does the expert speak? to offer information? to ask questions? What kinds of questions does the expert ask? How would you characterize the nature of the expert's talk?

4. How does the expert react to what the novice says?

5. How does the expert help the novice when the novice has trouble expressing an idea? Do you see examples of explicit talk about the language?

6. What happens when the expert and novice do not understand each other?

7. What kind of language errors do you notice?

8. What does the expert do when the novice makes a language mistake?

9. What types of assistance does the expert offer to the novice?

10. What are some examples of language play or mental rehearsal used by the novice?

• As you reflect upon the classroom you visited in Episode Two (or upon any other observation you made), describe the role of input, output, and meaningful interaction as you observed it.

Discuss and Reflect

Case Study I

Creating Real Conversational Models

Mr. Garretty has been teaching Spanish and French for over fifteen years in an urban middle school. He is very active in local, regional, and state organizations devoted to the teaching of foreign languages. His peers, both native and nonnative speakers of Spanish, consider him to be very proficient in his knowledge of and ability to use Spanish. He is committed to providing a Spanish language environment in which his students have many opportunities to develop their ability to use the language. He uses Spanish almost exclusively in his teaching.

Dr. Blanchard, professor of the foreign language teaching methods class at a local university, decided to send three Spanish Education majors to observe Mr. Garretty's class so that they could see how he manages communication in his classroom. Students were instructed to script out several brief episodes of conversation between Mr. Garretty and his students. They would then analyze these scripted episodes for characteristics of real conversational models.

The next week students returned to the methods class with the following script (Hall, 1995):

1 Teacher: Es música ↓ no ↑ música ↓ no ↑

2 Julio: no

3 T: es música ↓ es música ↓ es música ↓

4   ahora señor te gusta ↑ te gusta la música ↑

5 Julio: no me gusta ↓

6 T: no me gusta ↓

7 Julio: no me gusta ↓

8 T: no me gusta la música ↓ te gusta la música ↑

9   no me gusta la música ↓ te gusta la música ↑

10 Several Ss: I do sí sí yeah sí

11 Rafael: aw man where you goin ↓

12 T: sí me gusta la música ↓ te gusta la música ↑

13 Andrea: sí ↓

[. . .]

31 T: [loudly] es música de Gloria Estefan ↓

32 Several Ss: [unintelligible talk]

33   [T writes on board]

34 Rafael: If you'd speak English I'd understand

35 T: sí Gloria Estefan . . . Pon Poncherelo te gusta Gloria Estefan ↑

36 Ponch: sí ↓

37 T: sí ↓

38 Julio: who's Gloria Estefan ↑

39 Ponch: me sí gusta

40 T: sí ↓ me gusta me gusta Gloria Estefan... sí... me gusta Gloria Estefan

41 Rafael: Oh, that's the person who was singing that song... that's the person who was singing that song

Ask yourself these questions:

1. What purpose or objective does the teacher have in mind for conducting this conversational exchange?

2. What do the responses of the students indicate about the degree to which they understand the conversation and/or are motivated to engage in discussion?

3. Does this exchange reflect "real conversation" as described by Hall in this chapter?

4. What types of language-promoting assistance (as presented in Appendix 1.1) might the teacher have used to facilitate comprehension and to encourage students to speak?

To prepare the case:

Read the article by Hall (1995) for more detailed information regarding the classroom script featured here and other scripts; review the types of language-promoting assistance in Appendix 1.2 that the teacher might use to keep learners engaged in topical discussion; consult these sources of information regarding interaction in the classroom: Tracy (1994) and Richards (1996).

To prepare for class discussion, think and write about these topics:

- Analyze the script presented above for the characteristics of a real conversational model using the criteria suggested by Hall (1995): opening utterance, ellipsis, use of related lexical items, and reactions.

- Given the importance of input, how could the teacher begin this lesson by providing meaningful input and comprehension-checking activities before expecting students to speak?

- Teachers often require students to respond to questions in complete sentences so that they can practice various grammatical points and new vocabulary. As we saw in the script above, this goal on the part of the teacher caused problems in the conversational exchange. Students need to be able to talk in sentence form, yet a question-answer format does not always lend itself to responses in complete sentences without making the conversation seem unnatural. What type of activity might you design that would more naturally elicit a functional expression for talking about likes and dislikes in the language you teach? Try to elicit sentence-length utterances.

Case Study 2

Conducting a Cooperative Learning Task

Mrs. Gearheart has been teaching high school German for ten years in the Smith River School District. Her approach to teaching German is traditional and grammar-based. Believing that this approach is effective, she has not changed many aspects of her teaching since she began her career. Her classes are teacher-centered: she presents grammar rules, has students do mechanical exercises to learn the structures, and does some communicative practice as time permits. Approximately every other week, her students read a short text dealing with some aspect of German culture and answer comprehension questions. Mrs. Gearheart speaks German the entire class period except for giving grammar explanations and instructions. Her students speak German during grammar practice exercises.

Mrs. Gearheart noticed that she was the only one using German extensively in the classroom and looked for ways to increase student use of the language. Midway through the year, she attended a workshop for language teachers in which she saw demonstrations of various techniques for teaching communicative language use and involving students more in creative self-expression. Since the chapter her students were working on included vocabulary dealing with family, Mrs. Gearheart decided to have students interview one another in pairs in order to find out certain information about each other's families. She presented the task in English: "Choose a partner and interview one another in German to find out how many people are in the immediate family, what their relationships are, what their occupations are, and what they look like." She gave them fifteen minutes to complete the interviews. However, as Mrs. Gearheart began to circulate around the room, she found that students were confused. They had no idea how to form the questions in German, they were speaking in English, they were madly searching through verb charts and vocabulary lists in their books, and they seemed to dislike the idea of working in pairs.

Explore the following alternatives that Mrs. Gearheart could have used:

1. She could have asked students to write out the questions for homework and use them in class the next day to conduct the interviews.

2. She could have introduced the activity by giving examples of some questions students might form for use in the interviews.

3. She could have integrated grammar practice with functional use by providing more opportunities for students to use each grammar point through communicative use and interaction.

4. She could have provided more input in German through such strategies as presenting an authentic video of German native speakers describing their families.

• After having discussed the preceding alternatives, formulate your own list of probable causes for the difficulties Mrs. Gearheart's students are experiencing. Base your rationale on the theories presented in this chapter dealing with the role of input/output and social interaction. What advice or information would you give to Mrs. Gearheart to help her understand what was happening during peer interaction?

To prepare the case:

Consult the following sources dealing with pair/group work, student interaction, and organization of effective lessons: Ballman, T. (1998); Brooks & Donato (1994); Brooks, Donato, & McGlone (1997); Johnson & Johnson (1987). Observe a language lesson in which students are interacting with one another.

Now imagine that you are Mrs. Gearheart:

1. What would you do as you sense that students are having difficulties with the interviews?

2. What elements of your teaching would you begin to change as you learn more about current research in second language acquisition and its implications?

3. Interview an experienced language teacher and discuss the kinds of changes that s/he made over the years to update her/his approach to teaching. Describe these changes.

References

Adair-Hauck, B. (1995). Exploring language and cognitive development within the Zone of Proximal Development. Paper presented at the University of Pittsburgh.

Aljaafreh, A., & Lantolf, J. P. (1994). Negative feedback as regulation and second language learning in the zone of proximal development. *The Modern Language Journal, 78,* 465–483.

Antón, M., & DiCamilla, F. (1998). Socio-cognitive functions of L1 collaborative interaction in the L2 classroom. *The Canadian Modern Language Review, 54,* 314–342.

Appel, G., & Lantolf, J. P. (1994). Speaking as mediation: A study of L1 and L2 text recall tasks. *The Modern Language Journal, 78,* 437–452.

Ballman, T.L. (1998). From teacher-centered to learner-centered: Guidelines for sequencing and pre-senting elements of a foreign language lesson. In J. Harper, M.G. Lively & M.K. Williams (Eds.), *The coming of age of the profession: Issues and emerging ideas for the teaching of foreign languages* (pp. 97–111). Boston, MA: Heinle & Heinle.

Bialystok, E. (1982). On the relationship between knowing and using forms. *Applied Linguistics, 3,* 181–206.

Brooks, F. B. (1990). Foreign language learning: A social interaction perspective. In B. VanPatten & J. F. Lee (Eds.), *Second language acquisition-foreign language learning* (pp. 153–169. Clevedon, UK: Multilingual Matters.

Brooks, F. B., & Donato, R. (1994). Vygotskyan approaches to understanding foreign language learner discourse during communicative tasks. *Hispania, 77,* 262–274.

Brooks, F. B., Donato, R., & McGlone, V. (1997). When are they going to say "it" right? Understanding learner talk during pair-work activity. *Foreign Language Annals, 30,* 524–541.

Brumfit, C. (1983). The integration of theory and practice. In J. Alatis, H. Stern, & P. Stevens (Eds.), *Applied linguistics and the preparation of teachers: Toward a rationale* (pp. 59–73). Washington, D.C.: Georgetown University Press.

Campbell, R., & Wales, R. (1970). The study of language acquisition. In J. Lyons (Ed.), *New horizons in linguistics* (pp. 242–260). Harmondsworth, England: Penguin Books.

Canale, M., & Swain, M. (1980). Theoretical bases of communicative approaches to second language teaching and testing. *Applied Linguistics, 1,* 1–47.

Chomsky, N. (1965). *Aspects of the theory of syntax.* Cambridge, MA: MIT Press.

Clark, H. (1992). *Arenas of language use.* Chicago: University of Chicago Press.

Crookes, R., & Schmidt, R. (1991). Motivation: Reopening the research agenda. *Language Learning, 41,* 469–512.

Cross, D. (1991). *A practical handbook of language teaching.* London, England: Cassell Villiers House.

de Guerrero, M. C. M. (1994). Form and function of inner speech in adult second language learning. In J. P. Lantolf & G. Appel (Eds.), *Vygotskian approaches to second language research* (pp. 83–115). Norwood, NJ: Ablex Publishers.

Donato, R. (1994). Collective scaffolding. In J. Lantolf & G. Appel (Eds.), *Vygotskyan approaches to second language acquisition research* (pp. 33–56). Norwood, NJ: Ablex Publishers.

Donato, R., & McCormick, D. (1994). A sociocultural perspective on language learning strategies: The role of mediation. *The Modern Language Journal, 78,* 453–464.

Dörnyei, Z. (1994). Motivation and motivating in the foreign language classroom. *The Modern Language Journal, 78,* 273–284.

Duffy, G. G., & Roehler, L. R. (1986). The subtleties of instructional mediation. *Educational Leadership, 43,* 23–27.

Dulay, H., & Burt, M. (1977). Remarks on creativity in language acquisition. In M. Burt, H. Dulay, & M. Finnochiaro (Eds.), *Viewpoints on English as a second language* (pp. 95–126). New York: Regents.

Ellis, R. (1994). *The study of second language acquisition.* Oxford, England: Oxford University Press.

Ellis, R. (1997). *SLA research and language teaching.* Oxford, England: Oxford University Press.

Ely, C. M. (1986). Language learning motivation: A descriptive and causal analysis. *The Modern Language Journal, 70,* 28–35.

Frawley, W., & Lantolf, J. P. (1985). Second-language discourse: A Vygotskyan perspective. *Applied Linguistics, 6,* 19–44.

Gardner, R. C. (1985). *Social psychology and second language learning: The role of attitudes and motivation.* London, Ontario: Edward Arnold.

Gardner, R. C., & MacIntyre, P. (1993). A student's contributions to second-language learning. Part II: Affective variables. *Language Teaching, 26,* 1–11.

Gass, S. (1988). Integrating research areas: A framework for second language studies. *Applied Linguistics, 9,* 198–217.

Gass, S., & Selinker, L. (1994). *Second language acquisition.* Hillsdale, NJ: Lawrence Erlbaum.

Gillette, B. (1990). *Beyond learning strategies: A whole-person approach to second language acquisition.* Unpublished Ph.D. dissertation, University of Delaware, Newark, DE.

Gleason, J. B. (1985). *The Development of Language.* Columbus, OH: Charles E. Merrill Publishing Company.

Hall, J. K. (1999). The communication standards. In J. K. Phillips & R. M. Terry. *Foreign language standards: Linking reseach, theories, and practices* (pp. 15–56). Lincolnwood, IL: NTC/Contemporary Publishing Group.

Hall, J. K. (1997). A consideration of SLA as a theory of practice: A response to Firth and Wagner. *The Modern Language Journal, 81,* 301–306.

Hall, J. K. (1995). "Aw, man, where we goin'?":Classroom interaction and the development of L2 interactional competence. *Issues in Applied Linguistics, 6,* 37–62.

Halliday, M. A. K. (1994). *An introduction to functional grammar.* London: Edward Arnold.

Hymes, D. (1972). On communicative competence. In J. P. Pride & J. Holmes (Eds.), *Sociolinguistics* (pp. 269–293). Harmondsworth, England: Penguin Books.

Johnson, D. D., & Johnson, R. T. (1987). *Learning together and alone: Cooperation, competition, and individualization.* Englewood Cliffs, NJ: Prentice Hall.

Johnson, K. (1988). Mistake correction. *ELT Journal, 42,* 89–101.

Kanfer, R., & Ackerman, P. L. (1989). Motivation and cognitive abilities: An integrative/aptitude-treatment interaction approach to skill acquisition. *Journal of Applied Psychology Monograph, 74,* 657–690.

Krashen, S. (1982). *Principles and practice in second language acquisition.* Oxford, England: Pergamon Press.

Kuczaj, S. A., II. (1983). *Crib speech and language play.* New York: Springer-Verlag.

Lantolf, J. P. (1997). The function of language play in the acquisition of L2 Spanish. In W. R. Glass & A. T. Pérez-Leroux (Eds.), *Contemporary perspectives on the acquisition of Spanish* (pp. 3–24). Somerville, MA: Cascadilla Press.

Lantolf, J. P. (1994). Sociocultural theory and second language learning. *The Modern Language Journal, 78,* 418–420.

Lee, J. F., & VanPatten, B. (1995). *Making communicative language teaching happen.* San Francisco: McGraw-Hill.

Lightbown, P. (1983). Exploring relationships between developmental and instructional sequences in L2 acquisition. In H. W. Seliger & M. H. Long (Eds.), *Classroom oriented research in second language acquisition* (pp. 217–244). Rowley, MA: Newbury House.

Lightbown, P. (1985). Great expectations: Second-language acquisition research and classroom teaching. *Applied Linguistics, 6,* 173–189.

Lightbown, P., & Spada, N. (1996). *How languages are learned.* Oxford, England: Oxford University Press.

Long, M. H. (1981). Input, interaction and second language acquisition. In H. Winitz (Ed.), *Native language and foreign language acquisition* (pp. 259–278). *Annals of the New York Academy of Sciences No. 379.* New York: Academy of Sciences.

Long, M. H. (1983). Native speaker/Non-native speaker conversation in the second language classroom. In M. A. Clarke & J. Handscomb (Eds.), *On TESOL '82: Pacific perspectives on language learning and teaching* (pp. 207–225). Washington, D.C.: TESOL.

McCafferty, S. G. (1994). Adult second language learners' use of private speech: A review of studies. *The Modern Language Journal, 78,* 421–436.

McLaughlin, B. (1987). *Theories of second-language learning.* London: Edward Arnold.

Mehan, H. (1979). What time is it, Denise: Asking known information questions in classroom discourse. *Theory Into Practice, 28* (4), 285–294.

Munsell, P., & Carr, T. (1981). Monitoring the monitor: A review of second-language acquisition and second language learning. *Language Learning, 31,* 493–502.

Oxford, R. (1990). *Language learning strategies: What every teacher should know.* Boston: Heinle & Heinle.

Oxford, R. & Nyikos, M. (1989). Variables affecting choice of language learning strategies by university students. *The Modern Language Journal, 73,* 291–300.

Oxford, R., & Shearin, J. (1994). Language learning motivation: Expanding the theoretical framework. *The Modern Language Journal, 78,* 12–28.

Parr, P. C., & Krashen, S. D. (1986). Involuntary rehearsal of second language in beginning and advanced performers. *System, 14,* 275–278.

Piaget, J. (1979). *The development of thought.* New York: Viking.

Pica, T., Holliday, L., Lewis, N., & Morgenthaler, L. (1989). Comprehensible output as an outcome of linguistic demands on the learner. *Studies in Second Language Acquisition, 11,* 63–90.

Platt, E., & Brooks, F. B. (1994). The "acquisition-rich environment" revisited. *The Modern Language Journal, 78,* 497–511.

Ramsey, R. (1980). Learning-learning approach styles of adult multilinguals and successful language learners. *Annals of the New York Academy of Sciences, 345,* 73–96.

Reiss, M. (1985). The "good" language learner: Another look. *The Canadian Modern Language Review, 41,* 511–523.

Richards, J. C. (1996). Teachers' maxims in language teaching. *TESOL Quarterly, 30*, 281–296.

Rogoff, B. (1990). *Apprenticeship in thinking, cognitive development in social context.* New York: Oxford University Press.

Savignon, S. J. (1972). *Communicative competence: An experiment in foreign language teaching.* Philadelphia, PA: Center for Curriculum Development.

Scarcella, R. C., & Oxford, R. L. (1992). *The tapestry of language learning.* Boston, MA: Heinle & Heinle.

Schulz, R. A. 1991. Second language acquisition theories and teaching practice: How do they fit? *The Modern Language Journal, 5*, 17–26.

Selinker, L. (1974). Interlanguage. In J.H. Schumann & N. Stenson (Eds.), *New frontiers in second-language learning* (pp. 114–136). Rowley, MA: Newbury House.

Swain, M. (1985). Communicative competence: Some roles of comprehensible input and comprehensible output in its development. In S. Gass & C. Madden (Eds.), *Input in second language acquisition* (pp. 235–253). Rowley, MA: Newbury House.

Swain, M. (1995). Three functions of output in second language learning. In G. Cook & B. Seidlhofer (Eds.), *Principle and practice in applied linguistics: Studies in honour of H. G. Widdowson* (pp. 125–144). Oxford: Oxford University Press.

Tarone, E. (1983). On the variability of interlanguage systems. *Applied Linguistics, 4*, 142–163.

Tracy, K. (1994). Staying on topic: An explication of conversational relevance. *Discourse Processes, 7*, 447–464.

Tremblay, P. F., & Gardner, R. C. (1995). Expanding the motivation construct in language learning. *The Modern Language Journal, 79*, 505–518.

Tucker, G. R., Hamayan, E., & Genesee, F. H. (1976). Affective, cognitive, and social factors in second language acquisition. *The Canadian Modern Language Review, 32*, 214–226.

VanPatten, B. (1993). Grammar teaching for the acquisition-rich classroom. *Foreign Language Annals, 26*, 435–450.

VanPatten, B., & Cadierno, T. (1993). Input processing and second language acquisition: A role for instruction. *The Modern Language Journal, 77*, 45–57.

Vygotsky, L. S. (1978). *Mind in society: The development of higher psychological processes.* Cambridge, MA: Harvard University Press.

Vygotsky, L. S. (1986). *Thought and language.* Cambridge, MA: MIT Press.

Wells, G. (1998). Using L1 to master L2: A response to Antón and DiCamilla's 'socio-cognitive functions of L1 collaborative interaction in the L2 classroom.' *The Canadian Modern Language Review, 54*, 343–353.

Wen, X. (1997). Motivation and language learning with students of Chinese. *Foreign Language Annals, 30*, 235–251.

Wertsch, J. V. (1991). *Voices of the mind, a sociocultural approach to mediated action.* Cambridge, MA: Harvard University Press.

Wertsch, J. V. (1994). The primacy of mediated action in sociocultural studies. *Mind, Culture, and Activity, 1*, 202–208.

Wertsch, J. V., & Bivens, J. (1992). The social origins of individualmental functioning: Alternatives and perspectives. *Quarterly Newsletter of the Laboratory of Comparative Human Cognition, 14*, 35–44.

White, L. (1987). Against comprehensible input: The input hypothesis and the development of second language competence. *Applied Linguistics, 12*, 121–134.

White, L. (1989). *Universal grammar and second language acquisition.* Amsterdam/Philadelphia, PA: John Benjamins.

White, L., Spada, N., Lightbown, P., & Ranta, L. (1991). Input enhancement and question formation. *Applied Linguistics, 12,* 416–432.

Wood, D., Bruner, J. S., & Ross, G. (1976). The role of tutoring in problem solving. *Journal of Child Psychology and Psychiatry, 17,* 89–100.

Wong-Fillmore, L. (1985). *Second language learning in children: A proposed model.* Proceedings of a Conference on Issues in English Language Development for Minority Language Education. Arlington, VA, July 24. (ERIC Document Reproduction Service No. ED 273 149)

Young, D. J. (1990). An investigation of students' perspectives on anxiety and speaking. *Foreign Language Annals, 23,* 539–553.

CHAPTER 2

Contextualizing Language Instruction to Address Goals of the Standards for Foreign Language Learning

thandbook.
heinle.com

In this chapter you will learn about:

- chronological development of language teaching
- proficiency
- national standards (philosophy, development, goal areas, content standard, progress indicator, learning scenario)
- bottom-up/top-down approaches to teaching

Teach and Reflect: Developing a Learning Scenario; Contextualizing the Teaching of a Past Tense Grammar Point

- **Case Study 1:** Textbook Evaluation: A Look at the Use of Context in Exercises
- **Case Study 2:** Developing a Top-Down ESL Lesson

Conceptual Orientation

For decades, elementary school teachers have been combining language and academic content through techniques such as storytelling, games, role plays, and, more recently, integration of subject areas such as mathematics and geography. However, at subsequent levels of instruction, we have had a tradition of separating linguistic form from academic content and culture as students in higher language levels become cognitively able to analyze linguistic forms. Furthermore, various methods of language instruction (see Appendix 2.1) advocated separation of skills and a discrete-point approach to the teaching of grammar. Many teachers still allow their instruction to be driven by a textbook that is organized around a grammatical syllabus and devoid of stimulating content. Fortunately, the movement toward standards, the vision of foreign language as a subject area that can be related to other disciplines and to the world at large, and the advances in modern technology served as catalysts in bringing context back into language teaching.

A Historical View of Context in Foreign Language Instruction

Appendix 2.1 presents a chart that illustrates the chronological development of language teaching in terms of the key time periods when particular approaches and/or methods were being used. You may find it helpful to review the chart and explore the role of context in each method. The Audiolingual Method (ALM), which brought a new emphasis to listening and speaking, advocated teaching the oral skills by means of stimulus-response learning: repetition, dialogue memorization, and manipulation of grammatical pattern drills (Lado, 1964). Speaking in the ALM mode usually meant repeating after the teacher, reciting a memorized dialogue, or responding to a mechanical drill. Unfortunately, learners were seldom exposed to meaningful, contextualized input and were unable to transfer the memorized material into spontaneous communication. The cognitive approaches, first proposed in the 1960s, promoted more meaningful language use and creativity (Ausubel, 1968). This cognitive view was based largely on Chomsky's (1965) claims that an individual's linguistic knowledge does not reflect conditioned behavior but rather the ability to create an infinite number of novel responses. In this theoretical framework, learners must understand the rules of the language before they can be expected to perform or use the language. Although the cognitive approaches advocate creative language practice, extensive discussion about grammar rules (in either a deductive or an inductive mode) and mechanical practice often leave little time for communicative language use in real-world contexts.

> **?** **How did Chomsky define "competence" and "performance"? (See Chapter 1)**
>
> **?** **How did Canale and Swain (1980) expand upon the definition of communicative competence? (See Chapter 1)**

In the 1970s, greater attention was given to developing a more communicative approach to teaching language, focusing on the needs of the learners and on the nature of communication. In her support of a more communicative approach, Savignon stated that "the development of the learner's communicative abilities is seen to depend not so much on the time they spend rehearsing grammatical patterns as on the opportunities they are given to interpret, to express, and to negotiate meaning in real-life situations" (Savignon, 1997, p. xi). She further suggested the development of a communicative approach that includes appealing topics, a functional treatment of grammar, and emphasis on communication rather than on formal accuracy in the beginning stages.

Several methods for teaching language that were developed since the late 1970s reflect many of Savignon's ideas for a communicative approach. The Natural Approach, a modern-day version of the Direct Method, was Terrell's (1982) attempt to operationalize Krashen's theories in the classroom. Anchored in the philosophy that L2 learning occurs in the same way as L1 acquisition, the Natural Approach stresses the importance of authentic language input in real-world contexts, comprehension before production, and self-expression early on, and de-emphasizes the need for grammatical perfection in the beginning stages of language learning. Based on the same philosophy, the Total Physical Response Method (Asher, Kusudo, & de la Torre, 1974) uses activities directed to the learner's kinesthetic-sensory system (body movements). Learners initially hear commands in the foreign language, respond physically to the commands (e.g., run, jump, turn around, walk to the door), and later produce the commands orally and in writing. This method, which is often used as one instructional strategy for teaching vocabulary, has been shown to be very effective in enabling learners to acquire large amounts of concrete vocabulary and retain them over time (Asher, Kusudo, & de la Torre, 1974).[1]

Among the various humanistic or affective approaches to language instruction that place a top priority on the emotions or the affect of the learner are the Silent Way (Gattegno, 1976), Community Language Learning (Curran, 1976), and Suggestopedia (Lozanov, 1978). In many affective approaches, learners determine the content of what they are learning and are encouraged to express themselves from the start.

The Role of Context in Proficiency-Oriented Instruction

The definitions of communicative competence of the 1970s prompted new insights into the various aspects of language ability that needed to be developed in order for an individual to know a language well enough to use it. Early approaches to language instruction failed to specify levels of competence so that learners' progress could be measured or program goals could be articulated. Furthermore, there was a growing realization in the profession that perhaps rather than searching for one perfect method, we needed an "organizing principle" about the nature of language proficiency that could facilitate the development of goals and objectives in language teaching (Higgs, 1984). By the end of the 1970s, it was clear that a nationally recognized procedure for assessing language proficiency was needed as was some consensus on defining proficiency goals for second language programs. This need for standards in the area of foreign languages was brought to public attention by Senator Paul Simon of Illinois and other legislators, whose efforts led to the creation in 1978 of the President's Commission on Foreign Language and International Studies, with the support of President Jimmy Carter. In 1979, the Commission published its report, *Strength Through Wisdom,* which recommended that the profession develop foreign language proficiency tests to assess language learning and teaching in the United States. This report, together with recommendations by the Modern Language Association-American Council on Language Studies (MLA-ACLS) Task Force and the work of the Educational Testing Service (ETS), initiated a project whereby a proficiency scale and interview procedure used by the federal government would be adapted for use in academic contexts. In what came to be known as the Common Yardstick Project of the 1970s, ETS cooperated with organizations in Great Britain and Germany, representatives of the U.S. government, and business and academic groups to refine the proficiency scale and interview procedure for academic use (Liskin-Gasparro, 1984). This work, which was continued in 1981 by the American Council on the Teaching of Foreign Languages (ACTFL), in consultation with MLA, ETS, and other professional organizations, ultimately led to the development of the *ACTFL Provisional Proficiency Guidelines* in 1982. These guidelines, which were revised and refined in 1999, define what language

---

1. For additional ideas for using TPR as a strategy in teaching all skills, see Glisan (1986).

users are able to do with the language in speaking, listening, reading, and writing, at various levels of performance. The development of these guidelines, which marked a shift from a focus on methodology to a focus on outcomes and assessment, continue to have a great impact on language instruction. Although neither a curricular model nor a prescribed method in and of themselves, the guidelines provide instructional implications and organizing principles for discussing issues related to language teaching (Hadley, 1993). (See Appendix 2.2 for a historical overview of the development of the proficiency concept and Appendix 2.3 for the guidelines themselves.)

The proficiency model defines language ability in terms of three criteria: (1) functions: linguistic tasks performed such as asking for information, narrating past activities, or expressing opinions; (2) contexts/contents: the settings in which one uses language, for example, informal settings, transactional situations, formal settings, together with the topics or themes of conversation, such as topics related to self and to immediate environment (family, shopping, transportation, restaurant, etc.), concrete topics of personal and general interest, and abstract topics; and (3) accuracy: the precision of the message in terms of fluency, grammar, vocabulary, pragmatic competence, pronunciation, sociolinguistic competence (Buck, Byrnes, & Thompson, 1989). Language practice that is contextualized and reflects real-world use forms the foundation for an approach that seeks to develop proficiency.[2]

 The proficiency model defines language ability in terms of functions, contexts/contents, and accuracy.

An Introduction to the Standards for Foreign Language Learning (SFLL)

❑ The Developmental Process

An interest in standards in the academic disciplines was sparked by an initiative of the Bush administration and was continued under the Goals 2000 initiative of the Clinton administration. Visionary Goals 2000 (1994) described the competence that all students should demonstrate in challenging subject matter in grades four, eight, and twelve in seven subject areas, including foreign language. With its inclusion in Goals 2000, foreign language was brought into the K-12 core curriculum in the United States since many reform efforts and funding sources were tied to Goals 2000 (Sandrock, 1995). In 1993, foreign language education was the final subject area to receive federal funding to create national standards for levels K-12 (Lafayette & Draper, 1996). The National Standards in Foreign Language Education Project (1996) was a collaborative effort of ACTFL, the American Association of Teachers of French (AATF), the American Association of Teachers of German (AATG), and the American Association of Teachers of Spanish and Portuguese (AATSP). The standards framework was drafted by an eleven-member task force that represented a variety

---

2. The ACTFL Proficiency Scale will be described in detail in Chapter 8, and the oral proficiency interview procedure will be presented in Chapter 11.

of languages, levels of instruction, program models, and geographic regions. The task force shared each phase of its work with the profession as a whole, disseminating the drafts and seeking written comments, which were then considered as subsequent revisions were made. The final draft was published in 1996 and made available to members of the profession.

❐ Organizing Principles: Philosophy, Goal Areas, Standards

The work on proficiency during the past two decades placed the profession in an excellent position to define what students should know and be able to do with a foreign language they learn. Although influenced by the proficiency guidelines, the standards do not represent communication as four separate skill areas of listening, speaking, reading, and writing. Standards define the central role of foreign language in the learning experiences of all learners, and they have the potential for a lasting impact in the future by placing content and skill integration as the central focus for instruction. As it began its work, the task force developed a Statement of Philosophy that served as the foundation for the development of standards. This statement, which appears in Appendix 2.4, describes key assumptions that enabled the task force to identify five goal areas that reflect a rationale for foreign language education. These goals are known as the "5 Cs of foreign language education": Communication, Cultures, Connections, Comparisons, Communities. The standards document describes these goals in the following way:

 The Five Cs of foreign language education are Communication, Cultures, Connections, Comparisons, Communities.

Communication, or communicating in languages other than English, is at the heart of second language study, whether the communication takes place face-to-face, in writing, or across centuries through the reading of literature.

Through the study of other languages, students gain a knowledge and understanding of the *Cultures* that use that language; in fact, students cannot truly master the language until they also master the cultural contexts in which the language occurs.

Learning languages provides *Connections* to additional bodies of knowledge that are unavailable to monolingual English speakers.

Through *Comparisons* and contrasts with the language studied, students develop greater insight into their own language and culture and realize that multiple ways of viewing the world exist.

Together, these elements enable the student of languages to participate in multilingual *Communities* at home and around the world in a variety of contexts and in culturally appropriate ways (National Standards in Foreign Language Education Project, 1996, p. 27).

As Figure 2.1 illustrates, these five goals interconnect to suggest the richness of human language; no one goal can be separated from the other, nor is any one goal more important than another. Each goal area contains two to three content standards that describe the knowledge and abilities that all students should acquire by the end of their high school education in order to achieve the goals. Figure 2.2 illustrates the five goals and eleven standards. The standards as they relate to each topic will be explored in depth in subsequent chapters.

Figure 2.1   The Five C's of Foreign Language Study

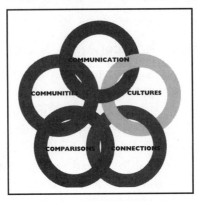

Figure 2.2   Standards for Foreign Language Learning

STANDARDS FOR FOREIGN LANGUAGE LEARNING

COMMUNICATION
Communicate in Languages Other Than English

Standard 1.1: Students engage in conversations, provide and obtain information, express feelings and emotions, and exchange opinions.

Standard 1.2: Students understand and interpret written and spoken language on a variety of topics.

Standard 1.3: Students present information, concepts, and ideas to an audience of listeners or readers on a variety of topics.

CULTURES
Gain Knowledge and Understanding of Other Cultures

Standard 2.1: Students demonstrate an understanding of the relationship between the practices and perspectives of the culture studied.

Standard 2.2: Students demonstrate an understanding of the relationship between the products and perspectives of the culture studied.

CONNECTIONS
Connect with Other Disciplines and Acquire Information

Standard 3.1: Students reinforce and further their knowledge of other disciplines through the foreign language.

Standard 3.2: Students acquire information and recognize the distinctive viewpoints that are only available through the foreign language and its cultures.

COMPARISONS
Develop Insight into the Nature of Language and Culture

Standard 4.1: Students demonstrate understanding of the nature of language through comparisons of the language studied and their own.

Standard 4.2: Students demonstrate understanding of the concept of culture through comparisons of the cultures studied and their own.

COMMUNITIES
Participate in Multilingual Communities at Home and Around the World

Standard 5.1: Students use the language both within and beyond the school setting.

Standard 5.2: Students show evidence of becoming life-long learners by using the language for personal enjoyment and enrichment.

Content standard = what students should know and be able to do

It is important to note that these standards are content standards, not performance standards, which address the issue of how well students demonstrate competency in subject matter (e.g., the *ACTFL Proficiency Guidelines*). Individual states and school districts have the responsibility for determining performance standards for their students and for answering the question, "How good is good enough?" However, in order to assist states and districts in this task, the standards document includes for grades four, eight, and twelve sample progress indicators that define student progress in meeting the standards but are not themselves standards. They apply to many languages, can be realistically achieved at some level by all students, provide many instructional possibilities, are assessable in numerous ways, and are designed for use by states and districts to establish acceptable performance levels for their students. The following is an example of a progression of performance indicators:

Goal area: Cultures

Standard: Students demonstrate an understanding of the relationship between the practices and perspectives of the cultures studied.

Sample progress indicators:

> **Grade 4:** Students use appropriate gestures and oral expressions for greetings, leave takings, and common classroom interactions.
>
> **Grade 8:** Students observe, analyze, and discuss patterns of behavior typical of their peer group.
>
> **Grade 12:** Students identify, examine, and discuss connections between cultural perspectives and socially approved behavioral patterns. (NSFLEP, 1996, pp. 46–47).

 Sample progress indicator = define student progress in meeting standards

To assist teachers in applying the standards to their classroom instruction, the standards document includes various examples of learning scenarios, each of which is a series of learner-centered activities based on a specific theme or unit of instruction and integrated so that one activity is the basis for the subsequent one (e.g., a listening activity provides the content for a small-group discussion). (See Teach and Reflect, Episode One of this chapter for a sample learning scenario.)

Learning scenario = series of learner-centered activities based on a specific theme and integrated so that one activity is the basis for the next.

In order to address the issue of "how well" students should be able to do the "what" from the content standards, ACTFL recently published its new *ACTFL Performance Guidelines for K–12 learners* (1999). These guidelines (see Appendix 2.4) describe language performance within the three modes of communication, as evidenced by students at the benchmarks of language development labeled Novice Range, Intermediate Range, and Pre-advanced Range. The language performance descriptions featured in these *Guidelines* are designed to help teachers understand how well students demonstrate language ability at various points along the language learning continuum (ACTFL Performance Guidelines for K–12 Learners, 1999).

❏ Focus on Context: The "Weave" of Curricular Elements

The Standards for Foreign Language Learning (SFLL) broaden the definition of the content of the language curriculum. Figure 2.3 depicts the elements that should be "woven" into language learning: language system, cultural traits and concepts, communication strategies, critical thinking skills, and learning strategies. In addition, other subject areas and technology are also important elements in a standards-driven curriculum.

Figure 2.3   The "Weave" of Curricular Elements

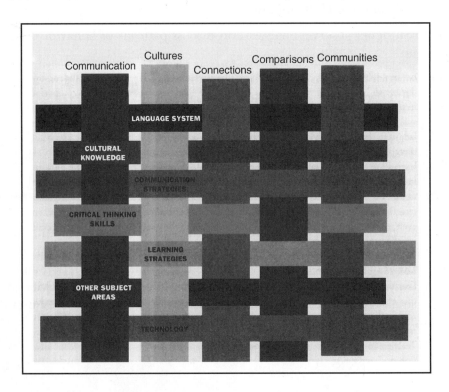

The *language system* goes beyond grammar rules and vocabulary by also including sociolinguistic elements of gestures and other forms of nonverbal communication, of discourse style, and "learning what to say to whom and when" (NSFLEP, 1996, p. 29). In addition to experience with the language system, learners must be able to identify key *cultural traits and concepts* that will facilitate sensitive and meaningful interaction. *Communication strategies* such as circumlocution, guessing intelligently, making hypotheses, asking for clarification, and making inferences will empower learners in their attempts to interact. In learning a foreign language, students use *critical thinking skills* as they apply their existing knowledge to new tasks, incorporate new knowledge, and identify and analyze issues in order to arrive at informed decisions and to propose solutions to problems. In assuming greater responsibility for their own learning, students use *learning strategies* such as organizing their learning, previewing new tasks, summarizing, using questioning strategies, and inferring information from a text. By exploring interesting and challenging content and topics, students can enhance their learning of the language while expanding their knowledge of other subject areas. Access to a wide range of forms of technology such as the World Wide Web, electronic mail, CD-ROM, and interactive video will enable learners to use their linguistic skills to establish interactions with peers and to learn about the contemporary culture of the target country.

Using the Standards Framework to Contextualize Teaching

As teachers address standards in their curricula and teaching, they reflect on their own philosophies of, or approaches to, language instruction. The methods of instruction presented earlier in this chapter can be categorized into one of two broader approaches to language teaching, based on one's theoretical understanding of how learners best learn a second language. The standards framework has implications for each of these approaches in view of the role of context that is brought to the learning experience.

❏ The Traditional Bottom-Up Approach: Skill-Based Approaches

Historically, foreign languages have been taught in the United States by means of a *bottom-up* approach: students learn grammar rules and vocabulary, and then later practice using them in communication. Rivers (1983) used the term *skill getting* to refer to the type of practice that helps students learn grammatical formations. Mechanical drills, such as substitution or transformation drills, for example, focus students' attention on correct forms without requiring them to attend to the message itself. In the skill-using phase, students use the learned structures in communicative activities designed to focus their attention on meaningful interaction. Littlewood (1980) suggested that classroom practice activities be sequenced so that meaning increasingly receives more focus. In his model, activities progress through the following stages: (1) primary focus on form; (2) focus on form, plus meaning; (3) focus on meaning, plus form; and (4) primary focus on meaning (cf. Hadley, 1993, p. 130). Hadley (1993) suggested that Type 1 activities should be kept to an absolute minimum if instruction is oriented to proficiency goals. Despite increasing attention to meaningful activities, the basic dichotomy between mechanical and communicative practice has remained relatively intact in language textbooks since the eras of both the Audiolingual Method and the cognitive approaches. However, the dichotomy's usefulness for the language learner has not gone unquestioned, particularly in light of the Vygotskian framework and sociocultural theory presented in Chapter 1 (Ballman, 1997; Walz, 1989).

The standards can help the teacher to incorporate more engaging content in a bottom-up approach. While maintaining a familiar sequence of instruction that is often organized around the textbook, the teacher might

- include additional information, practice, and activities related to the standards as each chapter or unit is explored (e.g., for practice of numbers, students read an authentic restaurant ad taken from the Internet);
- incorporate an increasing number of "synthesis" activities that integrate more than one skill area and address a particular standard (e.g., students send an e-mail message to a key pal abroad in order to find out information about peers in the target country);
- limit the number of mechanical, decontextualized textbook exercises and replace or revise them to bring meaning to the tasks as well as opportunities for student interaction and negotiation of meaning; and
- use some resources beyond the text to accommodate the gaps in context (e.g., video, Internet, visuals, stories).[3]

The focus on meaningful, contextualized teaching prompted some changes in the traditional bottom-up mechanical/communicative format of textbook exercises. In his review of textbook exercise formats, Walz found that textbooks are beginning to "contextualize" mechanical or skill-getting exercises in a wide variety of ways, such as by (1) connecting exercise sentences with the same situation or theme; (2) providing a context for the exercise in the form of information concerning people, activities, or descriptions; and (3) combining cultural aspects with language practice within the exercise (Walz, 1989, p. 161). Walz also points out that textbook authors have different ideas about what "contextualization" of an exercise means: "Contextualization, especially with respect to mechanical drills, does not seem to be the same as creating a context, which is the topic and situation of a communicative act that are necessary for understanding" (Walz, 1989, p. 162). Indeed, many "contextualized" exercises are simply disguised mechanical drills that do not require students to understand meaning in order to complete them. Walz recommends that textbook authors develop exercise contexts that must be understood in order to accomplish the task. Furthermore, Walz (1989) suggests that (1) sentences in mechanical drills be related in meaning and be introduced with a brief title in the directions; (2) contextualized meaningful drills have short directions and force students to make a choice when responding; and (3) most activities be communicative, with students' experience and opinions forming the context. (See Case Study 1 in this chapter for sample textbook exercises.)

❏ A Top-Down Approach: Theme- and Task-Based Approaches

A top-down or whole-language approach to language instruction resists reducing language to word lists, verb conjugations, discrete grammar points, or isolated linguistic elements (Adair-Hauck & Cumo-Johanssen, 1997). In a whole-language approach, learners are

---

3. These ideas were adapted from the four options for implementing the K-12 Standards for Foreign Language Learning, developed by Tom Welch, Jessamine County, Kentucky, Public Schools.

presented with a "whole" text (e.g., a story, poem, song, tape-recorded listening selection), are guided through comprehending its main ideas, explore these ideas through interaction with others, and then focus on specific details and/or linguistic structures (e.g., vocabulary, grammar). Learners manipulate language to communicate thoughts using higher-level skills before attending to discrete language structures with the use of lower-level skills. By means of activities such as negotiation of meaning and joint problem solving with the teacher and classmates, learners demonstrate performance before competence; that is, they participate in a more complex task than they are capable of completing without assistance (Rogoff, 1990). You will learn in a later chapter the specific implications of this approach for the teaching of grammar.

An example of this kind of human learning in another field is the first time one drives a car. Because of having ridden in a car, one knows a little about confining the car to a roadway, using the pedals and the steering wheel to control it. Thus one can begin initial interaction with the car and other drivers based on background knowledge. It requires some refinement to know how much pressure to put on the pedals, and it may require some instruction to know how and when to shift, but simply sitting in the car practicing pedal pushes over and over without having the engine running and being engaged on a roadway or parking area does not help one become a driver. Driving a car is, therefore, not an *object* of study but an *activity* in which to engage.

How does one implement a top-down or whole-language approach? Within the thematic unit being taught, the teacher might present a "text" to the class for the purpose of helping learners understand its meaning while discussing it. This "text" can be a story that is told, an authentic taped conversation or short reading, a piece of realia (a postcard, a letter, an invitation, etc.), or any verbal input given by the teacher. For example, in a chapter dealing with travel, learners might (1) listen to a public service announcement that gives advice to travelers; (2) read an advertisement on taking a cruise; or (3) listen to a story about a family vacation. If the vocabulary and grammar have been appropriately matched to the theme, then these initial authentic contexts contain examples of structures and words used naturally. In a Spanish version of the contexts given above, appropriate grammatical structures might include the future tense, the prepositions *por* and *para*, and the subjunctive used with adverbial expressions.

As students attend to the initial context, they are given tasks for demonstrating understanding of main ideas and/or particular details, such as selecting the main idea from a list of alternatives, creating a possible title for the text, responding to true-false statements, and finding specific pieces of information. The teacher leads the class in discussion for the purpose of relating new information to previously learned information, for heightening understanding of the text, or, in the case of a story, for recreating the text. While the text may contain new vocabulary and grammatical structures, students cope with the unknown by negotiating meaning with the teacher by asking questions, requesting clarification, and gleaning meaning from the context itself. Through exploration of the text, students indirectly learn vocabulary and grammar that can later become the focus of more directed and personalized practice. Thus a unit/chapter plan for integrating skills and culture might feature the organization shown on the next page.

Level of Instruction: Intermediate high school/college

Context: Travel

Functions: Making travel plans, getting a hotel room, discussing means of transportation

1. Students listen to an authentic conversation between an airline employee and a traveler. Students explore main ideas through discussion and true-false questions.

2. Students read an authentic advertisement on taking a cruise. They explore main ideas and offer their opinions.

3. Students listen to the teacher describe in the target language the forms of transportation in several target culture countries and the difficulties caused by pollution. Students see pictures and discuss information with the teacher.

4. Students practice new vocabulary, most of which they heard or read in one of the steps above, by means of a Total Physical Response (TPR) activity and interviews with classmates.

5. Students practice grammatical structures that were seeded in the initial contexts. Grammar is practiced in context by means of guided and open-ended activities and self-expression.

6. Students listen to an authentic conversation between a hotel clerk and a guest. They explore main ideas and some details and use this as a context for discussion and role play.

7. Students read an advertisement dealing with renting a car while vacationing. Same activities are done as in item 6 above.

8. Synthesis activities are used to bring together all skills and information in the unit/chapter: role plays, original conversations using the theme of travel, written compositions, and letters. Students read and explore a longer magazine article dealing with housing options when traveling abroad and listen to and explore a longer segment dealing with an airline advertisement. In exploring these longer segments, students are guided through them by means of various steps, ranging from identifying main ideas to expressing opinions and writing compositions.

The teacher/student interactive relationship described above is an element of what Jones calls "cognitive instruction," through which students process information in meaningful ways, take responsibility for their own learning, and become independent learners (Jones, 1986, p. 7). According to Jones (1986), this type of instruction can substantially alter the capability of the learner, especially the low-achieving student. As students and teacher work together to understand and explore new contexts through a scaffolding process, the teacher shows learners how to use various strategies to solve tasks (Duffy & Roehler, 1986). According to Bruner, "One sets the game, provides a scaffold to assure that the child's ineptitudes can be rescued or rectified by appropriate intervention, and then removes the scaffold part by part as the reciprocal structure can stand on its own" (Bruner, 1983, p. 60). A more interactive approach to language teaching also offers numerous opportunities for learners to develop and use a variety of strategies for understanding and creating language.

While top-down processing is still a new area of research, preliminary studies point to the likelihood that students of a top-down or whole-language approach may be able to acquire language at a higher and more successful rate than in the traditional bottom-up approach (Adair-Hauck & Cumo-Johanssen, 1997). One of the reasons for this may be that a bottom-up approach often allows little time in the unit for contextualized practice, since most of the time is spent analyzing small segments of language.

In summary, the information presented in this chapter highlights the importance of language learning experiences that meaningfully relate to real-world communication, the interests of learners, the content of other disciplines, and the target culture communities.

Teach and Reflect

Episode One

Developing a Learning Scenario

Part One: Read the following learning scenario and identify which goal areas and standards are addressed and how you can tell.

The Roman Family

When Ms. Bauer presents the Roman family to her first-year Latin class in Fairfax County, the students practice simple sentences aloud and answer questions in Latin regarding the members of the family, what they are wearing, and what they are doing in the picture. This leads to a discussion of the role of each family member in ancient Rome: the father as head of the household; the mother as the primary teacher of the daughter, who marries around the age of twelve; and the son as the student who learns to conduct business as his father does. Ms. Bauer then asks the students to discuss how the family roles in American culture are different and to give some of the reasons for these differences. Students who have a background in other cultures are encouraged to discuss the roles of family members of their culture. Ms. Bauer then introduces the students to a passage in Latin that discusses the Roman family, which the students are easily able to comprehend because of the prior oral and visual preparation. Finally, Ms. Bauer asks students to summarize what they noticed in the story with regard to adjectives that describe, respectively, female and male members of the family. Students describe what they noticed in the passage and how this relates to noun/adjective agreement and gender in the English language (NSFLEP, 1996, pp. 91–92).

Part Two: Choose one of the following themes and develop a learning scenario for the foreign language you teach. Remember to build the scenario around an interesting context and to integrate the skills and culture. Identify the standards addressed in the scenario (be sure that at least one standard in three goal areas is addressed). How much class time do you think it might take to complete this scenario?

> **Suggested themes:** education, celebrations, work and leisure time, the city, health and medicine, the environment, fine arts, tourism

(You might want to keep this learning scenario for Teach and Reflect activities in later chapters.)

Episode Two

Contextualizing the Teaching of a Past Tense Grammar Point

You are beginning a new unit/chapter that introduces a past tense in your target language. Unfortunately, your textbook is an outdated one that is organized around grammar points and has little contextual support. Vocabulary is included for leisure-time activities. Your task, as you plan, is the following:

1. Find a context in which the past tense can logically be studied. You might build on the theme of the given vocabulary.

2. Identify what students will need to know and be able to do by the end of the chapter/unit. Address the integration of skills and cultural understanding.

3. Identify what kind of introductory texts can be presented in a top-down fashion, keeping in mind the level of language complexity and the interest level of students. Include a description of a listening segment and a short reading that might be used. Your instructor may ask you to actually design these texts. How would students explore these texts?

4. What other vocabulary and grammar would you need to present in addition to the past tense, given the context being practiced? Remember that at least some of the vocabulary and grammar presented in the chapter should appear in the texts.

Discuss and Reflect

Case Study I

Textbook Evaluation: A Look at the Use of Context in Exercises

The Livingston Community School District adopts new textbooks every seven years. This year, textbooks will be ordered for the French program. Two of the five French teachers, Mr. Wallace and Ms. Moulin, were given the task of examining new textbook series for French I–IV. In their initial meeting about textbook selection, the two teachers agreed that one of the most important criteria for them is that the textbook program be highly contextualized, since their current text lacks interesting content.

As they examine each first-year textbook, Mr. Wallace and Ms. Moulin discover that there is a wide variety in the types of "contextualized" practice exercises presented in today's textbooks. They decide to analyze more closely the contexts of the speaking exercises in the text that they tentatively selected as their top choice. They examine the linguistic function of "making comparisons" found in Lesson 15. The exercises for this function follow.

Leçon 15: Chez les Hanin

(Lesson content: daily routines, the body, family life, health, reflexive verbs, making comparisons, work, time and space, day care)

La comparaison des adjectifs et des adverbes
Vous avez compris?

A. L'égocentrisme. Voilà une liste que Sandrine a faite pour se comparer à ses camarades de classe, à sa famille, et à ses amis. Elle a utilisé les symboles +, −, et = pour indiquer ses opinions. Interprétez sa liste.

> **Modèle:** intelligent(e): Martine +, Gauthier −
> Martine est plus intelligente que moi. Gauthier est moins intelligent que moi. (Je suis plus intelligente que Gauthier.)

1. beau (belle): Colette =, Danielle +, Valérie −
2. travailleur (travailleuse): mes frères −, ma mère =
3. riche: Bertrand +, Christophe −
4. fort(e) en maths: Annick +, Pierre −

[*English translation*]
Lesson 15: At the Hanin House

Comparison of Adjectives and Adverbs
Did You Understand?

A. Focus on self. Here is a list that Sandrine made in order to compare her classmates, family, and friends. She used the symbols +, −, and = to indicate her opinions. Interpret her list.

> **Model:** intelligent: Martine +, Gauthier −
> Martine is more intelligent than I. Gauthier is less intelligent than I. (I am more intelligent than Gauthier.)

1. pretty: Colette =, Danielle +, Valérie −
2. hard-working: my brothers and sisters −, my mother =
3. rich: Bertrand +, Christophe −
4. strong in math: Annick +, Pierre −

Continuons!

A. Comparez. Faites les comparaisons suivantes:

1. les chats et les chiens
2. les étudiants et les professeurs
3. les hommes et les femmes
4. la ville et la campagne

5. Los Angeles et New York
6. Alceste et Candide
7. Julie et Nicolas Hanin

[*English translation*]

Let's Continue!

A. Compare. Make the following comparisons:

1. cats and dogs
2. students and teachers
3. men and women
4. the city and the country

5. Los Angeles and New York
6. Alceste and Candide
7. Julie and Nicolas Hanin

B. La décision de Marie-Laure. Deux jeunes gens ont invité Marie-Laure au Bal du printemps. Elle ne peut pas décider quelle invitation elle va accepter.

1. **Marie-Laure compare.** Lisez la liste et comparez Marc à Antoine.

   Marc: intelligent / sérieux / gentil / bien équilibré / très grand / sportif / membre du club de foot / ne parle pas beaucoup / paie toujours / a une voiture de sport

   Antoine: intellectuel / artiste / branché / adore le rock / assez petit mais très beau / adore parler de politique / aime s'amuser / a beaucoup d'amis / n'a jamais d'argent / fume

   Modèle: Marc est plus sérieux qu'Antoine, mais Antoine adore parler de politique.

2. **La décision.** Quelle invitation est-ce que Marie-Laure doit accepter? Pourquoi?

[*English translation*]

B. Marie-Laure's decision. Two young men invited Marie-Laure to the spring dance. She can't decide which invitation she is going to accept.

1. **Marie-Laure compares.** Read the list and compare Marc to Antoine.

    Marc: intelligent / serious / kind / well-adjusted / very tall / athletic / member of the soccer club / doesn't talk too much / pays all of the time / has a sports car

    Antoine: intellectual / artist / "with it" / loves rock music / a little short but handsome / loves to talk about politics / loves to have a good time / has a lot of friends / never has money / smokes

    Model: Marc is more serious than Antoine, but Antoine loves to talk about politics.

2. **The decision.** Which invitation should Marie-Laure accept? Why?

Source: Heilenman, Kaplan, & Tournier, 1997

Ask yourself these questions:

1. What comments might Mr. Wallace and Ms. Moulin make as they discuss whether these exercises are "contextualized"?

2. Imagine that a textbook presents a sequence of practice exercises dealing with the function of "making comparisons," in which the tasks are ordered from mechanical practice initially to progressively more communicative language use, as in Littlewood's (1980) model. Where would each of these three exercises fit best according to Littlewood's sequencing of activities presented on page 33 of this chapter? Explain your rationale.

3. How does the use of "contextualization" in each exercise address the suggestions offered by Walz (1989), as described earlier in this chapter?

4. Mr. Wallace and Ms. Moulin find that the textbook also integrates the function of "making comparisons" in a reading dealing with day-care centers. Students are asked to compare specific characteristics of day care in the United States and day care in France. Given the lesson content provided at the beginning of this case study, in what other ways might this function be integrated into the lesson?

To prepare the case:

• Review the Standards for Foreign Language Learning (1996) presented earlier in this chapter and reflect on the implications they have for textbook evaluation; read Chapter 4 in Savignon (1997) on selection of materials; read Walz (1989) for an in-depth review of contextualized language practice in foreign language textbooks.

- Find a textbook written in the 1960s, one written in the early 1980s, and one written in the 1990s. Compare the three on these points:
  — meaningful contexts for presentation of language
  — sequencing of practice exercises in terms of student tasks
  — strategies to help students interact with and use the language presented
  — Describe the differences and similarities you find. Trace the changes in our understanding of how people learn languages, and show how these changes are reflected in the three textbooks you examined.

To prepare for class discussion, think and write about these topics:

Review the three exercises that present practice of the function "making comparisons." How might this function be taught in a top-down fashion in your target language? Use the suggestions provided earlier in this chapter and your own ideas to develop a plan.

Evaluating a textbook for use in a standards-based curriculum:

Now select a first-year textbook program for the foreign language you teach. Evaluate the program using the criteria below. Would you choose this text for your standards-based language program? Provide a rationale to convince your colleagues.

Textbook Evaluation Criteria

Rate each criterion on the following scale:

3 = Excellent   2 = Satisfactory   1 = Poor

1. Features an organization based on interesting topics and cultural contexts

2. Provides activities in which students talk to each other, share information and opinions, ask questions, and express feelings

3. Encourages students to negotiate meaning with one another

4. Provides authentic oral input (audio tapes, videotapes, CD-ROM programs) that has engaging content and tasks

5. Provides authentic written texts (newspaper/magazine articles, ads, poems, short stories) that have engaging content and tasks

6. Suggests strategies for comprehending and interpreting oral and written texts.

7. Includes pre-listening/pre-viewing/pre-reading tasks

8. Includes tasks in which students speak and write to an audience of listeners/readers

9. Provides contextualized and meaningful activities

10. Presents clear, concise grammar explanations that are necessary for communication.

11. Presents vocabulary thematically, in context, and with the use of visuals and authentic realia

12. Provides for integrated practice of listening, speaking, reading, and writing

13. Presents an accurate view of the cultures in which the target language is spoken

14. Includes visuals for presenting vocabulary and illustrating cultural aspects (overhead transparencies, pictures, slides, realia)

15. Provides opportunities for students to explore the products of the culture and their relationship to cultural perspectives

16. Provides opportunities for students to explore the practices of the culture and their relationship to cultural perspectives

17. Provides opportunities for students to use the target language to learn about other subject areas

18. Engages students in using the target language to learn about topics of interest

19. Provides opportunities for students to compare key features of the native and target languages in interesting ways

20. Provides opportunities for students to compare products, practices, and perspectives of the native culture and target cultures in interesting ways

21. Includes activities in which students use the target language with peers in other communities and target language regions (e-mail, World Wide Web, interactive video, field trips)

22. Provides opportunities for students to select authentic texts to explore for enjoyment and learning

23. Provides contextualized, performance-based achievement tests with scoring rubrics

24. Suggests strategies for assessing student progress in attaining standards

25. Integrates technology effectively into instruction (audiotapes, videotapes, interactive video, CD-ROM, World Wide Web, e-mail)

The evaluator/teacher may choose to add criteria of importance to specific language programs.

Case Study 2

Developing a Top-down ESL Lesson

Ms. Combes teaches an advanced class of English as a Second Language (ESL) for the English Language Institute in a northeastern state. Learners in her class speak Portuguese and Arabic. For the most part, they earn their living from commercial fishing, from working in restaurants, or from helping to develop computer software.

When the class began, the students told Ms. Combes that their biggest problem was listening to and understanding English as it was spoken to them by local native speakers and in the media. Ms. Combes decided to use taped segments from radio and television and recorded conversations of people in the community to help her students develop the necessary skills for listening in context.[4]

---

4. Thanks to Ms. Dee Messinger for the inspiration for this case.

As Ms. Combes planned the unit that presented the linguistic function/context of "ordering a meal," she decided to use a top-down approach and begin with an authentic conversation. She obtained permission from a restaurant owner and clients to record the conversational exchanges between a waitress and two college students having dinner. A transcription of the taped segment appears below. Ms.Combes now needs to plan how she will use the conversation as a basis for developing a lesson.

[Transcription of the taped conversation at the restaurant]

WAITRESS: Good evening, and welcome to the Red Snapper Restaurant. May I bring you anything to drink?

CLAUDIA: Sure. Do you have any diet sodas?

WAITRESS: Diet Coke and Slice.

CLAUDIA: Diet Coke, please.

HEATHER: Um . . . I'll just have some water.

WAITRESS: I'll be right back with your drinks. Here are the menus.

CLAUDIA: Gee, I hope we can find some light entrees on the menu. We've been exercising like crazy to get into shape! These restaurants use so much fat in their cooking.

HEATHER: Oh, look, they do have a section on the menu called "On the lighter side." These salads have only four hundred calories.

WAITRESS: Here's your water . . . and your Diet Coke. Uh . . . let me tell you about our specials for today. Our catch of the day is the golden trout, served with a butter sauce. Let's see . . . the second special is fresh lobster, served with rice.

CLAUDIA: No, no, we don't want anything too fattening. We'd like something low in fat but high in fiber . . . like these salads. I think I'll have the tuna/cole slaw/potato salad trio, but could you substitute additional tuna for the potato salad?

WAITRESS: Hmm . . . no potato salad, tuna instead . . . not a problem.

HEATHER: I'd like the Caesar salad with the dressing on the side, please.

WAITRESS: The Caesar salad usually has the dressing on it. Um . . . I don't think it's possible, but I'll check.

HEATHER: Gee, Claudia, do you think this waitress thinks we're weird since we're being so picky about our food?

CLAUDIA: Don't worry about it! Maybe she's just having a bad evening.

Ask yourself these questions:

1. What types of background knowledge might students need to understand the conversation?

2. What type of pre-listening work might be done in order to prepare students for the listening task?

3. What kinds of vocabulary and common grammatical structures are found in the conversation? Which words and structures might be most important in this context?

4. What types of cultural products, practices, and perspectives would students learn from this conversation?

5. How might comprehension be checked?

6. How might students be engaged in oral and written communication as a follow-up to listening?

7. What types of reading texts might Ms. Combes select as the unit is continued?

8. What types of synthesis activities might be used in order to integrate all skills and information? What standards would be addressed in these activities?

To prepare the case:

Read pages 177–189 on designing theme-based activities in the chapter by Williams, Lively, and Harper (1998); read Chapter 6 in Scarcella and Oxford (1992) on integrating language skills; read Chapter 5 in Galloway and Herron (1995) on listening; find a first-year textbook that presents lessons with an initial listening or reading segment and examine the manner in which grammar and vocabulary are taught.

To prepare for class discussion, think and write about these topics:

• Write a brief introduction for Ms. Combes's restaurant conversation in which you set the scene so that students will understand the context in which the conversation takes place.

• Select a grammar point from a textbook for beginning, intermediate, or advanced learners of the foreign language you teach. Describe how the grammar is contextualized in terms of functions, tasks, and the five goal areas of the standards. Offer additional ideas on how you might contextualize this particular grammar point—for example, by means of an initial taped segment, other functions and/or contexts, and so forth.

References

ACTFL Performance Guidelines for K–12 Learners. (1999). Yonkers, NY: American Council on the Teaching of Foreign Languages.

ACTFL provisional proficiency guidelines. Hastings-on-Hudson, NY: American Council on the Teaching of Foreign Languages. (1982).

ACTFL proficiency guidelines. Yonkers, NY: American Council on the Teaching of Foreign Languages. (1999).

Adair-Hauck, B., & Cumo-Johanssen, P. (1997). Communication goal: Meaning making through a whole language approach. In J. K. Phillips (Ed.), *Collaborations: Meeting new goals, new realities, Northeast Conference Reports* (pp. 35–96). Lincolnwood, IL: NTC/Contemporary Publishing Group.

Anthony, E. M. (1963). Approach, method, and technique. *English Language Teaching, 17,* 63–67.

Asher, J., Kusudo, J., & de la Torre, R. (1974). Learning a second language through commands: The second field test. *The Modern Language Journal, 58,* 24–32.

Ausubel, D. (1968). *Educational psychology: A cognitive view.* New York: Holt, Rinehart and Winston.

Ballman, T. L. (1997). Enhancing beginning language courses through content-enriched instruction. *Foreign Language Annals, 30,* 173–186.

Bruner, J. (1983). *Child's talk: Learning to use language.* New York: Norton.

Buck, K., Byrnes, H., & Thompson, I. (1989). *The ACTFL oral proficiency interview tester training manual.* Hastings-on-Hudson, NY: ACTFL.

Canale, M., & Swain, M. (1980). Theoretical bases of communicative approaches to second language teaching and testing. *Applied Linguistics, 1,* 1–47.

Chastain, K. C. (1988). D*eveloping second-language skills: Theory and practice.* San Diego: Harcourt Brace Jovanovich, Inc.

Chomsky, N. (1965). *Aspects of the theory of syntax.* Cambridge, MA: MIT Press.

Curran, C. (1976). *Counseling-learning in second languages.* Apple River, IL: Apple River Press.

Dandonoli, P., & Henning, G. (1990). An investigation of the construct validity of the ACTFL Proficiency Guidelines and oral interview procedure. *Foreign Language Annals, 23,* 11–22.

Duffy, G. G., & Roehler, L. R. (1986). The subtleties of instructional mediation. *Educational Leadership,* 43, 23-27.

Galloway, V., & Herron, C. (Eds.) (1995). *Research within reach II.* Southern Conference on Language Teaching. Valdosta, GA: Valdosta State University.

Gattegno, C. (1976). *The common sense of foreign language teaching.* New York: Educational Solutions.

Glisan, E. W. (1986). Total physical response: A technique for teaching all skills in Spanish. *Foreign Language Annals, 19,* 419–427.

Glisan, E. W. (1995). Listening. In V. Galloway & C. Herron(Eds.), *Research within reach II.* (pp. 61–83). Southern Conference on Language Teaching. Valdosta, GA: Valdosta State University.

Goals 2000: World-class education for every child. (1994). Washington, D.C.: U.S. Government Printing Office.

Hadley, A. O. (1993). *Teaching language in context.* Boston, MA: Heinle & Heinle.

Heilenman, L. K., Kaplan, I., & Tournier, C. T. (1997). *Voilà.* Boston, MA: Heinle & Heinle.

Higgs, T. V. (Ed.). (1984). *Teaching for proficiency, the organizing principle.* The ACTFL Foreign Language Education Series. Lincolnwood, IL: NTC/Contemporary Publishing Group.

Higgs, T. V., & Clifford, R. T. (1982). Teaching for proficiency: The organizing principle. In T. V. Higgs (Ed.), *Curriculum, competence, and the foreign language teacher.* The ACTFL Foreign Language Education Series (pp. 57–79). Lincolnwood, IL: NTC/Contemporary Publishing Group.

Hymes, D. (1974). *Foundation of sociolinguistics.* Philadelphia: University of Pennsylvania.

Jones, B. F. (1986). Quality and equality through cognitive instruction. *Educational Leadership, 43,* 4–11.

Lado, R. (1964). *Language teaching.* New York: McGraw-Hill.

Lafayette, R. C. & Draper, J. B. (1996). Introduction. In R. C. Lafayette (Ed.), *National standards: a catalyst for reform (pp. 1–8).* ACTFL Foreign Language Education Series. Lincolnwood, IL: NTC/Contemporary Publishing Group.

Liskin-Gasparro, J. E. (1984). The *ACTFL Proficiency Guidelines:* A historical perspective. In T. V. Higgs (Ed.), *Teaching for proficiency, the organizing principle.* The ACTFL Foreign Language Education Series (pp. 11–42). Lincolnwood, IL: NTC/Contemporary Publishing Group.

Littlewood, W. T. (1980). Form and meaning in language teaching methodology. *The Modern Language Journal, 64,* 441–445.

Lozanov, G. (1978). *Suggestology and outlines of suggestopedy.* New York: Gordon and Breach.

National Standards in Foreign Language Education Project.(1996). *National standards for foreign language learning: Preparing for the 21st century.* Lawrence, KS: Allen Press, Inc.

Rassias, J. A. (1983). *New dimensions in language training:* The Dartmouth College experiment. In J. W. Oller, Jr. & P. A. Richard-Amato (Eds.), *Methods that work: A smorgasbord of ideas for language teachers* (pp. 363–374). Rowley, MA: Newbury House.

Rivers, W. (1983). *Communicating naturally in a second language.* Chicago, IL: University of Chicago Press.

Rogoff, B. (1990). *Apprenticeship in thinking.* New York: Oxford University Press.

Sandrock, P. (1995). Foreign language education at the crossroads: Bringing coherence to the journey of a lifetime. In R. Donato & R. M. Terry (Eds.), *Foreign language learning: The journey of a lifetime.* ACTFL Foreign Language Education Series (pp. 167–188). Lincolnwood, IL: NTC/Contemporary Publishing Group.

Savignon, S. J. (1997). *Communicative competence: Theory and practice.* New York: McGraw-Hill.

Scarcella, R. C., & Oxford, R. L. (1992). *The tapestry of language learning.* Boston, MA: Heinle & Heinle.

Strength through wisdom: A critique of U.S. capability. A report to the President from the President's Commission on Foreign Languages and International Studies. (1979). Washington, D.C.: U.S. Government Printing Office.

Swender E. & Duncan, G. (1999). ACTFL performance guidelines for K–12 learners. *Foreign Language Annals, 31,* 479–491.

Terrell, T. (1982). The natural approach to language teaching: An update. *The Modern Language Journal, 66,* 121–132.

Walz, J. (1989). Context and contextualized language practice in foreign language teaching. *The Modern Language Journal, 73,* 160–168.

Williams, M. K., Lively, M. G., & Harper, J. (1998). Designing theme-based activities: Bringing ideas to speech. In J. Harper, M. Lively, & M. Williams (Eds.), *The coming of age of the profession* (pp. 177–189). Boston, MA: Heinle & Heinle.

thandbook.
heinle.com

CHAPTER 3

Organizing Content and Planning for Integrated Language Instruction

In this chapter you will learn about:

- new paradigm for instructional planning
- Oller's Episode Hypothesis
- classroom discourse: IRE vs. IRF
- authentic texts
- content-based instruction
- Atlas Complex
- state frameworks
- instructional goals
- lesson objectives
- advance organizers

Teach and Reflect: Planning for Instruction: Writing Daily Lesson Objectives; Designing a Unit of Instruction; Developing a Content-Based Level Five Foreign Language Class

- **Case Study 1: Does the Class Scheduling Format Make a Difference?**
- **Case Study 2: Using Learners' Needs to Plan for Instruction**

Conceptual Orientation

The impetus of *Goals 2000* (1994) was to provide a broad-based structure of goals that would prompt states and local school districts to rethink and redesign curriculum in ways pertinent to their local situations. State frameworks focus on national standards and specify benchmark tasks, and local school districts design a curriculum specific to their needs (Bartz & Singer, 1996). The national standards document depicts the relationship between the national, state, and local systems as shown in Figure 3.1. The set of documents at each level informs the others: "standards" at the national level provide the basis for "frameworks" at the state level, for "district curricula" at the school district level, and for the "lesson/unit plans" at the classroom level. More states are using the *SFLL* as the basis for the creation of state frameworks or standards, and school districts are using state frameworks to specify curricular goals and objectives.

Figure 3.1 The Relationships Among National, State, and Local Standards Documents

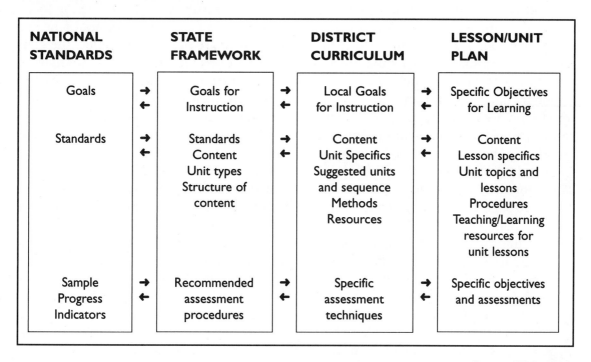

NATIONAL STANDARDS		STATE FRAMEWORK		DISTRICT CURRICULUM		LESSON/UNIT PLAN
Goals	→ ←	Goals for Instruction	→ ←	Local Goals for Instruction	→ ←	Specific Objectives for Learning
Standards	→ ←	Standards Content Unit types Structure of content	→ ←	Content Unit Specifics Suggested units and sequence Methods Resources	→ ←	Content Lesson specifics Unit topics and lessons Procedures Teaching/Learning resources for unit lessons
Sample Progress Indicators	→ ←	Recommended assessment procedures	→ ←	Specific assessment techniques	→ ←	Specific objectives and assessments

Source: SFLL, 1996.

As a beginning teacher, you will probably receive a written foreign language curriculum guide that outlines the content students are expected to learn by the end of the year, and that is consistent with the general purposes described for the entire school system and for the statewide framework. Curriculum guides are generally optional, although some states monitor their implementation more than others. Historically, curriculum guides have been nothing more than a list of the textbook's table of contents, consisting of a series of grammar points and sometimes including vocabulary themes such as weather expressions, numbers, kinship terms, and so on. However, more recently, curriculum design has been changing to reflect the content standards students should achieve at each level of instruction. Teachers use curriculum guides as they organize the content of the year-long course into unit and daily lesson plans.

In this chapter we will use the following terms as they relate to organizing content and planning for instruction:

- *Goal:* an aim or purpose of instruction, often stated in broad terms, as in the five goal areas of the *SFLL;* for example: "to gain knowledge of another culture"
- *Objective:* what the learner will be able to do with the language as a result of instruction, defined in terms of observable behavior; for example: "The learner will be able to invite a friend to go to a social event"; sometimes the term *outcome* is used to refer to an objective
- *Framework:* state document that describes goals and standards to be met by language programs

New Paradigm for Instructional Planning

A paradigm shift in curricular and daily lesson planning results from an increasing focus on standards-based goals and integrated language instruction. Figure 3.2 illustrates the old and new paradigms in instructional planning. Objectives are designed to reflect the content standards, that is, what students should know and be able to do with the language rather than the table of contents in the textbook. Interdisciplinary content and culture are no longer ancillary but rather the core of standards-driven curricula. Skills are integrated into lesson design by means of tasks that build on one another. The learner is given more responsibility for learning and is encouraged to use the foreign language to acquire new knowledge about topics of personal interest. The teacher assumes the role of a facilitator who guides instruction without being the sole source or expert transmitter of knowledge. This approach helps to dispel what Lee and VanPatten (1995) refer to as the "Atlas Complex," through which the teacher provides all information and students receive it. This type of planning assumes (1) the use of a wide variety of materials and tools that extend beyond the capabilities of a textbook; and (2) ongoing assessment of student progress toward addressing the standards through strategies such as completion of real-world tasks, exploration of content, and self-assessment. In this kind of planning, the teacher organizes learning for students so that they can know how and when to say what to whom, and so they and the teacher can know students are learning.

Figure 3.2   Paradigm Shift in Instructional Planning

	OLD PARADIGM	NEW PARADIGM
Objectives	Stated in terms of grammatical knowledge as provided in textbook	Stated in terms of what learners should know and be able to do with the language
Content/Culture	Content limited to bits and pieces of cultural information included in textbook; connections to other disciplines absent	Interdisciplinary and cultural connections; integration of cultural and academic content
Skills	Practice of individual skills: listening, speaking, reading, writing	Integrated practice of skills; skills build on one another
The Learner	Mostly passive and learns the material presented by the teacher	Actively engaged in learning and has opportunities to explore her/his own interests
The Teacher	The center of instruction and the audience for learners; students work to impress the teacher	Facilitates instruction and guides student learning; designs opportunities for cooperative learning; audience includes peers and community

Figure 3.2 (continued)

	OLD PARADIGM	NEW PARADIGM
Materials	Textbook as primary material	Textbook as one of many tools; others include authentic materials (tape recordings, videos, magazines, short stories, folklore), World Wide Web, visuals, realia
Assessment	Purpose to evaluate student achievement; focus on discrete-point grammar items, often out of context; primarily paper-and-pencil testing; learners provide one right answer	Purpose to assess progress in meeting standards and to improve instruction; assessment strategies include integration of skills for meaningful purposes, exploration of content, completion of real-world tasks, self-assessment by learners

Source: Adapted from Bragger & Rice, 1998.

 The new paradigm for planning assumes the use of a variety of materials beyond the textbook and ongoing performance assessments of student progress toward meeting the standards.

Integrating Skills and Organizing Content

Planning for language instruction in which skills are integrated requires the use of contextualized input, authentic texts, and interdisciplinary and cultural content.

❐ Characteristics of the "Text" as Input

In Chapter 2, you learned that a top-down approach uses whole language in the form of an initial oral or written text that provides the context or theme of the unit. As early as 1983, Oller maintained that certain kinds of texts are more easily internalized than others. According to Oller's Episode Hypothesis, "text (i.e., discourse in any form) will be easier to reproduce, understand, and recall, to the extent that it is motivated and structured episodically" (Oller, 1983, p. 12). Episodic organization has two aspects: "motivation," or affect, and logical structure. According to Oller (1983), a text that has "motivation" has an apparent purpose, holds the attention and interest of the listener or reader, introduces a conflict of some sort, and is not dull and boring. A text that is logically organized has the characteristics of a good story and connects meaningfully to our experience in the world (Oller, 1993). Carrell also found that text organization is an important factor in comprehension. Her research revealed that readers comprehend most effectively texts that feature the typical "problem-solution" type of organization (Carrell, 1984). In discussing the implications of the Episode Hypothesis for language teaching, Oller states that "perhaps second language teaching would be more successful if it incorporated principles of good story writing along with the benefits of sound linguistic analysis" (1983, p. 12). Unfortunately, language textbooks often still contain boring texts and dialogues that do not reflect real-world language or situations, although they usually contain multiple examples of the grammar being presented.

 "Text (i.e., discourse in any form) will be easier to reproduce, understand, and recall, to the extent that it is motivated and structured episodically."

Read the following example of a dialog from a beginning-level Spanish textbook (Terrell, Andrade, Egasse, 1998). Is it episodically organized? That is, does it reflect logical organization and motivation, according to Oller's definition? Does it captivate the interest of the reader? Is the context a real-world one?

[Los estudiantes] hablan de la ropa que llevan los estudiantes y la profesora.

E1: La blusa rosada de Lan es bonita, ¿no?

E2: Sí, es muy bonita, pero... ¿es rosada o roja?

E1: ¡Es rosada... !

E2: ¿De qué color son los pantalones de Alberto?

E1: Son grises. Y su camisa es anaranjada.

E2: *[Disgusted]* El color gris con el color anaranjado... ¡yuck!

E1: ¿Es morada la chaqueta de Luis?

E2: *[Unsure]* Eh... hummm... es azul... ¿no?

E1: Sí,... La chaqueta de Luis es azul.

E2: Pero el abrigo de la profesora... es morado, ¿no?

E1: ¡Correcto! ¡Y es muy elegante!

E2: *[Unconvinced]* ¿Elegante? Bueno, sí, un poquito...

[English translation]

[The students] talk about the clothing that the students and professor are wearing.

S1: . . . Lan's pink blouse is pretty, isn't it?

S2: Yes, it's very pretty, but . . . is it pink or red?

S1: It's red . . . !

S2: What color are Alberto's pants?

S1: They are gray. And his shirt is orange.

S2: *[Disgusted]* The color grey with the color orange . . . yuck!

S1: Is Luis's jacket purple?

S2: *[Unsure]* Uh . . . hmmm . . . it's blue . . . right?

S1: Yes, . . . Luis's jacket is blue.

S2: But the professor's coat is purple, right?

S1: Right! And it's very elegant!

S2: *[Unconvinced]* Elegant? Well, yes, a little . . .

Compare the dialog above to the following conversation that students hear on tape. The conversation comes from a 1996 intermediate-level Spanish textbook program (Glisan and Shrum, 1996). How does this conversation reflect the typical organization of a real conversation? Is the conversation "motivated"? Does it leave the listener wondering about anything at the end of the conversation?

Ud. va a escuchar una conversación breve entre Memo y Maite, dos estudiantes que acaban de conocerse. Ellos están en la residencia estudiantil.

MEMO: ¡Hola! ¿Qué tal? Mira, no conozco a mucha gente, pero si me permites me presento. Me llamo Guillermo, pero mis padres me dicen Memo. Tú, ¿cómo te llamas?

MAITE: Hola, Memo. Yo me llamo Maite y aunque nací en los EE.UU., mis padres son de España.

MEMO: ¡Ah sí!

MAITE: Mmmm.

MEMO: ¿De qué parte de España?

MAITE: Bueno, mi padre es del País Vasco, y mi madre es de Galicia.

MEMO: Ah, de Galicia... y dime, ¿llevan mucho tiempo aquí?

MAITE: Mmmm... aproximadamente unos treinta años, o algo así. Pero yo estoy muy contenta de haber nacido aquí.

MEMO: Mmm. Ya...

MAITE: Dime una cosa, ¿dónde vives tú? ¿Eres nuevo aquí en la universidad?

MEMO: Sí, éste es mi primer año. Estoy recién llegado de Chile y mi casa, bueno... vivo en un... vivo en un apartamento aquí como a dos cuadras en la calle Tremont. Creo que es el 791. Apenas llegué ayer, así que no me sé la dirección muy bien.

MAITE: Mmm, ¡qué coincidencia! Yo también vivo muy cerca de donde vives tú. Yo vivo en el 721 de la Tremont, ¡mmmm!

MEMO: Ah, ¡qué bien! Y dime... ¿qué vas a... qué vas a estudiar tú aquí?

MAITE: Bueno, me interesa mucho el periodismo.

MEMO: ¡Ajá!

MAITE: Bueno. Mucho, mucho, pero pues, no sé, todavía no estoy muy segura. Y tú, ¿qué es lo que quieres estudiar?

MEMO: Bueno, yo soy músico y quiero especializarme en música. Dime, ¿tú estás casada?

MAITE: No, soy soltera. ¿Y tú?

MEMO: También soltero, soltero, y estoy tratando de conocer gente porque...

MAITE: Mira, me tengo que ir porque me quedé en ver con una persona en biblioteca, ¿OK?

MEMO: OK, entonces, nos vemos luego.

MAITE: Mmmm... Hasta pronto.

MEMO: Chao.

MAITE: Chao.

[English translation]

MEMO: Hi! How are you? Listen, I don't know a lot of people, but if you'll let me, I'll introduce myself. I'm Guillermo, but my parents call me Memo. And you, what's your name?

MAITE: Hi, Memo. I'm Maite and, although I was born in the U.S., my parents are from Spain.

MEMO: Oh yes!

MAITE: Mmmm.

MEMO: From what part of Spain?

MAITE: Well, my father is from the Basque Country, and my mother is from Galicia.

MEMO: Oh, from Galicia . . . and tell me, have they been here a long time?

MAITE: Mmmm . . . approximately thirty years, or something like that. But I'm very happy to have been born here.

MEMO: Mmm. So . . .

MAITE: Tell me something, where do you live? Are you new at the university?

MEMO: Yes, this is my first year. I have recently arrived from Chile and my house, well . . . I live in . . . I live in an apartment about two blocks from here on Tremont Street. I think it's number 791. I just got here yesterday, so I don't know the address very well.

MAITE: Mmm, what a coincidence! I also live very close to where you live. I live at number 721 on Tremont, mmm!

MEMO: Oh, great! And tell me . . . what are you going to . . . what are you going to study here?

MAITE: Well, I'm interested a lot in journalism.

MEMO: Oh!

MAITE: Well, a lot, a lot, but well, I don't know; I'm still not very sure. And you, what do you want to study?

MEMO: Well, I'm a musician and I want to major in music. Tell me, are you married?

MAITE:	No, I'm single. And you?
MEMO:	I'm also single, single, and I'm trying to meet people because . . .
MAITE:	Listen, I have to go because I have to see someone in the library, OK?
MEMO:	OK, then, see you later.
MAITE:	Mmmm . . . See you soon.
MEMO:	Bye.
MAITE:	Bye.

❑ Teacher Input: Feedback or Evaluation?

Just as the type of oral or written text is critical in the instructional planning process, the nature of teacher input must also be considered as curricula and lessons are designed. In Chapter 1, you explored the importance of developing learners' interactional competence so that they are able to manage discussions in relevant ways. As Hall (1995) has pointed out, the rhetorical structure of most classroom talk is "IRE":

- The teacher *initiates* an assertion or asks a question.
- The student *responds.*
- The teacher *evaluates,* by giving an evaluative statement such as "very good" or by asking the same or similar question of another student (Mehan, 1979).

IRE can be used as a tool for finding out if learners have internalized a grammatical structure or set of vocabulary (e.g., in order to find out whether students can tell time in the foreign language, the teacher uses a cardboard clock with movable hands and asks students to tell what time is displayed on it). In this type of oral exchange, the teacher often asks *assessing questions* (i.e., questions that usually have one right answer or a predictable set of responses) and offers an evaluative response such as "very good," "right," "excellent" (Tharp & Gallimore, 1991). However, IRE does not exemplify communication in informal contexts outside the classroom, nor does it move the discourse forward or build meaning.

Reread the scripted classroom discourse sample that appears in Case Study 1 in Chapter 1. What are some examples of IRE in this script?

☞ IRE = input, response, evaluation (assessing questions)

In Krashen's Monitor Model (1982) presented in Chapter 1, a major component is the use of comprehensible input by the teacher in enabling learners to receive input that is interesting, a little beyond their current level of competence, and understandable through the use of background knowledge and contextual and extralinguistic cues. However, from the perspective of "talk-as-discursive-practice," this definition of input needs to be expanded to include the aspects of topic development and management (Hall, 1995). If learners are to acquire the skills necessary to be able to participate in conversations outside the classroom, then they must be exposed to more than the typical IRE sequences that occur in classrooms. Wells (1993) contrasts "IRE" to "IRF," which he defines as the type of classroom communication that focuses on making meaning and extending discourse, not on evaluating responses:

- The teacher *initiates* an assertion or asks a question.
- The student *responds.*
- The teacher *provides feedback* in order to encourage students to think and to perform at higher levels (e.g., "Tell me more! Are you saying that . . . ?").

In this discourse model, teachers use *assisting questions,* which encourage learners to think, which push learners to perform at higher levels, and which integrate content and topics (Tharp & Gallimore, 1991). Examples of assisting questions are: "What do you mean by that?"; "That's incredible!"; "Could you explain that a little more?" Furthermore, students need experience in using turn taking, which Hall (1996) notes is a primary communicative resource in speech-based instructional practices and a crucial part of the development of sociality. In classrooms dominated by IRE, learners do not have real opportunities to engage in turn taking, as the teacher controls who will speak and when. The implications of Hall's (1996) research is that, when planning for instruction, the teacher should simulate real conversations in the classroom and thereby help learners develop interactional strategies such as turn taking. This may mean that some opportunities must be provided for discussions during which students assume the responsibility for taking a conversational turn rather than raise a hand and wait to be called upon by the teacher.

Now examine the following script of classroom discourse. What examples of IRF are there? How does this script differ from the one you analyzed in Chapter 1?

Note: This is a transcript and an English translation of a discussion that takes place in a French I high school class. The prelude for this discussion is a question posed by the teacher: "What plans do you have for Thanksgiving vacation?" A student responds that he is going hunting. The teacher, who is a native of France and unfamiliar with the concept of hunting, asks him for additional information.

T: Tu vas chasser... pour... une personne?

Ss: *[Rires...]*

S1: Non... quelque... chose!

T: Tu veux dire un animal?

S1: Oui!

T: Hum... chasser *[she writes the verb* chasser *on the board]*

S1: Chasser. Euh... je... vais... euh... chasser... euh... dinde.

T: Ah! Tu vas chasser la dinde?

S1: Oui.

S2: *[In English] Shoot a turkey . . . that's not nice.*

Ss: *[Rires...]*

T: Non, mais c'est bon la dinde! Et puis, c'est un sport la chasse, n'est-ce pas?

S1: Oui, un sport.

T: *[Looking at the class]* Vous ne chassez pas?

Ss: NON!!!

T: Oh! Vous êtes protecteurs des animaux?

Ss: Non! *[Rires...]*

T: Vous mangez les animaux, non? Oui, on mange les animaux! En plus, c'est stupide une dinde, non?

S1: Hum... la dinde domestique... euh... *domesticated turkeys...* c'est stupide!

T: Ah? Mais la dinde sauvage est intelligente?

S1: ... oui... très intelligente. *[Rires...]*

[English translation]

T: You're going hunting . . . for . . . a person?

Ss: *[Laughter . . .]*

S1: No . . . some . . . thing!

T: You mean an animal!

S1: Yes!

T: Hum . . . to hunt *[she writes the verb* chasser *on the board]*

S1: To hunt. Eh . . . I'm . . . going . . . uh . . . to hunt . . . uh . . . turkey.

T: Ah! You're going to hunt turkey?

S1: Yes.

S2: *[In English]* Shoot a turkey . . . that's not nice.

Ss: *[Laughter . . .]*

T: No, but turkeys are nice! So . . . hunting is a sport, right?

S1: Yes, a sport.

T: *[Looking at the class]* The rest of you don't hunt?

Ss: NO!!!

T: Oh! You are animal protectors?

Ss: No! *[Laughter . . .]*

T: You eat animals, right? Yes, we eat animals! Besides, turkeys are dumb, aren't they?

S1: Hum . . . domesticated turkeys . . . uh . . . *domesticated turkeys* . . . are dumb!

T: Oh? But wild turkeys are intelligent?

S1: Yes, very intelligent. *[Laughter . . .]*

Source: Donato, 1998

 IRF = input, response, feedback (assisting questions)

❒ Authentic Materials

In order to build in context and meaning, an instructional plan must provide for the use of authentic materials. Galloway defined *authentic texts* as "those written and oral communications produced *by* members of a language and culture group *for* members of the same language and culture group" (Galloway, 1998, p. 133). According to Villegas Rogers and Medley, authentic materials reflect a "naturalness of form and an appropriateness of cultural and situational context" found in the language as used by native speakers (1988, p. 468). Authentic texts include realia, magazine and newspaper articles, literary excerpts, poems, audio recordings, videotapes, satellite broadcasts, radio programs, and so forth. Through exploring these materials, students have the opportunity to see and hear real language that serves a purpose. Another convincing reason to use authentic samples is for their richness in cultural content. Because these texts are prepared for native speakers, they reflect the details of everyday life in a culture as well as its societal values. Galloway suggests that "authentic texts, as total communicative events, invite observation of a culture talking to *itself*, not to outsiders; in its own context; through its own language; where forms are referenced to its own people, who *mean* through their own framework of associations; and whose voices show dynamic interplay of individuals and groupings of individuals within the loose general consensus that is the culture's reality" (1998, p. 133). We often have difficulty integrating culture into our teaching because we have stripped language of its authenticity and hence its culture.

 Authentic texts = "those written and oral communications produced *by* members of a language and culture group *for* members of the same language and culture group"

One of the challenges teachers often describe when using authentic texts is that these materials contain linguistic structures and vocabulary that students may not have already learned. Text is simply text, with varying levels of sophistication or complexity. Difficulty, as a concept, is involved with what learners are asked to do with the text. Thus difficulty level lies within the tasks that learners are asked to complete based on that material, and *not* within the text itself (Terry, 1998). Because of the richness of these materials, the teacher might use a particular text for the first time and ask students simply to identify certain pieces of information; s/he might present the same text at a later time and ask students to explore it in more depth. As Pusack and Otto (1996) point out, without early exposure to authentic texts, learners are ill prepared to interpret them when they are suddenly presented at a later stage in language study. In Chapters 5 and 6, you will learn more about how to use authentic materials in the classroom as a strategy for addressing the Cultures and Communication goal areas.

❒ Making Connections: Content-Based Instruction

Making connections with culture and other disciplines is at the heart of planning for standards-oriented instruction. Content-based instruction (CBI) is not new to language teaching, as it has been widely implemented in FLES (Foreign Language in the Elementary

School) and ESL (English as a Second Language) programs. CBI became the foundation of immersion and foreign language programs for K–12 students as early as the 1960s, and its success in immersion programs in Canada has been widely documented (Lambert, 1984). Research from foreign/second language immersion programs confirms that content-based approaches result in student attainment of advanced levels of proficiency (Genessee, 1998; Johnson & Swain, 1997). CBI uses the content, learning objectives, and activities from the school curriculum as the vehicle for teaching language skills, and it has been shown to result in enhanced motivation, self-confidence, language proficiency, and cultural literacy (Leaver & Stryker, 1989; Met, 1991). Although, historically, CBI has been implemented primarily at the elementary school level, its potential positive impact on secondary and post-secondary language instruction has been acknowledged (Glisan & Fall, 1991; Lafayette & Buscaglia, 1985). Glisan and Fall note that "the content-based instruction found in elementary immersion programs utilizes a key educational principle that advances all learning-increased time on task" (1991, p. 11). They suggest implementing CBI at the high-school level by offering content-based electives such as art, physical education, and music, in addition to foreign language classes.

> 🗝 **CBI uses the content, learning objectives, and activities from the school curriculum as the vehicle for teaching language skills.**

In acknowledging the new paradigm for teaching that is occurring as a result of the attention to standards, Bragger and Rice (1998) propose a developmental model for content-oriented instruction as a means of placing content and connections at the center of instructional planning. Learners are involved in researching less familiar contexts, and the teacher assumes the role of a facilitator. As Figure 3.3 illustrates, the model includes four stages of development that are not associated with a particular time frame and can correspond to any curricular levels. Stage 1 prepares learners for content connections and draws upon their receptive skills. Stages 2 and 3 focus on the development of the content connection, with progressive sophistication of the content and of the productive language skills. Stage 4 expands the content into unfamiliar areas. Bragger and Rice acknowledge that for learning to occur in this framework, "there must be familiarity with *either* the language needed to deal with the content *or* the content itself" (1998, pp. 200–201). During the planning process, the teacher must consider the linguistic level of the learner, the level of the input, and the familiarity of the content in setting the challenge level of learning experiences. For example, if the content in a particular task is familiar, the language level could be raised in order to stimulate learning; if the content is not familiar, it might be desirable to maintain the learner's current language level for the task in order to facilitate learning (Bragger & Rice, 1998). (In Chapter 4, you will have the opportunity to explore content-based instruction in greater detail as it relates to the Connections goal area of the standards.)

Figure 3.3 Developmental Model for Content-Oriented Instruction

	ACADEMIC CONTENT	OUTCOMES	CULTURAL CONTENT
	Standard 3.1: Students reinforce and further their knowledge of other disciplines through the foreign languages.		**Standard 3.2:** Students acquire information and recognize the distinctive viewpoints that are available only through the foreign language and its culture.
STAGE 1 (Preparing for content connections)	Links to content areas (e.g., math word problems, metric system)	RECOGNIZE UNDERSTAND	Links to cultural data (e.g., music, poems, folktales)
STAGE 2	Familiar academic content (e.g., human biology, geography)	UNDERSTAND TALK ABOUT PRESENT (word/phrase/sentence level)	Familiar (Equivalent) cultural content (e.g., short novel, health)
(Developing the content orientation) **STAGE 3**	Less familiar academic content (e.g., art history, genetics)	PRESENT (sentence/paragraph level) RESEARCH + PRESENT	Less familiar cultural content (e.g., short novel, history of film)
STAGE 4 (Expanding the content orientation)	Unfamiliar academic content (e.g., psychology, information theory)	RESEARCH + PRESENT	Unfamiliar cultural content (e.g., social structures, literature)

Source: Bragger & Rice, 1998.

Long-Term Planning for Instruction

❐ From State Framework to Year-Long Planning

Appendix 3.1 presents an excerpt from the state of Nebraska's framework that is based on the national standards (Nebraska Department of Education, 1996). You will note that the framework describes what learners are able to do at three levels of ability: beginning, developing, and expanding. School districts use these state frameworks as the basis for program and course development. At some point in your teaching career, you will be involved in writing a curriculum for a language program. Since long-term objectives must be valid regardless of which textbook is used, teachers should write a curriculum for any given level without reference to a particular textbook. The text should be adapted to reflect the objectives rather than vice versa.

Can you describe the connection between the national standards and the state framework in Appendix 3.1?

MacDonald has identified three steps in undertaking course-level planning:

1. Identifying (or reviewing) the central goals and purposes of the program or course you will be teaching.

2. Selecting course content, then organizing and sequencing to make it as coherent and teachable as possible.

3. Determining the amount of time to be spent on the various topics in the sequence. (1991, p. 66).

In the first step, language teachers identify the broader skills they want students to acquire in terms of the five goal areas and standards. As a second step, the teacher selects themes or contexts and linguistic functions, together with the grammar and vocabulary that students need to learn in order to attain the end-of-the-year goals. This course content is then organized and sequenced. Third, teachers decide how much time will be spent on each theme or topic. Appendix 3.2 is an example of an excerpt from a year planner for a Level 1 language class from the state of Nebraska (Nebraska Department of Education, 1996).

  Can you describe the relationship between the year planner in Appendix 3.2 and the state framework in Appendix 3.1?

❏ Unit Planning

In addition to course-level or year-long planning, you will also design the units of instruction to be presented throughout the year. A unit is usually a series of related lessons around a theme or a particular context. Some examples include family, shopping and bargaining, and daily routine/school activities. While units may correspond to unit divisions in the textbook, teachers often adapt the text in order to include other material and/ or address the needs of learners more effectively. Appendix 3.3 illustrates a unit planner for a unit on "Shopping at the Market" (Nebraska Department of Education, 1996). In developing a unit, the teacher (1) identifies the goals and standards to be addressed; (2) establishes a context; (3) develops the progress indicators (progress toward reaching the standards) and essential skills and knowledge needed; (4) designs the instructional strategies and assessments; and (5) identifies the resources to be used.

A unit is a series of related lessons around a theme or a particular context.

Daily Lesson Planning

❏ Writing Objectives

Working from the broader unit plans, language teachers organize the material to be presented in daily lessons. One of the most important aspects of planning a daily lesson is to identify the objective(s) that you want to achieve by the end of the class period. Effective objectives are measurable and describe what learners will be able to do in terms of observable behavior and when using the foreign language. For example, the objective may focus on learners' ability to accomplish some linguistic function—to communicate some real information. Examples of good objectives are that learners will be able to describe their daily routine, to identify prices of clothing given in a radio commercial, to compare the educational systems of the United States and target cultures, and to write an e-mail message to a "keypal" from a target country. Objectives use action verbs that represent desired student behavior. Verbs such as "learn" or "understand" are generally too vague for use in objectives. You may find it helpful to refer to Appendix 3.4 for Bloom's Taxonomy of Thinking Processes, which contains a list of action verbs that can be used in writing objectives. Appendix 3.5 illustrates the levels of Bloom's Taxonomy as applied to foreign language skills (Nebraska Department of Education, 1996). Objectives should also contain an indication of the realistic context in which students will be able to use the target language that they learn. Objectives should not consist of a listing of textbook exercises, although these may be a part of the instructional strategies.

Which of the following are appropriate lesson objectives?

1. The student will learn about modes of transportation.

2. The teacher will present ways to tell time.

3. The student will describe his or her family.

4. The student will understand how to form the future tense.

5. The student will identify numbers given in a taped airline announcement.

 An objective describes what learners will be able to do in/with the target language.

❒ The ACTFL Proficiency Guidelines and Design of Objectives

The teacher might use the *ACTFL Proficiency Guidelines* (1999) for designing objectives in two ways. First, the guidelines can be used to establish a performance level to be attained by the end of a given program. For example, teachers might establish "Intermediate-Mid" as the minimal speaking performance level to be attained by the end of a four-year high school sequence of study. In this case, the ACTFL guidelines would be used to develop broader objectives or outcomes that describe Intermediate-Mid proficiency. For example, proficiency-based objectives describe what the student should be able to do at this level:

- ask and answer questions related to personal needs and familiar topics
- participate in short conversations and express basic courtesy
- successfully handle a number of uncomplicated situations necessary for survival in the target culture

It is important to note that, while the proficiency guidelines can be helpful in establishing performance expectations, they are *not* curriculum and cannot be used verbatim as objectives since they are written as assessment descriptors for testers. The guidelines, particularly at the lower levels, tend to describe in detail negative aspects of performance, or what the speaker cannot do well. For example, in assessing the speech of an Intermediate-Low speaker, the guidelines state that "Their utterances are often filled with hesitancy and inaccuracies . . . Their speech is characterized by frequent pauses, ineffective reformulations and self-corrections " *(ACTFL Proficiency Guidelines–Speaking*, 1999, p. 3). Although the ACTFL guidelines are not suitable as statements of objectives, they can be helpful in setting expectations of learner performance.

Second, teachers might use proficiency principles for both unit and daily planning. Expected learner outcomes can be defined in terms of the *functions* learners can perform (lesson objectives), the specific *contexts* in which they can use the language, and the *accuracy* of their language (Swender, 1999).

 How were the terms *function, context/content,* and *accuracy* defined in Chapter 2?

❒ Designing a Daily Lesson Plan

Freeman (1996) points out the results of research that examined how teachers actually plan lessons, that is, what they thought about ahead of time for the lesson and what they were thinking about as they taught (Nunan, 1992). Findings revealed that teachers tend to visualize lessons as *clusters or sequences of activity* , tend to blend *content* with activity, and tend to focus on their *particular students* (Clark & Peterson, 1986; Freeman, 1996).

As a novice teacher, you will undoubtedly need to design daily lesson plans that are detailed in order to help guide you through the teaching process. A suggested format for developing the daily lesson plan appears on pages 64–65. This format illustrates the process the teacher follows during the planning phase, teaching phase, and reflective phase. Under the "Activities" section, possible segments of the lesson are listed. This approach is adapted from the one suggested by Ballman (1998, 1996).[1] The purpose of the "Setting the Stage" phase is to capture students' attention on the lesson context, to activate students' background knowledge, and to prepare students for the learning process. Ausubel, Novak, and Hanesian recommend the use of "advance organizers," that is, "appropriately relevant and inclusive introductory materials that are maximally clear and stable . . . introduced in advance of the learning material itself, used to facilitate establishing a meaningful learning set" (1978, pp. 170–171). Advance organizers, such as visuals and pre-listening/pre-reading activities, can be used to activate students' existing knowledge and facilitate meaningful learning. The "Providing Input/Engaging Learners" phase consists of presenting oral language in context, using visual support in the form of drawings, photos, and other visuals and/or written language, and incorporating comprehension check techniques to ensure comprehension. It also provides opportunities for learners actively to be involved in attending to the input and interacting with the teacher. "Guided Participation" is used here within a Vygotskian framework to refer to the scaffolded assistance offered to the learner (novice) by the teacher and/or peers (experts) in helping the learner to solve a problem or perform a task. The "Extension" phase denotes the opportunities for pairs/groups of students to participate in culminating activities that integrate multiple skills and standards. During the "Closure" stage, the teacher brings the lesson to a close by asking students to recall what they learned and/or by describing how the current lesson will be used as the basis for the next lesson. Note that every lesson may not feature all of the components. For example, on a day in which the teacher is presenting a story or a tape-recorded authentic segment, s/he may need more time to provide input. On the following day, the teacher may give much less input, as students are engaged in activities.

Planning Phase

    I. CONTENT:

        A. Context/Theme:

        B. Objectives: Learners will be able to. . .

        C. Standards addressed:

    II. LEARNERS: What do I need to know about the learners in order to plan instruction? What background knowledge do they need? What experiences, if any, have they had with this content? What special needs of my students need to be addressed in instruction?

Teaching Phase

    III. ACTIVITIES: (include materials) What are the teacher and learners doing? Possible instructional sequence:

        A. Setting the Stage

        B. Providing Input/Engaging Learners

---

1. See Ballman, 1996, for a "Model Five-Day Communicative Lesson Plan."

C. **Guided Participation**

D. **Extension**

E. **Closure**

Reflection Phase

IV. ADAPTATIONS TO LESSON: What changes did I have to make as I taught the lesson? Explain.

V. SELF-REFLECTION ON LESSON EFFECTIVENESS: Did I achieve my lesson objectives? How do I know? What worked especially well and why? What would I change if I were to teach this lesson again?

Teach and Reflect

Episode One

Planning for Instruction

Task A: Writing Daily Lesson Objectives

Use the Nebraska Foreign Language Frameworks Unit Planner in Appendix 3.3. Imagine that you are beginning this unit on "Shopping at the Market" in your Level 1 language class. Design Part I (Content) of the lesson plan presented earlier for the first TWO DAYS of this unit: describe the context/theme, the objectives (what learners will be able to do), and the standards addressed.

Task B: Designing a Unit of Instruction

Using the Year Planner in Appendix 3.2 and the Unit Planner in Appendix 3.3, design for a Level 1 language class another unit of instruction that reflects the goals of the year planner. Follow the format of the Unit Planner and include the title of the unit, the goals and standards addressed, the context, the progress indicators, the essential skills/knowledge needed, the assessments, the instructional strategies, and the resources. You may find it helpful to use a beginning-level textbook for some ideas, although be careful not to use the textbook as the primary resource.

Episode Two

Developing a Content-Based Level 5 Foreign Language Class

You are a high school foreign language teacher whose teaching assignment for next year includes a level 5 class. This is the first time that your program has had enough students for level 5, and you want to make the course a valuable experience that will motivate other students to take it in the future. You would like to design a content-based course instead of a skills-based one. What are some possibilities for incorporating content at this level in the high school curriculum? Use Bragger and Rice's Developmental Model for Content-Oriented Instruction (1998) presented in Figure 3.3 to give an example of the content you might integrate. Remember to include cultural content as well. Your instructor may ask you to work with one or two classmates on this assignment.

Discuss and Reflect

Case Study I

Does the Class Scheduling Format Make a Difference?[2]

Four students are all enrolled in the same Methods of Teaching Foreign Languages seminar at State University, in conjunction with their student teaching experience. Gabriel is teaching Spanish at Grand Forks High School where six classes meet for fifty minutes each day. Emily is teaching French at Rifton City High School which is on a block schedule: three classes meet for ninety minutes each on "A" day, and three other classes meet for ninety minutes each on "B" day. Li is teaching at Willowdale Middle School where two morning classes meet every day for one hour, and two other classes meet on the "A" day/"B" day schedule but each for 120 minutes. Conrad teaches at Cummings Middle School where his schedule is the same as Li's, except that on Mondays and Wednesdays the one-hour classes are in the morning; on Tuesdays and Thursdays the one-hour classes are in the afternoon, and on Fridays all classes meet for one hour each. The student teachers wrote the following comments in their journals at the beginning of the fall semester:

GABRIEL: I am so happy I will be student teaching in a school where I can see each student every day; I think it's important for them to practice in Spanish every day, especially since they are immersed in an English-speaking environment all day long. Besides that, I can keep in touch with them as people and know how they feel every day—something that's really critical for teenagers today. It gives me a chance to show I really care about what they learn and how they feel about it. Like today, when Cleo came into class, he was all happy because he made the winning goal at the soccer game last night. It was great to congratulate him this morning. I know there will be times when he misses that winning goal and I can at least let him know that I'm there for him.

EMILY: The block schedule is hard for me to get used to, since I went to a school that had forty-five-minute periods. My cooperating teacher has lots of activities planned for each session, though, and the students spend a lot of time practicing French. Today we had twelve different activities in one

2. See also Houston, Abrahamsen, Lucero, and Richardson, 1990

ninety-minute period for French I. So the students didn't feel like they were being taken from one activity to another, my cooperating teacher related three of the activities to the same reading selection and two more to a grammar point that was in the reading. Then we were able to have students introduce each other to a visitor from Congo and they practiced conversing using formal speech. I think students have a chance really to "get into" the language. But my cooperating teacher told me that the students who take French I this way will finish it in one semester and they won't be able to take French II until the next year in the fall. Won't they lose a lot? I worry about that. The good side is that when they start this in the seventh grade, they can finish French IV by the end of the tenth grade. So then what do they do? Study no French until college? I wonder if the school system will add French V and VI and hire new teachers—maybe there's going to be a job in that for me!

LI: I think I'm finally getting used to this schedule. First thing in the morning, two classes meet for an hour each, and these are classes that "somebody" decided were essential and students had to have every day. So what classes are they? Math and science of course! As a German teacher, I have a planning period and study hall! Then I get my first class of German I students for 120 minutes and then German II students for the next 120 minutes. The next day, I get my German III students and the ESL class. I love having the extra time to plan for my students since I see them only every other day, but I think sometimes two hours is too long. And then, sometimes I wish I could see the ESL students and the German I students every day, but the principal says math and science classes have the priority for the everyday schedule. I heard today that the teachers at Bellevue spent a year on this schedule and they all went to a board meeting to complain.

CONRAD: I was talking with Li, and my schedule is a lot more complicated than hers. I wonder who cooks these things up! My guess is that they think kids will be sleepy in the morning so the same classes shouldn't suffer all the time—but then wouldn't the students be more awake and do their best work in the morning? Of course, now, like in August, and again in April and May, it will be hot in the afternoons so I guess the same classes shouldn't have to be taught in the heat of the day. I'm really pretty happy about the schedule because I get the best of both kinds of classes, the short ones and the long ones, but gosh, there's so much to think about—and what if a student misses a day and then the schedule is different the next day, and what about days when school is cancelled due to a storm or power failure or some other emergency? Seems like it will be easy to get mixed up. I'll just go along with the system for now and see how it all pans out.

Ask yourself these questions:

1. What are the principles behind the various scheduling arrangements outlined?

2. What are the implications for each scheduling option for the school in general, and for foreign/second languages in particular?

3. How will teacher planning differ in each of these scenarios?

4. How will student learning differ in each of these scenarios?

The following is a schematic for the four-block model, also known as the 4 x 4 model, or the straight block model:

FIRST SEMESTER						
Course 1 (90 min.)	Passing (5–15 min.)	Course 2 (90 min.)	Lunch	Course 3 (90 min.)	Passing (5–15 min.)	Course 4 (90 min.)

SECOND SEMESTER						
Course 5 (90 min.)	Passing (5–15 min.)	Course 6 (90 min.)	Lunch	Course 7 (90 min.)	Passing (5–15 min.)	Course 8 (90 min.)

Source: ACTFL Professional Issues Report, 1996.

The following schematic is a sample of a rotating block schedule:

BLOCK A	BLOCK B
Course 1 Course 2 Lunch Course 3 Course 4	Course 5 Course 6 Lunch Course 7 Course 8
Week 1: Mon. / Block A Tues. / Block B Wed. / Block A Thurs. / Block B Fri. / Block A	Week 1: Mon. / Block B Tues. / Block A Wed. / Block B Thurs. / Block A Fri. / Block B

Source: ACTFL Professional Issues Report, 1996.

To prepare the case:

Read ACTFL's Professional Issues Report (1996), Block Scheduling and Second-Language Instruction; read Espitia (1998) for practical ideas on how to make block scheduling work; read Lapkin, Harley, and Hart, 1997; interview a teacher who teaches in at least two of the scheduling options listed by ACTFL. Summarize the comments you collect and compare them with those of your classmates.

To prepare for class discussion, think and write about these topics:

- Your first job is one in which you have the schedule Emily has. Using the principles for instructional design you studied in this chapter, develop a lesson for a ninety-minute period. Use the daily lesson plan format presented in this chapter.
- Emily mentions that the teachers at Bellevue dislike teaching according to the block schedule. In the following chart, administrators listed the problems they thought block scheduling would solve, teachers listed the benefits they found in the 4 x 4 block, and teachers and students listed their reasons for preferring the rotating block and for objecting to block scheduling.

Problems potentially solved by a 4 x 4 (administrators)[3]	Benefits from a 4 x 4 block (teachers)[4]	Reasons to prefer rotating block (teachers and students)[5]	Reasons to object to block scheduling[6]
• Classes too large • Too many classes per student and teacher • Too many failures • Too many dropouts • Too many teacher preparations • Too little individualized instruction • Inadequate variety of instructional methods • High level of stress for students and teachers • Too many truancies, absences, and tardies • Too many student-student and student-teacher conflicts • Class, lunch, and passing periods too short • Too much vandalism and inappropriate behavior	• 90-minute immersion benefits students • Fewer interruptions • Less clerical work • May interact with every student every day • Students can be moved to other classes sooner • Fewer students per teacher each semester • Less paperwork • Less grading • More students go on to advanced classes or study an additional language	• Time for development of key concepts • Time for greater diversity of activities • Time for greater variety of teaching techniques • Encourages teacher and student creativity • Encourages immediate application of new concepts	• Quality of daily interaction on an interpersonal level is diminished because teachers don't see students every day • Lower quality of in-class use of target language because students' attention spans are limited—they "tune out" even during interactive activities • After two years of block scheduling, students could not converse as freely as in traditional two-year cycle • Funding not available for fifth- and sixth-year classes, so students went to university language study with a two-year gap, diminishing the school's reputation and scholarship chances for future students

3. Remus, 1994; Steen, 1992
4. Schoenstein, 1994

5. Huff, 1995
6. Rorrer, 1998

Although the research on block scheduling is still incomplete, the ACTFL Profesional Issues Report (1996) shows that in terms of student contact hours and content mastery a one-semester ninety-minute block offers opportunities to teach less material than a two-semester traditional fifty-minute class; block scheduling generally requires more planning time. Schoenstein (1994) and Steen (1992) report that longer blocks of class time pose problems with continuity, retention, and attentiveness. On the other hand, Lapkin, Harley, and Hart (1997) found no difference between students who studied French in a half-day or in an eighty-minute block and those who studied in a traditional period, in terms of listening or speaking. They found some statistically significant benefits from the block schedule in reading and writing test results. In this study, all groups of students were seventh graders, and they spent the same amount of time studying French; only the distribution of that time varied. Some students in the compact schedule models had been away from the study of French for a semester at the time of some of the assessments.

- Having read the chart and the information following it, write what you believe are the positive and negative aspects of block scheduling.

Case Study 2

Using Learners' Needs to Plan for Instruction[7]

Ms. Kelly teaches English as a Second Language in a factory on a Native American reservation in the southwestern United States. Her class of eight adult students meets daily for an hour, and then she has another half hour of individual time with each student during the day. The students live and work within an English-speaking environment; Ms. Kelly's task is to teach them to read and write. In September, when she began her job, Ms. Kelly noted that the book that the plant manager had chosen for the students consisted of seven chapters, each twenty pages long. The semester was fifteen weeks long, which meant that she and her students would spend two weeks on each chapter, with about five days set aside for testing and cultural activities.

It is now the beginning of October, and Ms. Kelly has been reviewing the progress of her class. They appear to be right on schedule, having "covered" Chapters 1 and 2. The students' grades on her teacher-made tests have been good, and the students appear to have learned what is in the textbook. However, Ms. Kelly has noticed that their reading is still slow and full of hesitation and mispronunciation, and they don't recognize words from their reading when they see them in other written materials, such as newspaper articles. Students have complained that they are not learning much from their reading and writing lessons.

Ms. Kelly decided to interview the plant manager to find out more about why students were taking the course and to learn what kinds of reading and speaking they might have to do in their jobs. She learned that the students were paid on the basis of the number of pieces of wiring they completed each day and that they had quotas they were required to meet. If they were away from their stations, they had to complete "downtime" reports in order to justify the lower number of pieces produced that day. Otherwise, their paychecks would be reduced. The plant manager complained

---

7. Thanks to Susan B. Franks for the inspiration for this case.

that students often did not complete the reports accurately or that sometimes they simply did not fill them out, which meant that he had to dock their paychecks. Ms. Kelly discovered that the students did not understand the cards. Furthermore, other plant workers have been complaining that Ms. Kelly needs to "do something" with her students because they are leaving a mess on the breakroom tables, despite the numerous signs posted urging employees to clean up the area.

Ask yourself these questions:

1. Is the course learner centered, that is, does it address learner needs?

2. What do you think about the way Ms. Kelly matched the course content to the available time?

3. What could be the students' purpose for learning how to read and write English if they can already speak it well enough to live and work? Are there other people who may know what the learners need?

4. What situations would require these adult learners to read and write?

5. What implications do you see for language learning in the complaints of the plant manager and fellow workers?

What do you think of the following suggestions for Ms. Kelly?

1. Add worksheets to the students' daily assignments.

2. Interview the students to find out what they want and need to learn; then build lesson plans around their goals.

3. Find another book that is more interesting to the students.

4. Interview the plant manager to find out more specifically what materials the students need to be able to read and write.

5. Integrate a variety of authentic reading materials into instruction.

To prepare the case:

Read Chapters 10 and 11 of Lee and VanPatten (1995), which deals with comprehending and writing in a second language; read the section "Part One: Language and Communication Beyond the School Years" in Brecht and Walton (1995, pp. 113–132); learn about the use of "reading/writing workshops" for literacy instruction in the ESL classroom by reading Gee (1996).

To prepare for class discussion, think and write about the following topic:

Ms. Kelly finds an article that deals with the use of "reading/writing workshops," a way to organize a class for literacy instruction that may be varied "to meet the needs of your students and the amount of time you have" (Swift, 1993, p. 371). Key features of the workshop are that students make choices concerning the types of learning experiences they receive and that the tasks they perform become integrated into purposeful social activities.

Workshop activities include shared reading of a favorite class text, shared writing, mini-lessons to address issues that have surfaced as a need, individual writing, and conferencing with peers and the teacher. What are some specific strategies Ms. Kelly might incorporate in order to plan some of her classes as reading/writing workshops?

References

ACTFL Professional Issues Report. (1996). Block scheduling and second-language instruction. *ACTFL Newsletter 6* (2): 11–15. Yonkers, NY: The American Council on the Teaching of Foreign Languages.

ACTFL proficiency guidelines. (1986). Yonkers, NY: The American Council on the Teaching of Foreign Languages.

ACTFL proficiency guidelines—speaking. (1999). Yonkers, NY: The American Council on the Teaching of Foreign Languages.

Ausubel, D. P., Novak, J. D., & Hanesian, H. (1978). *Educational psychology: A cognitive view.* New York: Holt, Rinehart and Winston.

Ballman, T. L. (1996). Integrating vocabulary, grammar, and culture: A model five-day communicative lesson plan. *Foreign Language Annals, 29,* 37–44.

Ballman, T. L. (1998). From teacher-centered to learner-centered: Guidelines for sequencing and presenting the elements of a foreign language class. In J. Harper, M. Lively, & M. Williams (Eds.), *The coming of age of the profession* (pp. 97-111). Boston, MA: Heinle & Heinle.

Bartz, W. H., & Singer, M. K. (1996). The programmatic implications of foreign language standards. In R. C. Lafayette (Ed.), *National standards: A catalyst for reform.* The ACTFL Foreign Language Education Series (pp. 139–167). Lincolnwood, IL: NTC/Contemporary Publishing Group.

Bragger, J. D., & Rice, D. B. (1998). Connections: The national standards and a new paradigm for content-oriented materials and instruction. In J. Harper, M. Lively, & M. Williams (Eds.), *The coming of age of the profession* (pp. 191–217). Boston, MA: Heinle & Heinle.

Brecht, R. D., & Walton, A. R. (1995). The future shape of language learning in the new world of global communication: Consequences for higher education and beyond. In R. Donato & R. M. Terry (Eds.), *Foreign language learning: The journey of a lifetime.* The ACTFL Foreign Language Education Series (pp. 110–152). Lincolnwood, IL: NTC/Contemporary Publishing Group.

Carrell, P. L. (1984). The effects of rhetorical organization on ESL readers. *TESOL Quarterly, 18,* 441–469.

Clark, C., & Peterson, P. (1986). Teachers' thought processes. In M. Wittrock (Ed.), *Handbook of research on teaching,* 3rd ed. (pp. 255–296). New York: Macmillan.

Curtain, H. A., & Pesola, C. A. (1994). *Languages and children—Making the match.* White Plains, NY: Longman.

Donato, R. (1998). Personal communication.

Espitia, D. (1998). Making the block work for you! *Northeast Conference Newsletter, 43,* 45–53. Carlisle, PA: Northeast Conference on the Teaching of Foreign Languages.

Franks, S. A. (1992). *Whole language curriculum for non-reading, limited English-proficient Native American adult factory workers.* Unpublished doctoral dissertation. Virginia Polytechnic Institute and State University, Blacksburg, VA.

Freeman, D. (1996). Redefining the relationship between research and what teachers know. In K. M. Bailey & D. Nunan (Eds.), *Voices from the language classroom* (pp. 88–115). Cambridge: Cambridge University Press.

Galloway, V. (1998). Constructing cultural realities: "Facts" and frameworks of association. In J. Harper, M. Lively, & M. Williams (Eds.), *The coming of age of the profession* (pp. 129–140). Boston, MA: Heinle & Heinle.

Gee, R. W. (1996). Reading/writing workshops for the ESL classroom. *TESOL Journal, 5*(3*),* 4–9.

Genessee, F. (1998). Content-based language instruction. In M. Met (Ed.), *Critical issues in early second language learning* (pp. 103–105). Glenview, IL: Scott Foresman-Addison Wesley.

Glisan, E. W., & Fall, T. F. (1991). Adapting an elementary immersion approach to secondary and post-secondary language teaching: The methodological connection. In J. K. Phillips (Ed.), *Building bridges and making connections* (pp. 1–29). Burlington, VT: Northeast Conference on the Teaching of Foreign Languages.

Glisan, E. W., & Shrum, J. L. (1996). *Enlaces.* Boston, MA: Heinle & Heinle.

Goals 2000: Educate America Act. (1994). Washington, DC: Department of Education.

Hall, J. K. (1995). "'Aw, man, where we goin'?": Classroom interaction and the development of L2 interactional competence. *Issues in Applied Linguistics, 6*(2), 37–62.

Hall, J. K. (1996). The discursive formation of Spanish as a foreign language classroom community. Paper presented at AILA 1996, 11th World Congress of Applied Linguistics Symposium.

Houston, G. C., Abrahamsen, J. P., Lucero, M. D., & Richardson, L. L. (1990). *The Wasson Block Plan.* Roy J. Wasson High School, Colorado Springs, CO.

Huff, A. L. (1995). Flexible block scheduling: It works for us! *NASSP Bulletin, 79*(571), 19–22.

Johnson, K., & Swain, M. (1997). *Immersion education: International perspectives.* New York: Cambridge University Press.

Krashen, S. (1982). *Principles and practice in second language acquisition.* Oxford: Pergamon Press.

Lafayette, R., & Buscaglia, M. (1985). Students learn language via a civilization course—A comparison of second language classroom environments. *Studies in Second Language Acquisition, 7,* 323–342.

Lambert, W. E. (1984). An overview of issues in immersion education. In *Studies on immersion education: A collection for United States educators.* Sacramento, CA: California State Department of Education.

Lapkin, S., Harley, B., & Hart, D. (1997). Block scheduling for language study in the middle grades: A summary of the Carleton Case Study. *Learning Languages, 2*(3), 4–8.

Leaver, B. L., & Stryker, S. B. (1989). Content-based instruction for foreign language classrooms. *Foreign Language Annals, 22,* 269–275.

Lee, J. F., & VanPatten, B. (1995). *Making communicative language teaching happen.* New York: Mc-Graw Hill.

MacDonald, R. E. (1991). *A handbook of basic skills and strategies for beginning teachers.* White Plains, NY: Longman Group Ltd.

Mehan, H. (1979). What time is it, Denise: Asking known information questions in classroom discourse. *Theory Into Practice, 28*(4), 285–294.

Met, M. (1991). Learning language through content; learning content through language. *Foreign Language Annals, 24*(4), 281–295.

Nebraska Department of Education. (1996). *Nebraska K–12 Foreign Language Frameworks.* Lincoln, NE: Nebraska Department of Education.

Nunan, D. (1992). The teacher as decision-maker. In J. Flowerdew, M. Brock, & S. Hsia (Eds.), *Perspectives on second language teacher education* (pp. 135–165). Hong Kong: City Polytechnic of Hong Kong.

Oller, J., Jr. (1983). Some working ideas for language teaching. In J. Oller, Jr., & P. A. Richard-Amato (Eds.), *Methods that work* (pp. 3–19). Rowley, MA: Newbury House Publishers, Inc.

Oller, J., Jr. (1993). Reasons why some methods work. In J. W. Oller, Jr. (Ed.), *Methods that work* (pp. 374–385). Boston, MA: Heinle & Heinle.

Pusack, J. P., & Otto, S. K. (1996). Taking control of multimedia. In M. D. Bush (Ed.), *Technology-enhanced language learning.* The ACTFL Foreign Language Education Series (pp. 1–46). Lincolnwood, IL: NTC/Contemporary Publishing Group.

Remus, C. (1994). Telephone interview with Elizabeth Schollaert, Yorktown High School, Arlington, VA.

Rorrer, B. (1998, March 23). Personal communication.

Schoenstein, R. (1994). Block schedules: Building the high schools of the future? *Virginia Journal of Education, 88*(3), 7–12.

Steen, M. S. (1992). *Teaching foreign language on the block.* Unpublished response to request for information by Yorktown H.S., Arlington, VA.

Swender, E. (Ed.) (1999). *The ACTFL oral proficiency interview tester training manual.* Yonkers, NY: ACTFL.

Swift, K. (1993). Try reading workshop in your classroom. *The Reading Teacher, 46,* 366–371.

Terrell, T., Andrade, M., & Egasse, J. (1998). *Dos Mundos.* Columbus, OH: McGraw-Hill.

Terry, R. M. (1998). Authentic tasks and materials for testing in the foreign language classroom. In J. Harper, M. Lively, & M. Williams (Eds.), *The coming of age of the profession* (pp. 277–290). Boston, MA: Heinle & Heinle.

Tharp, R. G., & Gallimore, R. (1991). *The instructional conversation: Teaching and learning in social activity.* Washington, DC: National Center for Research on Cultural Diversity and Second Language Learning.

Villegas Rogers, C., & Medley, F. W., Jr. (1988). Language with a purpose: Using authentic materials in the foreign language classroom. *Foreign Language Annals, 21,* 467–478.

Wells, G. (1993). Reevaluating the IRF sequence. *Linguistics and Education, 5,* 1–38.

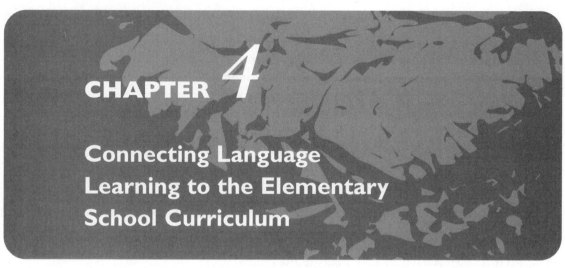

CHAPTER *4*

Connecting Language Learning to the Elementary School Curriculum

In this chapter you will learn about:

- critical period
- Piaget's stages of cognitive/ affective development
- mythic stage of development
- program models: FLES, FLEX, immersion
- content-based / content-enriched FLES
- content-obligatory / content-compatible objectives

- graphic organizers
- semantic maps
- Venn diagrams
- thematic webs
- Total Physical Response
- language experience chart approach
- cooperative learning
- learning centers
- global units

Teach and Reflect: Designing a Content-Based Elementary School Lesson; Developing a Storytelling Lesson

- **Case Study 1: Teaching First Grade Content in French**
- **Case Study 2: Implementing an Elementary School Program**

Conceptual Orientation

In recent years increasing attention has been given to introducing language instruction to students in the elementary grades. An early start provides increased time for learning and the opportunity to attain a functional level of language proficiency (Carroll, 1975). Much of the research in early language learning has focused on the outcomes of early language learning as compared to those of later language learning. This continues to be a key area of investigation as we seek to provide language learning experiences at the most optimal times during learners' cognitive and social development.

In this chapter you will encounter the following terms that relate to language programs in the elementary/middle school:

- FLES: Foreign Language in the Elementary School
- FLEX: Foreign Language Exploratory or Experience

These program models will be described later in the chapter.

 An early start provides increased time for learning and the opportunity to attain a functional level of language proficiency.

A Critical Period for Language Acquisition?

Much of the research in early language acquisition has examined the question: Is there a *critical period for language acquisition*; that is, "a time when the human brain is uniquely capable of acquiring language"? (Hoff-Ginsberg, 1998, p. 31). Studies indicate that the *neural plasticity* of the brain and the nature of cognitive abilities may provide answers to this question. According to research in neuropsychology, the brain of a younger learner is malleable and is shaped by its own activity, while the brain of an older learner is stable and is not as equipped to reorganize itself. Therefore, "the old brain encountering a new task must make do with the brain structure that has already been set" (Hoff-Ginsberg, 1998, p. 35). After the age of two, the development of the brain consists mainly of losing the synaptic connections that have not been used (Huttenlocher, 1994) and of tapping previously unused brain capacity for new tasks. As one matures, more of the brain is used for new functions, and there is less uncommitted capacity to access (Hoff-Ginsberg, 1998). Furthermore, Newport (1991) proposed that young children learn language better than adults because their cognitive abilities are limited. That is, it is easier for children because they analyze small chunks rather than longer segments of speech; adults have a more challenging analytical task because they extract and store larger chunks of information (Newport, 1991).

The research suggests that there may be multiple "critical periods" for different aspects of language (Seliger, 1978), particularly within informal learning environments:

- *Pronunciation/Accent:* A great deal of the research supports the claim that language learners who begin as children are able to achieve a more native-like accent than those who begin as adolescents or adults. Young children are able to mimic sounds and intonation patterns well, they are curious about different sounds and codes, and they are not self-conscious (Lipton, 1991). The critical age for pronunciation has been identified as being between six years (Long, 1990) and ten years (Thompson, 1991).
- *Competency in Syntax/Grammar:* Evidence indicates that children may also be more likely to acquire a higher level of competence in syntax, morphology, and grammar than older learners (Harley & Wang, 1997; Johnson & Newport, 1989). The critical age for syntactical/grammatical accuracy is likely to be later than for pronunciation—at around age fifteen (Patkowski, 1990). Some adult learners, however, may reach native

levels of grammatical accuracy in speech and writing (Ellis, 1994).

- *Language Proficiency:* Research suggests that younger learners may reach higher levels of functional proficiency than those who begin language learning at a later age. Cummins (1981) found that younger learners perform better on communicative tasks measuring interpersonal skills such as oral fluency and phonology.
- *Rate of Language Acquisition:* Adult language learners may have a greater advantage than younger learners where the rate of acquisition of language is concerned. Several studies have revealed older learners may acquire language faster and make more rapid progress than younger learners (Krashen, Long, & Scarcella, 1979; Snow & Hoefnagel-Höhle, 1978). This phenomenon is probably due to the fact that older learners experience more negotiation of meaning and they possess more fully developed cognitive skills, which equip them for the language learning task (Ellis, 1994).

Studies of bilingualism and cognition reveal that children who begin to study a second language in the early years reap cognitive, academic, and attitudinal benefits (Robinson, 1998). As supported by Vygotsky's theory of language as a mediator that guides thought and shapes social development (see Chapter 1), bilingual children develop a diversified set of abilities as they work to perceive, process, store, and recall information (Lapkin, Swain, & Shapson, 1990; Vygotsky, 1962). Accordingly, evidence indicates that immersion students perform better than their non-immersion counterparts in metacognitive processing, analysis, synthesis, and evaluation (Foster & Reeves, 1989). Children who have studied a foreign language score higher on standardized tests and tests of basic skills in English, math, and social studies than those who have not experienced language study (Rafferty, 1986). Additionally, according to Lambert and Klineberg (1967), the age of ten seems to be a crucial time in developing attitudes toward nations and groups perceived as "other." Children who are ten years of age appear to be more open toward people who are different from themselves than are fourteen-year-olds. Since they are in the process of proceeding from egocentricity to reciprocity, they are open to new information introduced during this time (Lambert & Klineberg, 1967; c.f. Robinson, 1998). Children between the ages of seven and twelve also demonstrate role-taking ability and seem to be the most open to learning about people from other cultures (Muuss, 1982).

In summary, there is evidence to suggest that the advantages of language study for younger learners include a heightened level of oral proficiency, more complex cognitive processing, higher performance on standardized tests and tests of basic skills, and a greater openness to other cultures. However, much of this research has been conducted with immersion students. There have been few empirical studies that have investigated the specific accomplishments of students in a traditional elementary school foreign language setting. Donato, Antonek, & Tucker (1994, 1996) and Tucker, Donato, & Antonek (1996) reported on the first three years of a Japanese FLES program in which K–12 North American students learned Japanese, a non-cognate language, by means of fifteen-minute daily lessons. Student progress was assessed by means of individual oral interviews with the children (using an adaptation of the ACTFL Oral Proficiency Interview and proficiency rating scale) and ratings of these oral samples and classroom performance according to the criteria of comprehension, fluency, vocabulary, pronunciation, and grammar. At the end of the first year of Japanese instruction, all students attained some degree of novice-level oral proficiency, while at the end of the second year, most students attained novice-level proficiency, and a few students demonstrated intermediate-level proficiency. At the end of both the first and second years of instruction, children scored highest in pronunciation and lowest in grammar. Furthermore, at the end of each year, children in grades 3–5 performed better than those in K–2 in comprehension, fluency, vocabulary, and grammar, but not in pronunciation. Although the older learners appeared to have performed better than the younger ones on several of the tests, the younger group did not do significantly poorer overall than the older group. Also, there was less variability among scores in the K–2 group; that is, the older learners exhibited a wider range of abilities, while the younger children made more uniform progress overall. At the end of the second year, all children were rated significantly higher on all five of the performance variables than in the first year. Also of interest was the fact that learners who attained higher levels of oral proficiency were not exclusively from the older group (Tucker, Donato, & Antonek, 1996). In the third year of the study, progress was assessed using the same instruments, but at three different times during the course of instruction in order to examine the learning curve (Donato, Antonek, & Tucker, 1996). While all children made progress in their language abilities, they did so in a differentiated manner; that is, some children made more progress in fluency, some more in vocabulary, and others more in pronunciation. Thus language acquisition did not develop in exactly the same way for all learners.

The results obtained in these empirical studies reveal the following about the effects of early language learning experiences in traditional classroom settings: (1) elementary school language learners make significant gains in pronunciation; (2) children in grades K–5 are able to demonstrate notable progress in developing oral proficiency over a two-year period of instruction; (3) since younger learners can generally keep up with older learners in the language learning process, being older may not be a distinct advantage for learning a language; (4) some evidence suggests that an early start in language learning may result in more uniform gains for the majority of learners, although this remains to be researched further by means of additional longitudinal studies; and (5) young learners demonstrate progress in language acquisition in differentiated ways (Donato, Antonek, & Tucker, 1994, 1996; Tucker, Donato, & Antonek, 1996).

The Elementary School Learner

Curtain and Pesola (1994) have defined the following key characteristics of elementary and middle school learners:

- *Preschool students (ages 2–4):* absorb languages effortlessly and imitate speech sounds well; are self-centered and do not work well in groups; respond best to activities relating to their own interests; have a short attention span; respond best to concrete experiences.
- *Primary students (ages 5–7, kindergarten, grades 1 and 2):* learn best through concrete experiences; are imaginative and respond well to stories of fantasy and dramatic play; learn through oral language and can develop good oral skills, pronunciation, and intonation when they have a good model; have a short attention span and require large-muscle activity; need structured and specific directions and regular routines.
- *Intermediate students (ages 8–10, grades 3–5):* are at their peak for being open to people different from themselves; begin to understand cause and effect; work well in groups; continue to need concrete learning experiences; often dislike working with classmates

of the opposite sex; learn well from imagination and stories that feature binary opposites (e.g., good vs. evil) and real-life heroes and heroines.

- *Preadolescent students (ages 11–14, grades 6–8):* experience cognitive and physical changes in their development; feel a need to assert their independence, develop their own self-image, and become members of a peer group; respond well to opportunities to learn about subjects of interest to them (Curtain & Pesola, pp. 69–70).

 What implications for instruction are suggested by the characteristics of elementary and middle-school learners?

Egan (1979) described the "mythic" stage of development in which children ages four/five to nine/ten make sense of the world by responding in terms of their emotions, such as love, hate, fear, and joy; and morals, such as good or bad. In order to plan effective learning experiences for children in the mythic stage, Egan (1979) suggests experiences that enable students (1) to interpret what they are learning in terms of their emotions and broad moral categories; (2) initially to build new information in terms of contrasting qualities, such as big/little and good/bad; and (3) to illustrate clear, unambiguous meaning, such as good or evil. Since children in the mythic stage are open to imagination and make-believe, Egan (1979) suggests the use of storytelling as an effective technique for instruction. The use of the technique will be discussed later in the chapter.

 Children in the mythic stage (ages four/five to nine/ten) are open to imagination and make-believe.

Program Models

As school districts across the nation are examining ways to expand language programs by introducing instruction at the elementary school level, they are faced with the need to choose from several different program models. There are three basic program models for early foreign language learning: FLES, FLEX, and immersion.[1] Figure 4.2 on page 82 presents the types of language programs and the goals and percent of class time spent in the foreign language per week. The Foreign Language in the Elementary School (FLES) model is a sequential, articulated program, the goals of which are:

- to develop functional proficiency in the second language (not as high as in immersion programs);

- to provide a meaningful context for teaching listening and speaking, with some reading and writing; and

- to build understanding and appreciation of the target cultures (Curtain & Pesola, 1994).

---

1. The term *FLES* (or *FLES**, as used by Lipton, 1998) is often used to refer in general to any type of language program at the elementary school level.

Figure 4.1 Developmental Characteristics of Children Ages 5–10

AGE	PHYSICAL	COGNITIVE	SOCIAL
5–6	• large and small motor skills still developing • very active • short attention span • fatigue easily	• need concrete objects as base for experience • still learning bulk of language • limited by "centration" • can classify along one dimension • think in terms of associating words with meanings	• egocentric • uninhibited • friendly • need structure • need praise • see self as physical traits • interact with peers more as friends • enjoy fantasy play
7–8	• refining large and small motor skills • longer attention span • on task longer	• greater ability to reason • interest in how/why relationships • reading and writing • language may be ahead of concepts • can construct a series (small to big) • can classify hierarchically • still need concrete experiences	• more separate sense of self • more reflective • go by rules • stronger friendships
9–10	• skills well developed	• reading and writing well established • can classify along more than one dimension • can think logically • can "conserve" • analyze work critically • still need concrete experiences	• increased autonomy • sensitive to differences • friendships are important and peer-oriented (same sex) • judgmental

Source: Rhodes, Curtain, & Haas, 1990

Figure 4.1 illustrates the physical, cognitive, and social characteristics of children ages five through ten (Rhodes, Curtain, & Haas, 1990).

Curtain and Pesola (1994) distinguish between *content-based* and *content-enriched FLES*. In *content-based* instruction, the foreign language teacher teaches certain parts of the regular elementary school curriculum through the foreign language; thus the subject content is the vehicle through which language is acquired. In *content-enriched* or *content-related* programs, the foreign language teacher uses concepts from the regular elementary school curriculum to enrich the language program with academic content, but these concepts may not be part of the prescribed curriculum for that grade level.

The Foreign Language Exploratory or Experience (FLEX) programs are designed to introduce learners to one or several languages and cultures at either the elementary or middle school levels. A minimal amount of instruction is provided, as little as once a week, for six to nine weeks a year (Hoch, 1998). Most FLEX programs address the following goals:

- introduction to language learning
- awareness and appreciation of foreign culture
- appreciation of the value of communicating in another language
- enhanced understanding of English
- motivation to further language study (Curtain & Pesola, 1994, p. 36).

In immersion programs, the foreign language is the vehicle for teaching academic content in the regular elementary school curriculum (e.g., mathematics, science, art) rather than the subject of instruction itself. In total immersion, all instruction is conducted in the foreign language; students learn to read in the foreign language first, then in English. In partial immersion programs, students receive instruction in the foreign language for up to fifty percent of the school day; reading and language arts are taught in English (Hoch, 1998). Curtain and Pesola (1994) identified the following goals common to immersion programs:

- functional proficiency in the second language, with children able to communicate in the second language on topics appropriate to their age level
- mastery of subject content material of the school district curriculum
- cross-cultural understanding
- achievement in English language arts comparable to or surpassing that of students in English-only programs (Curtain & Pesola, p. 31).

In immersion teaching, although language is simplified, it is not grammatically sequenced. Language reflects the themes and concepts of the elementary curriculum and the communicative and conceptual needs of the students. Reading instruction is based on previously mastered oral language. (See Haas, 1998, and Curtain & Pesola, 1994, for a discussion of early, late, double, continuing, and two-way immersion programs.)

 In immersion programs, the foreign language is the vehicle for teaching academic content in the regular elementary school curriculum rather than the subject of instruction itself.

Figure 4.2 Early Foreign Language Program Goals

PROGRAMS THAT ARE SEQUENTIAL • CUMULATIVE • CONTINUOUS • PROFICIENCY-ORIENTED • PART OF AN INTEGRATED K–12 SEQUENCE		
Program Type	**Percent of Class Time Spent in Foreign Language per Week**	**Goals**
Total Immersion Grades K–6	50–100% (Time is spent learning *subject matter* taught in foreign language; language learning per se incorporated as necessary throughout curriculum.)	To become functionally proficient in the foreign language. To master subject content taught in the foreign language. To acquire an understanding of and appreciation for other cultures.
Two-Way Immersion Grades K–6 (Also called two-way bilingual, dual language, or developmental bilingual education)	At least 50% (Time is spent learning *subject matter* taught in foreign language; language learning per se incorporated as necessary throughout curriculum. Student population is both native speakers of English and of the foreign language.)	To become functionally proficient in the language that is new to the student. To master subject content taught in the foreign language. To acquire an understanding of and appreciation for other cultures.
Partial Immersion Grades K–6	Approximately 50% (Time is spent learning *subject matter* taught in foreign language; language learning per se incorporated as necessary throughout curriculum.)	To become functionally proficient in the language (although to a lesser extent than is possible in total immersion). To master subject content taught in the new language. To acquire an understanding of and appreciation for other cultures.
Content-Based FLES Grades K–6	15–50% (Time is spent learning language per se as well as learning subject matter in the foreign language.)	To acquire proficiency in listening, speaking, reading, and writing the foreign language. To use subject content as a vehicle for acquiring foreign language skills. To acquire an understanding of and appreciation for other cultures.
FLES Grades K–6	5–50% (Minimum 75 minutes per week, at least every other day.) Time is spent learning language per se.	To acquire proficiency in listening and speaking (degree of proficiency varies with the program). To acquire an understanding of and appreciation for other cultures. To acquire some proficiency in reading and writing (emphasis varies with the program).

Figure 4.2 Early Foreign Language Program Goals (continued)

PROGRAMS THAT ARE NONCONTINUOUS AND NOT USUALLY PART OF AN INTEGRATED K–12 SEQUENCE		
FLEX Grades K–8 (Frequent and regular sessions over a short period of time or short and/or infrequent sessions over an extended period of time.)	I–5% (Time spent sampling one or more languages and/or learning *about* language—sometimes taught mostly in English.)	To develop an interest in foreign languages for future language study. To learn basic words and phrases in one or more foreign languages. To develop careful listening skills. To develop cultural awareness. To develop linguistic awareness.

Source: Rhodes, 1985; adapted and revised by Curtain & Pesola, 1994.

❐ Factors to Consider When Selecting a Program Model

Selecting a program model may be based on one or more of the following factors (Hoch, 1998):

1. Desired level of proficiency: As Curtain and Pesola (1994, pp. 29, 31) state, "language proficiency outcomes are directly proportional to the amount of time spent by students in meaningful communication in the target language. The more time students spend working communicatively with the target language, under the guidance of a skilled and fluent teacher, the greater will be the level of language proficiency that they acquire." Immersion programs enable students to attain the greatest amount of proficiency over time, FLES programs lead to some functional proficiency depending on the amount of instructional time, and FLEX programs are not designed with functional proficiency goals in mind because of the minimal amount of instructional time.

2. Length of sequence: Immersion programs require a commitment by the school district to invest in an uninterrupted sequence of language courses. Successful FLES programs are part of a sequential, well-articulated program that continues beyond the elementary grades to enable students to build on and strengthen the skills they had developed earlier. If school districts are unable to invest in long sequences of study, the FLEX model may be the best option as it offers a language experience without the same level of commitment in terms of sequence of courses.

3. Student population: FLES and FLEX models are generally chosen by districts that seek to provide language instruction to all children, as more students can be taught with fewer foreign language teachers. Immersion programs, however, may not be desired by parents who are not convinced that their children can learn as much subject content in a second language as in their own. Furthermore, immersion models require more resources and specialized language personnel.

4. Availability of resources: According to Met (1993, p. 3), "immersion requires teachers who are elementary trained and experienced in the grade level to be taught, who have near native proficiency in oral and written forms of the language, and who have a knowledge of the culture." Trained immersion teachers are usually not plentiful,

and districts may need to hire teachers from other countries and must be willing to provide ongoing in-service training. In addition, immersion programs often need assistance in accurately assessing target language skills of prospective teachers, developing and identifying effective textbooks and materials, and designing appropriate in-service education (Fortune & Jorstad, 1996). FLES programs require specialists with functional proficiency in the target language, an understanding of the nature of first- and second-language acquisition, and the ability to create their own instructional materials.

5. Community climate: For immersion programs to be successful, the parents and community must believe in the possibility that students can learn skills and subject content in a second language. In FLES programs, it is important that the regular classroom teachers view language as an important component of the curriculum rather than as a frill. Faculty, parents, and administrators need to provide input into scheduling so that they are not concerned about time for language being "taken away" from the other subject areas. Although FLEX programs may not require the degree of community support, it is necessary for everyone to acknowledge their educational value.

FLES Programs of the Past and Present

While elementary school language programs are being developed at an increasing rate, the profession is trying to avoid the problems experienced by the FLES programs of the 1960s. The heyday of audiolingualism brought with it a burst of enthusiasm, albeit short-lived, for elementary school language instruction. Unfortunately, despite government funding and public support, the new elementary school programs declined rapidly after 1964. Rosenbusch (1995) cites seven primary reasons for the demise of the FLES programs of the 1960s: (1) FLES teachers often lacked linguistic proficiency and skill in teaching young children. In 1961, a survey by Alkonis and Brophy indicated that in sixty-two elementary school language programs, the majority of teachers had no foreign language background; (2) FLES programs were begun quickly without sufficient coordination and planning; (3) program goals were unrealistic or inappropriate and promised too much linguistic fluency in too short a time; (4) few programs had a coordinator to provide supervision and articulation across levels; (5) FLES programs featured inappropriate methodologies as they relied on memorization and pattern drills often with little real communication (Lipton, 1998); (6) programs lacked adequate instructional materials; and (7) many schools made no attempt to assess student progress (Lipton, 1998, pp. 2–3). Lipton also notes that foreign language was separated from the rest of the curriculum.

However, there are many indications that today's elementary school language programs will not repeat the mistakes of the past. The revolution in language teaching over the past two decades has affirmed the importance of communicative language teaching. FLES programs are being planned and organized to match the age of the learners. New programs are emphasizing content-based learning that provides an integrated place for language in the elementary school curriculum. Culture and global connections are becoming integral components of the foreign language curriculum. New teacher training programs are enabling elementary school teachers to acquire proficiency in a foreign language and expertise in integrating language instruction into their curricula. (See Appendix 4.1 for an observation guide to assess the effectiveness of the elementary and middle school foreign language teacher.) More effective teaching materials that contextualize language instruction are appearing.

Strategies for Teaching Language to Elementary School Learners

Lipton (1998, p. 176) suggests the lesson plan format for FLES lessons, depicted in Figure 4.3, which builds in movement activities and variety:

Figure 4.3   A Typical Lesson Plan Format (Basic)

LESSON	TIME
(Goal or goals of the lessons, based on unit plans or learning scenarios and related to the five C's of the national FL standards)	
Warm-up of familiar material (greetings, health, weather, numbers, etc.)	3 minutes
New material, including culture	7 minutes
Change of pace (song, TPR, etc.)	2–3 minutes
Applications, including cultures, connections, comparisons, communication	8–10 minutes
Review of previous material	5 minutes
Productive and receptive activities	5–7 minutes
Summary and plans for follow-up	2–4 minutes
Peek at the next lesson	2 minutes

Source: Lipton, 1998.

 How does this lesson plan format compare with the one presented in Chapter 3?

Elementary school foreign language teaching features the use of a wide variety of approaches and techniques designed to involve students actively in language use. Since space permits the description of only a few of the most salient techniques, you may find it helpful to consult one or more of the references listed at the end of this chapter in order to explore other strategies in greater detail. Note that all of these techniques can be adapted and used effectively in secondary classrooms as well.

❐ Content-Based Instruction

In Chapter 3, you learned about the general concept of content-based instruction (CBI). CBI is, of course, an integral component of immersion instruction. However, content-based lessons can also be designed in FLES or content-enriched FLES programs. These lessons provide the means for contextualizing instruction and for integrating foreign language and elementary subject-content. In planning immersion lessons, the Montgomery County Public Schools in Maryland differentiates between two types of objectives according to the linguistic skills needed, the subject-content material, and the cognitive skills necessary to perform tasks: (1) *content-obligatory objectives* focus on the vocabulary (subject-content material), grammar, and language functions required for comprehension and mastery of a concept; and (2) *content-compatible objectives* focus on the vocabulary, grammar, and language functions that may be integrated logically into the content of a lesson but are not required for understanding or for mastery of a concept (Lorenz & Met, 1989). In Appendix 4.2, you will find a partial lesson plan for a Grade 1 mathematics lesson with these two kinds of objectives illustrated.

 Content-obligatory objectives focus on the vocabulary (subject-content material), grammar, and language functions required for comprehension and mastery of a concept.

 Content-compatible objectives focus on the vocabulary, grammar, and language functions that may be integrated logically into the content of a lesson but are not required for understanding or for mastery of a concept.

❐ Helping Students Link Language and Content

Graphic organizers, such as semantic maps, Venn diagrams, and thematic webs, can be an effective means of helping students organize subject-content topics and concepts. *Semantic maps* depict words or concepts in categories and show how they relate to each other. A key word or question is placed at the center of the map; students and teacher create the map together. In this way, students organize what they are learning and are able to see how it fits with the language and information previously learned (Curtain & Pesola, 1994). Appendix 4.3 illustrates a semantic map. *Venn diagrams* can be used for making comparisons and contrasts; they consist of two or more intersecting circles that depict relationships among concepts (see Appendix 4.4). In their planning for CBI, teachers also find it helpful to use *thematic webs,* a technique for organizing instruction around a central theme. Thematic webs enable the planner to extend the theme in various directions and flesh out the topic in meaningful categories (Pappas, Kiefer, & Levstik, 1990). See Appendix 4.5 for a sample thematic web.

graphic organizers = semantic maps, Venn diagrams, thematic webs

❐ Listening as the Impetus for Learning

At the elementary school level, listening is used as the vehicle through which students first begin to acquire language. Many studies show the benefits of providing an initial period of instruction in which students listen to input without being forced to respond in the target language (Postovsky, 1974; Winitz & Reeds, 1973). Through techniques such as *Total Physical Response* (TPR) (Asher, 1986), students in an acquisition-rich environment demonstrate understanding by responding physically to oral commands, then progress gradually to productive use. In addition to physical responses, in the beginning stages students give yes-no answers, choose the correct word, or manipulate visuals while listening to input. This "comprehension before production" stage allows students to "bind" or mentally associate input with meaning and instills the self-confidence necessary for producing language (Terrell, 1986).

In Chapter 2, you learned ways to contextualize language instruction by presenting an initial authentic oral or written segment. At the elementary school level, teachers use children's stories to provide an integrated-skills approach to acquisition. The teacher tells the story a number of times over an extended period of time, while also showing pictures and using gestures and mime to demonstrate meaning. After students hear the story numerous times, they are then involved through TPR and acting out story parts. Story mapping may be used to help students recall and visually organize the central theme and main components of a story setting, problem, characters, events, solution, or ending (Heimlich & Pittelman, 1986). A sample story map appears in Appendix 4.6.

Children's literature from the countries where the target language is spoken serves as an excellent source for story texts and provides another avenue for integrating culture into the program. In addition to helping students experience culture, *authentic literature* can serve as the foundation for a whole-language curriculum and appeals to children in Egan's (1979) mythic stage of learning, as described earlier. Pesola (1991) suggests the use of both folktales and contemporary children's literature in the elementary school classroom. Folktales, which present cultural information and describe solutions to human challenges, make effective stories since they come from a culture's oral tradition. Contemporary children's literature lets young students identify with the feelings and moral challenges faced by story characters (Pesola, 1991).

Egan (1992) suggests teachers use the following story form framework as they plan to use stories with children in the primary school years:

1. *Identifying importance.* What is most important about this topic? Why should it matter to children? What is affectively engaging about it?

2. *Finding binary opposites.* What powerful binary opposites best catch the importance of the topic (e.g., sad/happy, good/bad, threatened/secure)?

3. *Organizing content in story form.* What content most dramatically embodies the binary opposites in order to provide access to the topic? What content best articulates the topic into a developing story format?

4. *Conclusion.* What is the best way to resolve the dramatic conflict inherent in these binary opposites? What degree of mediation of these opposites is it appropriate to seek?

5. *Evaluation.* How can one know whether the topic has been understood, whether its importance has been grasped, and whether the content was learned? (Curtain & Pesola, 1994, pp. 204–205).

One of the ways in which the transition to reading from hearing a story or attending to other oral input is made is through the use of the *language experience chart approach*. This technique uses previously learned oral language as the basis for practicing reading and writing skills. The context is an experience that is shared by the class such as a field trip, story, film, or cultural experience. This technique features the following steps: (1) the teacher provides target language input that describes the shared experience, in a top-down fashion as described in Chapter 2; (2) the teacher checks comprehension through TPR and questions requiring one-word and then longer responses; (3) students retell the story or experience with the teacher's help as the teacher writes their account on large "language experience chart" paper (lined paper on an easel); (4) students copy this version into their notebooks; and (5) this permanent record is used for a variety of reading and writing tasks (Allen, 1970; Hall, 1970; Hansen-Krening, 1982). The language-experience chart approach has been used with success by both first- and second-language learners (Dixon & Nessel, 1983). This technique is particularly helpful to poor readers, who benefit from the progression from listening and speaking (while experiencing) to reading and writing.

❐ Cooperative Learning Strategies

The elementary school teacher uses a repertoire of techniques for actively involving children in learning. Through cooperative learning, in which students interact with one another in pairs and small groups in order to accomplish a task together, opportunities for using the target language are significantly increased. Research on cooperative learning by Johnson and Johnson (1987) suggests that the benefits of group and pair work include higher retention and achievement, development of interpersonal skills and responsibility, and heightened self-esteem and creativity. Cooperative learning is most successful when students depend on one another, participate in face-to-face interaction, take responsibility for the skills being learned by the group, use appropriate social skills (following directions, asking for help, taking turns), and analyze what is working and not working in the group activity (Johnson & Johnson, 1987). Kagan (1990) suggests that students assume roles such as the following when participating in a cooperative learning activity:

- *Gatekeeper/monitor* makes sure that each person participates and that no one individual dominates the group process.
- *Cheerleader/encourager* makes sure that the contributions of each member and the team as a whole are appreciated.

- *Taskmaster/supervisor* keeps the group on task and attempts to make sure each member contributes; s/he guides discussion or work.
- *Secretary/recorder* records team answers and supporting material; s/he can also be the team spokesperson who reports to the whole class.
- *Checker/explainer* checks that everyone agrees before a group decision is made; s/he checks that everyone understands the assignment and what is needed to finish.
- *Quiet captain* makes sure the group does not disturb other groups (Curtain & Pesola, 1994, p. 319).

 Through cooperative learning, students interact with one another in pairs and small groups in order to accomplish a task together.

The teacher should consider the following in planning activities: (1) the source of the message(s) to be exchanged; (2) the target language required to complete the activity; (3) how the language will be guided or controlled; (4) the provision for clearly defined turn taking; (5) how students will monitor the success of the activity; and (6) how the teacher will follow up on the activity in a communicative way (Curtain & Pesola, 1994, pp. 325–326). See Chapter 8 for more information regarding pair/group activities.

Other strategies used to provide hands-on experiences include the use of games, songs, rhymes, finger plays, role plays, demonstrations, chalkboard activities. See Curtain & Pesola (1994) and Lipton (1998) for numerous examples.

Another avenue for providing individual or small-group practice is the use of *learning centers,* which add variety and interest. The learning center is a designated area of the classroom that contains materials and directions for a specific learning task such as a game, listening activity, or reading. It may be a desk or group of desks, bulletin board, or computer center, but it always attracts attention because of its bright colors or attractive use of shapes and pictures (Glisan & Fall, 1991). The learning center should be thematically arranged, contain instructions for self-pacing, and allow for a range of student ability and interest levels.

 learning center = a designated area of the classroom that contains materials and directions for a specific learning task

❒ Learning Through Culture

Culture is a key component in a content-based elementary school language program, since it is integrated with all subjects in the curriculum. The next chapter introduces the Cultures goal area of the national standards and presents some strategies for engaging middle school students in exploring the products, practices, and perspectives of the target cultures. These same strategies can also be used at the elementary school level. Pesola

(1991) suggests that students explore cultural perspectives through the study of (1) cultural products such as traditional stories and legends, folk arts, visual arts and artists, musical arts and composers, and realia such as currency, coins, and stamps; and (2) cultural practices such as forms of greeting, use of gestures, recreational activities, home and school life, types of pets and attitudes toward pets, and how children and families move from place to place.

As described earlier in this chapter, the use of authentic literature can be an effective way to introduce many elements of cultural heritage in the classroom. The teaching of thematic units such as "Nutrition" or "Holidays" also provides the opportunity to present visual materials that show certain characteristics of the target culture—photographs, magazine pictures, and realia obtained from the target culture are rich in cultural information. Pesola suggests the following activities for integrating culture within the elementary school content areas:

- Social Studies: For display create banners or other items that reflect symbols used for the target city; celebrate an important holiday in the target city, preferably one that is not celebrated locally, or at least not celebrated in the same way.
- Mathematics and Science: Apply the concepts of shapes and symmetry to the folk arts and other visual arts from the target culture; use catalogs from the target culture for problem-solving mathematics activities involving budgeting and shopping.
- Art and Music: Replicate authentic crafts from the target culture in classroom art activities; incorporate typical rhythms from the target culture in the development of chants and rhymes to reinforce new vocabulary and concepts (Pesola, 1991, pp. 341–343).

See Pesola (1991) for other ideas on ways to integrate culture with these content areas.

Just as acquiring a language means more than knowing about its linguistic system, understanding another culture involves more than learning facts about it. Rosenbusch (1992) suggests the development of *global units* to help elementary school students develop a global perspective and deeper awareness of key issues in the target culture. For example, she describes a global unit dealing with "Housing," in which students compare housing in the native and target cultures through activities such as viewing and discussing slide presentations and making drawings, graphs, and housing models to illustrate similarities and differences. Students can gain a deeper awareness of the target culture by means of experiences in which they role play authentic situations or participate in "fantasy experiences" (Curtain & Pesola, 1994). For example, Curtain and Pesola (1994) describe an airplane fantasy experience in which children pretend that they are taking a trip, acting out each phase from checking baggage to finding their seats to landing. A truly integrated elementary school program carefully connects language and culture and provides many opportunities for students to learn about the culture through contextualized instruction and meaningful interaction.

 Global units help elementary school students develop a global perspective and deeper awareness of key issues in the target culture.

STANDARDS HIGHLIGHT: Making CONNECTIONS between Language and the Elementary School Curriculum

❐ The Connections Goal Area

The benefits of linking language and content have been explored in Chapter 3 and earlier in this chapter. The Connections goal area of the standards states that students should be able to "connect with other disciplines and acquire information" (National Standards in Foreign Language Education Project [NSFLEP], 1996, p. 49). The two Connections standards are the following:

- Students reinforce and further their knowledge of other disciplines through the foreign language.
- Students acquire information and recognize the distinctive viewpoints that are only available through the foreign language and its cultures (NSFLEP, 1996, pp. 50, 52).

When combined with other disciplines, knowledge of another language and culture shifts the focus from language acquisition alone to broader learning experiences. Students deepen their understanding of other subjects while they enhance their communicative skills and cultural awareness. Furthermore, as students learn a foreign language, they gain greater access to sources of information and a "new window on the world" (NSFLEP, 1996, p. 52). The foreign language can be used as the vehicle for acquiring new knowledge.

 Connections enable students to further their knowledge of other disciplines, acquire new information, and recognize the distinctive viewpoints that are available only through the foreign language and its cultures.

❐ Implications of the Connections Standards on Instruction

Teachers who are beginning to experiment with making connections with other areas of the curriculum should start with a simple connection such as addressing one small content piece of another subject (e.g., art, music, social studies, math). In lower levels of instruction, the foreign language teacher might continue the presentation of content introduced in science, mathematics, and social studies. For example, students in a science class might continue to explore weather, seasons, and temperatures in the foreign language (NSFLEP, 1996, p. 50). At various levels of instruction, students might read authentic documentation in the foreign language to support topics being explored (e.g., autobiographical accounts of historical figures, achievements of artists and musicians).

Pesola (1993) suggests the use of the *thematic center* as the starting point for developing interdisciplinary curricula. The thematic center features a theme or topic taken from the general school curriculum or from the literature or culture of the target language, around which the teacher develops the outcomes, activities, and materials for instruction. Choice of a thematic center depends on the curricular goals, the potential for integration of language and culture, and the interests of the students and teachers. The curriculum of a school year might consist of several related thematic centers. Pesola (1993) describes the following process that teachers might use as they develop curricula based on thematic centers:

1. Identify sources of outcomes
   a. lists of language functions (language necessary for dealing with the theme)
   b. inventory of cultural products, practices, and perspectives from the cultures in which the language is spoken
   c. lists of outcomes for the content areas of the curriculum

2. Choose a thematic center

3. Brainstorm potential content for the theme with special emphasis on potential for story form and storytelling

4. Choose outcomes for the theme
   a. language in use outcomes
   b. culture outcomes
   c. subject content outcomes: art, language arts, mathematics, music, physical education, science; social studies: economics, geography, history, political education/citizenship, sociology; across-the-curriculum areas: global education, multicultural education, thinking skills

5. Address the next level of decisions: activities, grammatical structures, vocabulary, materials, classroom setting, assessment

In addition to thematic centers or interdisciplinary units, the teacher might team teach a language course or a portion of it with a teacher from another subject area (e.g., history and foreign language). Individuals with language expertise who reside in the community might be invited to give presentations on certain content areas (e.g., art, music).

As students become more proficient in the target language, they could be expected to take more responsibility for their own acquisition of knowledge in areas of interest to them. They could find materials of interest, analyze the content, compare it to information available in their own language, and compare the linguistic and cultural characteristics (NSFLEP, 1996, p. 52). For example, students might research fashion, cars, music, art, and other topics of meaning and interest to them. Both the teacher and other students could learn new information as a result of students' research. The teacher acts as a coach, helping students to select materials and to interpret language appropriately; students become the content experts.

 How does this strategy address the Atlas Complex presented in Chapter 3?

Teach and Reflect

Episode One

Designing a Content-Based Elementary School Lesson

Design a content-based lesson that addresses ONE of the following learner outcomes:

- **Grade 1 Mathematics:** The student will identify halves, thirds, and fourths of region or set.
- **Grade 1 Science:** The student will classify objects by size, shape, and color.
- **Grade 1 Science:** The student will make accurate observations using the senses.
- **Grade 4 Mathematics:** The student will measure length (km and mm).
- **Grade 4 Science:** The student will describe how living things grow, age, and change in form and activity.
- **Grade 4 Science:** The student will illustrate how the relative position of the earth and sun cause changes in the seasons and in the length of day and night.

(Adapted from Curtain and Pesola, 1994, pp. 407–419.)

Assume that your lesson is twenty-five minutes in length and that this is the first day on this topic. Use the lesson plan format presented in this chapter or the one that appears in Chapter 3, being sure to include both content-obligatory and content-compatible language objectives, as described earlier in this chapter and as exemplified in Appendix 4.2. Plan your presentation and two or three student activities. As you plan the lesson, keep in mind the following ideas:

1. Design a lesson that is appropriate, given the developmental characteristics of your students (consult Figure 4.1 on page 80).

2. Present oral (not written) language.

3. Involve students in hands-on activities from the start of the lesson.

4. Do not lecture or overwhelm students with information they do not understand. They learn by being involved actively.

5. Use the target language. Make yourself understood by using realia, gestures, and mime.

6. Check comprehension often through TPR or short-response questions.

Your instructor may ask you to present a five-to-eight-minute segment of this lesson to the class.

Episode Two

Developing a Storytelling Lesson

Design a ten-minute storytelling lesson in which you present a story that is familiar to the children from their native culture (such as "Goldilocks and the Three Bears") or a simple, authentic children's story or folktale. Prepare visuals and realia as necessary for depicting meaning. Follow Egan's (1992) story framework planning guide and the suggestions given in this chapter for presenting the story orally and incorporating student involvement. Prepare a lesson plan, remembering that this is the first day using the story. Your instructor may ask you to present all or part of your story to the class. Be prepared to discuss how you would use the language experience chart approach to progress to reading after spending much time working with the oral version of the story.

Discuss and Reflect

Case Study 1

Teaching First Grade Content in French

Amy Guilderson and Georges Arnault have been teaching at the elementary school in Milford City for two years, ever since they began their teaching careers. Amy teaches physical education, and Georges teaches first grade. Georges is of French descent and grew up speaking French at home. Amy studied French in college and completed a semester-long study abroad experience in France before graduating. Amy enjoys the opportunity to speak French with Georges.

While having lunch together one day, they began talking about teaching their students some French. Georges had been reading some recent journal articles that presented the idea of combining foreign language and content-area instruction. They wondered what would happen if certain elements of physical education classes were taught in French. Excitedly, they launched into their experiment and agreed that Amy would use French to teach some lessons in physical education to the students in Georges' first grade class for a trial period of two weeks.

The interdisciplinary "exposure" lessons were so successful that Georges decided to teach some aspect of the elementary school *content* to his first graders in French. Since he grew up speaking French, he felt he had the language capability to do so. He also knew how to teach young children, having taught in the Milford City elementary schools for two years.

Georges asked Amy for a list of the words his students had learned from her, since he had been hearing his students exchange greetings in French for several days. He also had noticed that, on occasion, when they needed to count something, they counted in French. He was pleased that the students had learned how to use expressions of politeness such as "Excuse me" and "It's your turn" in French. They also knew how to ask someone what his or her name was and how to introduce themselves and their friends. Georges selected a portion of the content he would have taught in English over the next few weeks, and decided to teach some of it in French. He thought it might be interesting to incorporate some use of French in the mathematics portion of his class day. One of the upcoming curricular goals that he would be addressing was that students should be able to identify halves, thirds, and fourths of a region or set by the end of the year. He thus wanted to teach the most concrete and visually graphic portions of each day's math lesson in French.

Ask yourself these questions:

1. What are some dos and don'ts Georges should keep in mind as he teaches his students this math content?

2. What types of concrete experiences might work best in teaching halves, thirds, and fourths of a region or set?

3. How might Georges sequence activities involving listening, speaking, reading, and writing over the two-week period?

4. What are the academic and social benefits of this type of interdisciplinary instruction for the first graders?

5. How does Amy and Georges' project address the Connections goal area of the national standards?

To prepare the case:

Talk with an elementary school teacher to find out how this particular math skill is generally taught to first graders; read Chapter 9 of Curtain and Pesola (1994), which deals with planning for instruction; read Met (1991) for ideas about teaching content through language; read Chapter 9 in Lipton (1998), which deals with approaches used in teaching language at the elementary school level; read any selected chapter from Graham, Holt-Hale, and Parker (1998) for ways to involve students in movement activities.

To prepare for class discussion, think and write about these topics:

• Imagine that you are Georges and are planning your first lesson to teach this math concept. What is the content-obligatory language students will need to know? What is the content-compatible language you have selected?

• How might Amy and Georges expand their project so that students receive more content-based instruction in French? How would parents and school administrators be convinced that this plan is both beneficial academically and cost-effective?

Case Study 2

Implementing an Elementary School Language Program

The Pinecreek School District is a growing suburban school district that is quickly becoming well-known for its innovative educational programs. It recently began to address the national standards for the various content areas in an attempt to provide effective, cutting-edge instruction for the increasing numbers of youngsters moving into the area. Three years ago the district redesigned its foreign language program, instituting a fifth-grade exploratory program and updating its sequential program beginning in grade 6.

This year, the district began to investigate the merit of starting language instruction in first grade and continuing it through the elementary grades. A special task force comprised of teachers, parents, and administrators was appointed to research this issue and make recommendations to the school board. In an effort to pilot instruction in the early grades, the district followed the task force's suggestion and hired Ms. Marianne Howe, a teacher certified in both Spanish (K–12) and elementary education. Ms. Howe was hired as an itinerant teacher who traveled among four elementary schools, providing twenty-five-minute Spanish lessons to the two hundred students in grades 1–4. The objective of the FLES pilot program was to develop students' functional oral proficiency and to build cultural awareness. Ms. Howe's expertise in teaching Spanish and in working with young learners enabled her lessons to be very effective and well received by the students. In light of the success of the Spanish pilot program, the task force made the following recommendations to the school board regarding the implementation of a language program in the elementary grades:

1. Design a Spanish program for first grade to be implemented in year one and assign Ms. Howe to that grade level.

2. During year two, add French as an offering beginning in first grade. Hire one French teacher certified in French (K–12) and elementary education. During year three, add German as an offering beginning in first grade. Hire one German teacher certified in German (K–12) and elementary education.

3. Since the program must be cost-effective, ask for volunteers from the regular elementary school faculty to learn enough Spanish, French, or German so that they could begin to deliver language instruction in subsequent years (grades 2, 3, and 4). A group of volunteers from grades 2, 3, and 4 should begin to observe Ms. Howe in order to learn some Spanish and acquire strategies for teaching a foreign language. Using already employed elementary teachers will save funds that can then be used for materials and in-service training.

4. In each subsequent year of the project, continue instruction in the foreign language(s) at the next grade level so that the program is developed gradually from the bottom up.

5. Employ the services of experts in the area of elementary school language instruction to assess the program's effectiveness as it is being developed.

Ask yourself these questions:

1. What factors did the task force probably consider as they designed their proposal for an elementary school language program?

2. What elements of their proposal are effective, given the information presented in this chapter?

3. Based on the reasons for the decline in FLES programs of the 1960s, what aspects of the proposal might merit reconsideration?

To prepare the case:

Review the section of this chapter dealing with problems with FLES programs of the past; read Chapter 3 of Curtain and Pesola (1994), which deals with selecting and developing an elementary school language program model; interview an elementary school language teacher and/or an administrator in a district that has an effective language program in the early grades. Find out their views on what makes a program successful; read Chapter 6 of Lipton (1998), which deals with planning effective FLES programs; refer to Chapter 12 of this text to explore the use of distance education programs as a cost-effective means of providing language instruction in the elementary grades.

To prepare for class discussion, think and write about the following topics:

- What background information would you offer the task force concerning the qualifications of elementary school foreign language teachers? How would you address the issue of cost-effectiveness in employing new personnel?
- Create written testimony for the school board regarding your views of the proposal submitted by the task force. Support your views with research findings and other information you have read. Be prepared to answer questions.

References

Alkonis, N. V., & Brophy, M. A. (1961). A survey of FLES practice. *Reports and studies in the teaching of modern foreign languages, 1959–1961* (pp. 213–217). New York: The Modern Language Association of America.

Allen, R. V. (1970). *Language experience in reading.* Chicago: Encyclopaedia Britannica Press.

Asher, J. J. (1986). *Learning another language through actions: The complete teachers' guidebook.* Los Gatos, CA: Sky Oaks Publications.

Carroll, J. B. (1975). *The teaching of French as a foreign language in eight countries.* New York: John Wiley.

Cummins, J. (1981). Age on arrival and immigrant second language learning in Canada: A reassessment. *Applied Linguistics, 2,* 132–149.

Curtain, H. A., & Pesola, C. A. (1994). *Languages and children—Making the match.* White Plains, NY: Longman.

Dixon, C., & Nessel, D. (1983). *Language experience approach to reading (and writing): Language experience reading for second language learners.* Hayward, CA: Alemany Press.

Donato, R., Antonek, J. L., & Tucker, G. R. (1994). A multiple perspectives analysis of a Japanese FLES program. *Foreign Language Annals, 27,* 365–378.

Donato, R., Antonek, J. L., & Tucker, G. R. (1996). Documenting a Japanese FLES program: Ambiance and achievement. *Language Learning, 46,* 497–528.

Egan, K. (1979). *Educational development.* New York: Oxford University Press.

Egan, K. (1992). *Imagination in teaching and learning: The middle school years.* Chicago: University of Chicago Press.

Ellis, R. (1994). *The study of second language acquisition.* Oxford, UK: Oxford University Press.

Fortune, T., & Jorstad, H. L. (1996). U.S. immersion programs: A national survey. *Foreign Language Annals, 27,* 163–90.

Foster, K., & Reeves, C. (1989). FLES improves cognitive skills. *FLES News 2*(3), 4.

Glisan, E. W., & Fall, T. F. (1991). Adapting an immersion approach to secondary and postsecondary language teaching: The methodological connection. In J. K. Phillips (Ed.), *Building bridges and making connections*, Northeast Conference Reports (pp. 1–29). Burlington, VT: Northeast Conference on the Teaching of Foreign Languages.

Graham, G., Holt-Hale, S. A., & Parker, M. (1998). *Children moving*. Mountain View, CA: Mayfield.

Haas, M. (1998). Early vs. late: The practitioner's perspective. In M. Met (Ed.), *Critical issues in early second language learning: Building for our children's future* (pp. 43–48). Glenview, IL: Addison-Wesley.

Hall, M. A. (1970). *Teaching reading as a language experience*. Columbus, OH: Merrill.

Hansen-Krening, N. (1982). *Language experiences for all students*. Reading, MA: Addison-Wesley.

Harley, B., & Wang, W. (1997). The critical period hypothesis: Where are we now? In A. M. B. de Groot & J. F. Kross (Eds.), *Tutorials in bilingualism: Psycholinguistic perspectives* (pp. 19–51). Hillsdale, NJ: Lawrence Erlbaum.

Heimlich, J. E., & Pittelman, S. D. (1986). *Semantic mapping: Classroom applications*. Newark, DE: International Reading Association.

Hoch, F. S. (1998). A view from the state level. In M. Met (Ed.), *Critical issues in early second language learning: Building for our children's future* (pp. 5–10). Glenview, IL: Addison-Wesley.

Hoff-Ginsberg, E. (1998). Is there a critical period for language acquisition? In M. Met (Ed.), *Critical issues in early second language learning: Building for our children's future* (pp. 31–36). Glenview, IL: Addison-Wesley.

Huttenlocher, P. R. (1994). Synaptogenesis in human cerebral cortex. In G. Dawson & K. W. Fischer (Eds.), *Human behavior and the developing brain* (pp. 137–152). New York: Guilford Press.

Johnson, D., & Johnson, R. (1987). *Learning together and alone: Cooperation, competition, and individualization*. Englewood Cliffs, NJ: Prentice Hall.

Johnson, J., & Newport, E. (1989). Critical period effects in second language learning: The influence of maturational state on the acquisition of English as a second language. *Cognitive Psychology, 21,* 60–99.

Kagan, S. (1990). *Cooperative learning: Resources for teachers*. San Juan Capistrano, CA: Resources for Teachers.

Krashen, S. D., Long, M. A., & Scarcella, R. C. (1979). Age, rate and eventual attainment in second language acquisition. *TESOL Quarterly, 13,* 573–582.

Lambert, W. E., & Klineberg, O. (1967). *Children's views of foreign people*. New York: Appleton-Century-Crofts.

Lapkin, S., Swain, M., & Shapson, S. (1990). French immersion research agenda for the '90s. *Canadian Modern Language Review, 4,* 638–674.

Lipton, G. C. (1991). FLES (K–8) programs for the year 2000. *Hispania, 74,* 1084–1086.

Lipton, G. C. (1998). *Practical handbook to elementary foreign language programs*. 3d edition. Lincolnwood, IL: NTC/Contemporary Publishing Group.

Long, M. (1990). Input, interaction and second language acquisition. Unpublished doctoral dissertation. University of California at Los Angeles, Los Angeles.

Lorenz, E. B., & Met, M. (1989). *Planning for instruction in the immersion classroom*. Rockville, MD: Montgomery County Public Schools.

Met, M. (1991). Learning language through content: Learning content through language. *Foreign Language Annals, 24,* 281–295.

Met, M. (1993). *Foreign language immersion programs*. Washington, DC: Center for Applied Linguistics. (ERIC Document Reproduction Service No. ED 363 141).

Muuss, R. (1982). Social cognition: Robert Selman's theory of role taking. *Adolescence, 17*(65), 499–525.

National Standards in Foreign Language Education Project. (1996). *National standards for foreign language learning: Preparing for the 21st century*. Lawrence, KS: Allen Press, Inc.

Newport, E. L. (1991). Constraining concepts of the critical period for language. In S. Carey & R. Gelman (Eds.), *The epigenesis of mind: Essays on biology and cognition* (pp. 111–130). Hillsdale, NJ: Lawrence Erlbaum.

Pappas, C. C., Kiefer, B. Z., & Levstik, L. S. (1990). *An integrated language perspective in the elementary school.* New York: Longman.

Patkowski, M. (1990). Age and accent in a second language: A reply to James Emir Flege. *Applied Linguistics, 11,* 73–89.

Pesola, C. A. (1991). Culture in the elementary school foreign language classroom. *Foreign Language Annals, 24,* 331–346.

Pesola, C. A. (1993). Description of framework for curriculum development for FLES programs. Unpublished manuscript. Moorhead, MN: Concordia College.

Postovsky, V. (1974). Effects of delay in oral practice at the beginning of second language learning. *The Modern Language Journal, 58,* 5–6.

Rafferty, E. (1986). *Second language study and basic skills in Louisiana.* Baton Rouge, LA: Louisiana Department of Education.

Rhodes, N. (1985). Center for Applied Linguistics. Washington, DC.

Rhodes, N., Curtain, H. A., & Haas, M. (1990). Child development and academic skills in the elementary school foreign language classroom. In S. Magnan (Ed.), *Shifting the instructional focus to the learner,* Northeast Conference Reports (pp. 57–92). Middlebury, VT: Northeast Conference on the Teaching of Foreign Languages.

Robinson, D. W. (1998). The cognitive, academic, and attitudinal benefits of early language learning. In M. Met (Ed.), *Critical issues in early second language learning: Building for our children's future* (pp. 37–43). Glenview, IL: Addison-Wesley.

Rosenbusch, M. H. (1992). Is knowledge of cultural diversity enough? Global education in the elementary school foreign language program. *Foreign Language Annals, 25,* 129–136.

Rosenbusch, M. H. (1995). Language learners in the elementary school: Investing in the future. In R. Donato & R. M. Terry (Eds.), *Foreign language learning: The journey of a lifetime.* The ACTFL Foreign Language Education Series (pp. 1–36). Lincolnwood, IL: NTC/Contemporary Publishing Group.

Seliger, H. (1978). Implications of a multiple critical periods hypothesis for second language learning. In W. Ritchie (Ed.), *Second Language Acquisition Research* (pp. 11–20), New York: Academic Press.

Snow, C., & Hoefnagel-Höhle, M. (1978). The critical age for language acquisition: Evidence from second language learning. *Child Development, 49,* 1114–1128.

Terrell, T. D. (1986). Recent trends in research and practice: Teaching Spanish. *Hispania, 68,* 193-202.

Thompson, E. (1991). Foreign accents revisited: The English pronunciation of Russian immigrants. *Language Learning, 41,* 177–204.

Tucker, G. R., Donato, R., & Antonek, J. L. (1996). Documenting growth in a Japanese FLES program. *Foreign Language Annals, 29,* 539–550.

Vygotsky, L. (1962). *Thought and language.* Cambridge, MA: MIT Press.

Winitz, H., & Reeds, J. (1973). Rapid acquisition of a foreign language by the avoidance of speaking. *International Review of Applied Linguistics, 11,* 295–317.

CHAPTER 5

Integrating Language Study in the Middle School Curriculum

In this chapter you will learn about:

- the middle-level learner
- sequential vs. exploratory language programs
- Cultures and Comparisons standards

- practices, products, perspectives
- Kluckhohn Model
- culture capsules, assimilators, minidramas

> **Teach and Reflect: Unit and Lesson Design Around a Story, Myth, or Folktale; Developing Culture-Specific Examples of the Three Ps**
>
> - **Case Study 1: Exploratory vs. Sequential Middle School Programs**
> - **Case Study 2: Orderliness with Affection**

Conceptual Orientation

The teaching of foreign language at both the elementary and secondary levels in the United States received enthusiastic support at various periods in the past. However, prior to the last ten years, little attention was paid to the teaching of foreign language to junior high or middle school learners. Current emphasis on teaching language at this level is due in part to two factors: (1) a growing change in approach to teaching eleven- to fourteen-year-old learners, and (2) an attempt to begin language learning experiences as early as possible so that students benefit from a longer, uninterrupted period of language study.

Early in the twentieth century, the concept of the three-year junior high was adopted. This was to provide (1) attention to the needs of adolescents, (2) exploration of a wide variety of subjects, (3) individualization of teaching, and (4) better articulation between elementary and secondary education (Melton, 1984). As junior high schools were developed, however, many of them abandoned this original philosophy and became very similar to senior high schools. In 1920 Briggs stressed the importance of three key concepts in teaching the middle-level student: individualization, exploration, and articulation. These ideas have become the foundation for middle-level education, which today has taken on various organizational forms, from the traditional seventh-to-eighth grade junior high to the seventh-to-ninth grade intermediate school to the sixth-to-eighth grade middle school.

Despite the evidence that middle-school learners are different from their elementary and secondary counterparts, there is no empirical evidence that the grade-level organization affects learning or achievement (Johnston, 1984). What is most important is the quality of the middle-level program in providing opportunities for learners to explore not only many subjects, but also many approaches within a subject (Melton, 1984). Middle schools of the 1990s provide opportunities for students to explore content through a variety of experiences, such as discussion, discovery, experimentation, and cooperative learning. According to Nerenz, "good middle-level education allows students to experience old things in new ways and entirely new fields of learning in varied ways" (Nerenz, 1990, p. 95).

"Good middle-level education allows students to experience old things in new ways and entirely new fields of learning in varied ways."

The Middle-Level Learner

Eichhorn (1966) termed learners ages 11 to 14 as "transescents." Middle school children are different from elementary and high school learners because of the many physical, cognitive, and emotional changes that happen to them within a short period of time. Middle school learners are a diverse student group. As Mead maintains, they are "more unlike each other than they have ever been before or ever will be again in the course of their lives" (1965, p. 10). Rapidly occurring physical changes often accompany periods of restlessness and variable attention span (Nerenz, 1990). As Martin states, "Young adolescent students may have alternating periods of high energy and listlessness. They may need to squirm and move around, and may need to vent energy through physical exercise" (Martin, 1993, p. S–24). Middle-level learners are aware of their physiological changes and become preoccupied with self-image. Nerenz (1990) suggested that these feelings often make students sensitive to typical classroom discussions concerning physical descriptions, daily routines with reflexive verbs, vocabulary for parts of the body, comparisons of clothing sizes, body dimensions, and other similar topics that refer to appearance.

Egan (1979) characterizes middle school students as "romantic learners" who enjoy knowledge for its own sake, bringing a great deal of curiosity to the classroom. Middle school learners demonstrate a wide diversity of skills and abilities since, according to Maynard (1986), intellectual development from one learner to the next "ranges from the pre-operational cognitive level through the concrete level to the formal mature level of abstract thinking" (Egan, 1986, p. 21). Research by Epstein and Toepfer (1978) indicates that children between the ages of eleven and thirteen and a half experience a progressively slower period of brain growth, which may make them less able to acquire new cognitive skills and handle complex thinking processes. According to research by Piaget (1972) and Elkind (1974), the age of thirteen generally begins the stage of formal, abstract mental operations. However, people vary widely when they reach this stage, and some may enter adulthood without entering it. Thus the difficulty many middle school learners experience in understanding abstract grammatical concepts (such as verb conjugation) may be a reflection of cognitive maturity (Met, 1994).

The research of Andis (1981), Egan (1979), Johnston (1984), Lipsitz (1980), and Wiseman, Hunt, and Bedwell (1986) reveals that the middle-level learner views issues as either right or wrong, demonstrates a strong sense of justice and will work conscientiously for an important cause, is fascinated with the extremes of what exists and what is known, is able to memorize and retain massive amounts of detail, strives to define himself or herself as an individual, and gains identity by becoming part of a group. Middle school learners need to see a connection between language learning and their real lives and interests in order to be motivated to learn. Since these learners place much importance on peer norms, they are less accepting of differences and are susceptible to developing negative stereotypes of individuals from other cultures (Met, 1994). However, they tend to have more positive feelings toward foreigners when they know more about them and when they understand more about the "way other people think and feel" (Robinson, 1981, p. 106).

Language Instruction in the Middle School

Our standards call for language instruction for all students in grades K–12. Attainment of the standards requires an early start and an extended, uninterrupted sequence of foreign language learning. In recent years, school districts with high school language programs have begun to expand instruction into the middle school in an effort to pique students' interest about other languages and cultures, provide students with more time to study a language, and enable students to reach specific levels of oral proficiency (Adair-Hauck, 1992). Verkler (1994) examined the language competency and attitudes toward language study of middle school students enrolled in Spanish I and high school students enrolled in Spanish I. Her study indicated that middle school students demonstrated higher competencies in all four language skills than did their high school counterparts, and their attitude toward the foreign language learning experience was significantly more favorable (Verkler, 1994). She attributes these findings to the positive climate of the middle school, which fosters students' social, emotional, and academic needs, and to the tenets of second-language acquisition, which stress the key role of a positive and meaningful learning environment.

Middle schools are often organized around interdisciplinary teams, which consist of four to five teachers who serve approximately 100 to 120 students (Met, 1995). These teams meet often and regularly to plan jointly and to deliver instruction that integrates content from various subject areas. Teams develop *thematic units* that integrate content and skills around a specific theme, establish interdisciplinary connections, and provide opportunities for students to use critical thinking skills. Although teams have usually been comprised of teachers of mathematics, science, social studies, and English/reading/language arts, more innovative middle schools now include foreign language teachers (Met, 1995). Being part of teams enables foreign language teachers to integrate language instruction into the regular curriculum and helps teachers of other subject areas understand the role of language study.

❏ Middle School Language Program Design[1]

In its position statement on language instruction in the middle school, the National Council of State Supervisors of Foreign Languages (NCSSFL) suggests that the initial experience in foreign language, whether in elementary, middle, or senior high school, should (1) provide real language experiences for all students, (2) broaden students' educational background through language development and cross-cultural awareness, (3) foster healthy attitudes about people of other cultures through the interdisciplinary study of language and culture, and (4) provide motivation for continued language study during which there will be an opportunity for achieving higher levels of proficiency in the language (1994, p. 58). NCSSFL (1994) further asserts that, after the initial language experiences, a successful middle school program should have the following characteristics:

- The primary goal is the continual development of increasing proficiency in listening to, speaking, reading, and writing the foreign language.
- The program helps students develop an understanding of cultures in which the language is spoken and an ability to use language and behavior that is characteristic of authentic situations in those cultures.
- The program builds upon skills developed in any existing elementary foreign language experiences in the district.
- The program should be an integral part of the academic program of the school day, providing daily instruction.
- The foreign language offering should articulate with programs of the senior high school level (NCSSFL, 1994, pp. 59–60).

There has been little consistency in the type of language program developed for the middle school, due in part to the lack of consensus regarding the goals of language instruction at this level. Is the goal to offer exploration of languages and cultures or to begin to develop proficiency in a language? Accordingly, there is in the profession a divided opinion about whether middle school programs should be "exploratory" or "sequential."[2] Many middle school programs have been "exploratory," based on the middle school philosophy that students should have opportunities to explore a wide range of subjects. The term *exploratory*, however, has been interpreted in a variety of ways as indicated by the range of foreign language exploratory or foreign language experience (FLEX) programs: (1) a language readiness course that introduces students to how language works (vocabulary roots, grammar, syntax, etc.) (Adair-Hauck, 1992); (2) multiple minicourses in language or potpourri courses that expose students to several languages and focus on cultural awareness and limited survival skills; (3) an interdisciplinary course that focuses on topics from the perspective of more than one content area such as foreign language plus geography, social studies, history, and/or literature, enabling students to explore ideas from a new point of view (Nerenz, 1990); and (4) auxiliary language programs that take place outside of the school day and include before- and after-school programs, summer camps, immersion weekends, summer day programs, and ethnic Saturday or day schools (Curtain & Pesola, 1994). Kennedy and DeLorenzo (1994) argue that exploratory programs offer middle

---

1. See Curtain & Pesola (1994), pp. 435–460, for a guide to second languages in the middle grades, which includes detailed information on how to plan a middle school foreign language program.
2. See Wing (1996) for examples of middle school exploratory, sequential, and immersion programs.

school learners a "learner-friendly" way of beginning language study. In their view, effective exploratory courses include an introduction to linguistics, an option to explore several languages, development of survival language skills, fostering of strategies for language learning and readiness for language study, connections of other languages to English, exploration of cultures related to the languages being learned, and connection between languages and career paths (Kennedy & DeLorenzo, 1994, p. 70).[3]

Knop and Sandrock (1994) maintain that many of the goals of exploratory programs can be achieved as well by sequential language programs, which are more likely to enable students to acquire functional language ability in a cultural context, rather than talking in English about language and culture. They identify the following limitations of traditional exploratory programs: (1) students have a superficial exposure to many languages; (2) students often do not advance beyond rote memorization of vocabulary and sentences; (3) the same vocabulary is often taught in all of the languages, resulting in student boredom; (4) courses are frequently taught in English, particularly when cultural knowledge is the primary goal; (5) language potpourri courses are taught by teachers who may be less qualified in one language than another; and (6) students' choice of which language to study in a sequential course is an uninformed one, often based on the exploratory teacher's popularity or personality (Knop & Sandrock, 1994, pp. 78–79). These two viewpoints continue to be voiced even by state and local school district foreign language supervisors as they design middle school programs.[4] Met (1995) notes that the choice between exploratory and sequential programs is more often a result of school organization and scheduling than it is of educational philosophy.[5]

 The choice between exploratory and sequential programs is more often a result of school organization and scheduling than it is of educational philosophy.

☐ Teaching Strategies for Middle School Language Instruction

What is the ideal middle school environment? According to Beane (1986), it is one in which the adults are "nice"; that is, they know students' names and are interested in them as individuals. The curriculum should be lively and should contain activities that vitalize ideas through doing, making, creating, building, and dramatizing. Learners should have frequent opportunities to work together in pairs or in small groups. In their summary of the research on characteristics of effective middle school teachers, Johnston and Markle (1979) noted that, among other qualities, these teachers have a positive self-concept; demonstrate warmth; are optimistic, enthusiastic, flexible, and spontaneous; accept students;

---

3. For a comprehensive discussion about exploratory language programs, see Kennedy and DeLorenzo (1985).

4. See Met (1994) for the results of a survey conducted with state and local foreign language supervisors to ascertain the nature of exploratory and sequential course offerings in grades 6 to 8.

5. For a detailed discussion of middle school immersion continuation programs, see García, Lorenz, and Robison (1995).

demonstrate awareness of developmental levels; use a variety of instructional activities and materials; use concrete materials and focused learning strategies; incorporate indirectness in teaching; and incorporate "success-building" behavior in teaching.

 The middle school language curriculum should be lively and should contain activities that vitalize ideas through doing, making, creating, building, and dramatizing.

In her discussion of the role of foreign language in the middle school curriculum, Adair-Hauck suggests that a successful language program "will relate curricular objectives with the needs of the middle school learner" (1992, p. 15). The information presented here concerning the middle school learner points to the following curricular implications:

1. The classroom should be student-centered, with students encouraged to take risks, negotiate meaning, try new learning strategies, express their ideas, respect different points of view, interact with peers, and feel a sense of accomplishment and success.

2. The curriculum should be functionally, rather than grammatically, based, so that language is presented in terms of its social, interactive, and communicative use. Students should be engaged in real-world tasks that are meaningful and interesting to them.

3. A functional curriculum lends itself to a spiral approach to instruction in which previously taught material is recycled and new expressions and more complex language are integrated within a familiar framework. Material is recycled by presenting language in new contexts and by providing practice in various modalities of learning, such as aural, visual, and kinesthetic. A variety of classroom techniques and multimedia presentations should be used in the middle school language class.

4. To appeal to students' curiosity and fascination with adventure and drama, a top-down approach might be implemented in which culturally appropriate myths, folktales, science fiction, and adventure stories are presented (see Chapter 7).

5. To engage students more actively in their own learning, a Vygotskian approach (see Chapter 1) will enable learners to derive meaning and use the language by means of guided participation, scaffolding, and assisted problem solving.

6. This stage in students' development might also be an opportune time for connecting language and content through content-based instruction, by combining geography, history, social studies, and the arts (see Chapter 4).

7. Culture should be taught through a focus on the perspectives behind the products and practices, as suggested by the Cultures goal area of the standards, so that students understand *why* the people of the culture do what they do.

8. Each lesson should feature a balance between skill getting, skill using, and strategy training activities (Adair-Hauck, 1992). See Oxford (1990) for Strategy Inventory for Language Learning (SILL) through which students can become more self-confident and effective learners.

STANDARDS HIGHLIGHT: Integrating CULTURES and COMPARISONS into Middle School Language Instruction

❑ The Cultures Framework

Middle school language instruction should emphasize the acceptance of diversity, developing students' sensitivity to the differences they encounter in others, both within and beyond their classrooms, thus providing support for students' self-esteem (Met, 1995). The foreign language program is in a unique position to address the issue of diversity by exposing students to the cultures in which the foreign language is spoken. The Cultures goal area of the national standards states that students should be able to "gain knowledge and understanding of other cultures" (NSFLEP, 1996, p. 43). The two Cultures standards are:

- Students demonstrate an understanding of the relationship between the practices and perspectives of the cultures studied.
- Students demonstrate an understanding of the relationship between the products and perspectives of the cultures studied (NSFLEP, 1996, pp. 46–47).

Practices are the patterns of behavior accepted by a society; they represent knowledge of "what to do when and where" (e.g., how individuals address one another, the social "pecking order," the use of space, gestures, meal-time etiquette). *Products* refer to things created by members of the culture, both tangible (e.g., a house, an eating utensil, a painting, a piece of literature) and intangible (e.g., a system of education, a ritual, an oral tale, a dance). Practices and products are derived from the *perspectives* of the culture, that is, traditional ideas, attitudes, meanings, and values (NSFLEP, 1996, pp. 46–47). For example, in some Asian cultures, social hierarchy (a perspective) is very important and is based on age, education, and social status. In those cultures, people often exchange business cards (a product), which facilitate social interaction and are treated with respect (that is, one should not scribble another name or phone number on them). The information on the card affects the nonverbal behavior of those involved in communication (a practice) (NSFLEP, 1996, p. 46).[6] Figure 5.1 illustrates how the practices and products reflect the philosophical perspectives that form the world view of a cultural group, and it depicts the interrelatedness of these three cultural components. This model reflects the sociocultural framework posited by Fantini (1997), which consists of *sociofacts* (how people come together and for what purpose—practices), *artifacts* (things people make—products), and *mentifacts* (what people think or believe—perspectives). Since language is used to express cultural perspectives and to participate in social practices, language study offers students insights into a culture that are available in no other way. Although some cultural knowledge can be obtained from other kinds of courses, "only language study empowers learners to engage in direct interaction with members of other cultures" (NSFLEP, 1996, p. 45).

---

6. Not every product or practice may have a perspective that is easily identifiable. In this case, the teacher should be careful not to make up a possible perspective but to discuss with students the possibility that they would need to investigate with native speakers what the perspective is and that even native speakers may not know what the perspective is.

Figure 5.1 Cultural Practices, Products, Perspectives

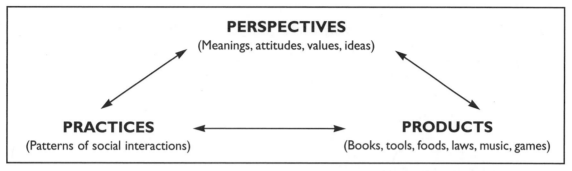

PERSPECTIVES
(Meanings, attitudes, values, ideas)

PRACTICES
(Patterns of social interactions)

PRODUCTS
(Books, tools, foods, laws, music, games)

Source: NSFLL, 1996.

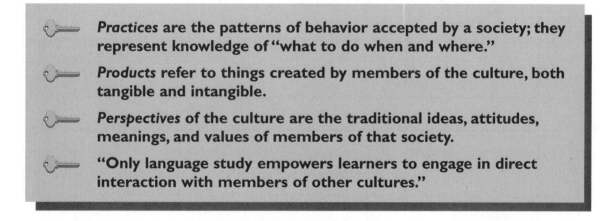

- *Practices* are the patterns of behavior accepted by a society; they represent knowledge of "what to do when and where."

- *Products* refer to things created by members of the culture, both tangible and intangible.

- *Perspectives* of the culture are the traditional ideas, attitudes, meanings, and values of members of that society.

- "Only language study empowers learners to engage in direct interaction with members of other cultures."

❏ The Comparisons Goal Area

The Comparisons goal area of the national standards states that students should be able to "develop insight into the nature of language and culture" (NSFLEP, 1996, p. 53). The two Comparisons standards are:

- Students demonstrate understanding of nature of language through comparisons of the language studied and their own.
- Students demonstrate understanding of the concept of culture through comparisons of the cultures studied and their own (NSFLEP, 1996, pp. 54, 56).

The second Comparisons standard can be addressed effectively with the Cultures standards as students analyze cultural practices, products, and perspectives between the target and native cultures. For example, as part of a thematic unit on "family and celebrations," middle school students studying French might explore how different cultures celebrate the birth of a baby. Students might imagine that they have a new baby in their family and are looking at the birth announcement. They might compare the two birth announcements shown in Figure 5.2. Through analysis and discussion, students might discover that the North American announcement focuses on the infant as an individual (even announcing her/his own birth) and places the parents' names last. The French announcement focuses more on family lineage, with parents' names first, while announcing both the birth and baptism.

Figure 5.2   Birth announcements (English and French)

An effective strategy for helping students to make cross-cultural comparisons is Ortuño's (1991) adaptation of the Kluckhohn model (Kluckhohn & Strodtbeck, 1961), as a way of analyzing a culture's value system. The model categorizes five basic concerns common to all human beings: (1) What is man's assessment of innate human nature (perception of self and others)? (2) What is man's relation to nature (world view)? (3) What is the temporal focus of life (temporal orientation)? (4) What is the group's principal model of activity (forms of activity)? (5) What is the modality of the group's relationships to others (social relations)? (Ortuño, 1991, p. 450). Figure 5.3 depicts the range of variations that exist across cultures within each of these value orientations. Students might use this framework for understanding their own culture and for comparing it to that of the target culture. For example, the dominant mode of activity in North American society is "doing,"

as individuals are judged primarily by what they can accomplish. In the non-Western world, the emphasis is on what a person *is* rather than what s/he *does*. Ortuño (1991) cautions that a given culture cannot necessarily be classified in one column of the chart in all five areas, although it might be plotted more on one side of the chart than on the other.[7] Also, the Kluckhohn model is not designed to make sweeping cultural generalizations, since much variation may also exist within a specific culture, but rather to account for dominant cultural patterns and perspectives.

Figure 5.3   The Kluckhohn Model

THE FIVE VALUE ORIENTATIONS AND THE RANGE OF VARIATIONS POSTULATED FOR EACH

Orientation	Postulated Range of Variations			
Human Nature	**Evil** mutable immutable	**Neutral** mutable	**Mixture of Good-and-Evil** immutable	**Good** mutable immutable
Man-Nature	Subjugation-to-Nature	Harmony-with-Nature		Mastery-over-Nature
Time	Past	Present		Future
Activity	Being	Being-in-Becoming		Doing

Source: Kluckhohn & Strodtbeck, 1961.

❐ Implications of the Cultures and Comparisons Standards for Instruction

For decades, culture has been divided into two areas: "big C" (formal) culture—the arts, literature, music, history; and "little c" (daily life) culture—the anthropological and sociological aspects such as social behavior, beliefs, housing, food, transportation (Brooks, 1975). Culture has been treated traditionally in the classroom in terms of imparting facts and information, as teachers often lack sufficient cultural experiences themselves and have difficulty integrating culture into the linguistic component of the language program. Galloway (1985) characterized four common approaches to teaching culture:

- *The Frankenstein Approach:* a taco from here, a flamenco dancer from there, a gaucho from here, a bullfight from there
- *The 4-F Approach:* folk dances, festivals, fairs, and food
- *The Tour Guide Approach:* the identification of monuments, rivers, and cities
- *The "By-the-Way" Approach:* sporadic lectures or bits of behavior selected indiscriminantly to emphasize sharp differences (cf. Hadley, 1993, p. 360)

---

7. However, Ortuño (1991) notes that the North American society can be traced straight down the right-hand column.

At the heart of the cultural framework posited by the national standards is the importance of helping students to relate cultural practices and products to each other and to their cultural perspectives. The following are a few examples of instructional strategies for integrating culture instruction at the middle and high school levels. Because *Teacher's Handbook* advocates integration of culture into the teaching of the other standards and skills, additional instructional strategies will be addressed within each of the subsequent chapters.

- Visual Literacy: Students look at a scene from the target culture (e.g., a street scene with traffic lights) or a magazine advertisement and discuss the possible practices and products depicted and the perspectives to which they relate.
- Integration of Language and Culture: As students learn vocabulary, they see and discuss culturally authentic visuals/realia[8] so that they acquire both language and cultural concepts. For example, in a lesson on housing, students look at photos of various types of housing from the target cultures, name features of them, and compare and contrast them with each other and with housing from their own cultures.
- Semantic Mapping: As presented in Chapter 4, semantic maps can be used to associate word clusters graphically around an idea, key word, or concept. Words can be grouped thematically according to cultural practices and products. See Appendix 5.1 for a sample semantic map based on the concept of the bullfight.
- Use of Authentic Documents: Students discover information dealing with practices and products by analyzing documents such as movie listings, restaurant ads, bus/subway schedules, invitations, and so on. For example, students might read a restaurant ad from a Spanish-speaking country and discuss why the restaurant's hours are different from the hours of a North American restaurant (cultural perspectives and comparisons).
- Investigation of Cultural Truths:
  - E-mail surveys: Students communicate with their target language counterparts and investigate information about their daily routines, school, and interests, and compare these data to their own responses.
  - Culture capsules (Taylor & Sorenson, 1961): Students hear a brief description that illustrates a difference between American culture and the target culture, discuss the difference, perform role plays based on the ideas, and integrate this information into activities that incorporate other skills.
  - Culture assimilators (Fiedler, Mitchell, & Triandis, 1971): Students listen to a description or watch an incident of cross-cultural interaction in which miscommunication occurs between an American and a member of the target culture. They choose from a list of alternatives an explanation of the episode and finally they read feedback paragraphs that explain whether each alternative is likely and why (see Appendix 5.2 for an example of a culture assimilator).
  - Cultural minidramas (Gordon, 1974): Students listen to, watch, or read a series of episodes in which miscommunication is taking place; each successive episode reveals additional information, with the exact problem in understanding revealed in

---

8. *Realia* (cultural products) are real items or objects from the target culture, such as menus, train tickets, newspaper articles, party invitations, eating utensils, and toys.

the last part. Students are led in discussion in order to understand how misunderstandings arise when wrong conclusions are reached about the target culture on the basis of one's own cultural understanding.

As the profession strives to provide language instruction for all students and at all levels, increasing attention will need to be given to the unique needs of the middle-level learner. Furthermore, clear goals will need to be articulated for this level of language instruction so that there is a smooth transition from elementary to middle to high school language courses and so that one level builds effectively on the next.

Teach and Reflect

Episode One

Unit and Lesson Design Around a Story, Myth, or Folktale

In Chapter 4, you designed a storytelling lesson appropriate for elementary school students. Now select a culturally authentic story, myth, or folktale that you will present to a middle school class in your target language. First, design a unit plan built around the story you select (use the unit plan design model presented in Chapter 3.) Second, design a lesson plan for the first day devoted to this story. Follow the lesson plan format presented in Chapter 3. Be sure to include your objectives for the lesson and to prepare visuals and realia to help demonstrate meaning. Your instructor may ask you to present part of your lesson to the class.

Episode Two

Developing Culture-Specific Examples of the Three Ps

Create three age-appropriate examples of products, practices, and perspectives for the cultures of the foreign language you are preparing to teach. For the first example, begin with the product and match a practice and perspective to it. For the second, begin with the practice and match a product and perspective to it. For the third, begin with the perspective and match a product and practice to it. Into what types of middle school lessons might these examples be integrated? How do these examples relate to the Kluckhohn Model for Cross-Cultural Awareness?

Discuss and Reflect

Case Study I

Exploratory vs. Sequential Middle School Programs

Mr. Freeman is Chair of the Foreign Language Department in the Stonecrest Area School District. His district currently offers an exploratory language potpourri course in the sixth grade, in which students experience nine weeks of "Phenomenon of Language," nine weeks of French, nine weeks of German, and nine weeks of Spanish. In seventh grade, students choose one language and take what the district calls an "exploratory" course, but it is really a shortened version of Level One. Instruction is given on a six-day rotation—students take language on days one, two, and three and have other classes on days four, five, and six. In eighth grade, students take the traditional Level One class and continue the sequence in grades nine through twelve.

The language teachers in Mr. Freeman's department have complained about the curriculum design for the following reasons:

1. In the sixth grade language potpourri exploratory course, teachers are often expected to teach languages they don't know themselves; for example, Ms. Alvarez had to teach not only Spanish, in which she is certified, but also French and German, languages in which she has no expertise.

2. In the seventh grade exploratory program, teachers feel that students are without language instruction for too many days in a row (sometimes a week) with the six-day rotation schedule. Also, they feel that the goals of this program are poorly defined, as students end up being exposed to the same material in eighth grade.

3. In the eighth grade Level One program, teachers say that some students are bored since they have already learned a lot of the vocabulary in seventh grade, while others demonstrate little mastery over the material taught in seventh grade.

Parents in the district have been pushing for language instruction to be introduced in the fifth grade, and Mr. Freeman and his faculty have been asked to present a proposal to the school board for redesigning the program to include fifth grade as the starting point.

Ask yourself these questions:

1. Why do you think that teachers are being asked to teach languages in which they lack competence?

2. What are the benefits of an exploratory potpourri language course? What might be some shortcomings?

3. Why do you think programs might be designed around a six-day rotation schedule?

To prepare the case:

Read about ways to expand middle school instruction in Adair-Hauck (1992); observe an exploratory middle school language class and interview the teacher to find out her/his views concerning the program's effectiveness; read the published debate concerning exploratory vs. sequential language programs in the special middle school edition of *Foreign Language Annals, 27,* 1994 (pp. 69–88).

To prepare for class discussion, think and write about the following topics:

- Design one program option that introduces language in grade five and begins with a year of exploratory study. Define "exploratory" so that it addresses the possible short-comings of the traditional exploratory course as presented in this chapter.
- Design another program option that features sequential language courses beginning in grade five.
- Prepare a written report to the school board in which you justify offering foreign languages beginning in grade five. Describe how this will affect the rest of the language curriculum. Address the following issues:
  - rationale for foreign languages in grades five and six
  - expected outcomes/goals of language study in the middle school
  - fitting of foreign languages into the existing curriculum
  - fitting of foreign languages into the school day
  - time allotment

Case Study 2

Orderliness with Affection

Ms. Carson won several awards for teaching excellence in the Jefferson School District. Her high school students like her clear explanations of rules and the logical step-by-step drills they practice, leading to their written and oral production of French. For years, parents in the district have asked for French classes in Carver Middle School. This year, the school district granted their request and selected Ms. Carson to teach the classes, given her past record of success. In addition to teaching her three classes of French at Washington High School, Ms. Carson drives five miles a day to teach two first-year French classes at Carver Middle School. Since the school district uses a seven-period day, Ms. Carson has five classes, one period for travel, and a planning period.

Ms. Carson is very excited about working with young language learners. In fact, she strongly supported the parents' efforts over the years to persuade the school district to offer the French classes. During the summer, she planned her lessons for the middle school classes very carefully and taught the first month of class in a very orderly and methodical manner. Each time the students must learn something new, Ms. Carson explains the rule and elaborates on it in great detail. She then has the students practice it by using repetition drills, substitution drills, and, finally, writing drills requiring the students to fill in the blanks on practice sheets she prepares for them each night. Then she asks the students to make sentences using the new information they have learned and, finally, to interview each other using the new language. Ms. Carson is a no-nonsense teacher whose classes are structured and filled with on-task activity. Ms. Carson is surprised that, after the first month of class, the students have not settled down and continue to be restless and inattentive, in her opinion. At Carver Middle School's Open House last week, several parents reported to Ms. Carson that the students have told them how orderly their French class is. The parents also reported that the students like Ms. Carson but do not feel that Ms. Carson likes them very much.

Ask yourself these questions:

1. How would you describe Ms. Carson's approach to language teaching?

2. Given what you know about middle school learners, what characteristics of her students might Ms. Carson need to address?

3. What effect do you think Ms. Carson's daily schedule might have on her instruction, if any?

What do you think of the following alternatives for Ms. Carson?

1. Appear before the school board and ask them to abandon the middle school program because the students are not cognitively ready for language learning.

2. Ask one of her third- or fourth-year high school students to team teach with her in the middle school since the addition of one extra person in the role of teacher will better enable her to monitor the students' behavior.

3. Use fewer repetition drills and more small group work and open discussion.

4. Study middle school curriculum and human development in order to understand the needs of middle school learners.

To prepare the case:

- Recall your own school experience and a favorite teacher you had when you were eleven to thirteen and a half. Try to answer these questions:
  - What did you like best about your teacher?
  - What were some of the things you did in that teacher's class that you especially liked and especially didn't like?
- Interview a middle school student to find out what s/he likes about the way her/his favorite teachers teach. Ask the same questions you asked yourself; read the article by Ralph (1994), "Middle and Secondary L2 Teachers Meeting Classroom Management Challenges Via Effective Teaching Research."

To prepare for class discussion, think and write about the following topics:

- Describe the classroom behavior of a restless student whom you have observed. Postulate some reasons for the student's behavior.
- Assuming the perspective of a middle school language learner, rank the activities listed in Figure 5.4 according to how relaxed or anxious they might make you feel. Use the five-point scale, from moderately anxious (1) to moderately relaxed (5).

FIGURE 5.4 Ranking of Anxiety Level on Scale of 1 to 5

MODERATELY RELAXED			MODERATELY ANXIOUS	
5	4	3	2	1

_____ Read orally in class.

_____ Repeat individually after the instructor.

_____ Speak in front of the class.

_____ Read silently in class.

_____ Open discussion based on volunteer participation.

_____ Work in groups of three or four.

_____ Write your work on the board.

_____ Interview each other in pairs.

_____ Present a prepared dialogue in front of the class.

_____ Compete in class games by teams.

_____ Write a composition at home.

_____ Listen to questions and write answers to the questions.

_____ Role play a situation spontaneously in front of the class.

_____ Repeat as a class after the instructor.

_____ Work on projects (i.e., newspapers, filmstrips, and photo albums).

_____ Speak individually with the instructor in his/her office.

_____ Give an oral presentation or skit in front of the class.

_____ Do exercises in the book.

_____ Work in groups of two and prepare a skit.

_____ Write a composition in class.

Source: Young, 1990.

Now compare your ranking for Figure 5.4 with Figure 5.5, which was developed from research with university-level students. Describe the similarities and differences you find in your ranking.

FIGURE 5.5 Activities Arranged by Anxiety Level by Means

ANXIETY LEVEL	MEAN	ACTIVITY
Moderately Relaxed	4.54	1. Read silently in class.
	4.38	2. Repeat as a class after the instructor.
	4.05	3. Write a composition at home.
Neither Anxious	3.94	4. Do exercises in the book.
Nor Relaxed	3.90	5. Work in groups of three or four.
	3.69	6. Work on projects (i.e., newspapers, filmstrips, and photo albums).
	3.53	7. Compete in class games by teams.
	3.53	8. Repeat individually after the instructor.
	3.51	9. Open discussion based on volunteer participation.
	3.50	10. Interview each other in pairs.
	3.30	11. Work in groups of two and prepare a skit.
	3.26	12. Read orally in class.
	3.13	13. Listen to questions and write answers to the questions.
	3.07	14. Speak individually with the instructor in his or her office.
	3.02	15. Write a composition in class.
Moderately Anxious	2.83	16. Write your work on the board.
	2.47	17. Present a prepared dialog in front of the class.
	2.26	18. Give an oral presentation or skit in front of the class.
	2.23	19. Speak in front of the class.
	2.12	20. Role play a situation spontaneously in front of the class.

Source: Young, 1990.

References

Adair-Hauck, B. (1992). Foreign languages in the middle schools: A curricular challenge. *Pennsylvania Language Forum, 64*, 12–18.

Andis, M. F. (1981). Early adolescence. Skills essential to learning television project. (Working paper) Bloomington, IN: Agency for Instructional Television.

Beane, J. A. (1986). A human school in the middle. *Clearing House, 60*, 14–17.

Briggs, J. B. (1920). *The junior high school.* New York: Houghton Mifflin.

Brooks, N. (1975). The analysis of language and familiar cultures. In R. C. Lafayette (Ed.), *The cultural revolution.* Reports of the Central States Conference on Foreign Language Education (pp. 19–31). Lincolnwood, IL: NTC/Contemporary Publishing Group.

Curtain, H., & Pesola, C. A. (1994). *Languages and children: Making the match.* White Plains, NY: Longman.

Egan, K. (1979). *Educational development.* New York: Oxford University Press.

Egan, K. (1986). *Teaching as story telling.* Chicago: The University of Chicago Press.

Eichhorn, D. H. (1966). *The middle school.* New York: Center for Applied Research.

Elkind, D. (1974). *Children and adolescents: Interpretive essays on Jean Piaget.* London: Oxford University Press.

Epstein, H. T., & Toepfer, C. F., Jr. (1978). A neuroscience basis for reorganizing middle school education. *Educational Leadership, 36,* 656–660.

Fantini, A. E. (Ed.). (1997). *New ways in teaching culture.* Arlington, VA: TESOL.

Fiedler, F. E., Mitchell, T., & Triandis, H. (1971). The culture assimilator: An approach to cross-cultural training. *Journal of Applied Psychology, 55,* 95–102.

Galloway, V. B. (1985). A design for the improvement of the teaching of culture in foreign language classrooms. ACTFL project proposal. Yonkers, NY: ACTFL.

García, P. A., Lorenz, E. B., & Robison, R. E. (1995). Reflections on implementing middle school immersion programs: Issues, strategies, and research. In R. Donato & R. M. Terry (Eds.), *Foreign language learning: The journey of a lifetime.* The ACTFL Foreign Language Education Series (pp. 37–75). Lincolnwood, IL: NTC/Contemporary Publishing Group.

Gordon, R. L. (1974). *Living in Latin America: A case study in cross-cultural communication.* Skokie, IL: NTC/Contemporary Publishing Group.

Hadley, A. O. (1993). *Teaching language in context.* Boston, MA: Heinle & Heinle.

Johnston, J. H. (1984). A synthesis of research findings on middle level education. In J. H. Lounsbury (Ed.), *Perspectives: Middle school education, 1964–1984* (pp. 134–156). Columbus, OH: Middle School Association.

Johnston, J. H., & Markle, G. (1979). What research says to the middle level practitioner. National Middle School Association, 16–17.

Kaplan, I. (1997). Activities to integrate culture into the classroom. Paper presented at the American Association of Teachers of Spanish and Portuguese Pedagogy Summit, Breckinridge, CO.

Kennedy, D. F., & DeLorenzo, W. E. (1994). The case for exploratory programs in middle/junior high school. *Foreign Language Annals, 27,* 69–73.

Kennedy, D. F., & DeLorenzo, W. E. (1985). *Complete guide to exploratory foreign language programs.* Lincolnwood, IL: NTC/Contemporary Publishing Group.

Kluckhohn, F. R., & Strodtbeck, F. L. (1961). *Variations in value orientations.* Evanston, IL: Row, Peterson. Rpt. 1976, Westport, CT: Greenwood.

Knop, C. K., & Sandrock, P. (1994). The case for a sequential second language learning experience at the middle level. *Foreign Language Annals, 27,* 77–83.

Lipsitz, J. S. (1980). The age group. In M. Johnson (Ed.), *Toward adolescence: The middle school years* (pp. 7–31). Seventy-ninth Yearbook of the National Society for the Study of Education, pt. 1. Chicago: University of Chicago Press.

Martin, T. (1993). Turning points revisited: How effective middle-grades schools address developmental needs of young adolescent students. *Journal of Health Education* Supplement, S-24–S-27.

Maynard, G. (1986). The reality of diversity at the middle level. *Clearing House, 60,* 21–23.

Mead, M. (1965). Early adolescence in the United States. *Bulletin of the National Association of Secondary School Principals, 49,* 5–10.

Melton, G. E. (1984). The junior high school: Successes and failures. In J. H. Lounsbury (Ed.), *Perspectives: Middle school education, 1964–1984* (pp. 5–13). Columbus, OH: Middle School Association.

Met, M. (1994). Current foreign language practices in middle schools. *Foreign Language Annals, 27,* 43–58.

Met, M. (1995). Foreign language instruction in the middle schools: A new view for the coming century. In R. Donato & R. M. Terry (Eds.), *Foreign language learning: The journey of a lifetime.* The ACTFL Foreign Language Education Series (pp. 76–110). Lincolnwood, IL: NTC/Contemporary Publishing Group.

National Council of State Supervisors of Foreign Languages. (1994). Foreign language programs and the middle school of the nineties. A position statement. *Foreign Language Annals, 27,* 59–68.

National Standards in Foreign Language Education Project (NSFLEP). (1996). *National standards for foreign language learning: Preparing for the 21st century.* Lawrence, KS: Allen Press, Inc.

Nerenz, A. G. (1990). The exploratory years: Foreign languages in the middle-level curriculum. In S. Magnan (Ed.), *Shifting the instructional focus to the learner.* Northeast Conference Reports (pp. 93–126). Middlebury, VT: Northeast Conference on the Teaching of Foreign Languages.

Ortuño, M. M. (1991). Cross-cultural awareness in the foreign language class: The Kluckhohn Model. *The Modern Language Journal, 75,* 449–459.

Oxford, R. (1990). *Language learning strategies: What every teacher should know.* New York: Newbury House Publishers.

Piaget, J. (1972). Intellectual evolution from adolescence to adulthood. *Human Development, 15,* 1–12.

Ralph, E. G. (1994). Middle and secondary L2 teachers meeting classroom management challenges via effective teaching research. *Foreign Language Annals, 27,* 89–103.

Robinson, G. (1981). *Issues in second language and cross-cultural education: The forest through the trees.* Boston, MA: Heinle & Heinle.

Seelye, H. N. (1997). *Teaching culture: Strategies for intercultural communication.* Lincolnwood, IL: NTC/Contemporary Publishing Group.

Taylor, H. D., & Sorenson, J. (1961). Culture capsules. *The Modern Language Journal, 45,* 350–354.

Verkler, K. W. (1994). Middle school philosophy and second language acquisition theory: Working together for enhanced proficiency. *Foreign Language Annals, 27,* 19–42.

Wing, B. H. (1996). Starting early: Foreign languages in the elementary and middle schools. In B. H. Wing (Ed.), *Foreign languages for all: Challenges and choices.* Northeast Conference Reports (pp. 21–55). Lincolnwood, IL: NTC/Contemporary Publishing Group.

Wiseman, D. G., Hunt, G. H., & Bedwell, L. E. (1986). Teaching for critical thinking. Paper presented at the Annual Meeting of the Association of Teacher Educators, Atlanta, GA.

Young, D. J. (1990). An investigation of students' perspectives on anxiety and speaking. *Foreign Language Annals, 23,* 539–553.

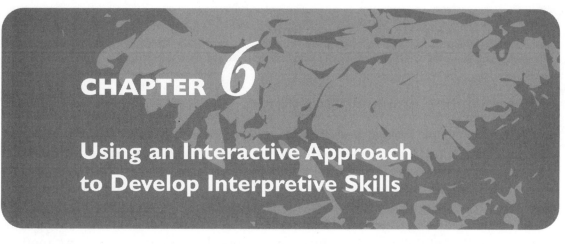

CHAPTER *6*

Using an Interactive Approach to Develop Interpretive Skills

In this chapter you will learn about:

- three communicative modes
- interpretive mode for teaching listening, reading, viewing
- interactive model for developing listening and reading
- interaction with authentic oral and written texts

Teach and Reflect: Using the Interactive Model to Explore an Authentic Written Text; Using the Interactive Model to Explore an Authentic Taped Segment

- **Case Study 1: But the Students Don't Understand What I'm Saying**
- **Case Study 2: Reading Aloud**

Conceptual Orientation

Historically, communicative ability in a foreign language has been described in terms of the four skills of listening, speaking, reading, and writing. As you learned in Chapter 2, instructional methods such as the Audio-Lingual Method (ALM) even fostered the teaching of the four skills separately and in a prescribed sequence (Chastain, 1988). Communication in the world, however, occurs as skills are used in concert, not in isolation, and it is shaped by a specific cultural context. Listening and reading are often catalysts for speaking and/or writing; discussion often leads to written communication; and all of these aspects of communication occur within a specific set of cultural perspectives that govern patterns of interaction among individuals and interpretations of the message. Therefore, comprehension and interpretation involve both cognitive processes (integration of all skills) and social processes such as discussing possible text messages with others. For example, you may have approached the task of reading this chapter by first taking some notes about and/or discussing your background knowledge and the information you hope to learn. You might take notes as you read the chapter; after reading you will probably discuss the information with your classmates. You will have used all skills both cognitively and socioculturally as you explore the new information presented in the chapter.

Framework of Communicative Modes

The standards define communication by means of three communicative modes that emphasize the context and purpose of the communication and thus depict the four skills as working in an integrated fashion. The framework is based on the model proposed by Brecht and Walton (1995), the purpose of which is to illustrate how one participates in "cultural discourses." Figure 6.1 illustrates the framework.

The interpersonal mode. This mode features active negotiation of meaning among individuals, regardless of skill modality. Since participants observe and monitor one another, they can make clarifications and adjustments in their communication. Communication can be realized through face-to-face conversation and written correspondence. Thus all four skills of listening, speaking, reading, and writing can be involved in the interpersonal mode. This mode will be explored further in Chapters 7 and 8.

The interpersonal mode features two-way oral or written communication and negotiation of meaning.

The interpretive mode. This mode focuses on the appropriate cultural interpretation of meanings that occur in written and oral form when there is no possibility of negotiation of meaning with the writer or speaker. Interpretation can occur in activities such as listening to an authentic news broadcast, reading a novel, or viewing a film. Clarification of meaning is not possible since the creator of the text is absent or not accessible. Interpretation involves listening, reading, and viewing skills. However, it goes beyond the traditional idea of "comprehension," since interpretation also involves the listener's/reader's ability to "read (or listen) between the lines" and bring her/his own background knowledge and ideas to the task (NSFLEP, 1996, pp. 32–33). Since the interpretive mode does not provide for active negotiation between the listener and speaker or the reader and writer, it may also require a deeper knowledge of culture to gain an appropriate cultural interpretation of a text.

In interpretive communication, clarification of the message is not possible.

The presentational mode. This mode features formal, one-way communication to an audience of listeners or readers. Speaking and/or writing skills are involved, and no direct opportunity exists for active negotiation of meaning between the presenter and audience. Examples include giving a speech or oral report, preparing a paper or story, and producing a newscast. Substantial knowledge of the language and culture is necessary since the goal is to ensure that the audience will be able to interpret the message (NSFLEP, 1996). This mode will be explored further in Chapters 8 and 9.

> **The presentational mode features formal, one-way communication to an audience of listeners or readers.**

As shown in Figure 6.1 on page 122, successful communication in all three modes requires knowledge of cultural products, practices, and perspectives so that understanding of the appropriate patterns of social interaction and encoding of meaning can occur.

 STANDARDS HIGHLIGHT: Exploring the Interpretive Mode Through Listening, Reading, Viewing

Few would dispute the claim that comprehension is necessary in order for language acquisition to occur. In order to communicate effectively, learners must understand what is being said. To function successfully with a target language, learners depend upon their ability to comprehend the spoken and written word. Empirical studies have shown that the higher the level of listening comprehension ability the higher the oral proficiency skills and overall language abilities (Feyten, 1991). A similar positive relationship has been found to exist between reading ability and language acquisition (Krashen, 1984; Stotsky, 1983).

Historically, interpretive skills have received less attention in language teaching than have the interpersonal skills. Due in part to a lack of knowledge about interpretive processes, teachers often assumed that comprehension would occur on its own. More recently, however, the profession has recognized that merely exposing learners to oral or written input is not sufficient and that explicit teaching of interpretation strategies is needed (Rubin, 1990).

The Process of Interpretive Communication: Listening and Reading Skills

Listening and reading comprehension involve both cognitive and social processes. Listening and reading are active cognitive processes that require an interplay between various types of knowledge. Listeners and readers draw upon four types of competencies as they attempt to comprehend an oral or a written message:

1. grammatical competence: knowledge of morphology, syntax, vocabulary, and mechanics

2. sociolinguistic competence: knowing what is expected socially and culturally by native speakers of the target language

Figure 6.1 Framework for the Communicative Modes

	INTERPERSONAL	INTERPRETIVE	PRESENTATIONAL
Definitions	Direct oral communication (e.g., face-to-face or telephonic) between individuals who are in personal contact Direct written communication between individuals who come into personal contact	Receptive communication of oral or written messages Mediated communication via print and non-print materials Listener, viewer, reader works with visual or recorded materials whose creator is absent	Productive communication using oral or written language Spoken or written communication for people (an audience) with whom there is no immediate personal contact or which takes place in a one-to-many mode Author or creator of visual or recorded material not known personally to listener
Paths	Productive abilities: speaking, writing Receptive abilities: listening, reading	Primarily receptive abilities: listening, reading, viewing	Primarily productive abilities: speaking, writing, showing
Cultural knowledge	Knowledge of cultural perspectives governing interactions between individuals of different ages, statuses, backgrounds Ability to recognize that languages use different practices to communicate Ability to recognize that cultures use different patterns of interaction	Knowledge of how cultural perspectives are embedded in products (literary and artistic) Knowledge of how meaning is encoded in products Ability to analyze content, compare it to information available in own language and assess linguistic and cultural differences Ability to analyze and compare content in one culture to interpret U.S. culture	Knowledge of cultural perspectives governing interactions between a speaker and his/her audience and a writer and his/her reader Ability to present crosscultural information based on background of the audience Ability to recognize that cultures use different patterns of interaction
KNOWLEDGE OF THE LINGUISTIC SYSTEM The use of grammatical, lexical, phonological, semantic, pragmatic, and discourse features necessary for participation in the Communicative Modes.			

Source: SFLL, 1996.

3. discourse competence: the ability to use cohesive devices such as pronouns, conjunctions, and transitional phrases to link meaning across sentences, as well as the ability to recognize how coherence is used to maintain the message's unity

4. strategic competence: the ability to use a number of guessing strategies to compensate for missing knowledge (Canale & Swain, 1980).

Much of the research in L2 listening and reading cognition is based on studies conducted in L1 (Rubin, 1994; Joiner, 1986; Bernhardt, 1986).[1] Listeners and readers rely upon the types of knowledge described earlier as they perform a variety of tasks in the comprehension process. Some tasks or subskills reflect *top-down processing* (see Chapter 2), in which meaning is derived through the use of contextual clues and activation of personal background knowledge about the content of the text. These subskills include identifying key ideas and guessing meaning through a process that Goodman (1967) calls a "psycholinguistic guessing game." In his description of a top-down approach to reading, Goodman states that "efficient reading does not result from precise perception and identification of all elements, but from skill in selecting the fewest, most productive cues necessary to produce guesses which are right the first time" (cf. Chastain, 1988, p. 223).

Other tasks or subskills reflect *bottom-up processing* (see Chapter 2), in which meaning is understood through analysis of language parts. Simply put, the listener or reader processes language in a sequential manner, combining sounds or letters to form words, then combining words to form phrases, clauses, and sentences of the text (Goodman, 1967). Bottom-up subskills include discriminating between different sounds or letters, recognizing word-order patterns, recognizing suprasegmental patterns or sentence structures, translating individual words, and looking at word endings.

Top-down skills can be an effective way for readers to interpret texts since reading in a foreign language is not solely determined by oral language use, as is the case in the native language. Bottom-up processing is essential in order to learn to read the native language, since oral language is already firmly in place and learning to read depends in large part on a child's phonological awareness of a language s/he already speaks. In a foreign language, a learner can often read aloud a text (decode phonologically) without knowledge of the words s/he has decoded. Therefore, in L1 orality comes before literacy, while in L2 literacy may lead to and improve orality.

The current view of the interpretive skills is that the listener/reader arrives at meaning by using both bottom-up and top-down processing in concert. According to Scarcella and Oxford, "Listening can best be understood as a highly complex, interactive operation in which bottom-up processing is interspersed with top-down processing, the latter involving guessing" (1992, p. 142). Similarly, in their discussion of the reading process, Swaffar, Arens, and Byrnes state that reading comprehension "results from interactive variables that operate simultaneously rather than sequentially" (1991, p. 21). There is evidence to suggest that learners perceive top-down strategies to be the more immediate strategies needed for comprehension and bottom-up strategies to be necessary in "repairing" comprehension in the face of difficulty (Vogely, 1995). This finding is supported by Eskey's (1986) interactive reading model, which proposes that readers use both (1) lower-level "identification" skills through which they recognize words and structures necessary for decoding; and (2) higher-level "interpretive" skills through which they reconstruct meaning of whole parts of the text. Both of these skill types are interactive in that they blend into one as the reader or listener attaches meaning to a text and makes it a part of what s/he knows (Eskey, 1986).

In addition to the cognitive processes described earlier, listening and reading comprehension also involve a "social" process. In her sociocognitive view of second-language

---

1. For a comprehensive review of first- and second-language listening and reading research, see Wing, 1986.

reading, Bernhardt (1991) proposes that readers interact with the features of a text, select the features that they feel are important for processing the information, and then use selected features to reconstruct the text and interpret the message.[2] This process involves a different concept of "text," one that includes not only linguistic elements, but also the text's pragmatic nature, its intentionality, its content, and its topic (Bernhardt, 1991). Furthermore, a great deal of comprehension and interpretation is based on the experiences the learner brings to the text. The learner gains new insights about the meaning of a text as a result of discussions s/he has with others. This social view of comprehension reflects the sociocultural view of language learning and instruction posited in Chapter 1 of *Teacher's Handbook*, in which comprehension (i.e., learning) is at least in part constructed through interaction with members of a community. In the world outside the classroom, comprehension does not occur in a vacuum, but rather is socioculturally constructed.

 Top-down and bottom-up processes are used together in the comprehension task.

The Viewing Process

The interpretive mode relates not only to listening to an oral message and reading a written text, but also to viewing videos, movies, plays, and television programs. The viewing medium provides a unique way of bringing the target cultures into the classroom and making learning more meaningful and stimulating. Through video, for example, learners can "witness the dynamics of interaction as they observe native speakers in authentic settings speaking and using different accents, registers, and paralinguistic cues (e.g., posture, gestures)" (Secules, Herron, & Tomasello, 1992, p. 480). Although multimedia research in second-language learning is still in its infancy, an increasing number of studies have verified the effectiveness of video instruction in the classroom (Secules, Herron, & Tomasello, 1992; Hanley, Herron, & Cole, 1995; Price, 1990). Students who view videos demonstrate greater listening comprehension than do students who do not view them (Price, 1990; Secules, Herron, & Tomasello, 1992). Videos have been found to have a positive effect on the learning of grammar in the foreign language (Ramsay, 1991). In addition, studies have indicated that videos that are shown as advance organizers prior to the reading of a passage facilitate the retention of cultural information in the written text (Herron & Hanley, 1992) and that videos are more effective advance organizers than are pictures used with teacher narratives (Hanley, Herron, & Cole, 1995).

Swaffar and Vlatten (1997) propose that the viewing process should begin with silent viewing during which students explore the possible messages and cultural perspectives implied by the visual images. Then, as students are exposed to sound, they verify whether their visual comprehension matches their understanding of what they hear. They engage in comprehension tasks and use the new information they learn through the viewing as the basis for discussion, role playing, and creative writing (Swaffar & Vlatten, 1997). Thus the

---

2. See Bernhardt (1991) for detailed information regarding the process of second-language reading.

viewing process becomes one of predicting and anticipating the meaning of the visual images and then comparing these predictions to what is understood in the oral message. In Chapter 12, you will explore in further detail the selection of videotexts and their integration into language instruction.

Research on the Variables Involved in Comprehension and Interpretation

Research documents a number of variables that affect comprehension and interpretation of a text, be it oral or written. These variables relate to (1) reader-based factors such as familiarity with the topic, use of strategies, purpose for listening/reading/viewing; and (2) text-based factors such as text length, text organization, content of the text, vocabulary (Knutson, 1997).

❐ Reader-Based Factors

The first variable is the key role that *topic familiarity* plays in facilitating comprehension, regardless of the learner's proficiency level (Schmidt-Rinehart, 1994). This variable has been explored in Chapter 2 in terms of the importance of context and background knowledge in understanding input. The degree to which the reader or listener is able to merge input with previously acquired knowledge structures, or schemata, determines how successful s/he will be in comprehending (Minsky, 1982). This linking of new and existing knowledge helps the listener or reader make sense of the text more quickly. The key role of topic/context has been verified by many studies in listening (Chiang & Dunkel, 1992; Bransford & Johnson, 1972) and in reading (Hanley, Herron, & Cole, 1995; Herron & Hanley, 1992; Nunan, 1985; Lee, 1986a; Mueller, 1980; Omaggio, 1979). These experiments have shown that language users provided with prior contextual assistance, such as pictures, video segments, or scripts, comprehend more accurately than they do in the absence of such support. The use of contextual and background information aids understanding by limiting the number of possible text interpretations.

A second variable is the degree to which the reader or listener uses *strategies* in comprehending and interpreting a text. In both listening and reading, prediction of forthcoming input, or the "activation of correct expectancies," is one characteristic of native listener and reader processing (Oller, 1983, p. 10). Many studies support the claim that learners who interact with the text through strategies such as predicting, skimming, scanning, and using background knowledge comprehend much better than learners who fail to use these strategies (Vandergrift, 1997; Bacon, 1992a; Barnett, 1988a; Carrell, 1985; Palinscar & Brown, 1984).

In her study examining how beginning-level Spanish students used strategies to comprehend authentic radio broadcasts, Bacon (1992b) found significant differences in strategy use between upper and lower achievers. Figure 6.2 summarizes the characteristics of successful versus less successful listeners, as reflected in Bacon's (1992b) study.

Figure 6.2 Summary of Characteristics of Successful Versus Less Successful Listeners

SUCCESSFUL LISTENERS	LESS SUCCESSFUL LISTENERS
1. Showed greater flexibility: Greater number and range.	1. Showed less flexibility: Tended to stick with one or two strategies.
2. Not reluctant to rely on English when other strategies failed.	2. Unlikely to mention using English as a comprehension strategy.
3. Could verbalize their strategies for controlling input.	3. Expressed frustration with input.
4. Showed interest in understanding and learning.	4. Seemed to lose interest easily.
5. Able to summarize and add detail.	5. Unable to summarize, or seemed satisfied with little information.
6. Effectively used personal, world, or discourse knowledge.	6. Overdependent on previous knowledge.
7. Controlled comprehension process.	7. Distracted by unknown vocabulary or extraneous factors.
8. Used monitor *marginally* more successfully to help revise a hypothesis or choose between alternative interpretations. More realistic in evaluation of comprehension.	8. Used monitor, but not particularly successfully. Easily discouraged or overconfident of comprehension.
9. Were conscious of losing attention to meaning and could refocus.	9. When they lost their attention to meaning, had trouble refocussing.

Source: Bacon, 1992b.

Vandergrift (1997) recently examined the types of reception strategies that students at the novice and intermediate levels of oral proficiency used in their social interaction with target language speakers. Figure 6.3 presents and defines these strategies and provides examples. Her study revealed that the novice speakers demonstrated a higher use of kinesics, global reprises, and hypothesis testing in English to clarify meaning or ask for additional input than did their intermediate-level counterparts. Intermediate-level speakers used global reprises and hypothesis testing in the target language, and the use of kinesics was less obvious; their use of uptaking (defined in Figure 6.3) reflected their higher level of linguistic knowledge and ease in interacting in the target language (Vandergrift, 1997, p. 500).

Evidence suggests that students benefit from direct strategy training in listening (Bacon, 1992b; Rost & Ross, 1991), reading (Barnett, 1988b; Carrell, 1989; Hosenfeld, 1984; Kitajima, 1997), and language learning in general (Oxford, 1990). For example, in Rusciolelli's (1995) study, Spanish students received training in using the following strategies in reading: pre-reading activities, skimming, scanning, identifying unknown words, contextualized guessing (relating words by analyzing parts of speech and by linking them to the context), looking up words in the dictionary, and writing a summary. This research revealed that after the strategy training, students demonstrated an increased use of guessing unknown words by analyzing the part of speech and by relating words to the context and a decreased use of accessing the dictionary. Furthermore, two additional strategies that students used more often than they did prior to training were (1) skimming for main ideas and (2) using illustrations and titles as clues to meaning (Rusciolelli, 1995). Similarly, in listening, Thompson and Rubin (1993) conducted a study in which they taught students

Figure 6.3 Reception Strategies Used in Interactive Listening: Definitions and Examples

TYPOLOGY OF LISTENER FEEDBACK MOVES AND LIKELY SPEAKER RESPONSE(S)			
Strategy	**Stage**	**Definition**	**Speaker Response**
Global Reprise	I	Listener asks for repetition, rephrasing, simplification, or simply states that nothing was understood.	Repeat or rephrase entire utterance or segment.
Continuation Signal	I	Listener requests no elaboration or repetition and indicates current status of understanding with an overt statement or a nonverbal gesture.	Continue.
Lexical Reprise	II	Listener asks a question about a specific word; may include repetition of word with questioning intonation.	Repeat or rephrase entire utterance or segment.
Fragment Reprise	II	Listener asks a question about a specific part of the previous discourse; may include repetition.	Repeat or rephrase specific part of utterance.
Lexical Gap	II	Listener asks a question about a specific word or term, often requesting a repeat for the word.	Same response as above.
Positional Reprise	II	Listener refers to a position in the previous utterance that was not understood.	Same response as above.
Hypothesis Testing	III	Listener asks specific questions to verify what was heard and indicates a propositional understanding (or misunderstanding) of the utterance.	Confirm if hypothesis check is true or plausible. Provide other information if listener's hypothesis is false.
Forward Inference	III	The listener overtly indicates current understanding by asking a question using established information given by the interlocutor.	Answer question, confirm assumption if consistent with story/conversation, modify assumption or add information to clarify misunderstanding.

Source: Vandergrift, 1997.

learning Russian to choose from among a set of strategies for viewing a video segment. Their research revealed that strategy training improves listening comprehension and that students can be taught to choose their own strategies effectively (Thompson & Rubin, 1993).

A third variable that affects comprehension and interpretation is the *purpose* for listening/reading/viewing, that is, the nature of the task. Reading (and also listening and viewing) with a purpose means "approaching texts with a specific perspective or goal" (Knutson, 1997, p. 51). Munby identified two kinds of reading that involve different goals and skills. Extensive reading, usually for pleasure, requires the ability to understand main ideas, find specific information, and read quickly. Intensive reading, most often for information, requires the ability to read for details, understand implications, and follow relationships of thought throughout a text (Munby, 1979). Knutson suggests strategies such as the following for providing learners with specific purposes for reading: asking learners to read from a particular point of view (e.g., that of a detective, child, etc.); providing a reason for reading that reflects a real-word situation (e.g., looking through movie listings to find an appealing movie to see); giving groups of students a task to complete based on reading (e.g., students plan a trip after reading brochures, timetables, and maps; and listening to weather and traffic reports); guiding students in text analysis of rhetorical devices such as register and audience; developing language literacy by engaging students in reading and discussing literature; and providing opportunities for learners to learn new information and pursue their own interests and enjoyment through interpretive tasks (Knutson, 1997, pp. 51–55).

 Which national standard does this last activity address?

 Reader-based factors include topic familiarity, comprehension strategies, and the purpose of the task.

❏ Text-Based Factors

A fourth variable relates to the *length of text* presented for comprehension and interpretation. In beginning-level classes, students are typically given shorter, edited texts to listen to or read. Learners who process shorter texts are more likely to use word-for-word processing strategies since the demands on memory permit greater attention to detail (Kintsch & van Dijk, 1978; Swaffar, Arens, & Byrnes, 1991). Some evidence suggests that longer texts may actually be easier for students to comprehend because they are more cohesive and interesting to students, though requiring more top-down processing (Allen, Bernhardt, Berry, & Demel, 1988). More research is clearly needed in this area to verify the relationship between text length and the ease of comprehension.

A fifth variable in the comprehension/interpretation process pertains to the *organization of the oral or written text* presented. Traditionally, the difficulty of texts has been judged on the basis of the simplicity of grammatical structures and the familiarity of the vocabulary. According to Lee (1987), this may be due to the fact that we have often tested comprehension itself on the basis of grammar and vocabulary recognition rather than on the reader's/listener's interaction with the text's message. However, empirical studies have shown that exposure to texts with unfamiliar grammar and vocabulary does not significantly affect comprehension (Lee, 1987). Other factors, such as the quality of the text itself in terms of factual consistency and coherence, as well as the background knowledge and motivation of learners, may be more important considerations for teachers when selecting texts (Swaffar, Arens, & Byrnes, 1991). Research reveals that text structure is an important factor in comprehension (Riley, 1993; Roller, 1990). Riley found that texts that are organized according to a "story" format (those that have a beginning event, introduction of a conflict, development or attempt to resolve the conflict, outcome, and ending) have a positive effect on L2 readers' ability to recall the text (Riley, 1993, p. 417). The effect of text structure, however, may also be contingent on the language level of the learner, since in Riley's (1993) study, text structure made the biggest difference in comprehension for the Level Two students. Riley (1993) attributes this to the findings of Roller (1990), which suggest that structure is most important in comprehending "moderately difficult texts"; that is, texts in which the ideas are fairly unfamiliar and require the reader to depend upon text structure to determine which ideas are more important than others. If the language of the text is too difficult for the reader, then structure may not be utilized; if the language is simple, text structure may also be less important (Roller, 1990).

 How does the "story" format discussed here relate to Oller's Episode Hypothesis presented in Chapter 3?

A sixth variable relates to the *content of the text*. Is the content interesting, relevant to students' interests and instructional objectives? Does the content provoke a topic to be discussed and ideas to be shared? Or does the content relate to the subject areas of the school curriculum (see Chapter 3 for discussion of CBI)? The quality of the content will affect how successfully students will be engaged in exploring the text.

A seventh variable involves the treatment of *new vocabulary*. The use of vocabulary lists with definitions does little to help the reader build vocabulary or comprehend more effectively while reading (Bensoussan, Sim, & Weiss, 1984; Johnson, 1982). More effective teacher strategies present new words in terms of their thematic and discourse relationship to the text instead of in terms of dictionary definitions, and use pre- and post-reading discussion to link text information to the readers' background knowledge (Grellet, 1981; Nuttall, 1982). According to Swaffar, Arens, & Byrnes, readers should be encouraged to build their own vocabulary banks, since not all students need to learn the same words. They also suggest in-class vocabulary practice that provides opportunities for students to "find additional words that relate to the same semantic category . . . ; identify how the same words are redefined by different contexts . . . ; increase awareness of pronounceability, and identify affixes, suffixes, or parts of speech" (1991, p. 68). The research indicates that background knowledge helps to facilitate comprehension more effectively than does knowledge of vocabulary (Johnson, 1982).

Text-based factors include the length of text, organization of text, content of text, and treatment of new vocabulary.

According to the research presented above, we should take into consideration the following variables when we provide opportunities for students to comprehend and interpret oral and written texts: (1) topic familiarity and background knowledge of the learner; (2) strategies that learners use in the comprehension task; (3) purpose for listening/reading/viewing, i.e., the nature of the task; (4) length of text; (5) organization of the text; (6) content of the text; and (7) treatment of new vocabulary. Although empirical research often provides implications for classroom instruction, such as the ones described earlier, practice often lags behind the research. In two recent surveys that compared the questions that language instructors have about listening comprehension and the questions being addressed by L2 listening research, Berne (1996, 1998) discovered a gap between L2 listening research and actual classroom practice. Her studies revealed that, while L2 research tends to examine the effects that different variables have on listening performance, the questions teachers ask tend to focus on specific instructional strategies or learner behavior (Berne, 1996; Berne, 1998). Berne suggests that the gap between research and practice in the area of interpretive skills (i.e., listening, reading, and viewing) be closed through attempts such as encouraging L2 listening researchers to create materials for teaching interpretive skills, offering opportunities for collaboration between researchers and teachers, increasing the emphasis placed on the interpretive skills in methods courses, encouraging teachers to seek out pertinent research more regularly, and engaging language instructors in collaboration on classroom research in this area (1998, pp. 176–177).

Use of Authentic Materials

 What was the definition of "authentic materials" given in Chapter 3?

Chapter 3 introduced the concept of using authentic materials in order to establish a meaningful context and reflect real-world culture. Empirical studies have confirmed the positive results gained by listeners and readers who are given opportunities to interact with authentic oral or written texts. In listening comprehension, for example, Herron and Seay (1991) conducted an experiment with intermediate-level French students to test the effect of using tapes of authentic radio segments as a substitute for other types of communicative oral activities and grammar practice. They concluded that students who listened to the tapes demonstrated significantly greater listening comprehension than students who did not interact with the authentic segments. In a similar vein, Bacon's (1992b) study with beginning-level Spanish students who were exposed to authentic radio broadcasts showed that beginning-level students can successfully comprehend authentic, unedited discourse.

In reading, Vigil (1987) found significant differences in comprehension with beginning language students who read unedited authentic texts. Their comprehension skills increased, and their oral and written language performance also improved. Similarly, Young's (1993) study revealed that students studying Spanish in Levels One through Four all comprehended significantly more from an authentic passage than from the edited ones; furthermore, the majority responded more favorably to the authentic passage. As a result, Young suggests that "students would benefit more from reading authentic texts, having cultural information written in English, or reading edited texts written with the characteristics often found in authentic texts such as bold headings, subheadings, pictures, obvious rhetorical organization, and so on, than from reading edited texts that lack these characteristics and are typically found in first- and second-year language textbooks" (1993, p. 451). The results of these and other studies indicate that authentic texts should be used more extensively given their positive effects on listening, reading, and viewing skills (see, for example, Bacon, 1989, and Weissenrieder, 1987).

While authentic materials are often thought to refer primarily to newspaper and magazine articles or news broadcasts, many other types of oral and written texts appropriate to specific age groups can be used effectively, including literary texts. Shook defines literature as "more than just *informational* in nature, but rather . . . compelling; that is, *it makes the reader reflect inwardly,* personally" (1996, p. 202). Earlier chapters of *Teacher's Handbook* have explored various possibilities for using folktales, stories, and legends. Christensen (1990) suggests the use of authentic teenage adventure novels because of their potential for sustaining interest by means of suspense, intrigue, fast action, and cliff-hanging chapter endings.[3] In addition to serving as a source of cultural context, literature provides opportunities for students to use their cognitive skills, develop their language abilities, and interact with one another through sharing ideas.

Rice (1991) suggested three ways for the profession to combine more successfully the teaching of language and literature:

1. Define what we want students to do with literature and identify the skills they need: for example, trace a plot, describe characters, generate a poem that has similar sounds to the one they read.

2. Introduce literature from the beginning levels of language instruction, designing the reading task according to students' abilities: for example, beginning classes might figure out sound patterns of a poem, associate actions with emotions or responses, or set up opposition between male and female characters in a story.

3. Interrelate the proficiency concepts of function, context, and accuracy in developing an approach to teaching literature: for example, the literary equivalent of context might be the genre or type of text; function might be the operations the reader must perform in order to read or critique a particular type of text; and accuracy might include the vocabulary, grammar, and cognitive skills necessary for carrying out the functions.

In selecting texts for beginning FL learner-readers, Shook (1996) suggests that teachers choose literary texts that express the basic, shared cultural beliefs of the target culture. The

---

3. Teachers of Spanish may be particularly interested in Christensen's (1990) ideas about using *Las aventuras de Hector,* a teenage adventure-novel series from Spain.

texts do not have to be direct descriptions of values but can indirectly reflect or hint at values. The teacher should select subsequent literary texts that build upon the knowledge of the native and target cultures already explored by the readers' interaction with previous texts (Shook, 1996). Galloway (1992) suggests that, as students explore literary texts, they need frequent comprehension checks, and guidance in sorting information, assigning meaning, formulating and testing hypotheses, and integrating new ideas. Reading tasks that build strategies will help students to overcome grammatical, lexical, and cultural difficulties and enable them to acquire new information and perspectives (Shook, 1996).

Galloway suggested a four-step reading process for using authentic texts to guide learners' cross-cultural discovery (see Appendix 6.1 for the task formats that can be designed for each stage):

1. Thinking Stage: Readers are oriented to the text through the L2 by means of predicting and exploring cross-cultural similarities and differences in the topic or context. Readers examine their own native cultural framework (C1) and compare it to that of the second-language culture (C2).

2. Looking Stage: Readers anticipate the nature and context of the text, its organization, and its structure. They are introduced to aspects of C2 that might be different from what they expect, and they consider possible C2 meanings and associations.

3. Learning Stage: Readers discover and examine cross-cultural contrasts, form and test hypotheses, expand the C2 framework through analysis, gain insight regarding the C1 framework, and target C2 areas for further research.

4. Integrating Stage: Readers disengage from the text to use, internalize, and reflect on linguistic and cultural information and insights gained through the previous stages. They apply new L2 and C2 learning to new contexts and make new hypotheses (Galloway, 1992, pp. 109–113).

 How might this framework for guiding cross-cultural discovery relate to the cultures framework of the SFLL?

Implications for Teaching Listening, Reading, Viewing

If we adopt the definition of reading as proposed by Swaffar, Arens, and Byrnes and extend it to listening and viewing, then L2 reading and listening comprehension are functions of "cognitive development, the ability to think within the framework of the second language" (1991, p. 63). According to their framework and the results of the studies described earlier, research points to the following implications for teaching the interpretive skills:

1. Students' comprehension may increase if they are trained to use strategies such as activation of background knowledge and guessing.

2. Students need pre-reading, pre-listening, and pre-viewing activities that prepare them for the comprehension/interpretation task.

3. Text appropriateness should be judged on the basis of text quality, interest level, and learners' needs.

4. Authentic materials provide an effective means for presenting real language, integrating culture, and heightening comprehension.

5. Vocabulary must be connected to text structure, student interest, and background knowledge in order to aid retention and recall.

6. Students should be taught to interact with the text through the use of both bottom-up and top-down processes.

7. The information gained through interpreting a text can be used as the basis for interpersonal and presentational communication.

8. Comprehension assessment should engage the learner in a hierarchy of procedures through which s/he interacts with the text.

The Role of the Interpretive Mode Across Instructional Levels

In Chapters 4 and 5, you learned about the key role that the listening skill plays in teaching foreign language to elementary and middle school students. Listening is used as the vehicle for language acquisition and serves as a springboard for integrating other skills and content. Elementary and middle school teachers use many techniques for improving listening comprehension, such as gestures, TPR, exploration of visuals and realia, and hands-on student participation.

For elementary school children, the transition from listening and speaking to reading is made through the use of the language experience chart approach, as described in Chapter 4. At both the elementary and middle school levels, culturally appropriate stories, myths, folktales, science fiction, and adventure stories can be presented to combine cultural understanding and the teaching of reading. Chapter 5 presented an approach for using an oral or a written text as the context for a thematic unit while integrating the practice of all skills and culture.

At the middle/junior high school and high school levels and beyond, listening should also play a prominent role if students are to acquire language. Learners need to attend to large amounts of comprehensible input in the target language, and they benefit from training in strategy development. Authentic input provides the context and meaning stage for the story-based approach to grammar instruction that is presented in Chapter 7. The various types of authentic oral or written texts, as described in earlier chapters, can be presented to students at all levels of instruction. Beginning language learners benefit from experience in top-down processing or listening/reading/viewing for the gist, since this activity discourages the word-for-word decoding that often occurs in early language learning. However, the research discussed earlier in this chapter refutes the notion of consistently matching text length and text type to particular levels of instruction or to students' proficiency levels. For example, beginning-level students should not just be given short texts dealing with concrete information, such as menus and advertisements. Instead, students should be given the opportunity to use the information in the text, that is, grammar, vocabulary, and discourse markers that connect ideas as a tool for achieving comprehension. In addition, by listening/reading/viewing from various perspectives, students can also gain additional insights about the text and the author's intent. Thus this type of interactive listening, reading, and viewing not only develops comprehension skills but can also enable students to learn new ideas and improve global language ability.

An Interactive Model for Integrating the Three Modes of Communication

A model is presented here for developing students' communicative skills, using integration of the three modes of communication as the framework. The modes and skills are integrated as students are engaged in interaction with oral and written texts and with one another. Figure 6.4 illustrates the integrative aspects of the three modes in this model: (1) through the interpretive mode, students acquire new information and explore cultural perspectives as a result of listening to, reading, or viewing an authentic text; (2) through the interpersonal mode, students share information and reactions with one another and organize the ideas found in the text; (3) through the presentational mode, students use their new knowledge and perspectives as they create an oral or written product. As depicted in Figure 6.4, interaction in this model can begin with any of the three modes; for example, a reading might be the springboard for discussion and for doing an oral presentation on a particular topic; a two-way discussion might prompt the viewing of a video-text and lead to further sharing of ideas; a letter to the editor of a newspaper might serve as the basis for discussion and for listening to a news broadcast. Thus the communicative skills and strategies students might use are reiterative and non-linear in nature. In addition, they reflect both cognitive and social processes.

Figure 6.4   Integrating the Three Modes of Communication

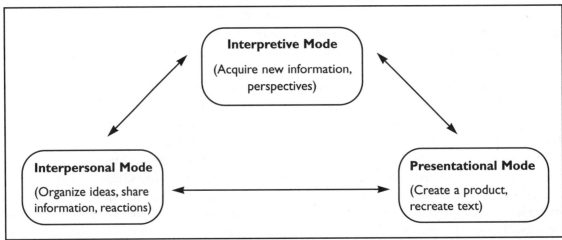

Source: Adapted from SFLL, 1996.

In the first edition of *Teacher's Handbook,* Shrum and Glisan present a model for teaching listening and reading through the use of the following six steps, which integrate the receptive skills with speaking and writing:

I. Pre-listening/Pre-reading
II. Identify main elements
III. Identify details
IV. Organize/revise main ideas/details
V. Recreate text
VI. React to text/explore intertextuality (Shrum & Glisan, 1994, pp. 120–121)

In this model, students begin with an oral or written text; analyze it in a linear fashion in order to comprehend it, moving from main ideas to details; make a summary of it; react to it by sharing personal ideas; and then compare the text to another text in order to compare ideas and discourse organization.

This model has been adapted in this second edition of *Teacher's Handbook* to address the reiterative nature of the three modes of communication and the close integration of skills. The strength of the six-step model has been maintained in the new model introduced here. Figure 6.5 presents the new Interactive Model for Integrating the Three Modes of Communication according to the mode, class activities, discourse format, and purpose for each stage. This model engages students in interaction with the text, helps them build strategies for comprehending and interpreting a text, and provides ways for them to use their newly acquired knowledge and skills in meaningful tasks. The model is interactive and procedural in nature, guiding the learner as s/he interacts with the text by using both bottom-up and top-down processes. It is also integrative, since it provides opportunities for students to combine skills from the three modes and cultural perspectives as they derive meaning from the text, recreate the text, and react to the text in a personal way. Note that students are guided through the text by means of five phases of interaction:

I. Preparation   IV. Application
II. Comprehension   V. Extension
III. Interpretation

Although Figure 6.5 begins with the interpretive mode to illustrate the process; communication could begin with any of the three modes, as illustrated in Figure 6.4.

The interactive model outlined in Figure 6.5 can be implemented with any type of oral or written text. See Chapter 12 for a web-based module using the interactive model. The amount of time spent on each mode will depend on the length and nature of the text as well as on the instructional objectives. Appendix 6.2 presents an example of how an authentic reading can be used as the impetus for communication in all three modes.

Teachers should spend sufficient time in the preparation phase so that students have the necessary skills, background knowledge, and motivation for the comprehension/interpretation task. This phase should include:

1. activation of prior knowledge about the content of the text;

2. some instruction about the content of the text, especially if unfamiliar to learners; and

3. some attention to the language of the text, particularly on new vocabulary (see earlier section in this chapter dealing with the treatment of new vocabulary).

One issue that teachers confront when teaching listening and reading is how much of the native versus target language to use when exploring oral or written texts with their students. Studies have shown that learners receive higher comprehension scores when they are tested in their native language (Wolf, 1993). In a recent study by Davis, Glass, and Coady (1998), undergraduate and graduate students of Spanish demonstrated significantly higher recall of a written text when tested in their native language. The results of their investigation led these researchers to conclude that the language of recall affects FL readers' performance in terms of (1) the amount of textual information recalled accurately and (2) the number of inferences, elaborations, and metacognitive statements produced (Davis, Glass, & Coady, 1998). Their findings support Lee's earlier conclusion that "assessing comprehension with a target language task may limit learners' ability to demonstrate what they [have] comprehended" (1986b, p. 353). When the native language is used to check for comprehension and recall, comprehension skill is not confused with productive use of the target language (Lee, 1986b; Swaffar, Arens, & Byrnes, 1991; Tan & Ling, 1979). It might be beneficial to conduct the pre-listening and pre-reading activities in the native language, particularly if students require new background information prior to the listening or reading task. Clearly, the decision to use either the native or target language for each phase of the interactive model presented here must be made by each teacher after considering the level of students' proficiency and the task to be accomplished. It is advantageous to use the target language to the maximum extent possible, while realizing that occasional use of the native language may be both necessary and helpful in guiding students in strategy use and in checking their comprehension.

This chapter presented the overall framework of the communicative modes together with a model for developing communicative skills by integrating the modes. The focus here was on the interpretive mode as the processes underlying reading, listening, and viewing were discussed and implications for instruction were explored. Each of the next three chapters will examine a particular aspect of the other two modes—interpersonal and presentational—in an effort to explore specific issues relating to grammar, speaking, and writing. These modes and skills will be analyzed somewhat separately in order to help the reader focus on particular issues one at a time. However, keep in mind that the approach of *Teacher's Handbook* is that the modes and skills be taught in an integrative manner, using the model presented in this chapter and other strategies.

Teach and Reflect

Episode One

Using the Interactive Model to Explore an Authentic Written Text

For this activity, you will need to select a targeted level of instruction: elementary school, middle/junior high school, high school, or beyond.

Figure 6.5 An Interactive Model for Integrating the Three Modes of Communication

MODE	CLASS ACTIVITIES	DISCOURSE FORMAT	PURPOSE
Interpretive	PREPARATION PHASE: Students preview the text, establish a purpose, predict meaning, activate background knowledge, preview unfamiliar content, anticipate new vocabulary and text language. COMPREHENSION PHASE: Students skim for the gist, scan for specific information.	Authentic text—written, video, audiotape Story about real or imagined experience Class story about common experience Current events Interdisciplinary content[4]	Acquire new information Explore cultural perspectives Pique student interest
Interpretive + Interpersonal	INTERPRETATION PHASE: Students create a list of main ideas and match them to sections of text. Students match main ideas to key details. Students read/listen/view "between the lines." Students create visuals of cultural products, practices, perspectives. Students ask each other questions about the content of the text. Students share their opinions of and reactions to the text.	Pair/Small group discussion, interviewing	Organize and discuss main ideas and details Connect main ideas and details Discuss cultural products, practices, perspectives Identify key discourse markers (word order, transitional words, parts of speech) and/or specific linguistic features
Presentational	APPLICATION PHASE: Students create a written summary of text and/or design an oral/video presentation. Students create a follow-up product such as a letter, advertisement, new beginning or ending for text, visuals.	Written/Oral summary of text Product (visual, oral, written)	Use new information to complete a task or create a product
Interpretive (revisited)	EXTENSION PHASE: Students analyze features of two texts and compare content and organization.	Authentic text—written, video, audiotape	Compare text to another text (discourse, organization)

Source: Shrum & Glisan, original material, 1994; modified, 1999.

---

4. Thanks to June K. Phillips for ideas on story formats for the interpretive mode.

Option 1: Select an authentic magazine or newspaper article of at least 750 words.

Option 2: Select an authentic literary text (folktale, story, novel excerpt, poem, etc.).

Check the text for the characteristics of good episodic organization. First, decide how this text might be used in a particular thematic unit in order to address short- and long-range objectives. Second, design a plan for teaching the text by using the interactive model presented in this chapter. Begin with the interpretive mode and then integrate interpersonal and presentational communication. Remember that you may need to devote a portion of several class periods in order to complete your work on the text. For each day you plan to spend on the reading, describe what students will do in all stages of the procedure. Your instructor may ask you to present an element of your plan to the class.

Episode Two

Using the Interactive Model to Explore an Authentic Taped Segment

For this activity, you will also need to select a targeted level of instruction: elementary school, middle/junior high school, high school, or beyond.

Option 1: Select an authentic segment on audiotape or videotape (conversation, commercial, news report, song, etc.).

Option 2: Semiscript your own taped conversation: Give two native speakers a particular situation or subject to discuss (for example, ask them to pretend that they are two students who meet for the first time while standing in the registration line); ask the speakers to talk spontaneously for two to three minutes. Do not prepare a written script, since the conversation should be as natural as possible.

Next, decide how this segment might be used in a particular thematic unit in order to address short- and long-range objectives. Then design a plan for teaching the segment by using the interactive approach presented in this chapter. Begin with the interpretive mode and then integrate interpersonal and presentational communication. Describe what students will do in each stage of the procedure. Your instructor may ask you to present to the class your taped segment and an element of your lesson.

Discuss and Reflect

Case Study 1

But the Students Don't Understand What I'm Saying

Mr. Cosgrove and Ms. Sturgeon teach German at Warrington High School, an urban, multicultural school district in the eastern section of a large city. They began their teaching careers twenty-five years ago when they accepted their present positions at the high school. Although they are good friends and work together cordially on school committees, Mr. Cosgrove and Ms. Sturgeon do not employ similar approaches to teaching. Mr. Cosgrove believes in a teacher-centered classroom in order to maintain effective control of his classes. His instructional plans are grammar oriented, for he feels that knowing a language means understanding the rules and English equivalents of target-language vocabulary. Although his command of German is very good, Mr. Cosgrove uses the language only during his presentation of dialogues and during the practice of grammar exercises. Since he feels that beginning-level students have great difficulty understanding spoken German, he translates everything he says into English. Mr. Cosgrove's daily plans follow the textbook organization fairly closely. Students do some communicative practice as provided in the textbook, although rarely in pairs or groups. Mr. Cosgrove attended a few workshops over the years, but he doesn't agree with teaching strategies that propose that Level One students be given the opportunity to communicate extensively. He feels that Level One students need to learn the grammar first and then in later levels can apply the rules to meaningful communication. The school administration assigns Mr. Cosgrove primarily Level One and some Level Two classes to teach, for they feel that the upper levels should be given to teachers who keep abreast of innovations in teaching.

Ms. Sturgeon, on the other hand, uses a communicative approach to teaching and provides ample opportunities for students to hear the target language and to interact with one another. She organizes her units around contexts and functions and makes sure that meaning is at the center of every activity. She has changed many elements of her teaching over the years as a result of attending numerous workshops and conferences. Her teaching load consists of Levels Three, Four, and Five.

The differences in teaching philosophy resulted in high levels of frustration for Mr. Cosgrove's Level One and Two students when they initially entered Ms. Sturgeon's Level Three classes. They wanted Ms. Sturgeon to translate everything the way that Mr. Cosgrove did, and they resented the amount of time spent having to listen to the target language. Ms. Sturgeon also experienced frustration as she felt that she could never really introduce upper-level kinds of activities, since these students had not acquired basic-level listening and speaking skills. For many years now, she has been dealing with this problem and, on occasion, has discussed it with Mr. Cosgrove, who steadfastly refused to change his approach, feeling justified that the students liked German and felt confident in their understanding of it when they finished his class.

However, at the start of this academic year, Mr. Cosgrove was convinced that he needed to make some changes in his teaching. Over the summer he had gone to Germany for several weeks to visit his son, who was spending two years there engaged in business. Although his son knew virtually no conversational German when he went to Germany, he told his father that he learned to speak German by hearing the real language spoken and by reading it in newspapers and magazines. His son was so convincing in his argument that Mr. Cosgrove resolved to ask Ms. Sturgeon to help him make some changes in his teaching. He also acknowledged that his teaching had not reflected recent approaches to language instruction because he was afraid that the new strategies wouldn't work and that he would lose enrollments. Ms. Sturgeon was thrilled with Mr. Cosgrove's new position, and, recognizing his professional and emotional vulnerability, she sought ways that they could both improve their teaching.

Ask yourself these questions:

1. What do you think the listening process is like for students in Mr. Cosgrove's classes?

2. What do you think the listening process is like for students in Ms. Sturgeon's classes?

3. What are some ways Ms. Sturgeon and Mr. Cosgrove might seek change in neutral and non-threatening ways?

To prepare the case:

- Read Rubin (1994) for a review of second-language listening comprehension research; read Herron and Seay (1991) for information about the effectiveness of authentic listening texts; read Berne (1998) for a discussion of the gap between L2 listening research and classroom practice; interview an experienced high school foreign language teacher to find out what s/he does when students fail to understand what has been said.

- Mr. Cosgrove and Ms. Sturgeon look to the national standards for some guidance about the role of comprehension in the communication process. How do the three modes shed light on the role of comprehension in communication? What are some implications for classroom practice?

To prepare for class discussion, think and write about these tasks:

- Imagine that you are Ms. Sturgeon and are helping Mr. Cosgrove to use authentic materials in teaching listening comprehension. Give him some guidance with respect to the following issues related to using authentic texts: (1) advantages of authentic, unedited texts over edited texts; (2) initial perception by students that they will have difficulty comprehending authentic texts; (3) how to match the comprehension task to the level of the students' language abilities.

- In addition to using audiotapes in German to provide oral input in his classroom, what other resources might Mr. Cosgrove use in order to expose his students to authentic spoken German? How might these resources be integrated into instruction?

Case Study 2

Reading Aloud

For twelve years, Ms. Boone has been teaching French at Big Sky High School in a rural Midwestern town. One of the first things she noticed about her students when she began teaching was the transference of students' regional English accent to their French pronunciation. She began to ask her students to read aloud in French to help them practice their pronunciation. Generally, her procedure is to introduce the activity by telling students that it's time to practice pronunciation. Sometimes she puts them through some practice exercises, repeating words that have a particularly troublesome sound. Then she models for the students a short sentence she selected that embodies the sound and asks for whole-class repetition. Finally, she asks individuals to read aloud subsequent sentences that also contain the troublesome sound.

Ms. Ariel teaches in the same school as Ms. Boone and has roughly the same amount of teaching experience, but Ms. Ariel teaches Spanish. Ms. Boone and Ms. Ariel belong to the same walking group, which meets after school for a mile walk around the track. One day as they walked, Ms. Boone asked Ms. Ariel how she used reading aloud for pronunciation practice. Ms. Ariel replied that she did not use it at all for pronunciation practice and wondered how one could use such a strategy for pronunciation. Of course, she said, the main purpose of reading aloud was for students to comprehend the language and then discuss what it meant; even the students listening to the oral reader could use the reading to figure out meaning. That day, in fact, her students had read aloud a passage from *Mosén Millán*, and their understanding of the novel was enhanced by having done so.

Both Ms. Boone and Ms. Ariel were so surprised that they had used a technique by the same name for entirely different purposes that they decided to ask their students what they did in their minds as they read aloud in class.

Ask yourself these questions:

1. What are some possible metacognitive strategies that Ms. Boone's students are using during oral reading? How about Ms. Ariel's students?

2. How do the activities in the classes of Ms. Boone and Ms. Ariel fit the descriptions of reading provided in this chapter?

3. Do you agree with Ms. Ariel's statement that her students' comprehension was enhanced by listening to their classmates read aloud? Explain.

To prepare the case:

Read Bacon (1992b) for information about the metacognitive strategies learners use while listening; interview a beginning and an advanced language student to find out what they think about while they are reading aloud; interview a beginning and an advanced language student to find out what they think about while someone else is reading aloud.

To prepare for class discussion, think and write about these tasks:

Conduct your own mini-experiment. Ask a student to read a paragraph aloud; ask two other students to listen and then to answer the following questions. Summarize your findings.

1. What was the first thing you did to make sense of this paragraph?

2. Did you do anything else to help you understand at any point during the listening?

3. At any point during the listening, did you change your mind regarding what this passage was about or what to listen for?

4. What can you remember hearing?

5. Can you remember anything else that you heard? Any new information?

6. Did you learn anything new? Any new information?

7. Do you remember anything else?

8. Do you remember any new words?

9. On a scale of one-to-ten, how confident are you that you understood this passage?

10. On a scale of one-to-ten, how much did you already know about this topic?

(Adapted from Bacon, 1992a)

- Write a description of the effectiveness or ineffectiveness of using reading aloud as a strategy in your foreign language classroom.

References

Allen, E. D., Bernhardt, E. B., Berry, M. T., & Demel, M. (1988). Comprehension and text genre: An analysis of secondary school foreign language readers. *The Modern Language Journal, 72,* 163–187.

Bacon, S. M. (1989). Listening for real in the foreign-language classroom. *Foreign Language Annals, 22,* 543–551.

Bacon, S. M. (1992a). The relationship between gender, comprehension, processing strategies, and cognitive and affective response in foreign language listening. *The Modern Language Journal, 76,* 160–178.

Bacon, S. M. (1992b). Phases of listening to authentic input in Spanish: A descriptive study. *Foreign Language Annals, 25,* 317–334.

Barnett, M. (1988a). Reading through context. *The Modern Language Journal, 72,* 150–159.

Barnett, M. (1988b). Teaching reading strategies: How methodology affects language course articulation. *Foreign Language Annals, 21,* 109–119.

Bensoussan, M., Sim, D., & Weiss, R. (1984). The effect of dictionary usage on EFL test performance compared with student and teacher attitudes and expectations. *Reading in a Foreign Language, 2,* 262–276.

Berne, J. E. (1996). Current trends in L2 listening comprehension research: Are researchers and language instructors on the same wavelength? *Minnesota Language Review, 24*(3), 6–10.

Berne, J. E. (1998). Examining the relationship between L2 listening research, pedagogical theory, and practice. *Foreign Language Annals, 31,* 169–189.

Bernhardt, E. B. (1986). Reading in the foreign language. In B. H. Wing (Ed.), *Listening, reading, writing: Analysis and application,* Northeast Conference Reports (pp. 93–115). Middlebury, VT: Northeast Conference on the Teaching of Foreign Languages.

Bernhardt, E. B. (1991). *Reading development in a second language: Theoretical, empirical, and research perspectives.* Norwood, NJ: Ablex.

Bransford, J. D., & Johnson, M. K. (1972). Contextual prerequisites for understanding: Some investigations of comprehension and recall. *Journal of Verbal Learning and Verbal Behavior, 11,* 717–726.

Brecht, R. D., & Walton, A. R. (1995). The future shape of language learning in the new world of global communication: Consequences for higher education and beyond. In R. Donato & R. M. Terry (Eds.), *Foreign language learning: The journey of a lifetime,* The ACTFL Foreign Language Education Series (pp. 110–152). Lincolnwood, IL: NTC/Contemporary Publishing Group.

Canale, M., & Swain, M. (1980). Theoretical bases of communicative approaches to second language teaching and testing. *Applied Linguistics, 1,* 1–47.

Carrell, P. (1985). Facilitating ESL reading by teaching text structure. *TESOL Quarterly, 19,* 727–752.

Carrell, P. (1989). Metacognitive awareness and second language reading. *The Modern Language Journal, 73*, 121–134.

Chastain, K. (1988). *Developing second language skills—Theory and practice.* San Diego, CA: Harcourt Brace Jovanovich.

Chiang, C. S., & Dunkel, P. (1992). The effect of speech modification, prior knowledge, and listening proficiency on EFL lecture learning. *TESOL Quarterly, 26*, 345–374.

Christensen, B. (1990). Teenage novels of adventure as a source of authentic material. *Foreign Language Annals, 23*, 531–537.

Davis, J. N., Glass, W. R., & Coady, J. (1998). Use of the target language versus the native language to assess foreign/second language reading comprehension: Still an issue? Unpublished manuscript.

Eskey, D. E. (1986). Theoretical foundations. In F. Dubin, D. E. Eskey, & W. Grabe (Eds.), *Teaching second language reading for academic purposes* (pp. 3–23). Reading, MA: Addison-Wesley.

Feyten, C. (1991). The power of listening ability: An overlooked dimension in language acquisition. *The Modern Language Journal, 75*, 173–180.

Galloway, V. (1992). Toward a cultural reading of authentic texts. In H. Byrnes (Ed.), *Languages for a Multicultural World in Transition.* Northeast Conference Reports (pp. 87–121). Lincolnwood, IL: NTC/Contemporary Publishing Group.

Glisan, E. W., & Shrum, J. L. (1996). *Enlaces: Cuaderno de práctica.* Boston, MA: Heinle & Heinle.

Goodman, K. S. (1967). Reading: A psycholinguistic guessing game. *Journal of the Reading Specialist, 6*, 126–135.

Grellet, F. (1981). *Developing reading skills. A practical guide to reading comprehension exercises.* Cambridge: Cambridge University Press.

Hanley, J. E. B., Herron, C. A., & Cole, S. P. (1995). Using video as an advance organizer to a written passage in the FLES classroom. *The Modern Language Journal, 79*, 57–66.

Herron, C. A., & Hanley, J. (1992). Using video to introduce children to a foreign culture. *Foreign Language Annals, 25*, 419–426.

Herron, C. A., & Seay, I. (1991). The effect of authentic oral texts on student listening comprehension in the foreign language classroom. *Foreign Language Annals, 24*, 487–495.

Hosenfeld, C. (1984). Case studies of ninth grade readers. In J. C. Alderson & A. H. Urquhart (Eds.), *Reading in a foreign language* (pp. 231–249). London, UK: Longman.

Johnson, P. (1982). Effects on comprehension of building background knowledge. *TESOL Quarterly, 16*, 503–516.

Joiner, E. G. (1986). Listening in the foreign language. In H. S. Lepke (Ed.), *Listening, reading, writing: Analysis and application,* Northeast Conference Reports (pp. 43–70). Middlebury, VT: Northeast Conference on the Teaching of Foreign Languages.

Kintsch, W., & van Dijk, T. A. (1978). Towards a model of discourse comprehension and production. *Psychological Review, 85*, 363–394.

Kitajima, R. (1997). Referential strategy training for second language reading comprehension of Japanese texts. *Foreign Language Annals, 30*, 84–97.

Knutson, E. M. (1997). Reading with a purpose: Communicative reading tasks for the foreign language classroom. *Foreign Language Annals, 30*, 49–57.

Krashen, S. D. (1984). *Writing: Research, theory and application.* New York: Pergamon Press.

Lee, J. F. (1986a). Background knowledge and L2 reading. *The Modern Language Journal, 70*, 350–354.

Lee, J. F. (1986b). On the use of the recall task to measure L2 reading comprehension. *Studies in Second Language Acquisition, 8*, 83–93.

Lee, J. F. (1987). Comprehending the Spanish subjunctive: An information processing perspective. *The Modern Language Journal, 71*, 51–57.

Minsky, M. (1982). A framework for representing knowledge. In J. Haugeland (Ed), *Mind design* (pp. 95–128). Cambridge, MA: MIT Press.

Mueller, G. A. (1980). Visual contextual cues and listening comprehension: An experiment. *The Modern Language Journal, 64*, 335–340.

Munby, J. (1979). Teaching intensive reading skills. In R. Mackay, B. Barkenson, & R. R. Jordan (Eds.), *Reading in a second language* (pp. 142–158). Rowley, MA: Newbury House.

National Standards in Foreign Language Education Project (NSFLEP). (1996). *National standards for foreign language learning: Preparing for the 21st century*. Lawrence, KS: Allen Press.

Nunan, D. (1985). Content familiarity and the perception of textual relationships in second language reading. *RELC Journal, 16*, 43–51.

Nuttal, C. (1982). *Teaching reading skills in a foreign language*. Practical Language Series, 9. London, UK: Heinemann.

Oller, J. W. (1983). Some working ideas for language teaching. In J. W. Oller & P. A. Richard-Amato (Eds.), *Methods that work* (pp. 3–19). Rowley, MA: Newbury House.

Omaggio, A. C. (1979). Pictures and second language comprehension: Do they help? *Foreign Language Annals, 12*, 107–116.

Oxford, R. (1990). *Language learning strategies: What every teacher should know*. Boston, MA: Heinle & Heinle.

Palinscar, A., & Brown, A. (1984). Reciprocal teaching of comprehension-fostering and comprehension-monitoring activities. *Cognition and Instruction, 1*, 117–175.

Price, J. (1990). Improving foreign language listening comprehension. In J. A. Alatis (Ed.), *Georgetown University Roundtable on Languages and Linguistics 1990: Linguistics, language teaching, and language acquisition: The interdependence of theory, practice, and research* (pp. 309–316). Washington, DC: Georgetown University.

Ramsay, R. (1991). French in action and the grammar question. *French Review, 65*, 255–266.

Rice, D. B. (1991). Language proficiency and textual theory: How the twain might meet. *ADFL Bulletin, 22*, 12–15.

Riley G. L. (1993). A story structure approach to narrative text comprehension. *The Modern Language Journal, 77*, 417–432.

Roller, C. M. (1990). The interaction between knowledge and structure variables in the processing of expository prose. *Reading Research Quarterly, 25*, 79–89.

Rost, M., & Ross, S. (1991). Learner use of strategies in interaction: Typology and teachability. *Language Learning, 41*, 235–273.

Rubin, J. (1994). A review of second language listening comprehension research. *The Modern Language Journal, 78*, 199–221.

Rusciolelli, J. (1995). Student responses to reading strategies instruction. *Foreign Language Annals, 28*, 262–273.

Scarcella, R. C., & Oxford, R. L. (1992). *The tapestry of language learning*. Boston, MA: Heinle & Heinle.

Schmidt-Rinehart, B. C. (1994). The effects of topic familiarity on second language listening comprehension. *The Modern Language Journal, 78*, 179–189.

Secules, T., Herron, C., & Tomasello, M. (1992). The effect of video context on foreign language learning. *The Modern Language Journal, 76*, 480–490.

Shook, D. J. (1996). Foreign language literature and the beginning learner-reader. *Foreign Language Annals, 29*, 201–216.

Shrum, J. L., & Glisan, E. W. (1994). *Teacher's handbook: Contextualized language instruction*. Boston, MA: Heinle & Heinle.

Stotsky, S. (1983). Research on reading/writing relationships: A synthesis and suggested directions. *Language Arts, 60*, 627–642.

Swaffar, J., Arens, K., & Byrnes, H. (1991). *Reading for meaning*. Englewood Cliffs, NJ: Prentice Hall.

Swaffar, J., & Vlatten, A. (1997). A sequential model for video viewing in the foreign language curriculum. *The Modern Language Journal, 81*, 175–188.

Tan, S., & Ling, C. (1979). The performance of a group of Malay-medium students in an English reading comprehension test. *RELC, 19,* 81–89.

Thompson, I., & Rubin, J. (1993). Improving listening comprehension in Russian. Report submitted to U.S. Department of Education, International Research and Studies Program. Grant #PO17A00032.

Vandergrift, L. (1997). The Cinderella of communication strategies: Reception strategies in interactive listening. *The Modern Language Journal, 81,* 494–505.

Vigil, V. D. (1987). Authentic text in the college-level Spanish I class as the primary vehicle of instruction. Unpublished doctoral dissertation, University of Texas, Austin.

Vogely, A. (1995). Perceived strategy use during performance on three authentic listening comprehension tasks. *The Modern Language Journal, 79,* 41–56.

Weissenrieder, M. (1987). Listening to the news in Spanish. *Foreign Language Annals, 71,* 18–27.

Wing, B. H. (Ed.). (1986). *Listening, reading, writing: Analysis and application.* Northeast Conference Reports. Middlebury, VT: Northeast Conference on the Teaching of Foreign Languages.

Wolf, D. F. (1993). A comparison of assessment tasks used to measure FL reading comprehension. *The Modern Language Journal, 77,* 473–489.

Young, D. J. (1993). Processing strategies of foreign language readers: Authentic and edited input. *Foreign Language Annals, 26,* 451–468.

CHAPTER **7**

Using a Story-Based Approach to Teach Grammar

by Bonnie Adair-Hauck, Ph.D. (University of Pittsburgh), Richard Donato, Ph.D. (University of Pittsburgh) and Philomena Cumo-Johanssen (World Languages Educational Consultant, Pittsburgh, Pennsylvania).[1]

In this chapter you will learn about:

- explicit/implicit grammar explanations
- story-based language learning
- guided participation for grammar explanations

- The Pace Model: Presentation, Attention, Co-Construct, Extension

Teach and Reflect: Examining Grammar Presentations in Textbooks; Designing a Story-Based Language Lesson
- **Case Study 1: Using a Story-Based Approach to Teach Reflexive Verbs**
- **Case Study 2: Using Songs to Foreshadow Grammar**

Conceptual Orientation

In this chapter, you will explore a story-based approach to the teaching of grammar in a standards-based foreign language curriculum. The SFLL (NSFLEP, 1996) emphasize that "communication" is at the core of second-language learning. Communication has been defined as the personal expression, interpretation, and negotiation of meaning where information, feelings, and ideas are exchanged in talk, gesture, and writing (Lee & VanPatten, 1995). Communication also involves the development of close relationships between individuals as they use language to create social bonds, show sympathy or understanding, and support each other. This type of communication is referred to as *phatic communication* and contrasts sharply with communication that is aimed primarily at exchanging information in verbal transactions. Furthermore, communication involves

---

1. These individuals were asked to co-author this chapter since their research in the teaching of grammar supports the premise of contextualized language instruction espoused in *Teacher's Handbook*.

private talk, or "communication with the self," to plan, organize, and evaluate one's thinking and doing (Brooks & Donato, 1994; Brooks, Donato, & McGlone, 1997) as discussed in the section on private speech in Chapter 1. As you learned in Chapter 6, the standards further refine this definition by organizing our language-using activities into the interpersonal, interpretive, and presentational modes. Each mode specifies how language is used in the process of communication. In the past, a traditional classroom with its emphasis on grammatical competence and explicit knowledge of language rules did not provide occasions for learners to "communicate" in the ways communication is currently being defined and understood by psycholinguists, applied linguists, materials developers, and the language teaching profession. Unfortunately, many learners who spend years learning the formal properties of the language (sound system, verb conjugations, rules of syntax, vocabulary lists, etc.) could not, in the end, exchange information, express ideas or feelings, construct and control problem solving, or develop and nurture a social relationship in a second-language (Adair-Hauck & Cumo-Johanssen, 1997; Barnes, 1992; Hall, 1995, 1999).

Cooper underscores the important role of communication when he states that "it is through communication that we are able to improve our world, to prosper and enjoy it (1993, p.43)." Communicating, in Cooper's broad sense of the word, involves more than Chomsky's (1965) notion of linguistic or grammatical competence; indeed, communication requires both communicative and interactional competence (Mehan, 1979; see Chapter 1) and the ability to use language in a variety of ways and for a variety of purposes. In the most general terms, the SFLL capture the notions of communicative and interactional competence by stressing the need to "know how, when, and why to say what to whom" (NSFLEP, 1996, p. 11).

Added to this goal is the need to provide learners with opportunities to reflect on the language system they are learning to use. Teachers committed to providing communicative and interactive language learning experiences for their learners often find it a challenge to integrate what is called "grammar instruction" or "focus on form" into their classrooms. The standards stress that knowledge of the language system including grammar, vocabulary, phonology, and pragmatic and discourse features, undergirds the accuracy of communication. Researchers agree that "focus on form" (Long, 1991) can be beneficial to learners and is critical to making progress as language users (Adair-Hauck & Donato, 1994; Ellis, 1988; Herron & Tomasello, 1992; Lightbown & Spada, 1990; Long, 1991; Salaberry, 1997). Liskin-Gasparro illustrates what teachers attempt to do when they focus students' attention on form for purposes of accurate communication: Teachers are "supplying information about how the language works when one or more students experience what we might call communicative urgency, a need to say something and, thus, a desire for grammatical information" (1999).

The rationale for teaching grammar is multi-faceted. The first reason is theoretically motivated. As the Variable Competence Model (Bialystok, 1982; Ellis, 1988; Tarone, 1983) states, depending on the social and communicative context, a learner draws on both their automatic (non-analyzed) and controlled (analyzed) language knowledge. Ellis (1988) advises that analyzed knowledge regarding the grammar can develop into automatic or non-analyzed knowledge if the learner is placed into interactional situations that call for a two-way negotiation of meaning between learners. The second reason for the teaching of grammar relates to the dynamics of classroom practice and, particularly, to the background knowledge of the learners. Learners in middle school and high school are already literate and therefore have established expectations concerning language instruction (Celce-Murcia, 1991) and language use. Grammar instruction can also be beneficial because it raises learners' consciousness concerning the differences and similarities of L1 and L2 (Rutherford, 1988) and thus can directly address the Comparisons goal of the SFLL. In this respect, grammar instruction can be used as a "linguistic map," with reference points or "rules of thumb" to assist learners as they explore the "topography" of the new language.

However, we need to remember that understanding grammatical structures apart from their use and function is pointless unless one wants to be a linguist and describe a language scientifically without necessarily becoming a communicatively competent user of that language. Like road signs, grammatical structures take on meaning only if they are situated in a context, in people, and in connected discourse. Furthermore, Krashen (1982) reminds us that grammatical structures will become internalized only if the learners are placed in a situation in which they need to use the structures for communicative purposes. Consequently, an important role of the teacher is to create learning situations in which the learners feel a need to call upon and make use of the grammar in order to comprehend and communicate in the target language.

 Grammatical structures will become internalized only if the learners are placed in a situation in which they need to use the structures for communicative purposes.

The Explicit/Implicit Controversy

Although many researchers agree on the benefits of some grammar instruction, how to teach grammar has met with little agreement. Grammatical structures will become internalized only if the learners are placed in a situation in which they need to use the structures for communicative purposes (DeKeyser & Sokalski, 1996; Fotos & Ellis, 1991; Salaberry, 1997; Shaffer, 1989; VanPatten & Cadierno, 1993). Furthermore, research on focus on form is often conducted in highly controlled laboratory settings and rarely tested against the realities of the language classroom with real teachers and learners and all that this implies (Ellis, 1998). The controversy has become particularly acute in the framework of communicative language teaching, which has consistently underscored the importance of stressing meaning over form. For years, our profession has been grappling with polarized views concerning the teaching of grammar within a communicative framework. An *explicit* method of grammar instruction involves direct teacher explanations of rules followed by related manipulative exercises illustrating these rules. Many of us have probably experienced this method of grammar instruction, since most textbooks present grammar in this fashion. Unfortunately, many of the textbooks' manipulative drills are grounded in shallow and artificial contexts (Walz, 1989) that have little importance to the real concerns of learners. Thus these practice opportunities are meaningless to learners and are not capable of engaging their commitment to learning, their imaginations, or their desire to communicate using the forms they are learning (Brooks & Donato, 1994). It is common for teachers to observe that these mechanical, repetitive drills often result in unmotivated and lethargic responses in learners, no matter how much context is given in the directions or how much personalization is provided.

Another potential problem with explicit grammar instruction is that it implies a direct instructional and authoritative role on the part of the teacher. Conversely, this practice assigns a passive role on the part of the learners. Learner interaction takes place, if it occurs at all, only after the teacher's grammatical explanations and after several practice exercises that consist of disconnected sentences unrelated to an overall theme. Addressing the lack of learner motivation to learn forms, Rivers (1983) advocated that skill-getting should be stressed before skill-using, but this practice has the disadvantage of requiring learners to master a skill or to learn a grammatical form before experiencing its relevance in a communicative encounter (see Chapter 2 for a discussion on the differences between skill-getting and skill-using activities). This linear model of teaching a form before using a form has distinct disadvantages in terms of fostering learner desire to use the form, of assisting their understanding of the form in question, and of providing a valid reason for learning the particular grammar point.

On the other side of the instructional dichotomy, *implicit* grammar explanation as presented by Krashen (1985), Terrell (1977), and Dulay and Burt (1973) rejects the need for any explicit focus on form. These researchers argue that learners can acquire language naturally if they are provided with sufficient comprehensible input from the teacher and that grammatical development follows its own natural, internal syllabus. If learners are exposed to a sufficient amount of language that interests them and is globally understandable to them, they will eventually be able to hypothesize and determine how the structures work, as well as the language's systematicity, function, and meaning. Theoretically, learners should be able to do the hypothesizing and language analysis on their own. However, research has shown that some learners do not attend to or "induce" the teacher's grammatical agenda in these implicit, inductive lessons.[2] This implicit approach clearly places little importance on instruction, reducing the teacher to a provider of input rather than explanation, as discussed in the explicit approach. Herron and Tomasello (1992) also state that the inductive method cannot guarantee that the learner will discover the underlying concepts or that the induced concepts will actually be correct. Furthermore, the implicit/inductive approach can be frustrating to adolescent or adult learners, many of whom have already become analytical with regard to the rules that govern their native languages. These learners also often want to hasten the learning process by consciously comparing and contrasting their own native language rules to the rules that govern the new target language.

Reformulating Grammar Instruction

Although explicit and implicit instruction are clearly opposite approaches to teaching and learning, they both share some notable deficiencies. Neither approach acknowledges the critical role of the teacher in negotiating and constructing explanations of how the new

---

2. For a discussion of the implicit/explicit dichotomy, see Adair-Hauck and Donato (1994); and Adair-Hauck, (1993).

language works, and neither approach acknowledges the contributions and backgrounds that the learners bring to the instructional setting for collaborating with the teacher on constructing an explanation. Moreover, neither approach recognizes how learning takes place among people in the real world, outside of the classroom. A Vygotskian approach to instruction (see Chapter 1) indicates that learning is a dynamic, reciprocal, and interactive process.[3] However, our profession has been offered only two dichotomous approaches to learning and processing information, neither of which recognizes the mutually responsive interactions that are fundamental to learning as it occurs naturally between humans in everyday life (Brown, Collins, & Duguid, 1989; Forman, Minnick & Stone, 1993; Lave & Wenger, 1991, Rogoff, 1990).

Therefore, we believe it is time to begin a serious reappraisal regarding the teaching of grammar and a new vision that goes beyond dichotomies in approaches. In this chapter, we are advocating a story-based and guided participatory approach (Adair-Hauck, 1993; Rogoff, 1990) that contrasts with both traditional explicit or implicit teaching.[4] In many ways, this alternative approach can reconcile the explicit/implicit polarized views, as shown in Figure 7.1.

FIGURE 7.1 Story-Based and Guided Participation: An Alternative Approach to Grammar Instruction

IMPLICIT EXPLANATIONS	GUIDED PARTICIPATION	EXPLICIT EXPLANATIONS
Learners analyze the grammar explanation for themselves.	*Teachers and learners* collaborate on and co-construct the grammar explanation.	*Teacher* provides explanation for learners.

Source: Adair-Hauck, 1993.

For a number of reasons that will be discussed later in this chapter, we believe that a story-based and guided participatory approach might hold the key to dramatic improvements in teaching grammar.

Basic Principles of Story-Based Language Teaching

Before discussing some practical applications of this approach, we should discuss some basic principles of story-based and guided participatory teaching. Many specialists in first-language literacy development have been exploring the implications of story-based language teaching for the past decade. Likewise, researchers in cognitive psychology have been investigating guided participation in the areas of science, math, and social studies. Unfortunately, foreign language education has been lagging behind these other

---

3. All work in this area is to some degree rooted in the research of theorists such as Vygotsky (1978) and Leontiev (1981). For examples of supporting research, see Lave (1977); Cole (1985); Newman, Griffin, and Cole (1989); Rogoff (1990); Wertsch (1991); Tharp and Gallimore (1988, 1991); Kowal and Swain (1994).

4. The term *guided participation* was first coined by Rogoff (1990).

disciplines. First, we will discuss some basic principles of a story-based approach to grammar instruction, and then we will discuss how to use guided and joint problem solving to enhance grammar explanations.

Goodman stated that "language is language only when it is whole" (cf. Fountas & Hannigan, 1989, p. 134).[5] According to Goodman (1986), the whole is always viewed as being greater than the sum of its parts, and it is the whole that gives meaning to the parts. In terms of grammar instruction, words, phrases, or sentences are not linguistic islands unto themselves; on the contrary, these linguistic elements gain meaning only when they are placed in context and when used in conjunction with the whole. According to Goodman, once learners experience the whole, they are then better prepared to deal with the analyses of the parts (Fountas & Hannigan, 1989).

We should acknowledge that Goodman is primarily addressing the needs of first-language learners. However, research in first-language acquisition has often acted as a catalyst for theoretical advancement in second-language acquisition, including the development of language literacy skills. For example, concepts such as the importance of comprehensible input, the role of interaction, and the notion of scaffolding in both **motherese** and **caretaker speech** are all derived from theories of first-language development (Ellis, 1988; Hatch, 1983; Hawkins, 1988). Furthermore, many second-language specialists (Celce-Murcia, 1991; Hughes & McCarthy, 1998; Kramsch, 1993; Nunan, 1991) emphasize the importance of content-based instruction, authentic texts for listening and reading comprehension, and the need for connected discourse in grammar instruction, all of which emphasize the importance of whole texts rather than fragmented speech in second-/foreign-language classrooms.

Conceptually, then, we need to reappraise our orientation to grammar instruction. Teaching approaches have all too often focused on fragmented discourse and artificial mechanical exercises. Many language programs stress a bottom-up or transmission approach by emphasizing the "bits and pieces" of language (word lists, verb conjugations, or isolated linguistic elements). A transmission, or language differentiation approach, usually results in what Goodman calls "non-language," which can be characterized as being unnatural, cognitively undemanding, and dull (Cummins, 1984). Moreover, words, phrases, or sentences do not take on meaning when viewed in isolation from each other; on the contrary, these linguistic elements gain meaning only when used in connected discourse forming a coherent whole. Therefore, if words take on their meanings when used in connection to each other, learners will need to experience "whole" contextualized language (stories, legends, poems, listening selections, cartoons, songs, recipes, etc.) with an emphasis on meaning-making and sense-making before a focus on form can be a productive instructional activity (Long, 1991). In this way, a story-based language approach stresses natural discourse and encourages learners to comprehend meaningful and longer samples of discourse from the very beginning of the lesson. Once learners experience the whole, they are better able to deal with the parts (Adair-Hauck & Donato, 1994; Adair-Hauck & Cumo-Johanssen, 1997; Fountas & Hannigan, 1989; Freeman & Freeman, 1992; Hughes & McCarthy, 1998).

---

5. As early as the first quarter of this century, Vygotsky and Piaget, both constructionists of sorts, stressed that the whole is always greater than and gives meaning to its parts. However, unlike Piaget, Vygotsky stressed that language and social interaction lead to cognitive development.

A story-based language approach stresses natural discourse and encourages learners to comprehend meaningful and longer samples of discourse from the very beginning of the lesson.

By introducing the lesson with a whole text, the teacher foreshadows the grammar explanation through the use of integrated discourse that will highlight the critical grammar structures to be taught. Galloway and Labarca explain that foreshadowing of new language elements is beneficial, for it provides "learners with a 'feel' for what is to come and can help learners cast forward a familiarity net by which aspects of language prompt initial recognitions and later, gradually, are pulled into the learner's productive repertoire" (1990, p. 136). In this way, the story or text highlights the functional significance of the grammatical structure before the learners' attention is focused on form. This approach agrees with Ausubel, Novak, and Hanesian's (1968) idea of using advance organizers to assist the learners by providing an "anchoring framework" for the new concepts to be learned. Unlike many classroom textbooks, which may offer a group of disconnected sentences or a "contextualized" drill (Walz, 1989), a story-based and guided participatory approach invites the learner to comprehend and experience the functions and purposes of language through integrated discourse, in the form of a story. This practice is in agreement with Krashen's Input Hypothesis, which stresses the importance of comprehensible input that "contains structures a little beyond our current level of competence" (Krashen, 1982, p. 21). As a result, from the very beginning of the lesson, the teacher and learners are engaged in authentic use of language through joint problem-solving activities and interactions to render the story comprehensible. By using pictures, mime, and gestures, the teacher scaffolds (see Chapter 2) and guides the learners eventually to comprehend the story or other sample of connected discourse. Once comprehension is achieved, the teacher can then safely turn the learners' attention to various linguistic elements.

Foreshadowing of new language elements provides learners with a "feel" for what is to come.

Storytelling is particularly adaptable to second-language instruction, since it is natural to tell stories orally, stressing listening comprehension, followed by role plays and then reading and writing activities. Oller (1983) reminds us that the episodic organization represented in stories aids comprehension and retention. Furthermore, using "multiple passes" and recycling the story line through picture displays, TPR activities, or role-playing scenarios deepen comprehension. The framework of the story provides a continuous flow of mental images that help the learners to assign meaning and functions to the forms they hear. After these initial activities and interactions have helped the learners to understand the meaning of the discourse, the teacher turns the learners' attention to specific language forms or structure. This approach is in agreement with Celce-Murcia's suggestion concerning grammar instruction for ESL learners, when she states that "one of the best times for them [the learners] to attend to form is after comprehension has been achieved and in conjunction with their production of meaningful discourse" (1985, p. 301).

 "One of the best times for them [the learners] to attend to form is after comprehension has been achieved and in conjunction with their production of meaningful discourse."

A Model for Integrating Form in a Story-Based Language Approach

Focus on form has recently become the topic of intense research and has been shown to be an important design feature of language teaching (Ellis, 1998; Fotos, 1994; Kowal & Swain, 1994; Long, 1991; Spada & Lightbown, 1993; Swain, 1995, 1998; VanPatten & Cadierno, 1993). The theories of learning espoused in the *Teacher's Handbook* emphasize the importance of creating a zone of proximal development with the learner so that what the learner currently needs help with will emerge as independent, automatic performance at a later time. Grammar teaching can also be viewed in this way and is no less an interactive process between expert and novice than any other aspect of developing communicative ability in learners. *Learners need to be guided to reflect on the language they use to create their own meanings.*

 Learners need to be guided to reflect on the language they use to create their own meanings.

 What is the Zone of Proximal Development (Chapter 1)?

No language teaching should be driven by grammar instruction alone, nor should grammar instruction be literally interpreted to mean instruction on morphology (e.g., adjective or subject-verb agreement, rules for pluralization, etc.) or meaningless manipulation of forms. When the teacher focuses on form, attention is drawn to the formal properties of the language, which include its sound system, word formation, syntax, discourse markers, and devices for relating one sentence to another, to name a few; our colleagues who teach reading in the elementary schools call this form of instruction "Language Arts." Classes that focus on language form for the purpose of increasing comprehension and meaning have been shown to result in greater language gains than classes in which no focus on form is available or in which forms are learned as meaningless structures (Lightbown & Spada, 1990). Therefore, the issue is not whether a teacher should focus on form; instead, the issue is how, when, and where to focus on form in a lesson that will ultimately clarify this important design feature of foreign language instruction.

The following is a model for contextualizing interactions with learners about the forms of language. The model is called PACE (Donato & Adair-Hauck, 1994), an acronym for the four steps we have developed for integrating formal instruction in the context of a story-based language lesson.

P: PRESENTATION of Meaningful Language

This step represents the "whole" language you are presenting in a thematic way. It can be an interesting story (folktales and legends work well), a TPR lesson, a recorded authentic listening segment, an authentic document, or a demonstration of a real-life, authentic task, such as playing a sport, making a sandwich, or doing a science experiment. Even materials from the textbook chapter (narratives, dialogues, stories) may be used if they are found to be interesting and episodically organized. Stories that include stageable actions and events are well suited for the presentation since the meanings of these texts can be made transparent and comprehensible through dramatization, actions, or TPR storytelling. The Presentation does not consist of isolated, disconnected sentences illustrating the target form in question; instead, it is thematic, contextualized, story-based language intended to capture learner interest and provide opportunities for the teacher to create comprehension through negotiation of meaning (see Chapter 1). Care should also be taken to ensure that the presentation adequately presents the structure in question and that the structure is appropriate to the learners' developmental level. The structure should appear often enough during the Presentation to be salient to the learners without making the language sound unnatural or stilted. Authentic stories, documents, or listening segments can guarantee naturalness and often contain naturally occurring repetitions, for example, the story of Goldilocks and the three bears.

The Presentation should also be interactive. By scaffolding participation in the activity, teachers can guide learners through the new element of the language to be learned. This scaffolded, guided participation during the presentation of the text may take the form of learner repetitions of key phrases cued by the teacher during a storytelling session, learner-teacher role reversal in a TPR activity, cloze exercises based on listening segments, K-W-L activities,[6] or discussions that anticipate the content of a reading. The goal here is to enable learners to stretch their language abilities by comprehending new elements of the target language in meaningful texts through the help and mediation of the teacher. This step may last for part of a class, an entire class session, or even several class sessions, depending on the story selected and the sequencing of its presentation. For example, a storytelling lesson may contain pre-storytelling activities focusing on prior knowledge, content, cultural references, and language, dramatization, pair-work comprehension checks, or story-retelling exercises. The length of time required depends on the nature of the story and the amount of negotiation work required to charge the language with meaning.

---

6. K-W-L activities are a way to organize classroom tasks around learners' background knowledge and their goals for learning. From the learners' perspective, "K" stands for "what I know already"; "W" stands for "what I want to know"; and "L" stands for "what I have learned." For instance, if the topic is grasshoppers, the "K" activities might include making a list on the board of everything learners know about grasshoppers; the "W" activities might include the creation of a list of questions students have about grasshoppers, e.g., "How long do grasshoppers live?"; and the "L" activities might include a videotaped presentation of a skit students wrote about the life of a grasshopper.

A: ATTENTION

This step focuses the learners' attention on some aspect of the language used during the Presentation activity. In this step, the teacher highlights some regularity of the language. This can be achieved in several ways. Teachers can ask questions about patterns found in a written text or about words and phrases repeated in a story. Overhead transparencies of example sentences from the Presentation story can be prepared, with important words and phrases circled or underlined. The point to this step is to get learners to focus attention on the target form without needless elaboration or wasted time. Another purpose of this step is to ensure that learners are indeed focused on the grammatical element chosen for discussion. Recall that research has shown that learners do not always process or attend to input in ways that we expect (Herron & Tomasello, 1992). As an example of this, Adair-Hauck (1993) found that when learners were presented with contextualized sentences (examples taken from "Le lion et la souris" story with sentences both in the present and in the past using the new past-tense verb form) and were asked by the teacher what they noticed about these sentences, the learners were unable to answer. Instead, they responded with puzzled looks. However, when the teacher provided responsive and graduated assistance and included the words *aujourd'hui* (today) and *hier* (yesterday), which are semantic, not syntactic, clues, the learners were able to articulate the differences in the meanings of the sentences. After paying attention to the *semantic clues* (focus on meaning), the learners were able to attend to the *syntactic clues* (focus on form). This classroom-based observation highlights the important role of the teacher in guiding and assisting the learners *to attend to* the lesson objective.

C: CO-CONSTRUCT AN EXPLANATION

Learners and teacher should be co-constructors of grammatical explanations. After learners focus attention on the target form, the teacher assists them in raising their awareness about the target structure and enables them to contrast the structure with what they know about their own language. This phase directly addresses the Comparisons goal area and addresses it at a time when language comparisons are appropriate and can be discussed in a meaningful context. During this step, learners are guided to hypothesize, guess, make predictions, or come to generalizations about the target form, all higher-order thinking skills requiring observation, evaluation, analysis, and synthesis. Co-constructing an explanation requires teacher questions that are well chosen, clear, and direct. Questions are powerful tools in the hands of teachers who can adjust their questioning "in flight" to meet the emergent understandings of their learners. For example, asking learners questions such as "What words do you hear or see repeated in the text, and what could they mean?" "What pattern do you see in this group of words?" and "How do certain words change as their meanings change?" is a way to help learners draw insights from the language they hear and understand. These cognitive "probes" help learners discover regular grammatical patterns, sound systems, word order, unique cultural meanings of words, or language functions. Additionally, questions cannot be predicted in advance and need to be responses to learner contributions. Learners should also be encouraged to ask the teacher and each other questions if the explanation is to be truly co-constructed and negotiated. As learners hypothesize and generalize about the target form, teachers build upon and extend the learners' knowledge without overwhelming them with superfluous grammatical detail. Hypothesis testing can also be conducted, with teachers leading learners in trying out their new knowledge by applying their generalizations to new situations. Teachers need to be aware that the help they provide is graduated and may range from brief hints about the target form to explicit instruction if needed (Aljaafreh, 1992; Aljaafreh & Lantolf, 1994).

It is important to note that, unlike guided induction techniques, that rely primarily on teacher questioning, a co-constructed explanation is not an inquisition; instead, co-constructed explanations recognize that learners may not be able to perceive the formal properties of language on the basis of the teacher's questions alone. What is obvious to an expert language user is often a mystery to the novice. A co-constructed explanation is as participatory for the teacher as it is for the learners; that is, teachers need to assess the abilities of their learners and assist them by providing as well as eliciting information when necessary. As Tharp and Gallimore (1988) point out, teaching is responsive assistance and cannot be reduced to series of actions to be performed in the same order in every instructional circumstance. By listening closely to learner contributions during this step, teachers can assess how much help is needed to attain the concept. In time, some learners may be able to work in small groups on their own grammar problems and report back to the class about their discoveries (Fotos & Ellis, 1991).

E: EXTENSION ACTIVITY

Focus on form is only useful if this knowledge can be pressed into service by the learners in a new way at a later time. In story-based language teaching, the teacher never loses sight of the "whole." Therefore, the Extension Activity provides learners with the opportunity to use their new skill in creative and interesting ways while at the same time integrating it into existing knowledge. The Extension Activity should be interesting, be related to the theme of the lesson in some way, and, most important, allow for creative self-expression. Extension activities are not worksheets on which learners use the target form to fill in blanks of disconnected sentences; instead, they can be information-gap activities, role-play situations, dramatizations, games, authentic writing projects, paired interviews, class surveys, out-of-class projects, or simulations of real-life situations. The possibilities are endless, as long as the learners have the chance to try to use the target form in ways that they see as useful, meaningful, and connected to the overarching theme of the lesson. Moreover, the Extension phase of the lessons allows the teacher to address other Goal areas of the Standards such as Cultures, Communities and Connections. The Extension activity could address cultural perspectives embodied in the story (West & Donato, 1995), bring learners into contact with target-language members of the community for further investigations of the story's country of origin, or link the story's theme to an academic subject area. The Extension Activity closes the circle of the PACE lesson and puts the "whole" back into story-based language teaching (see Figure 7.2).

FIGURE 7.2 PACE: A Story-Based and Guided Participatory Approach to Language Instruction

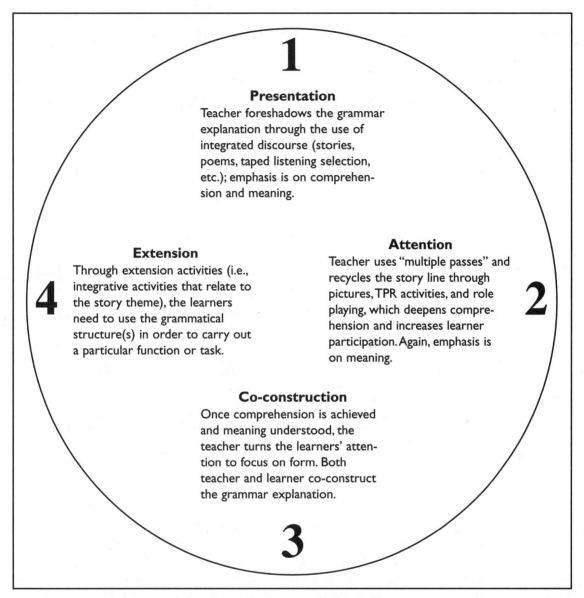

1

Presentation
Teacher foreshadows the grammar explanation through the use of integrated discourse (stories, poems, taped listening selection, etc.); emphasis is on comprehension and meaning.

Extension
Through extension activities (i.e., integrative activities that relate to the story theme), the learners need to use the grammatical structure(s) in order to carry out a particular function or task.

4

Attention
Teacher uses "multiple passes" and recycles the story line through pictures, TPR activities, and role playing, which deepens comprehension and increases learner participation. Again, emphasis is on meaning.

2

Co-construction
Once comprehension is achieved and meaning understood, the teacher turns the learners' attention to focus on form. Both teacher and learner co-construct the grammar explanation.

3

Source: Donato & Adair-Hauck, 1994; Adair-Hauck & Cumo-Johanssen, 1997, p. 43.

Elements of Story-Based Language Learning

Figure 7.3 summarizes the differences between a story-based language approach and the traditional approach to teaching grammar. The earlier discussion should have led you to the conclusion that language learning is a thinking process or, from the learners' viewpoint, a challenging and intellectual guessing game. Teachers need to design cognitively demanding activities that will encourage learners to hypothesize, predict, take risks, make errors, and self-correct (Fountas & Hannigan, 1989). By doing so, the learners become active participants in the learning process. All the story-based and guided participatory activities described later in this chapter have a common denominator—they all encourage the learners to be active thinkers and hypothesizers as they collaborate in language-learning activities with the teacher or with their peers.

Figure 7.3 Teaching of Grammar: Story-Based/Guided Participation vs. Traditional Approach

STORY-BASED/GUIDED PARTICIPATION	TRADITIONAL APPROACH
1. Use of higher skills and language before moving to procedural skills	1. Sequencing of tasks from simple to complex
2. Instructional interaction between Teacher ("expert") and Learners ("novices")	2. Little teacher/learner interaction; teacher-directed explanation
3. Richly implicit explanation (guided participation)	3. Explicit explanation of grammar
4. Encourages performance before competence (approximations encouraged)	4. Learner must master each step before going to next step (competence before performance).
5. Learners participate in problem-solving process and higher-order thinking skills (opportunity for learners' actions to be made meaningful).	5. Learners are passive and rarely participate in constructing the explanation.
6. Language and especially questions must be suitably tuned to a level at which performance requires assistance.	6. Few questions—mainly rhetorical
7. Lesson operationalizes functional significance of grammatical structure before mechanical procedures take place.	7. The functional significance of a grammatical point often does not emerge until end of lesson.

Source: Adair-Hauck & Donato, 1994, p. 20.

Whether listening to a storytelling activity, co-constructing a grammar explanation, or collaborating with peers during an extension activity, the learners are actively discovering and hypothesizing about the target language. This approach concurs with the framework for the Communication Standard that advises that learners be engaged in cognitively challenging activities that encourage them to use communication strategies, such as guessing intelligently, deriving meaning from context, asking for and providing clarification, making and checking hypotheses, and making inferences, predictions, and generalizations. Moreover, all the classroom activities described following encourage functional and interactional use of language by giving the learners opportunities to share information, ask questions, and solve problems collaboratively.

Finally, a distinguishing theme of a story-based and guided participatory approach to grammar instruction is that learning needs to be integrated, contextualized, and meaning-centered (Pearson, 1989). In Appendix 7.1, we have included a sample story-based language lesson to teach the past definite in French with *avoir* (story suggested and edited by Terry [1986] and based on a well-known Aesop's fable). The lesson begins with a story,

"The Lion and the Mouse," which foreshadows the functional significance of the grammar point. All the subsequent classroom activities—for example, role-playing, paired activities to retell the story, and team activities using graphic organizers—are contextualized and relate to the theme of "The Lion and the Mouse." In this way, the unit is contextualized and integrated, which enables the instructional events to flow naturally. As noted earlier, integrated and meaning-centered activities facilitate comprehension and retention on the part of learners. Furthermore, the extension activities encourage learners to integrate meaning, form, and function while experiencing language in context.

It should be mentioned that creating integrated and meaning-centered activities is probably one of the most difficult aspects of story-based language teaching, since many textbooks still stress context-reduced practice and fragmented materials. The following activities will provide you with suggestions on how to incorporate integrated and story-based language activities into your classroom. See the *Teacher's Handbook* website at **http://thandbook.heinle.com** for a video of a sample PACE lesson.

❏ Designing a Contextualized Story-Based Language Lesson

One of the first steps in designing a story-based lesson is to select an appropriate text for the learners and for your instructional purposes. Text selection is not an easy task, given the many texts that exist, their contents, and their complexity. Interactive storytelling, rather than "story-reading," is an excellent way to make use of the myriad of stories that exist in the target-language cultures. Through storytelling, natural simplifications can occur, and teachers can shape the story to be within the learners' zones of proximal development. A few guiding principles of selecting a good text for a PACE lesson are the following:

1. Do you like the text and find it appealing?

2. Will the learners enjoy the story you selected? Is it an age-appropriate story dealing with issues, experiences, and themes that reflect the lives of your learners? Does the story incite imagination or reflection?

3. Does the story lend itself to "stageable actions"?

4. Does the story suggest connections to academic content?

5. Does the story represent some aspect of the target culture that you will address?

6. Does the story present stereotypes or reasonable and fair depictions of the target-language culture?

7. Is the language accessible or can it be made accessible through story-telling simplifications to the learners' current stage of linguistic development?

8. Is the theme of the story one that can be expanded upon and extended into various activities?

9. Does the story adequately represent a grammatical structure on which you will later focus?

10. Does the story lend itself to addressing some of the goal areas of the SFLL?

As a comprehension check, the teacher might play the "I Have: Who Has" game with students (Polette, 1991). This is an **attentive listening comprehension** game. The game can be constructed from any story and can be played as a whole-class activity or in groups. The teacher constructs a number of questions concerning the setting, character, major events, and final outcome of the story. The learner who has the starred card reads the first question. For the "Le lion et la souris" story, the first question is "Where does the story take place?" The learner holding the card with the answer reads it and then provides the next question. By listening carefully, the learners should be able to respond correctly and thereby retell the story.

Creative extension activities are critical, for they afford the learners plenty of opportunities to develop skills in *interpersonal* communication. In a constructive approach, the learners need to have opportunities to create and construct their own thoughts in the second language. Extension activities also encourage learners to collaborate and cooperate in meaningful, interpersonal contexts. Although these activities may be challenging for learners, through story-based language learning activities they are able to express their own thoughts with more confidence, and their listening, reading, and writing skills improve (Adair-Hauck, 1993).

 Creative extension activities afford learners opportunities to develop interpersonal communication.

Extension activities often incorporate graphic organizers (such as story mapping, character mapping, or discussion webbing) to serve as anchoring devices to help learners organize their thoughts and ideas concerning the story. Vygotsky (1978) would argue that these graphic organizers may be viewed as mediating devices as well as psychological tools to organize the learners' higher psychological processes such as perception, attention, and memory. Story mapping or character mapping can be accomplished in pairs or in groups. During story-mapping activities, learners work together to construct the principal elements of the story. The story map encourages learners to focus on the principal characters, problems, major events, and solutions to the problem. For character-mapping activities, learners focus on a number of elements, such as the character's physical, as well as intrinsic traits, and the character's good and bad actions. For sample PACE lessons and accompanying story-based activities in French, German, Japanese, and Spanish, see Appendix 7.1 and other relevant materials at **http://thandbook.heinle.com.**

At some point, the teacher will want to move the lesson from mere comprehension activities to activities that stimulate the learners' critical thinking skills. These activities encourage learners to analyze the events of the story and then to draw conclusions about the story. Alvermann suggests that critical thinking activities should be carried out collaboratively and cooperatively since "some of the best thinking results in a group's collaborative efforts" (1991, p. 91).

Discussion webbing (Alvermann, 1991) is a critical thinking activity that can be developed for any story. Discussion webbing moves learners from *what happened* in the story to *why it happened*. For example, using the "Lion and the Mouse" story, the teacher can develop a discussion-webbing activity around the question "Should the mouse help the lion?"

Discussion webbing encourages the learners to think about an even number of yes/no answers. Finally, the learners try to form a consensus on the best reason WHY the mouse should or should not help the lion. This encourages the learners to look at both sides of an issue. Later, the groups can share their results from the discussion-webbing activity. For sample discussion-webbing activities, see Appendix 7.1.13 and the web site.

> ⚷— **Discussion webbing moves learners from *what happened* in the story to *why it happened*.**

And finally, the teacher may want to integrate an intertextual activity as a way to encourage learners to move beyond the mere recalling of events to higher critical thinking skills. During intertextual activities, learners working in pairs or groups analyze the components of stories by juxtapositioning two different texts or stories. Intertextual links can be made at various levels, that is, by juxtaposing characters, content, plot development, style, and so on. (Bloome & Egan-Robertson, 1993). A Venn diagram is often used as a graphic organizer (Christenbury & Kelly, 1983; Edwards, 1989; Redmond, 1994) to help learners analyze their thoughts. Note again that learners are encouraged to work in participatory groups during these intertextual activities since a story-based approach emphasizes meaning-making and the *interpersonal* nature of language and literacy. For sample intertextual activities, see Appendix 7.1.1 and PACE lessons at **http://thandbook.heinle.com.**

Many teachers might wonder how learners with limited L2 resources will be able to participate in some of the more challenging story-based activities. For example, discussion webbing and intertextual activities tap into learners' higher critical thinking skills; therefore, during these activities learners use their cognitive processes to concentrate on comparing and contrasting, analyzing, and synthesizing new information gleaned from the story with their prior background knowledge. In order to participate in these "immersion-type" activities, learners exploit a variety of compensation strategies to communicate their ideas in L2. As a result, their productive use of L2 varies. For example, some learners feel comfortable mixing L1 and L2, other learners seek assistance from the teacher or a more capable peer, and other learners feel more comfortable consulting a resource such as a dictionary (Adair-Hauck, 1996). The teacher creates a "social context" that *assists and supports* learners in activities that they would be unable to do alone or unassisted. According to Vygotsky, instruction (assisted performance) leads to development (unassisted performance): "Therefore the only good kind of instruction marches ahead of development and leads it. It must be aimed not so much at the ripe, but at the ripening functions" (1986, p. 188).

To illustrate this point, one of the foreign language teachers who uses a story-based approach encourages her learners to negotiate meaning in L2 using discourse strategies such as comprehension checks and clarification requests. To do so, she decorates her room with large, colored, laminated signs highlighting discourse facilitators, such as: "Répétez, s'il vous plaît"; "Comment?"; "Je n'ai pas saisi ça"; "Comment dit-on ___ en français?"; "Comment dirai-je ____?", and so on. She explained that in this way she is providing assistance to her learners and, at the same time, is decorating her classroom with the "curriculum."

Elementary/intermediate level learners certainly will make some grammatical errors while participating in these extension activities. As learners work in groups, the teacher needs to serve as a participant observer for the various groups by providing assistance (e.g., requisite vocabulary, verb tense, etc.) when necessary. But in many instances learners are capable of expressing their opinions regarding the events/outcomes of the story, even if those opinions are at times not grammatically perfect. Frustration on the part of the teacher and/or learners will be reduced if the teacher places an emphasis on *meaning-making or sense-making* as the learners try to create and construct meaning during these interpersonal and socially mediated activities.

As a debriefing activity, the teacher may want to focus attention on some common or frequently made errors. It is important to note that in a natural second-language setting, error correction tends to be limited to errors regarding meaning, including vocabulary choice, rather than on pronunciation and grammar. Errors that do not interfere with meaning tend to be overlooked by native speakers (Lightbown & Spada, 1993). Unfortunately, in many formal second-language classroom settings, accuracy has precedence over meaningful communication, and, therefore, errors are frequently corrected. Too much error correction can stifle leaner motivation (Hadley, 1993), but, on the other hand, a teacher has the responsibility to bring to the learners' attention commonly made or persistent errors (Lalande, 1984).

A collaborative approach to error correction is advantageous since it includes the learners in the learning process. For example, during the debriefing session, the teacher can remind the learners that errors are a natural part of language development (Lightbown & Spada, 1993). In the natural second-language setting, errors regarding *meaning* would prompt a native speaker to correct or to ask for clarification. For purposes of instruction, the teacher may want to identify errors that interfere with meaning as **strong errors;** for example, a student might say *Il a travaillé en Europe* (He worked in Europe), when the learner really wants to say *Il a voyagé en Europe* (He traveled in Europe). This error involving vocabulary choice would negatively affect meaning and therefore would require a correction, or at least a clarification request, from a native speaker. Also, depending on the second-language in question, certain grammar or pronunciation errors may interfere with meaning, such as *Elle veut aller à la boîte* instead of *Elles veulent aller à la boîte*. In this example, the pronunciation error of the verb changes the meaning from "She wants to go to the disco" to "They want to go to the disco," thus interfering with meaning. It is thus classified as a strong error.

By contrast, a weak error includes poor grammar usage or pronunciation but does not affect meaning; for example, *Il a resté toute la journée* instead of *Il est resté toute la journée*. This is a weak error since it does not interfere with meaning and probably would not be corrected by a native. Learners enjoy collaborating with the teacher and investigating which of their mistakes; are strong or weak errors (Adair-Hauck, 1995; Vavra, 1996). Using an overhead projector to show sample contextualized mistakes, the teacher can illustrate to the learners contextualized mistakes; that is, errors in meaningful exchanges with longer stretches of discourse. Rather than identifying discrete-point errors, the learners can work in peer groups to investigate whether the errors are strong or weak mistakes, and why. They can then use problem-solving techniques to correct the errors.

Another strategy that encourages learners to pay attention to accuracy is to show elementary- or intermediate-level students a sample OPI intermediate-level interview of a young adult in English (Adair-Hauck, 1996). Before viewing the OPI interview, the teacher briefly discusses the *ACTFL Oral Proficiency Guidelines* for novice-, intermediate-, advanced-, and superior-level speakers. This explanation may have to be conducted in L1, depending on the level of the learners. Then the learners view the OPI interview and discuss with their teacher why the interviewee is at the intermediate or advanced level and which accuracy structures the interviewee needs to work on in order to receive the higher rating. Furthermore, the class can discuss what language functions or tasks the interviewee was able to carry out during the interview. In this way, the teacher crystallizes the importance of the functions and grammatical structures embedded in the curriculum. As Christenbury succinctly explains, "Grammar and usage cannot be taught effectively if students see no real need for it and if teachers cannot persuade them to see the need" (1996, p. 12).

❐ Moving to Independent Practice

At some point, the teacher will want the learners to practice the target language independently. Ideally, group activities or working together on an interpersonal level will have prepared the learners to function independently or on an intrapersonal level (Vygotsky, 1978). As an independent extension activity, the teacher may ask learners to create a different ending to the story. Learners may also use the story-mapping technique to create their own stories. A number of foreign language teachers have reported that learners enjoy creating humorous stories or "spoofs" related to the story in class. As a final *presentational* activity, learners can share their stories either with their class or with other members of the community (e.g., younger learners in the district, target-culture student exchange groups, etc.).

Voices of the Learners

Before concluding, one should acknowledge the thoughts and opinions of learners regarding story-based language learning activities for foreign language learners. Adair-Hauck (1993) conducted a three-month, classroom-based research project using a story-based approach to teach intermediate-level French to a class of twenty learners ranging from fifteen to sixteen years of age. At the end of the project, learners' responses were overwhelmingly positive. For example, when asked, "Was it easier to learn French by listening to stories?" ninety percent of the learners answered "yes," one learner answered "no," and one learner answered "yes" and "no." Learners' qualitative responses to the question "What did you like most about the storytelling activities?" were particularly enlightening. One perceptive learner commented, "I liked learning with pictures and props. That way, if there was something I didn't understand, then I knew what it was." Another learner responded, "I liked the storytelling activities because they had a good effect. You seem to remember things better if you have something to do with the words you are learning." Finally, one learner made this comment regarding a positive, affective climate: "I liked the fact that it gets the class into the story and it makes it more fun. I think I learn better when I enjoy the class."

Teach and Reflect

Episode One

Examining Grammar Presentations in Textbooks

In preparation for this activity, examine at least two textbooks in the target language. Decide whether the textbooks use an explicit or implicit approach to grammar explanation. To do so, answer the following questions for each textbook:

1. Does the textbook offer some form of grammatical analysis? If so, is the textbook advocating direct and explicit or indirect and implicit grammar explanations?

2. When is the teacher supposed to focus the learners' attention on form or on grammatical structures—at the beginning of the chapter, the middle, the end, or not at all?

3. Analyze the role assigned to the learner regarding grammar explanations; that is, is the learner a passive listener during the explanation? Is the learner supposed to be an active hypothesizer? Is the learner supposed to hypothesize alone or in collaboration with others?

4. Now identify a particular language function, such as asking and giving directions, making purchases, or describing people or things. (Turn to the chapter that focuses on your selected language function.) How does the chapter relate language function to form? Hint: Are "skill-getting" activities emphasized before "skill-using" activities, or vice-versa?

5. Examine the chapter to see if the learners are exposed to meaningful, integrated discourse. If so, how—through stories, poems, songs, videotapes, or drama? And when—at the beginning, the middle, or the end of the chapter?

6. In your opinion, how well does the chapter integrate (1) meaning—the thoughts and ideas of the message being conveyed; (2) form—the various linguistic or grammatical elements; and (3) function—the way to carry out a particular task by exploiting the appropriate grammatical structures?

7. In your estimation, is one particular dimension—meaning, form, or function—emphasized more than the others? If so, which one? Can you offer an explanation of why one dimension might be emphasized at the expense of the others?

Episode Two

Designing a Story-Based Language Lesson

You are now going to design a lesson that emphasizes a story-based language approach to grammar instruction. First, you need to identify a particular linguistic function, for example, asking questions, making purchases, or describing people or things. Think of an appropriate context in which you would need to use this function. Then decide which structures should be incorporated into the lesson so that the learners are capable of carrying out the function. Using the following steps as guidelines, decide how you are going to PACE the story-based language lesson.

1. Identify an integrated discourse sample that foreshadows the selected linguistic function, context, and accuracy structures. Remember that the "text" can be in the form of a story, poem, taped listening selection, advertisement, videotaped interview, and so on. Consult the section on selecting a text before doing this step.

2. Decide what you need to do to help learners comprehend the meaning of the "text." For example, will you aid the learners' comprehension if you use visuals, mime, gestures, and props? Gather all necessary supplemental materials. This phase is critical to the success of the lesson. Be creative!

3. Demonstrate for your fellow classmates how you plan to introduce the story-based language text. Even if your classmates do not know your target language, see if you can convey the general meaning or significance of the text. (Make use of those props!)

4. Discuss how you would use "multiple passes" to recycle the story line. In other words, what kind of TPR activities, role-playing scenarios, or other activities would be appropriate to deepen the learners' comprehension? Remember that at this stage the learners will become more participatory.

5. Write a short description of how you would focus the learners' attention on form. What "hints" or "helping questions" are you going to ask? In other words, how do you plan to "co-construct" the explanation?

6. Now design at least three extension activities that relate to the selected context. (Note: Use the extension activities that are in Appendix 7.1.1 and following as guidelines.) These activities should create a need for the learners to use the identified accuracy structures. In doing so, the learners will develop a fuller understanding of the function of the grammar structures.

Discuss and Reflect

Case Study 1

Using a Story-Based Language Approach to Teach Reflexive Verbs

Mr. West, a French teacher, has learned about a new way to incorporate grammar teaching into a story-based language lesson. He is anxious to try out this new approach since the textbook he uses, which serves as the basis of his district's curriculum, is grammar driven. He has not yet succeeded in doing more than presenting the "grammar-rule-of-the-day" and completing the textbook exercises with his classes. Mr. West previews the chapter and sees that he will need to teach reflexive verbs. He picks a context for this new structure, the morning routine. For his presentation, Mr. West writes the French equivalent of the following sentences on the board:

I wash my son's face.	I wash myself.
I get my son up.	I get up.
I look at my son.	I look at myself in the mirror.
I brush my son's hair.	I brush my hair.

Mr. West reads the sentences aloud, hoping that the class will perceive the non-reflexive/reflexive contrast in the two columns. The learners seem bored, uninterested, and unchallenged. He then asks a question: "What do you see here?" The learners are bewildered and silent until Mr. West calls on Mike, who says, "French sentences beginning with *Je*." "These learners are clueless about these sentences and completely confused," Mr. West thinks to himself. He decides to abandon the questioning and delivers a lesson in English on the formation and use of French reflexive verbs. Because of this experience, he thinks that learners are unable to think about the target language and that all that can be done to ensure "learning" is to lecture learners on the rules they need to know.

Ask yourself these questions:

1. Why are the learners bored and uninterested?

2. How would you evaluate Mr. West's PRESENTATION? Does it satisfy the requirements of a PRESENTATION in the PACE model? Why or why not?

3. What would you have done when Mike responded with "French sentences beginning with *Je*"?

4. How do you think the learners were feeling about Mr. West's lesson?

To prepare the case:

Review the PACE models presented in this chapter and on the web site; examine one or more textbooks in the language you teach to see how reflexive verbs are presented; read Celce-Murcia (1985), Walz (1989), and Larsen-Freeman (1991) for further information about the role of grammar in contextualized teaching.

To prepare for class discussion, think and write about these topics:

What PRESENTATION would you choose for contextualizing a lesson on reflexive verbs? How would you develop this lesson?

Case Study 2

Using Songs to Foreshadow Grammar

Mr. Kruse teaches French at a suburban high school near a large Pennsylvania city. Most of his learners have had little, if any, experience with other cultures, nor have they interacted with foreigners who live in the area, except for visitors invited to the classroom. Their life experiences and their curiosity about and interest in other cultures are very limited, as evidenced in the few, mundane questions they ask when confronted with a visitor from another country. While in France last summer, Mr. Kruse bought several CDs, one of which was an American Cajun recording that was then popular in France. In an attempt to stir his learners' interest and to show French influence on American culture, Mr. Kruse decided to plan a grammar lesson using one of the songs from this recording. The words to this song follow, both in French and in English:

CAJUN TELEPHONE STOMP	CAJUN TELEPHONE STOMP
O bébé, j'avais essayé De causer aujourd'hui. 'Y avait quelque chose qui est arrivé Et moi, j'ai commencé d'être fâché.	O baby, I tried To talk to you on the phone today. Something strange happened And I started to get mad.
Sur le téléphone de l'autre cîté, 'Y avait une 'tite voix mal enregistrée. "Après le beep," c'est ça il dit, "Laisse ton message, 'ya personne ici."	On the other end of the line, There was a little voice, a bad recording "After the beep," that's what it said, "Leave your message, there's no one home."
Quoi c'est ça, il dit "le beep"? C'est pas Cadien, ni poli, S'il n'est pas là, quoi faire sa voix? O yé yaille, mon coeur fait mal.	What is this, it said "the beep"? That's not Cajun, nor polite, If no one's there, why is this voice? O yé yaille, it makes me sad.
Après dix fois avec cette voix maudite Ç'a commencé de ma faire rire, J'ai oublié á qui je veux parler Et enfin, j'ai accroché.	After hearing that darn voice ten times, It started to make me laugh, I forgot who I was calling And finally, I hung up.

Source: *Cajun Conja*, by Beausoleil.

Ask yourself these questions:

1. What information concerning the recording artist might learners need to know?

2. What vocabulary might learners need to know in order to understand the context?

3. What work might be done in advance to prepare the learners for listening to the recording?

4. What cultural information might be learned from this song?

5. What grammar might be targeted?

6. What types of activities might be designed to target the grammar?

7. What types of activities might the PACE Model or a cyclical approach to teaching this grammar include?

8. What creative activities might be explored, based on this model?

To prepare the case:

Find a music magazine in the target language and read some articles on modern music; read a brief history of Cajun culture and music or of the music characteristic of the target cultures that you teach; refer to the PACE Model presented in this chapter; read the sections of Hadley (1993) that deal with the role of context in comprehension and learning; listen to current hit songs by other recording artists.

To prepare for class discussion, think and write about the following topics:

Describe the differences and similarities you find in the songs you heard, emphasizing the style, content, and cultural aspects of the recordings so that learners working in groups might create a song of their own; sing a song as your context, select a grammar point, and design two contextualized activities that will integrate the meaning, form, and function.

References

Adair-Hauck, B. (1993). *A descriptive analysis of a whole language/guided participatory versus explicit teaching strategies in foreign language instruction.* Unpublished doctoral dissertation, University of Pittsburgh.

Adair-Hauck, B. (1995). Are all grammar errors created equal? Seminar presented at Millersville University Summer Graduate Program in French, Millersville, PA.

Adair-Hauck, B. (1996). Practical whole language strategies for secondary and university level FL learners. *Foreign language Annals, 29,* 253–270.

Adair-Hauck, B., & Cumo-Johanssen, P. (1997). Communication goal: Meaning making through a whole language approach. In J. Phillips (Ed.), *Collaborations: Meeting new goals, new realities,* Northeast Conference Reports (pp. 35–96). Lincolnwood, IL: NTC/Contemporary Publishing Group.

Adair-Hauck, B., & Donato, R. (1994). Foreign language explanations within the zone of proximal development. *Canadian Modern Language Review, 50,* 532–557.

Aljaafreh, A. (1992). *The role of implicit/explicit error correction and the learner's zone of proximal development.* Unpublished doctoral dissertation, University of Delaware, Newark.

Aljaafreh, A., & Lantolf, J. (1994). Negative feedback as regulation and second-language learning in the zone of proximal development. *The Modern Language Journal, 78,* 465–483.

Alvermann, D. (1991). The discussion web: A graphic aid for learning across the curriculum. *The Reading Teacher, 45,* 92–98.

Ausubel, D., Novak, J., & Hanesian, H. (1968). *Educational psychology: A cognitive view.* New York: Holt, Rinehart and Winston.

Barnes, D. (1992). *From communication to curriculum.* Porthsmouth, NH: Boynton/Cook.

Bialystok, E. (1982). On the relationship between knowing and using forms. *Applied Linguistics, 3,* 181–206.

Bloome, D., & Egan-Robertson, A. (1993). The social construction of intertextuality in classroom reading and writing lessons. *Reading Research Quarterly, 28*(4), 305–334.

Brooks, F., & Donato, R. (1994). Vygotskyan approaches to understanding foreign language learner discourse during communicative tasks. *Hispania, 77,* 262–274.

Brooks, F., Donato, R., & McGlone, J. (1997). When are they going to say it right? Understanding learner talk during pair-work activity. *Foreign Language Annals, 30,* 524–541.

Brown, J., Collins, A., & Duguid, P. (1989). Situated cognition and the culture of learning. *Educational Researcher, 1,* 32–41.

Celce-Murcia, M. (1985). Making informed decisions about the role of grammar in language teaching. *Foreign Language Annals, 18,* 297–301.

Celce-Murcia, M. (1991). Grammar pedagogy in second and foreign language teaching. *TESOL Quarterly, 25,* 459–479.

Chomsky, N. (1965). *Aspects of the theory of syntax.* Cambridge: MIT Press.

Christenbury, L. (1996). The great debate (again): Teaching grammar and usage. *English Journal, 85*(7), 11–12.

Christenbury, L., & Kelly, P. (1983). Questioning: A path to critical thinking. *TRIP: Theory and Research in Practice.* Urbana, IL: National Council of Teaching of English. (Eric Document Reproduction Service No. ED 226–372).

Cole, M. (1985). The zone of proximal development: Where culture and cognition create each other. In J. V. Wertsch (Ed.), *Culture, communication and cognition: Vygotskian perspective* (pp. 146–161). New York: Cambridge University Press.

Cooper, D. (1993). *Literacy: Helping children construct meaning.* Boston: Houghton Mifflin Company.

Cummins, J. (1984). Language proficiency, bilingualism and academic achievement. *Bilingualism and Special Education: Issues in Assessment and Pedagogy.* San Diego: College-Hill.

DeKeyser, R., & Sokalski, K. (1996). The differential role of comprehension and production practice. *Language learning, 46,* 613–642.

Donato, R., & Adair-Hauck, B. (1992). Discourse perspectives on formal instruction. *Language Awareness, 2,* 73–89.

Donato, R., & Adair-Hauck, B. (1994). PACE: A model to focus on form. Paper presented at the American Council on the Teaching of Foreign Languages, San Antonio, Texas.

Dulay, H., & Burt, M. (1973). Should we teach children syntax? *Language Learning, 23,* 245–258.

Edwards, A. (1989). Venn diagrams for many sets. *New Scientist, 121,* 51–56.

Ellis, R. (1988). *Classroom second-language development.* Englewood Cliffs, NJ: Prentice Hall.

Ellis, R. (1998). Teaching and research: Options in grammar teaching. *TESOL Quarterly, 32*(1), 39–60.

Forman, E., Minnick, N., & Stone, A. (1993). *Contexts for learning.* New York: Oxford University Press.

Fotos, S. (1994). Integrating grammar instruction and communicative language use through grammar consciousness-raising tasks. *TESOL Quarterly, 28,* 323–351.

Fotos, S., & Ellis, R. (1991). Communicating about grammar: A task-based approach. *TESOL Quarterly, 25,* 605–628.

Fountas, I., & Hannigan, I. (1989). Making sense of whole language: The pursuit of informed teaching. *Childhood Education, 65,* 133–137.

Freeman, Y., & Freeman, D. (1992). *Whole language for second-language learners.* Portsmouth, NH: Heineman Educational Books.

Galloway, V., & Labarca, A. (1990). From student to student: Style, process and strategy. In D. Birckbichler (Ed.), *New perspectives and new directions in foreign language education* (pp. 111–158). Lincolnwood, IL: NTC/Contemporary Publishing Group.

Goodman, K. (1986). *What's whole in whole language.* Portsmouth, NH: Heineman Educational Books.

Hadley, A. O. (1993). *Teaching language in context.* Boston, MA: Heinle & Heinle.

Hall, J. K. (1995). "Aw man, where are we goin'?" Classroom interaction and the development of L2 interactional competence. *Issues in Applied Linguistics, 6*(2) 37–62.

Hall, J. K. (1999). The communication standard. In J. Phillips (Ed.), *Foreign language standards: Linking research, theories, and practices* (pp. 15–56). Lincolnwood, IL: NTC/Contemporary Publishing Group.

Hatch, E. (1983). *Psycholinguistics: A second-language perspective.* Rowley, MA: Newbury House.

Hawkins, B. (1988). *Scaffolded classroom interaction and its relation to second-language acquisition for minority children.* Unpublished doctoral dissertation, University of California, Los Angeles.

Herron, C., & Tomasello, M. (1992). Acquiring grammatical structures by guided induction. *The French Review, 65,* 708–718.

Hughes, R., & McCarthy, M. (1998). From sentence to discourse: Discourse grammar and English language teaching. *TESOL Quarterly, 32,* 263–287.

Kowal, M., & Swain, M. (1994). Using collaborative language production tasks to promote learners' language awareness. *Language Awareness, 3*(2), 73–93.

Kramsch, C. (1993). *Context and culture in language teaching.* Oxford: Oxford University Press.

Krashen, S. (1982). *Principles and practice in second-language acquisition.* Oxford: Pergamon.

Krashen, S. (1985). *The input hypothesis.* New York: Longman.

Lalande, J. (1984). Reducing composition errors: An experiment. *Foreign Language Annals, 17,* 109–117.

Larsen-Freeman, D. (1991). Teaching grammar. In M. Celce-Murcia (Ed.), *Teaching English as a second or foreign language* (pp. 279–295). Boston, MA: Heinle & Heinle.

Lave, J. (1977). Cognitive consequences of traditional apprenticeship training in West Africa. *Anthropology and Education Quarterly, 8,* 177–180.

Lave, J., & Wenger, E. (1991). *Situated learning: Legitimate peripheral participation.* Cambridge, MA: Cambridge University Press.

Lee, J., & VanPatten, B. (1995). *Making communicative language teaching happen.* New York: McGraw Hill, Inc.

Leontiev, A. (1981). The problem of activity in psychology. In J. V. Wertsch (Ed.), *The concept of activity in soviet psychology* (pp. 37–71). Armonk, NY: M. E. Sharpe.

Lightbown, P., & Spada, N. (1990). Focus on form and corrective feedback in communicative language teaching. *Studies in Second-language Acquisition, 12,* 429–448.

Lightbown P., & Spada, N. (1993). *How languages are learned.* New York: Oxford University Press.

Liskin-Gasparro, J. (1999) Personal communication as reviewer of *Teacher's Handbook.*

Long, M. (1991). The least a second-language acquisition theory needs to explain. *TESOL Quarterly, 24,* 649–666.

Mehan, H. (1979). *Learning lessons.* Cambridge, MA: Harvard University Press.

National Standards in Foreign Language Project. (1996). *Standards for foreign language learning: Preparing for the 21st century.* Lawrence, KS: Allen Press.

Newman, D., Griffin, P., & Cole, M. (1989). *The construction zone: Working for cognitive change in school.* New York: Cambridge University Press.

Nunan, D. (1991). *Language teaching methodology.* New York: Prentice Hall.

Oller, J., Jr. (1983). Some working ideas for language teaching. In J. Oller, Jr. and P. Richard Amato (Eds.), *Methods that work* (pp. 3–19). Rowley, MA: Newbury House.

Pearson, D. (1989). Reading the whole-language movement. *Elementary School Journal, 90,* 231–241.

Polette, N. (1991). *Literature-based reading.* O'Fallon, MO: Book Lures, Inc.

Redmond, M. L. (1994). The whole language approach in the FLES classroom: Adapting strategies to teach reading and writing. *Foreign Language Annals, 27,* 428–444.

Rivers, W. (1983). *Communicating naturally in a second-language.* Chicago: University of Chicago Press.

Rogoff, B. (1990). *Apprenticeship in learning.* Oxford: Oxford University Press.

Rutherford, W. (1988). Grammatical consciousness raising in brief historical perspective. In W. Rutherford & M. Sharwood Smith (Eds.), *Grammar and second-language teaching* (pp. 15–18). New York: Harper.

Salaberry, R. (1997). The role of input and output practice in second-language acquisition. *Canadian Modern Language Review, 53,* 422–453.

Shaffer, C. (1989). A comparison of inductive and deductive approaches to teaching foreign languages. *The Modern Language Journal, 73,* 395–403.

Sharwood Smith, M. (1988). Consciousness raising and the second-language learner. In W. Rutherford & M. Sharwood Smith (Eds.), *Grammar and second-language teaching* (pp. 51–84). New York: Harper.

Spada, N., & Lightbown, P. (1993). Instruction and the development of questions in L2 classrooms. *Studies in second-language acquisition, 15,* 205–224.

Swain, M. (1995). Three functions of output in second-language learning. In G. Cook & B. Seidholfer (Eds.), *Principles and practices in applied linguistics* (pp. 125–144). Oxford: Oxford University Press.

Swain, M. (1998). *The output hypothesis and beyond.* Unpublished manuscript. University of Toronto, OISE.

Tarone, E. (1983). On the variability of interlanguage systems. *Applied Linguistics, 4,* 142–163.

Terrell, T. (1977). A natural approach to second-language acquisition and learning. *The Modern Language Journal, 61,* 325–337.

Terry, R. M. (1986). *Let Cinderella and Luke Skywalker help you teach the* passé composé *and the* imparfait. Hastings-on-Hudson, NY: ACTFL Materials Center.

Tharp, R., & Gallimore, R. (1988). *Rousing minds to life: Teaching, learning and schooling in social context.* New York: Cambridge University Press.

Tharp, R., & Gallimore, R. (1991). *The instructional conversation: Teaching and learning in social activity.* Washington, DC: National Center for Research on Cultural Diversity and Second-Language Learning.

VanPatten, B. & Cadierno, T. (1993). Explicit instruction and input processing. *Studies in Second-Language Acquisition, 15,* 225–241.

Vavra, E. (1996.) On not teaching grammar. *English Journal, 85*(7), 32–37.

Vygotsky, L. S. (1978). *Mind in society: The development of higher psychological processes.* Cambridge, MA: Harvard University Press.

Vygotsky, L. S. (1986). *Thought and language.* Cambridge, MA: MIT Press.

Walz, J. (1989). Context and contextualized language practice in foreign language teaching. *The Modern Language Journal, 73,* 161–168.

Wertsch, J. (1991). *Voices of the mind.* Cambridge, MA: Harvard University Press.

West, M., & Donato, R. (1995). Stories and stances: Cross-cultural encounters with African folktales. *Foreign Language Annals, 28,* 392–406.

CHAPTER 8

Developing Oral Interpersonal and Presentational Communication

In this chapter you will learn about:

- ACTFL oral proficiency scale
- strategies for helping students interact orally
- interpersonal mode of communication
- presentational mode of communication
- task-based instruction
- cooperative learning and interactive activities

- information-gap activities
- jigsaw activities
- use of imagination
- simulations
- integrating speaking into the teaching of literature and culture
- effect of feedback on performance

Teach and Reflect: Creating Information-Gap Activities for Various Levels of Instruction; Integrating Speaking with Oral or Written Texts

- **Case Study 1: Defining Groups for Cooperative Learning Activities**
- **Case Study 2: Friday Is Culture Day**

Conceptual Orientation

Although the speaking skill received a great deal of attention since the onset of audiolingualism in the 1950s, the profession struggled to understand how students learn to speak a foreign language, what they should be taught to say, and which classroom strategies are most effective in teaching speaking.

Speaking from a Proficiency Perspective

The concept of proficiency as developed and explored over the past decade generated even more discussion concerning the role of speaking in the curriculum. What can we expect students at each level to be able to say in the foreign language? What classroom strategies might enable students to develop skill in speaking? The current concept of proficiency describes the competencies that enable us to define in more specific terms what it means to know a language. Liskin-Gasparro's statement, "If you can't use a language, you don't know a language" (1987, p. 26), reflects the basic idea underlying proficiency. As explained in Chapter 2, proficiency is the ability to use language to perform language functions within a variety of contexts/contents and with a given degree of accuracy. In Chapter 2 of the *Handbook* you read a summary and reviewed Appendix 2.2 which contains a brief historical summary of how the proficiency concept came about; you will find it helpful to review this chart in order to understand more fully the development of the proficiency concept.

The *ACTFL Guidelines* in Appendix 2.3 provide detailed information about the performance characterized for listening, speaking, reading, and writing at each major border and sublevel of the scale. These criterion-referenced descriptions are experientially based, describing how speakers typically function at various levels of ability. Figure 8.1 illustrates the four major levels of the rating scale in the form of an inverted pyramid, showing that language facility increases exponentially, rather than arithmetically; in other words, it takes progressively more language ability to climb from one level to the next. Figure 8.2 illustrates the assessment criteria for each major level in terms of functions, context, content, and accuracy. The criteria also include *text type* (the last column on the chart), which refers to the kind of discourse being produced, from words to sentences to paragraphs to longer stretches of discourse. At this point, you will find it beneficial to familiarize yourself with the major levels of the rating scale. Teachers who experience training in using the OPI to elicit speech samples and rate proficiency and those who work in proficiency-oriented programs are able to develop reasonably accurate intuitions and predictions about their students' levels of proficiency (Glisan & Foltz, 1998, p. 14). ACTFL conducts a rigorous training and practice program for those who wish to qualify as official oral proficiency testers and to be certified to conduct interviews and accurately rate the speaking skill (Swender, 1999). Chapter 11 discusses the interview procedure itself and its significance to classroom testing.

Figure 8.1 Inverted Pyramid Showing Major Levels of the ACTFL Rating Scale

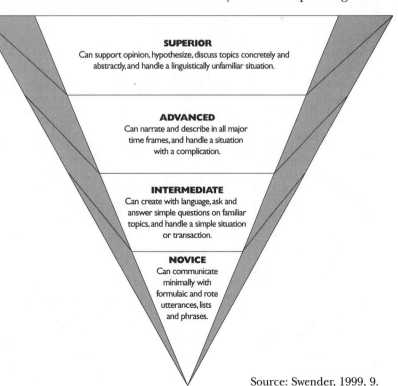

SUPERIOR
Can support opinion, hypothesize, discuss topics concretely and abstractly, and handle a linguistically unfamiliar situation.

ADVANCED
Can narrate and describe in all major time frames, and handle a situation with a complication.

INTERMEDIATE
Can create with language, ask and answer simple questions on familiar topics, and handle a simple situation or transaction.

NOVICE
Can communicate minimally with formulaic and rote utterances, lists and phrases.

Source: Swender, 1999, 9.

Figure 8.2 Assessment Criteria—Speaking

PROFICIENCY LEVEL*	GLOBAL TASKS AND FUNCTIONS	CONTEXT / CONTENT	ACCURACY	TEXT TYPE
Superior	Discuss topics extensively, support opinions and hypothesize. Deal with a linguistically unfamiliar situation.	Most formal and informal settings / Wide range of general interest topics and some special fields of interest and expertise.	No pattern of errors in basic structures. Errors virtually never interfere with communication or distract the native speaker from the message.	Extended discourse
Advanced	Narrate and describe in major time frames and deal effectively with an unanticipated complication.	Most informal and some formal settings / Topics of personal and general interest.	Understood without difficulty by speakers unaccustomed to dealing with non-native speakers.	Paragraphs
Intermediate	Create with language, initiate, maintain, and bring to a close simple conversations by asking and responding to simple questions.	Some informal settings and a limited number of transactional situations / Predictable, familiar topics related to daily activities.	Understood, with some repetition, by speakers accustomed to dealing with non-native speakers.	Discrete sentences
Novice	Communicate minimally with formulaic and rote utterances, lists, and phrases.	Most common informal settings / Most common aspects of daily life.	May be difficult to understand, even for speakers accustomed to dealing with non-native speakers.	Individual words and phrases

[*A rating at any major level is arrived at by the **sustained performance** of the functions of the level, within the contexts and content areas for that level, with the degree of accuracy described for the level, and in the text type for the level. The performance must be sustained across **ALL** of the criteria for the level in order to be rated at that level.]

Source: Swender, 1999, 31.

What kind of effect does classroom instruction have on the development of students' oral proficiency? First, instruction does make a difference, enabling learners to develop proficiency more rapidly and precisely than they would if they were merely exposed to the language (Ellis, 1990). Several states implemented proficiency requirements for graduation from high school. For example, in Pennsylvania, one of fifty-three requirements of all students for graduation from high school is that they converse at a minimum proficiency level of Intermediate-Low, as defined by the *ACTFL Guidelines,* in at least one language other than English (Pennsylvania Department of Education, 1993). Results of studies on what levels of proficiency can be expected after two years of secondary school study have been consistent: two studies (Glisan & Foltz, 1998; Huebner & Jensen,1992) showed that Level 2 students of Spanish rated from Novice-Mid to Novice-High. After four years of study, however, results were mixed with the mean rating for Level 4 students in the Glisan and Foltz study approaching Intermediate-Low, but in the Huebner and Jensen study the mean rating was Intermediate-Mid. In Russian, Thompson (1996) showed that forty percent of the university students tested reached Intermediate-Low after two years of study. In German, forty percent of the students were Intermediate-High or better after four semesters (Tschirner, 1992). Perhaps the most significant finding revealed by these studies is the range of oral proficiency levels attained by students in a given level of study. This is corroborated by Magnan's (1986) study, which found that proficiency levels form "bands" at each level of study and that the bands overlap from one level or year of study to the next. Magnan concludes that "this banding and overlapping reminds us that the process of language learning is a continuum on which learners progress at different rates, regardless of course boundaries" (1986, p. 432). Of importance is that these studies indicate the extended period of time that it takes most learners to progress from one level of proficiency to the next and the variation of levels attained by learners who experience the same number of years of instruction. If a teacher is unfamiliar with the proficiency concept and simply reads the proficiency guidelines, s/he may think that her/his students attained a much higher level of proficiency than they actually have. Thus, these research findings and proof through face-to-face proficiency testing should provide us with a realistic view of what is reasonable in terms of our expectations regarding our students' levels of proficiency.

> ⚷ "... language learning is a continuum on which learners progress at different rates, regardless of course boundaries.

What implications for teaching can we glean from proficiency? The proficiency concept does not propose a single method of instruction, but rather offers an organizing principle that can help teachers establish course objectives, organize course content, and determine what students should be able to do upon completion of a course or program of study. As Bragger states, proficiency "has provided educators with a framework into which methodology, curriculum, classroom techniques and testing can fit with relative ease, and which allows for flexibility, teacher and student individuality, and variety" (1985, p. 43). What are the characteristics of a proficiency-oriented classroom in which students learn how to speak a foreign language? Hadley proposes the following hypotheses about how classroom instruction might best be organized:

Hypothesis 1: Opportunities must be provided for students to practice using the language in a range of contexts likely to be encountered in the target culture.

Corollary 1: Students should be encouraged to express their own meaning as early as possible in the course of instruction.

Corollary 2: A proficiency-oriented approach promotes active communicative interaction among students.

Corollary 3: Creative language practice (as opposed to exclusively manipulative or convergent practice) must be encouraged.

Corollary 4: Authentic language should be used in instruction wherever and whenever possible.

Hypothesis 2: Opportunities should be provided for students to carry out a range of functions (tasks) likely to be necessary for dealing with others in the target culture.

Hypothesis 3: The development of accuracy should be encouraged in proficiency-oriented instruction. As learners produce language, various forms of instruction and evaluative feedback can be useful in facilitating the progression of their skills toward more precise and coherent language use.

Hypothesis 4: Instruction should be responsive to the affective as well as the cognitive needs of students, and their different personalities, preferences, and learning styles should be taken into account.

Hypothesis 5: Cultural understanding must be promoted in various ways so that students are sensitive to other cultures and prepared to live more harmoniously in the target-language community (Hadley, 1993, p. 77).

 The proficiency concept does not propose a single method of instruction, but rather offers an organizing principle for planning course objectives and organizing course content.

These hypotheses support the research presented in Chapter 1 of *Teacher's Handbook* concerning the language learning process. Current research points to the need to provide opportunities for students to hear a great deal of comprehensible language, to use the language in meaningful interaction with others, to negotiate meaning in cooperation with others, and to participate in an environment that encourages and motivates self-expression in a non-threatening way (Gass & Magnan, 1993; Krashen, 1982; Long, 1983; Vygotsky, 1978). In recent years, classrooms began to incorporate these characteristics of proficiency-oriented teaching. Indeed, Rollman (1994) compared 1976 and 1993 German classes and found that student talk had increased in 1993 as had the use of the target language as the language of instruction.

Proficiency-based classrooms provide students with ample opportunities to use the target language in authentic ways. Taylor (1983) identified five basic characteristics of communication in real-language situations:

1. Participants must be able to comprehend meaning conveyed beyond the sentence level.

2. The purpose of the exchange is to bridge some information gap; that is, to enable one speaker to acquire new information from another speaker.

3. Participants have the choice of what to say and how to say it.

4. Participants have an objective in mind while they are speaking.

5. Participants have to attend to many factors at the same time, such as remembering what was said, following shifts in topic, and knowing when to take turns speaking.

Providing a classroom environment that is conducive to language use in the world means that teachers must modify their traditional ways of interacting with students. Bragger (1985) describes typical teacher behaviors that should be modified as we attempt to provide the type of classroom described earlier. She bases her suggestions on the behaviors of trained testers in oral proficiency interview situations and on their awareness of their own classroom behaviors as teachers. According to Bragger (1985), teachers should

- attempt to take part in real conversation with students, without interrupting while they are speaking and without correcting while they are trying to communicate; rather, teachers might keep track of repeated errors made by students and, at the conclusion of the conversation or communicative activity, comment on the general patterns of errors made;
- listen to the content of what students are saying rather than listen exclusively to the structural accuracy;
- use a normal rate of speech when talking to students, use authentic language, and speak to students as naturally as they would to native speakers of the language.

Bragger's recommendations are supported by current research described in Chapter 3 on I-R-E (Input-Response-Evaluation) and I-R-F (Input-Response-Feedback). Further, Tharp and Gallimore (1988) and their associates (Goldenberg, 1991; Rueda, Goldenberg, & Gallimore, 1992; Patthey-Chavez, Clare, & Gallimore, 1995) proposed instructional conversations (ICs) in order to foster learning in ways related to Vygotsky's (1978) Zone of Proximal Development. As described in Hall, an IC has the following characteristics:

- *modeling,* in which the teacher lets students listen as s/he narrates paragraph-length thought, allowing them to hear linkages of ideas, construction of an argument, or defense of a position. Then s/he guides the students in the same tasks, decreasing teacher help as student control of the language increases.
- *feeding back,* or telling students that their performance matches or does not match the explicit model.
- *contingency managing,* or rewarding positive performance by students, and closely connecting rewards to feedback.
- *directing,* or focusing learners' attention on what is to be learned in a task or activity.
- *questioning,* or assisting the learner's performance by asking questions that activate background knowledge, or assessing how much progress the student has made in performing without assistance.
- *explaining,* explicitly showing how new information applies in new contexts, or organizing new information for learners.

- *task structuring,* arranging tasks so that learners may perform them, moving from tasks they can do only with assistance to tasks they can do independently (Hall, 1999, pp. 30–32).

You may find it helpful to match these characteristics to the steps of the PACE model described in Chapter 7.

 STANDARDS HIGHLIGHT: Using the INTERPERSONAL and PRESENTATIONAL Modes to Develop Oral Communication Skills

In Chapter 6, you explored the interpretive mode of communication, which refers to one-way communication that happens when learners listen to or read a variety of print and non-print materials. In Chapter 7 and in the present chapter, you were introduced to the interpersonal mode, which refers to two-way interactive communication (NSFLEP, 1996). A third aspect of communication is the presentational mode, which refers to one-way communication in a one-to-many mode—one person produces language in oral or written form for an audience. Although the creator of the message may be present, s/he is not personally known or accessible to the audience. In learning how to communicate in this mode, students will use primarily the productive skills of speaking and writing. In this chapter you will learn more about this mode with regard to speaking, and in Chapter 9 you will explore writing as it relates to this mode.

Classroom Strategies for Teaching Speaking

In Chapters 6 and 7, you explored standards-driven ways to integrate the teaching of grammar, listening, and reading with the speaking skill. In Chapter 9, you will learn strategies for integrating writing with speaking and the other skills. Below are sample techniques for interactive speaking that are based on the research findings presented in Chapter 1, as well as on the implications of proficiency introduced in this chapter. These activities may be adapted for use with elementary school, middle school, high school, and post-secondary classes. Note that these activities often address both the interpersonal and presentational modes of communication: students interact with one another to perform a task (interpersonal mode) and then present this information to an audience (presentational mode). Furthermore, they are often based on or can lead to an interpretive task.

The reader is encouraged to review the information from Chapter 1 dealing with negotiation of meaning, which is a vital concept in developing oral communication skills. In the spirit of sociocultural theory, *Teacher's Handbook* advocates an approach to teaching oral skills that actively engages learners in negotiating meaning.

Task-Based Instruction

In Chapter 2, you explored the various types of communicative activities and exercises that engage students in practice of language structures and communication. The research shows that students who perform communicative drills or activities (with a focus on meaning and some focus on form) tend to focus on the manipulation aspect of the activity and not on the communication itself (Brooks, 1990; Kinginger, 1990). Indeed activities classified as "communicative" often consist of questions asked by the teacher and answers supplied by students (Lee, 1995). Studies dealing with the nature of classroom tasks confirmed that when pair/group work entails negotiation of meaning, students perform a greater number of content clarifications, confirmation checks, and comprehension checks (Doughty & Pica, 1986; Porter, 1986). According to Crookes and Gass (1993a, 1993b), the language students use in these types of interaction plays a vital role in language acquisition. A strategy for restructuring the traditional question-answer type of class discussion is *task-based instruction,* which enables students to interact with others by using the target language as a means to an end (Lee, 1995). Task-based instruction enables learners to use the language with a purpose so that language is not merely the object of manipulation or drill (Lee, 1995; Richards, Platt, & Weber, 1985). Task-based activities are carried out as the result of processing or understanding language (Richards, Platt, & Weber, 1985). An example is the drawing of a map while listening to a tape, where production of language may or may not be involved (Lee, 1995, p. 440). Although there are various types of task-based activities, they usually emphasize that communication (1) is the expression, interpretation, and negotiation of meaning; (2) requires two or more autonomous participants; and (3) should focus on the learners' use of the language, not the instructor's (Lee, 1995, p. 440). One type of task-based activity is task-based discussion, which promotes self-expression, interpretation, and negotiation of meaning among learners (Lee, 1995). Figure 8.3 shows a sample task-based discussion activity that uses a discussion question as the springboard for communication. Lee suggests the following steps for recasting questions into a task-based discussion format:

1. Identify a desired outcome: What information are students supposed to extract from the interaction?

2. Break down the topic into subtopics: What are the relevant subcomponents of the topic?

3. Create and sequence concrete tasks for learners to do, for example, lists, charts, tables: What tasks can the learners carry out to explore the subcomponents?

4. Build in linguistic support, either lexical or grammatical or both: What linguistic support do the learners need? (Lee, 1995, p. 441).

 Task-based instruction enables students to interact with others by using the target language as a means to an end.

Cooperative Learning and Interactive Activities

In cooperative learning, students work in pairs or in small groups of four or five to help one another complete a given task, attain a goal, or learn subject matter. Each person in the group has a responsibility, and students depend on one another as they work to

Figure 8.3   Activity H

ACTIVITY H. HOW HAVE TRADITIONAL ROLES CHANGED?

Step 1. Work in pairs or in groups of three. The instructor will assign one of the following to each pair or group:

    a. Prepare a list of actions, attitudes, and qualities that characterize the traditional role of the man in the family. Careful. What past tense will you need to do this?

    b. Prepare a list of the actions, attitudes, and qualities that characterize the contemporary role of the man in the family.

Step 2. Write your list on the board and compare it to those of your classmates. As you do, fill in the following chart with the ideas each group presents.

THE MAN'S ROLE	
In the past	**Today**

Step 3. Repeat Steps 1 and 2 but this time, focus on the role of a woman in traditional and contemporary families. That is, first make lists and then fill in the following chart.

THE WOMAN'S ROLE	
In the past	**Today**

Step 4. As a class, contrast the traditional roles men and women play in the family with their more contemporary roles. Have their roles changed? How? Why?

Step 5. Optional. Prepare a written summary of the class discussion using the information in the two tables.

Source: Lee, 1995, 444.

 What makes this discussion "task-based"?

complete their task. Students learn to work together and respect their classmates. They are also encouraged to develop their own abilities and identities. The teacher may give points or some form of credit to the entire group for achieving the objectives and may also give individual students credit for their contributions. Extensive research on cooperative learning by Johnson and Johnson (1987) suggests that this technique often produces higher achievement, increases retention, and develops interpersonal skills. Cooperative learning also has been shown to promote higher self-esteem and acceptance of differences, as well as to foster responsibility. Furthermore, it encourages creativity by giving students opportunities to observe the problem-solving approaches and cognitive processing strategies of others (Kohn, 1987). According to Johnson, Johnson, and Holubec (1988), cooperative learning provides the vehicle for teaching students to process skills that are needed to work effectively within a group. By using process observers and peer feedback on group processing skills, students begin to analyze and improve the group interaction. Figure 8.4 is an example of a questionnaire designed to encourage students to think about the group process and their own participation (Scarcella & Oxford, 1992). Of particular benefit to foreign language study, cooperative learning activities teach students how to ask questions and negotiate meaning, skills that have traditionally been neglected in the classroom (Honeycutt & Vernon, 1985). In addition, there is evidence to suggest that students in the honors foreign language class are eager to learn in a cooperative setting and experience success and increased motivation (Szostek, 1994).

Figure 8.4 Questionnaire: Conversational Skills

IN TODAY'S ACTIVITY	OFTEN	SOMETIMES	NEVER
1. I checked to make sure that everyone understood what I said.			
2. I gave explanations whenever I could.			
3. I asked specific questions about what I didn't understand.			
4. I paraphrased what others said to make sure that I understood.			
5. I encouraged others to speak by making such remarks as "I'd like to know what _____ thinks about that" and "I haven't heard from _____ yet" and "What do you think, _____?"			

Source: Scarcella and Oxford, 1992, 158.

 In cooperative learning tasks, each person in the group has a responsibility, and students depend on one another as they work to complete their task.

❒ Examples of Cooperative Learning Activities

Cooperative learning activities can range from the simple think-pair-share task described below (Kagan 1989) to a more complex simulation activity, as described later. The following are only a few of the many types of cooperative learning activities:[1]

- *peer tutoring* (Fotos & Ellis, 1991; Gaier, 1985; Kagan, 1989): Teammates teach each other simple concepts in content areas such as math, science, or language arts. Richard-Amato (1988) suggests using this for a content-area class that includes ESL students.
- *think-pair-share* (Kagan, 1989): Students use the following response cycle in answering questions: (1) they listen while the teacher poses a question; (2) they are given time to think of a response; (3) they are told to pair with a classmate and discuss their responses; and (4) they share their responses with the whole group.
- *jigsaw* (Kagan, 1989): Each member of the group assumes responsibility for a given portion of the lesson. These members work with the members from the other groups who have the same assignment, thus forming "expert groups." Eventually, each member must learn the entire lesson by sharing information with others in the group. Figure 8.5 depicts a sample jigsaw activity, together with suggestions for how to form teams and expert groups. Slavin (1987) describes a form of Student Team Learning, called Student Teams-Achievement Division (STAD), in which students assemble in teams of four or five to learn the material covered in a lesson presented by the teacher and later take a quiz on the learned material. The team's overall score is determined by the extent to which each student improved over her/his past performance.
- *information-gap activities* (Johnson, 1979; Walz, 1996): One student has information that another one does not have but needs. For example, pairs of students might be given the task of finding an hour that they both have free this week to play a game of tennis. Each student might have a copy of her/his schedule of activities for the week, and each has to ask questions in order to find out when the other person is free. As they share the information, the students eventually find the time slot that is available for both of them. Figures 8.6 (Dreke & Lind, 1986), 8.7 (Freed & Bauer, 1989), 8.8 (adapted from Freed & Knutson, 1989), and 8.9 (Hadfield, 1984 c.f. Walz 1996) are sample information-gap activities in German, Spanish, French, and English, respectively. Figure 8.10 is an example of a generic information-gap activity in Spanish which students must communicate with each other so that they both have the same picture (Brooks, Donato, & McGlone, 1997).

---

1. For a review of many research-based activities that use cooperative learning in the college classroom, refer to Cook (1991).

Figure 8.5A Sample Jigsaw Activity

The teacher will cut out the four sections of the house. Give each group only *one* of four sections.

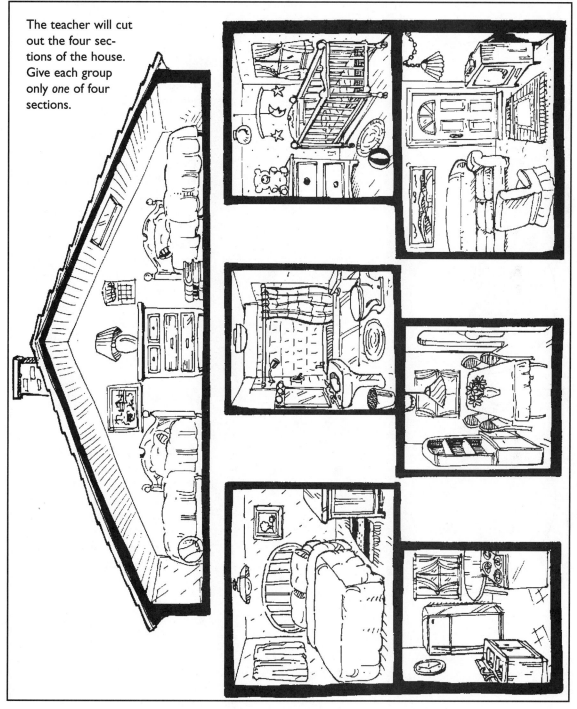

Source: Fall, 1991.

Figure 8.5B   Jigsaw Activity for Four Groups of Students

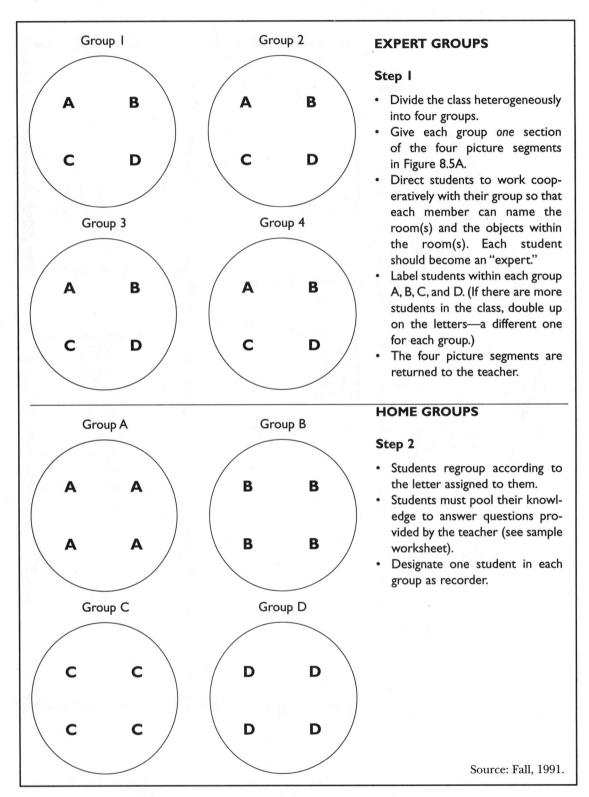

Group 1

Group 2

A   B
C   D

A   B
C   D

Group 3

Group 4

A   B
C   D

A   B
C   D

Group A

Group B

A   A
A   A

B   B
B   B

Group C

Group D

C   C
C   C

D   D
D   D

EXPERT GROUPS

Step 1

- Divide the class heterogeneously into four groups.
- Give each group *one* section of the four picture segments in Figure 8.5A.
- Direct students to work cooperatively with their group so that each member can name the room(s) and the objects within the room(s). Each student should become an "expert."
- Label students within each group A, B, C, and D. (If there are more students in the class, double up on the letters—a different one for each group.)
- The four picture segments are returned to the teacher.

HOME GROUPS

Step 2

- Students regroup according to the letter assigned to them.
- Students must pool their knowledge to answer questions provided by the teacher (see sample worksheet).
- Designate one student in each group as recorder.

Source: Fall, 1991.

Figure 8.5C   Jigsaw Activity Worksheet

Group _____

Names _____   _____

_____   _____

Each member of your group has seen one part of a house. You will need to work together to answer the following questions:

1. How many rooms are in the house?   _____

2. How many bathrooms are there?   _____

3. How many bedrooms are there?   _____

4. How many of the following did you see?

beds	_____	pictures	_____
tables	_____	sinks	_____
clocks	_____	doors	_____
chairs	_____	toys	_____
dressers	_____	pillows	_____
lamps	_____	bookshelves	_____
rugs	_____	waste baskets	_____
windows	_____		

5. How many children might live in this house?   _____

6. Do you think the children are older or younger?   _____

Variations: Selected readings may be given, or research assignments may be made, including biographies (each group studies one facet of the person's life) or cultural studies (each group studies one facet of a particular country or culture).

Target Language Use: To encourage use of the target language, give each student 5–10 bingo chips. Each time a student uses English, he or she must place a chip in a pile. Students receive bonus points depending on the number of chips they still have at the end of the activity.

Process Objectives: Students will work cooperatively.
    Students will engage in peer teaching.

Content Objectives: Students will communicate in the target language.
    Students will recall and/or name vocabulary items or basic facts and information.

Source: Fall, 1991.

Figure 8.6A Besitzverhältnisse

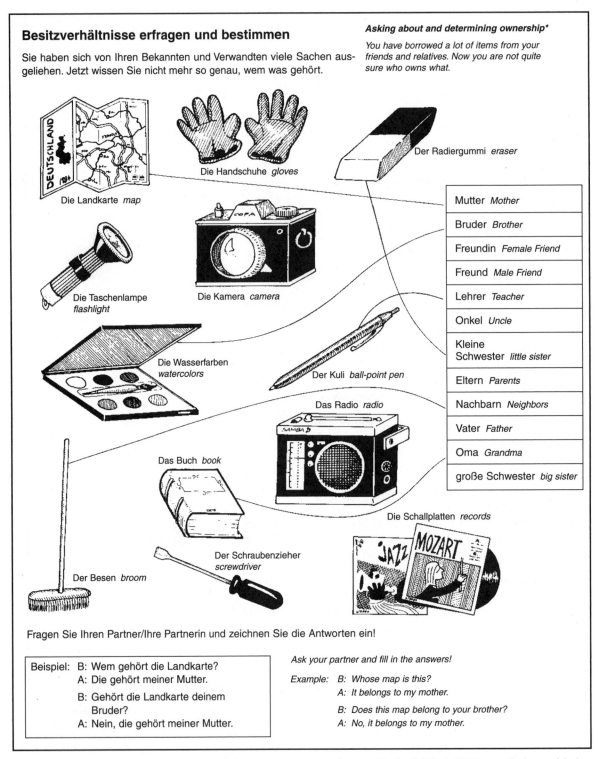

Besitzverhältnisse erfragen und bestimmen

Sie haben sich von Ihren Bekannten und Verwandten viele Sachen ausgeliehen. Jetzt wissen Sie nicht mehr so genau, wem was gehört.

Asking about and determining ownership*

You have borrowed a lot of items from your friends and relatives. Now you are not quite sure who owns what.

Die Landkarte *map*

Die Handschuhe *gloves*

Der Radiergummi *eraser*

Die Taschenlampe *flashlight*

Die Kamera *camera*

Die Wasserfarben *watercolors*

Der Kuli *ball-point pen*

Das Radio *radio*

Das Buch *book*

Der Besen *broom*

Der Schraubenzieher *screwdriver*

Die Schallplatten *records*

Mutter	*Mother*
Bruder	*Brother*
Freundin	*Female Friend*
Freund	*Male Friend*
Lehrer	*Teacher*
Onkel	*Uncle*
Kleine Schwester	*little sister*
Eltern	*Parents*
Nachbarn	*Neighbors*
Vater	*Father*
Oma	*Grandma*
große Schwester	*big sister*

Fragen Sie Ihren Partner/Ihre Partnerin und zeichnen Sie die Antworten ein!

Beispiel: B: Wem gehört die Landkarte?
A: Die gehört meiner Mutter.
B: Gehört die Landkarte deinem Bruder?
A: Nein, die gehört meiner Mutter.

Ask your partner and fill in the answers!

Example: B: *Whose map is this?*
A: *It belongs to my mother.*
B: *Does this map belong to your brother?*
A: *No, it belongs to my mother.*

Source: Dreke & Lind, 1986, translations added.

Figure 8.6B Besitzverhältnisse

Besitzverhältnisse erfragen und bestimmen

Sie haben sich von Ihren Bekannten und Verwandten viele Sachen ausgeliehen. Jetzt wissen Sie nicht mehr so genau, wem was gehört.

Asking about and determining ownership*

You have borrowed a lot of items from your friends and relatives. Now you are not quite sure who owns what.

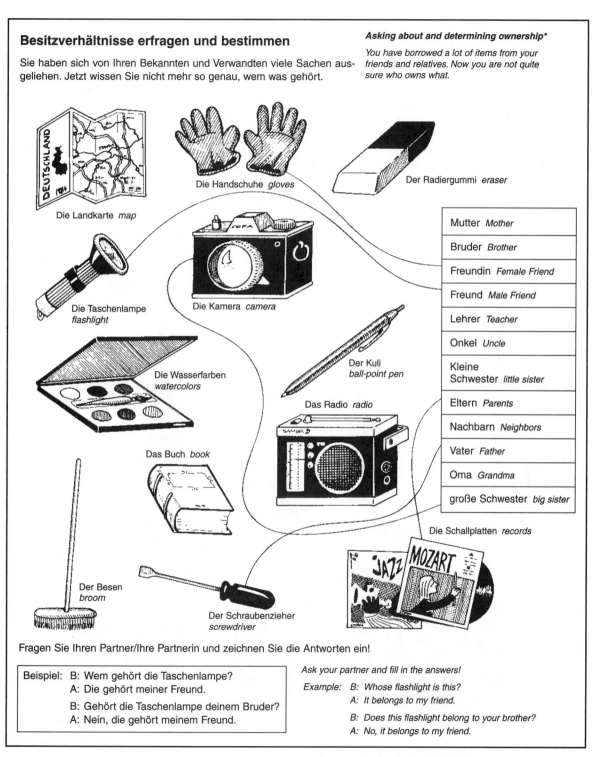

Die Handschuhe *gloves*

Der Radiergummi *eraser*

Die Landkarte *map*

Die Taschenlampe *flashlight*

Die Kamera *camera*

Die Wasserfarben *watercolors*

Der Kuli *ball-point pen*

Das Radio *radio*

Das Buch *book*

Der Besen *broom*

Der Schraubenzieher *screwdriver*

Die Schallplatten *records*

| Mutter *Mother* |
| Bruder *Brother* |
| Freundin *Female Friend* |
| Freund *Male Friend* |
| Lehrer *Teacher* |
| Onkel *Uncle* |
| Kleine Schwester *little sister* |
| Eltern *Parents* |
| Nachbarn *Neighbors* |
| Vater *Father* |
| Oma *Grandma* |
| große Schwester *big sister* |

Fragen Sie Ihren Partner/Ihre Partnerin und zeichnen Sie die Antworten ein!

Beispiel: B: Wem gehört die Taschenlampe?
A: Die gehört meiner Freund.

B: Gehört die Taschenlampe deinem Bruder?
A: Nein, die gehört meinem Freund.

Ask your partner and fill in the answers!

Example: B: Whose flashlight is this?
A: It belongs to my friend.

B: Does this flashlight belong to your brother?
A: No, it belongs to my friend.

Source: Dreke & Lind, 1986, translations added.

Figure 8.7A   La sala de estar

La sala de estar

Context

In this activity you will work with another student to describe the location of furniture in a room. You will carry out a telephone conversation between an interior designer and a client. One of you will work with a completed floor plan and the other will work with the blank plan. Both of you may consult the *Lista de Muebles* (List of Furniture).

First Student

You are the interior designer. You must call your client and indicate what furniture you have chosen and where it should be placed. Since this is a phone conversation, you must give instructions with words alone. Do not look at or point to your partner's diagram.

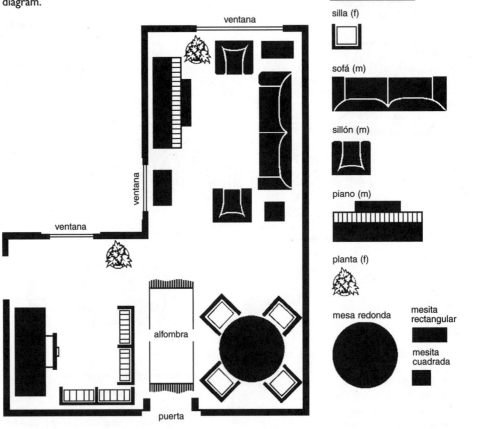

Source: Freed & Bauer, 1989.

Figure 8.7B   La sala de estar

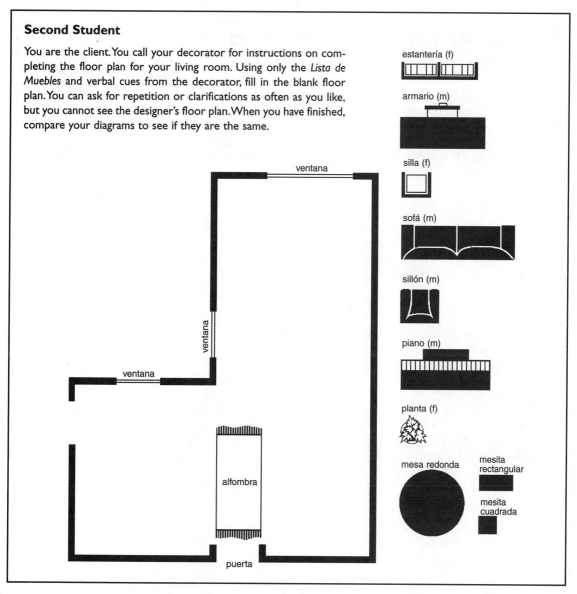

Second Student

You are the client. You call your decorator for instructions on completing the floor plan for your living room. Using only the *Lista de Muebles* and verbal cues from the decorator, fill in the blank floor plan. You can ask for repetition or clarifications as often as you like, but you cannot see the designer's floor plan. When you have finished, compare your diagrams to see if they are the same.

estantería (f)

armario (m)

silla (f)

sofá (m)

sillón (m)

piano (m)

planta (f)

mesa redonda

mesita rectangular

mesita cuadrada

ventana

ventana

ventana

alfombra

puerta

Source: Freed & Bauer, 1989.

Figure 8.8A   La géographie de l'Afrique francophone

La géographie de l'Afrique francophone

Context

You will work with a partner on this activity to practice learning the geography of French-speaking sub-Saharan Africa. One of you will have a map of Africa with names of Francophone countries filled in. The other will receive a blank map.

First Student

You have the completed map. Your task is to give instructions to your partner on where each country is located. The only country on your partner's map is Niger, so that must be your point of departure.

Source: Adapted from Freed & Knutson, 1989.

Figure 8.8B   Second Student's Map

Second Student

You have a blank map. Your partner will tell you where to write in each country name. He or she will begin using Niger as a point of reference. You can ask for repetition or clarification as often as you like, but you can't look at his or her map.

When you have finished, compare maps to check for accuracy.

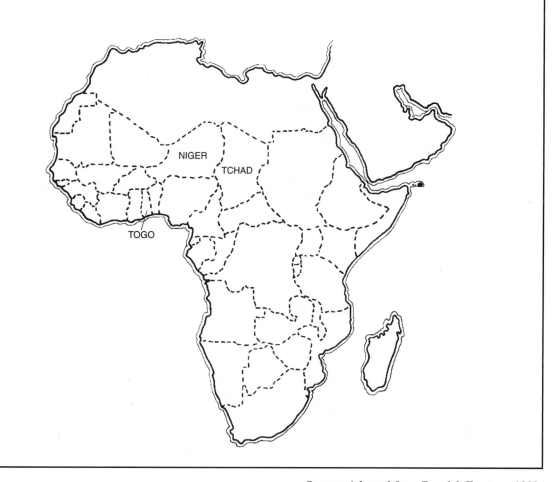

Source: Adapted from Freed & Knutson, 1989.

Figure 8.9A   Where Are My Glasses?

Source: Walz, 1996.

Figure 8.9B   Where Are My Glasses?

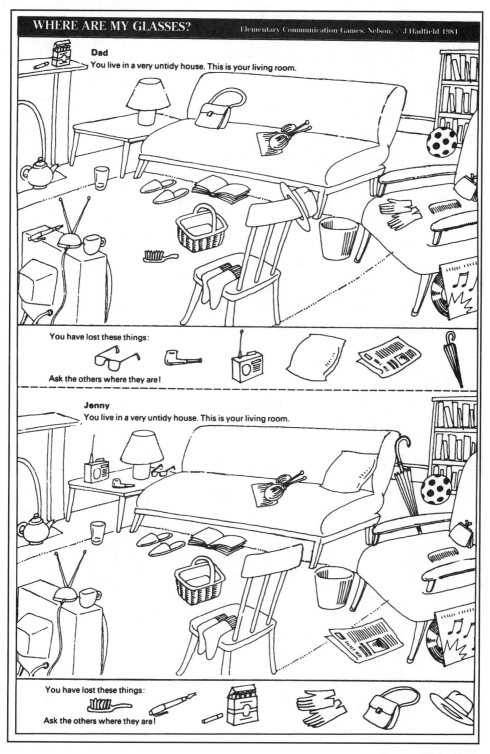

Source: Walz, 1996.

Figure 8.10 Jig-Saw

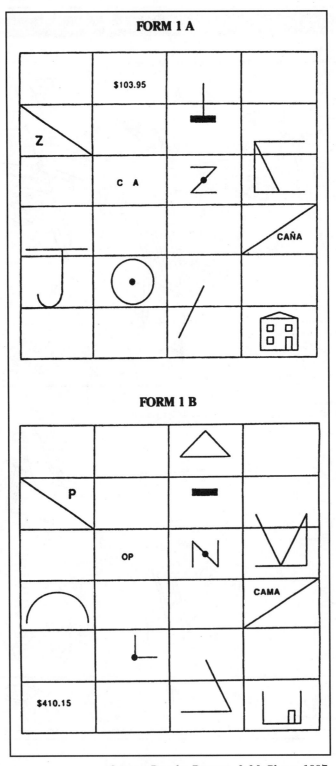

Source: Brooks, Donato, & McGlone, 1997.

Brooks describes another type of information-gap activity: "There are two parts to a whole diagram or picture, Part A and Part B. When both parts are superimposed, they form a complete diagram. One student receives Part A, the other Part B. The teacher then asks the students to talk to one another in the foreign language to find out how their part of the diagram is both different from and similar to that of the partner and to draw in or add the missing information so that, by the end of their conversation, they both have replicas of the same master diagram" (Brooks, 1992, p. 67).

When teachers use an information-gap activity for they first time, they must realize that students need sufficient opportunities to become comfortable with this type of task. If the teacher explains the task, models with another student what learners are to do, and then provides several similar but different tasks, students find these tasks more productive and enjoyable than other kinds of practice, and teachers find that students begin to use the language more to exchange information. It is important to do several similar activities so that students can become comfortable managing the intrapersonal communication— that is, figuring out within their own minds how they will sustain their involvement in the task (Brooks, Donato, & McGlone, 1997, p. 526).

 In information-gap activities, one student has information that another one does not have but needs.

Figure 8.11 illustrates how the same jigsaw activity used in 8.5 can be adapted for use as an information-gap activity of the kind described above. This type of information-gap task can be created by drawing a picture, diagram, or arrangement of items on a sheet of paper. After the master is drawn, the two parts (or three parts for three-way jigsaws) can then be drawn so that when superimposed, they form the complete picture or diagram (Brooks, 1992). Information-gap activities provide a good opportunity for students to learn how to ask for clarification, how to request information, and how to negotiate when faced with misunderstandings.[2] (See Appendix 8.1 for sources of published information-gap activities.)

- *problem solving* (Long & Crookes, 1986): Group members must share information in order to solve a problem, such as how to find lost luggage at an airport.
- *storytelling:* students recreate a familiar story, add more details, change the ending, or create a story with visuals.
- *cooperative projects* (Kagan, 1989): Group members work together to complete a group project such as a presentation, composition, or art project. Oxford (1992) describes the "Heritage Project," a successful cooperative model for teaching culture in language classes, in which students design a culture-related project and have a large degree of freedom in topic choice, grouping, implementation, and time management.[3]

---

2. Recent high school and college textbooks include numerous pair and small-group tasks, including information-gap activities (Dreke & Lind, 1986; Freed & Bauer, 1989; Freed & Knutson, 1989;) and strategic interaction (DiPietro, 1987).

3. For many ideas on long-term task-oriented projects, see Fried-Booth (1986).

Figure 8.11A   What's Missing?

- Your partner has a picture that is identical to yours except that it is missing the seven objects numbered on your picture. Tell your partner (or describe) what is missing and where he or she should draw it.
- Draw the objects that are missing from your picture as your partner tells you what to draw and where to draw it.
- When completed, both pictures should be identical.

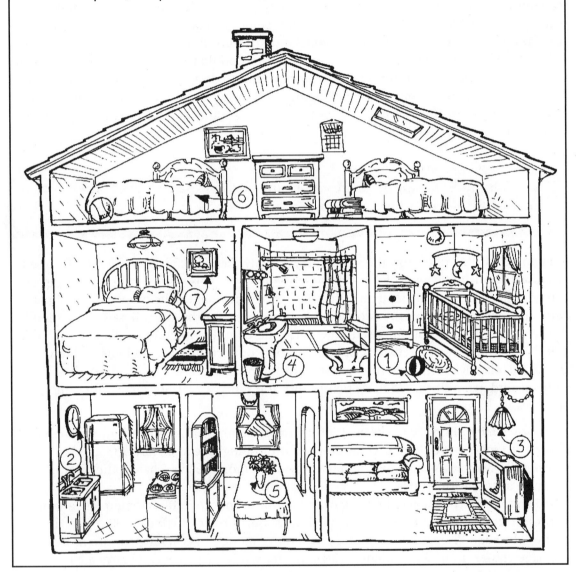

Source: Fall, 1991.

Figure 8.11B What's Missing?

- Your partner has a picture that is identical to yours except that it is missing the seven objects numbered on your picture. Tell your partner (or describe) what is missing and where he or she should draw it.
- Draw the objects that are missing from your picture as your partner tells you what to draw and where to draw it.
- When completed, both pictures should be identical.

Source: Fall, 1991.

- *movement activities* (Bassano & Christison, 1987): Students get up from their seats and walk around the room in order to obtain information from classmates. For example, students might have a list of ten activities in the present tense and would ask classmates whether or not they do each activity (wake up at 6:00 A.M., eat breakfast every morning, etc.); students share the information with the class afterward.
- *paired activities and interviews:* Students interview each other for specific information and share their findings with the class.[4]
- *conversation cards* (Bonin & Birckbichler, 1975): Working in groups of three, two students ask each other questions according to cues on their cards while the third student checks for accuracy, helps the other two students, and might also report back to the class. Fleak (1992) suggests that the third student use a monitor sheet that contains suggested correct linguistic forms and possible answers; the sheet can also be given to all students as they check their responses in class or at home.
- *role plays:* Students act out situations such as a restaurant scene or a visit to a doctor. Beginning students can be given role-play cards with vocabulary/grammar hints provided, intermediate-level students can practice role plays around survival situations, and advanced-level learners can present role plays around a problematic situation in which someone must solve a conflict or persuade someone else to do something within a culturally specific context (DiPietro,1987; Hadley, 1993).

It is advantageous to present the situation card in the native language so that students completely understand the task and so that they are not given the target language words and expressions that they are being asked to generate in the role play. However, when preparing role plays, students benefit from well-organized instructions and guidance, such as a model situation and hints concerning vocabulary and grammar use. The extent to which the teacher offers specific suggestions will depend on the cognitive and linguistic levels of the students. Younger learners, for example, require more structured role play directions in order to help them focus their ideas.

Richards describes the following procedure for using role play with intermediate-level learners:

1. Learners participate in a preliminary activity in which the topic and situation are introduced.

2. They then work through a model dialogue on a related topic that provides examples of the type of language that will be required.

3. Assisted by role cards, learners perform the role play.

4. Learners listen to recordings of native speakers performing the role play with the role cards.

5. Follow-up activities exploit the native speaker performance.

6. The entire sequence is then repeated with a second transaction on the same topic. (Richards, 1985, pp. 85–88)

---

4. The next section in this chapter describes ways to configure small groups by placing students together who represent a cross-section of the class in terms of level of performance, race/ethnicity, and sex. This same procedure could be used in configuring heterogeneous pairs of students.

- *open-ended free conversations:* Students are given a list of topics related to their lessons and told to select the topic and let the conversation flow from there, consistent with the topicalization hypothesis, according to which, choice of topic allows for more natural flow of language (Ellis, 1990; Hatch, 1978; Kinginger, 1994; Long, 1983; Wells, 1985).
- *sharing opinions, debating, narrating, describing, explaining:* These activities are particularly useful as students move into the advanced level of study, since they provide the impetus for self-expression, use of paragraph-length and extended discourse, and manipulation of more sophisticated vocabulary and grammatical structures.

Norman (1996) outlines a set of classroom activities designed to promote spontaneous oral interaction for students in the English as a Foreign Language (EFL) classroom. The activities are based on the initial reading of texts such as diaries, newspaper articles, poems, and drama scenes (interpretive mode). Students work together to explore the texts and share reactions (interpersonal mode), after which they create a presentation or product such as a drama activity or newscast (presentational mode) (Norman, 1996, pp. 598–602).

❏ Conducting Cooperative Learning Activities

Grouping Students

Research in cooperative learning shows that the most effective way to configure small groups is to put together four students who represent a cross-section of the class in terms of level of past performance in the subject area, race or ethnicity, and sex (Slavin, 1986). Slavin suggests that "a four-person team in a class that is one half male, one half female, and three quarters white, one quarter minority might have two boys and two girls and three white students and one minority student. The team would also have a high performer, a low performer, and two average performers" (1986, p. 16). Students are assigned to groups or teams by the teacher, since they tend to choose partners who are like themselves.

When a class does not evenly divide up into groups, a student can be assigned a role as a "floater." Floaters can have several functions, such as collecting information from each group (for example, during paired interviews), eavesdropping and reporting back to the class what s/he discovered, or serving as an observer of group processing. In this way, the extra student can contribute to the class at the end of the activity or during group reporting (Donato, 1992).

Teaching Group Interaction Skills

In conducting cooperative learning tasks, the teacher often must teach the interaction skills that are lacking or in need of improvement, such as taking turns at talking. Kramsch suggests that teachers use the following strategies for encouraging students to take control of turn-taking as they would in natural discourse:

- Tolerate silences; refrain from filling the gaps between turns. This will put pressure on students to initiate turns.
- Direct your gaze to any potential addressee of a student's utterance; do not assume that you are the next speaker and the student's exclusive addressee.

- Teach the students floor-taking gambits; do not grant the floor.
- Encourage students to sustain their speech beyond one or two sentences and to take longer turns; do not use a student's short utterance as a springboard for your own lengthy turn.
- Extend your exchanges with individual students to include clarification of the speaker's intentions and your understanding of them; do not cut off an exchange too soon to pass on to another student (Kramsch, 1987, p. 22).

 Teach students how to manage their talk during group interaction.

The teacher usually finds it necessary to teach "gambits" or strategies for opening and closing conversations (e.g., "Hi! Nice to see you!"; "Well, I have to leave now. I promised to meet someone at the library.") and conversational routines used in managing turn-taking and topics (e.g., "I understand what you're saying, but I think that . . . ") (Keller and Warner, 1979).

Structuring Group Tasks

The following are helpful guidelines for structuring cooperative learning and interactive activities:

1. Limit the size of the group; groups are most effective when they are no larger than five.

2. Motivate the activity with drama, actions, or visuals.

3. Set clear goals and describe outcomes clearly for the students.

4. Prime the students with the target language they need to accomplish the activity so they will know exactly how to say what they need to say.

5. Give directions and a model.

6. Set a time limit to help students feel accountable and to make the best use of the time available. Use a kitchen timer with a loud bell or buzzer to provide a neutral timekeeper and a clear signal for the end of the activity.

7. Circulate among the students throughout the activity to offer assistance and check progress.

8. Elicit feedback at the end of the activity (Knop, 1986).

 Define group tasks and set time and membership limits before the group begins.

Detailed attention must be given to providing clear directions and examples before the task is begun (Johnson, Johnson, & Holubec, 1988). Modeling the task with another student in front of the class (and talking about the task while it is performed) is another good way to provide support for the activity. While students are engaged in group activities, the teacher acts as both a process observer and a resource person. At the conclusion of the group activity, the groups report back to the whole class on their progress and on the process, thus helping the teacher to plan for future activities. Circulating around the room to monitor progress and making students responsible for reporting back to the class after the activity will encourage students to use the target language and may prevent them from reverting to the use of the native language. See Appendix 8.2 for a description of Donato's (1992) "Talk Scores," a technique for monitoring and evaluating group speaking activities. Appendix 8.3 presents self- and peer-assessment for presentational speaking, and Appendix 8.4 is a self-assessment for an interactive speaking interview with a classmate.

Curtain and Pesola suggest that the elementary school foreign language teacher ask questions similar to the following when designing pair activities and cooperative learning tasks. These questions are also applicable to tasks done at higher levels of instruction.

1. What is the source of the message to be exchanged? Is there an information or opinion gap?

2. What language will be required to complete the activity? How much of it will need to be practiced or reviewed?

3. How is the language to be used—guided or controlled?

4. What provision is made for clearly defined turn taking? Does each partner have an opportunity to participate approximately equally?

5. Is the activity self-correcting? Can the partners find out immediately if they have been successful? Is there a way for the partners to monitor their own accuracy?

6. How can the teacher follow up on the activity in a communicative way? (Curtain & Pesola, 1994, pp. 325–326)

Student Discourse in Pair/Group Activities

While the research shows the effectiveness of group work (Sharan & Shaulov, 1990), researchers in foreign language education began to look at what kind of discourse students use in paired and small-group communication settings. A series of studies illuminates the ways student mediate their work on tasks in pairs and small groups over time (Donato & Brooks, 1994; Brooks, Donato, & McGlone, 1997; Liskin-Gasparro, 1996; Platt & Brooks, 1994). The following excerpt from a jigsaw activity illustrates the strategies students use when they participate in a problem-solving task of this kind for the first time:

249 **J:** uh well, now I'm even more confused

250 **K:** ha! ha!

251 **J:** see, I have um

okay let me try to do this in Spanish

I'll at least put up the effort

253   En mi papel yo tengo muchos espacios algunos tienen películas otros están blancos [On my paper, I have many spaces, some have movies, others are blank.]

254 **K:**   uh huh

255 **J:**   y uh yo pienso que tú tienes un blancos donde yo tengo películas [And, uh, I think you have blanks where I have movies.]

256 **K:**   uh huh

257 **J:**   ¿entiendes? [Do you understand?]

258 **K:**   uh sí

259 **J:**   Y but that's not happening

. . .

264 **J:**   I think um you're supposed to draw in what I have and I'm supposed to draw um um

(Brooks, Donato, & McGlone, 1997, pp. 524–525).

Through classroom speech samples such as the excerpt shown here, researchers identified four mediational strategies students use during pair-work activity: talk about talk, talk about task, the use of English, and whispering to self.

Typical student language in pairs includes: talk about talk, talk about task, the use of English, and whispering to self.

When participants talk about their own talk, sometimes called *metatalk,* they use statements such as "*¿Cómo se dice* 'through'?" ("How do you say 'through'?"), or "That's a good word for that." (Brooks, Donato, & McGlone, 1997, p. 528). This talk about talk is also accompanied by *talk about task* when students say things like "I don't know if I'm right," or "*¿Tú quieres mi hablar mi hablo en español y tú oye oír?*" ("You want me to speak and you listen?") (Brooks, Donato, & McGlone, 1997, p. 529). As students think, act, and speak through a task, they mediate their work with the language that is available to them, most likely the *native language.* In the second language classroom this use of English is often distressing to teachers. Szostek (1994) pointed out that in her study insufficient time had been spent on preparing students for managing group dynamics, and they resorted to English for these exchanges. Brooks, Donato, and McGlone (1997) explain that use of English is normal and does not necessarily mean that target language use will not be achieved. They explain that students are learning to use the target language for such tasks, but they must start with the native language and move toward use of the target language as they resolve the problem of the task. Across time, English use diminishes.

A final strategy identified by these researchers is *whispering to the self.* This mediation behavior appears early in L1 language acquisition, mostly when communication is difficult and thinking is verbal, and it is suppressed in adults except when under communicative duress. The subjects in the Platt, Brooks, and Donato studies used this mediational tool in the native and the target language, and its use diminished over time as the tasks and how to resolve them became more familiar. In sum, these studies indicate that if the purpose and function of learner language during problem-solving tasks is not clearly understood, learners might not be given the strategic opportunities that can lead to their successful performance of tasks using the target language; that is, they might have difficulty ever "saying it right" during such tasks (Brooks, Donato, & McGlone, 1997).

 How does "whispering to the self" relate to the concepts of "private speech" and "mental rehearsal" discussed in Chapter 1?

Examining student discourse within the context of an oral proficiency interview, Liskin-Gasparro also found that students use a number of communicative strategies to manage discourse: asking for assistance, switching languages, transliteration (guessing that Spanish *ropa* must mean "rope" when it really means "clothing"), reconstructing the message, circumlocution or description, approximation (use of a near synonym), coining words, and abandoning the message (1996, pp. 320–322). Advanced learners use more strategies that were based on the L2, abandoning those based on L1.

Imaginative Activities

Sadow developed a number of imaginative activities for the language classroom in which students are asked to "solve a problem they would not normally have to face, concoct a plan they would never have dreamt of on their own, reconstruct the missing parts of stories, and act in outlandish ways" (1987, p. 33). According to Sadow, imaginative activities have the following characteristics:

1. Students work from the known to the unknown.

2. The problem is deliberately ambiguous.

3. Any logical response to the problem is acceptable.

4. Role play is commonly used.

5. Listening skills are crucial at several points in the activity.

6. The teacher sets up the activity and then withdraws.

7. There is a summing up or debriefing following student discussion (1987, pp. 33–34).

When students first begin to do imaginative work, Sadow (1987) suggests that they work with structured paired activities such as rewriting conversations or dialogs to change the characters, perhaps by switching male and female or altering age and status. Beginning-level students might be engaged in activities such as designing a mask with unusual facial features, designing half-built houses, or inventing a job interviewer they would like to encounter (Sadow, 1987). At the intermediate and advanced levels, challenging problem-solving activities can be presented that promote interaction and critical thinking through what Sadow (1994) termed *concoctions*. Students are presented with an unusual problem to solve creatively; for example, students might create a new animal, plan model cities, invent a heroine for a country that lacks one, and write plays with happy endings (Sadow, 1994, p. 242). The following is a sample "concoction," the script of which is normally read by the teacher to the students in the target language: "After weeks of hiking through uninhabited, thick woodlands and open prairie, climbing step mountainside, boating down wild rivers and across quiet lakes, you have finally reached the long-sought coast. Your explorations have been a great success, and you expect to be heroes and heroines when you finally return home. But first you must draw a complete map of your travels. Draw your route as accurately as possible, pointing out places that are especially beautiful or especially difficult to cross. Be sure to invent names for all the places you've passed through" (Sadow, 1994, p. 242). Following the reading of the script, comprehension checks are conducted, and students work on the task in groups of three to five for fifteen to forty-five minutes; then each group presents its work to the entire class while designated secretaries record the reporting. Appropriate comments or questions in the whole-class format are then followed by writing activities or interrelated activities in subsequent classes (Sadow, 1994, pp. 250–251). Many kinds of imaginative activities can be based on stories that students have heard or read, and they can recreate and adapt these stories or create their own versions, consistent with the presentational mode of the Communications goal area.[5]

Simulations

Another category of activities through which students combine language use and imagination is the *simulation*. In the world outside the language classroom, job trainees often experience simulations in order to prepare themselves for the real situations they will encounter later (e.g., the airline pilot's training simulator is a mock cockpit that gives the trainee the impression of flying a real airplane) (Crookall & Oxford, 1990a). In the language classroom, a simulation is a mock situation through which participants use their linguistic skills and cultural knowledge to gain a deeper understanding of how communication occurs in the world outside the classroom. Simulation reduces students' level of anxiety by allowing students to make mistakes that might be less acceptable in real-world communication and helps build a positive self-image (Gardner & Lalonde, 1990; Harper, 1985). Simulation strategies enable the teacher to (1) increase motivation and interest, (2) convey and reinforce information, (3) develop language skills, (4) change attitudes, and (5) teach and evaluate language and cultural awareness (Greenblat, 1988). Through simulations, students can also experience the culture of the target language as they interact in the simulation culture (Saunders & Crookall, 1985).

Simulation activities that integrate reading and writing include the writing of letters, resumes, and dialog journals. Letters can consist of genuine writing tasks in which students write letters to editors, ask travel agents for information, make complaints to hospitals or stores, and extend invitations to others (Crookall & Oxford, 1990a). Swain (1994) suggests a simulation activity in which students apply for a job by writing and submitting resumes; a panel of students selects the best applicants for the jobs. In dialog journals, students record their thoughts and feelings and submit their entries to a class journal for possible publication (Crookall & Oxford, 1990a).

---

5. For a wealth of activities designed to promote divergent thinking and language production, consult Sadow (1982).

Simulations also include games and role plays. A game might not represent a game as it occurs in the world outside the classroom, but it might simulate processes such as decision making and problem solving. An example of a simulation/game is the "island game," which Crookall and Oxford describe as follows: "The scene is an island upon which you, the participants, have been marooned. In order to escape from the island you must make decisions on what information to reveal, what destination you wish to go to, whom you wish to go with, and the like. This involves weighing complex sets of data on the above questions as well as on your own and others' personal profiles. There is no single correct solution to the problem" (1990b, p. 253). The game is in three stages: (1) a preparation stage in which participants complete their own personal profiles; (2) the game itself, which involves planning an escape from the island; and (3) the debriefing, or discussion, about the final escape (Crookall & Oxford, 1990a, pp. 253–259). The use of computerized language learning simulation is discussed in Chapter 12.

In a role play (see earlier section in this chapter), participants take on and act out specified roles within some simulated aspect of a real social situation. Role plays are always a type of simulation, but simulations do not necessarily have to involve role play. The tasks involved in conducting classroom simulations and games include presenting new language, preparing students for the task, setting up the task, giving instructions, organizing and managing groups, establishing the teacher's role, and evaluating the task after it is completed.

Speaking and the Study of Literature and Culture

In Chapters 6 and 7, you explored strategies for guiding students through oral and written texts and using these texts as springboards for discussion and creative extension activities. One of the advantages to the interactive model for teaching listening and reading presented in Chapter 6 is that it helps students understand the text and feel comfortable with it *before* being asked to engage in creative speaking. The difficulty students often experience in trying to discuss readings, particularly literary texts, is that their reading level is usually higher than their speaking level. Therefore, they cannot communicate orally in the same style or at the same level as the text. The interactive model compensates for this difference in skill level by encouraging students to express their thoughts in their own words or at their own speaking level, while using parts of the text prose for additional support. Breiner-Sanders (1991) suggests that, when beginning to use reading as a basis for conversation, teachers select reading materials that are targeted more closely to students' speaking level, in order to help them gain confidence in discussing texts. Iandoli describes an approach to teaching oral communication with literature study that includes the following activities:

1. extensive pre-reading discussion in groups to enable students to make predictions about the text;

2. group discussion of the text and development of text interpretations;

3. brief oral synopses or interpretations of the reading without notes;

4. personalized questions and answers;

5. text-specific questions and answers;

6. dramatic reenactment of the text (Iandoli, 1991, pp. 481–484).

The sample progress indicators of the *SFLL* offer ideas for integrating speaking with the study of literature and culture. Elementary school students can tell or retell stories orally or in writing. Students in the middle grades can prepare oral or written stories or summaries of plot and characters of age-appropriate literature. High school students can create stories or poems, short plays, or skits based on personal experiences and exposure to themes, ideas, and perspectives from the target culture. In this way, the performance of learners in a presentational mode weaves together culture and literature (NSFLEP, 1996, pp. 41–42; see also Appendix 3.1).

Sadow (1987) suggests the use of simulations or reenactment of scenes from a literary passage or historical event as a strategy for integrating speaking with the study of literature and history. According to Cazden (1992), reenactments or performance activities stimulate discussion as the groups plan and decide upon an interpretation of the text, and then later, in the post-performance discussion when the small groups' interpretive decisions are explained and compared.[6] These activities provide opportunities for students to use the target language in preparing their reenactments while interacting with the text and assimilating text language into their linguistic repertoire.

Undoubtedly, students cannot be taught to communicate effectively without an understanding of the target culture. *Teacher's Handbook* advocates the close integration of culture and contextualized language use. Chapters 3 and 5 present ways to integrate culture in the curriculum planning and lesson design processes.[7] In Chapters 6 and 7, you explored ways in which culture can be integrated in an initial authentic context—story, conversation, written text—and used as the basis for communication. Chapters 9 and 11 will present additional ideas for integrating culture with writing and testing, respectively.

In Chapter 6 you were introduced to Galloway's (1992) four-stage model for guiding students through an authentic text for the purpose of cross-cultural discovery. In the fourth stage, *integrating*, students might use speaking as they transfer and reflect on cultural information and insights acquired through the first three stages. Sample integrating task formats are that students:

- role play a scenario using appropriate cultural and linguistic protocols, given the context;
- verbally support or refute a position from the point of view of a native from the target culture, using citations from an authentic text;
- debate an issue from the viewpoints of both the native and target cultures;
- analyze a possible target language utterance by determining the likelihood that it would have been said at all and identifying the type of speaker from whom it might have come; and
- respond to open-ended questions relating to cultural information they discovered in an authentic text.

(Galloway, 1992, pp. 120–121)

A series of cross-level collaborative projects was recently undertaken to address the standards in classroom practice (Phillips, 1997). Two of the projects exemplify how speaking can be effectively integrated into exploration of cultures, comparisons of language and

---

6. For an extensive treatment of simulation/gaming activities, consult Crookall and Oxford (1990a).

7. You might find it helpful to review the strategies for teaching culture presented in Chapter 5.

cultures, communication with native speakers, connections to other disciplines, and interaction with target language communities. Haas and Reardon (1997) designed and taught an interdisciplinary unit on Chile to a seventh-grade Spanish class.[8] Speaking was integrated in various ways as students (1) discussed in Spanish slides and literary texts (including poetry) dealing with Chile; (2) presented oral reports on Chile based on research; (3) interviewed a guest informant from Chile; and (4) as a culminating activity, visited a Chilean bakery in their local community and interacted with the store owners in Spanish making purchases, asking questions about a food preparation demonstration, etc. (See the Chapter 10 video segment on the *Teacher's Handbook* web site for the bakery visit.) Schwartz and Kavanaugh (1997) taught a unit on immigration to a ninth-grade Spanish class through the study of conditions in Guatemala and the viewing of various video materials. Speaking was incorporated by means of (1) oral presentations on library research completed dealing with various aspects of Guatemalan culture; (2) discussion of video segments *(El norte)*; (3) role plays from video scenes; (4) interviewing a Guatemalan informant; (5) debate on immigration to the United States.

Providing Useful Feedback in Speaking Activities

The type of feedback that language teachers have traditionally given students has been in response to the correctness of language use. A "very good" awarded by the teacher undoubtedly means that the student used accurate grammar, vocabulary, and/or pronunciation, or used the designated linguistic pattern being practiced. Oral feedback given by the teacher in the classroom can generally be of two types: (1) error correction and (2) response to the content of the student's message, much as in natural conversation. In classrooms that focus on negotiation of meaning (as defined in Chapter 1), the teacher includes feedback that helps learners figure out meaning, make themselves understood, and develop strategies for interacting effectively in groups (Platt & Brooks, 1994).

 In Chapter 3, what did the discussion of IRE/IRF reveal about the nature of teacher feedback?

Summarizing the research since 1970, Mings drew these four conclusions about error correction: (1) different types of errors are made by learners; (2) they do not all produce identical consequences; (3) they originate from a variety of causes; and (4) learner errors serve a very useful purpose in interlanguage development (1993, p. 176). Some researchers (Vigil & Oller, 1976) maintain that lack of error correction may lead to fossilization, or aspects of the interlanguage that are never eliminated. On the other hand, Terrell (1985) posited that correcting students' errors directly does not help them correct their mistakes in the future, may frustrate students, and may cause them to focus on language form rather than on meaning. Lightbown and Spada affirm that within a communicative contextual base, form-focus activities and correction in context is beneficial (1990, p. 443).

---

8. A key component of this project was that students corresponded to Chilean keypals by means of e-mail letters.

In a recent study with French immersion students in grades four and five, Lyster and Ranta (1997) examined the effect of teacher correction strategies on student *uptake,* that is, how the student incorporates teacher feedback into subsequent utterances. There are two types of student uptake: (a) uptake that results in "repair" of the error which the feedback addressed and (b) uptake that results in an utterance that is still in need of repair (Lyster & Ranta, 1997, p. 49). Students demonstrate uptake through repetition of the teacher's feedback that includes the correct form, incorporation of the correct form (provided by the teacher) into a longer utterance, self-correction, and peer correction. Lyster and Ranta (1997) believe that student-generated repairs may help learners to retrieve target language knowledge that already exists in some form and may help them to revise their hypotheses about the target language.

The Lyster and Ranta study identified six types of teacher feedback:

1. *explicit correction:* The teacher corrects the student, indicating clearly that what the student said was incorrect (e.g., "You should say . . . ").

2. *recasts:* The teacher reformulates all or part of a student's utterance minus the error. Recasts are implicit and are not introduced by "You should say . . . "; they may focus on one word, grammatical modification, or translation of the student's use of L1 (e.g., S: "I go not to the movies last night." T: "Oh, you *didn't go* to the movies last night.").

3. *clarification requests:* The teacher identifies a problem in either comprehensibility or accuracy or both, using phrases such as "Pardon me?" or "What do you mean by X?"

4. *metalinguistic feedback:* The teacher makes comments or asks questions about the form of the student's utterance without providing the correct form. These comments indicate that there is an error somewhere (e.g., "Can you find your error?" or "It isn't said in that way.") This feedback includes some grammatical metalanguage that refers to the nature of the error (e.g., "It's masculine").

5. *elicitation:* The teacher repeats part of the student's utterance and pauses to allow the student to complete the utterance at the place where the error occurred (e.g., S: "I had already went to the library." T: "I had already _____."); the teacher uses questions to elicit correct forms (e.g., "How do we say 'X' in French?"); or the teacher asks students to reformulate their utterance.

6. *repetition:* The teacher repeats the student's erroneous utterance, usually changing the intonation to highlight the error (e.g., S: ". . . many money." T: ". . . *many* money?").

(Lyster & Ranta, 1997, pp. 46–48)

The teachers in Lyster and Ranta's (1997) study used recasts more than any other strategy for correcting errors (fifty-five percent of the time), with the other strategies occurring in the following order of decreasing frequency: elicitation (fourteen percent), clarification request (eleven percent), metalinguistic feedback (eight percent), explicit correction (seven percent), and repetition (five percent). Interestingly, recast was the strategy that proved least likely to lead to uptake: only thirty-one percent of the recast strategies led students to make attempts at repairing their utterances. Explicit correction led to uptake only fifty percent of the time. Clarification requests, metalinguistic feedback, and repetition were effective strategies for eliciting uptake from students (eighty-eight percent, eighty-six percent, and seventy-eight percent, respectively). The most effective strategy with respect to uptake was elicitation: in all cases elicitation led to uptake (Lyster & Ranta, 1997).

A strategy such as a clarification request focuses on the message while signaling to the student that there is a problem, most likely due to a grammatical or vocabulary error. The following is an example of an exchange between a Spanish teacher and a student where a clarification request is made by the teacher:

Teacher: Estoy cansada hoy, clase. Trabajé hasta muy tarde anoche. ¿Qué hicieron Uds. anoche? Sí, Susana, ¿qué hiciste tú? [I'm very tired today, class. I worked until very late last night. What did all of you do last night? Yes, Susana, what did you do?]

Student: Pues, tú no hiciste nada. [Well, you didn't do anything.]

Teacher: ¿Quién? ¿Yo? Sí, yo hice mucho anoche. [Who? Me? Yes, I did a lot last night.]

Student: ¡Oh! Yo no hice nada. [Oh! I didn't do anything.]

In this exchange, the focus on form happened in a meaningful context, as it resulted from misunderstanding. It was not arbitrary or dependent on the teacher's hidden grammatical agenda. When errors are treated in this way, students must think about what went wrong in communication while they are developing strategies for negotiating meaning.

In highly communicative or group activities, the teacher might do best to keep a mental note of patterns of errors and use them as the focus for subsequent language activities. Kramsch (1987) suggests extensive use of natural feedback rather than overpraising everything students say. Statements such as "Yes, that's interesting," "I can certainly understand that!" "That's incredible!" and "Hmm, that's right" show students that you are listening to what they're saying, and this strategy encourages students to focus more on meaning. When conversing with the class as a follow-up to group interaction, Kramsch (1987) also proposes that teachers give students explicit credit for their contributions by quoting them ("As X just said, . . ."). In this way, teachers are not taking credit for what students have said by using it to suggest their own ideas.

At more advanced levels of study, where one of the goals is to refine language use, students can be given increasingly greater responsibility for their accuracy. The following are a few ideas that merit further research:

- peer editing of oral language samples: The teacher records role plays or situations that students enact in the classroom, after which pairs of students listen to the tapes in order to correct linguistic errors and identify ways to improve their message's content.
- teacher feedback: At certain designated times throughout the year or semester, perhaps following speaking exams, the teacher might give helpful feedback to each student concerning progress made in speaking. This feedback would include patterns of errors that merit attention, with specific suggestions on how to improve accuracy.
- error tracking system: As a class group, students listen to tapes of themselves and, with the teacher's help, compile a listing of the kinds of errors they hear. They focus on eliminating certain errors over a specified period of time and agree on a system to check and reward their efforts.

Clearly, a great deal of research is still needed in order to understand more fully the role of oral feedback. The research presented here points to the following implications regarding error correction and feedback in the classroom:

1. Students benefit most when the feedback they receive focuses on comprehensibility of the message itself, not just on accuracy of form.

2. The feedback strategies that lead to negotiation of form most effectively are elicitation, clarification requests, metalinguistic feedback, and repetition.

3. Student-generated repairs may help learners to access target language forms and revise hypotheses about the target language.

4. In order to focus on fluency and comprehensibility of speech, it is best to avoid trying to coerce correction of errors in speaking and to allow the interaction to develop as it would in natural discourse.

5. Teacher feedback should include comments that help the student to focus on negotiation of meaning.

6. Students should be made increasingly more responsible for their language accuracy so that their oral proficiency can improve.

This chapter presented many ideas for developing oral skills in the interpersonal and presentational modes. Keep in mind that the approach of *Teacher's Handbook* is that all three modes should be integrated closely, as described in the model presented in Chapter 6.

Teach and Reflect

Episode One

Creating Information-Gap Activities for Various Levels of Instruction

Create the following information-gap activities in the language you teach, according to the following instructions:

1. Elementary school level: Design an information-gap activity that would be appropriate for elementary school children. You might create this for the content-based lesson you designed in the **Teach and Reflect** section of Chapter 4, or you could create it for practice within another context. Decide what the purpose of the activity is and how it relates to your unit objectives. Include specific directions for students and your procedure for grouping students; that is, what will you do if you don't have an even number? Your instructor may ask you to present your activity to the class.

2. Secondary school level: Using a chapter from a textbook suggested by your instructor, create an information-gap activity to provide speaking interaction among your students. Decide what the purpose of the activity is and how it relates to your chapter or unit objectives. What functions/contexts will students practice? What grammar and vocabulary are integrated? Include specific

directions for students and your procedure for grouping students; that is, what will you do if you don't have an even number? Your instructor may ask you to present your activity to the class.

Episode Two

Integrating Speaking with Oral or Written Texts

For this activity, you will work from the authentic reading or taped segment that you prepared in the **Teach and Reflect** section of Chapter 7. Another option is to work with a literary reading, such as a short story. Design three activities for integrating speaking as a follow-up to exploration of the oral or written text:

1. an interactive activity, such as a movement activity, paired interview, or role play

2. an imaginative activity, such as changing the text or reenacting a part of the text

3. a culture-based activity, such as a culture minidrama or culture capsule

Identify the objective of each activity and the communicative mode (interpersonal, presentational, or combination). Include instructions to the students and your procedure for grouping students, if applicable. Your instructor may ask you to present one or more of these activities to the class.

Discuss and Reflect

Case Study I

Defining Groups for Cooperative Learning Activities

Today is the first of four teacher work/in-service days for Hans Klaus in the new school year. His principal, Mark Henry, called him in July to tell him that he would have a combined class of German II (fifteen students) and German III (five students). Although he tried to convince him to establish two separate classes, using every pedagogically sound argument he could think of, the principal could not change the situation, except by not offering German III at all. Mr. Klaus rejected that choice, of course.

Now, as he ponders the class list, he is thinking about how he will handle the two ability levels of the class, especially in speaking tasks. Mr. Klaus regularly assigns his students short speaking tasks that can be completed in pairs or small groups—sometimes as many as four tasks during a class period. How, he asks himself, will a German III student be able to talk with a German II student? Then, as he recalls the performance of the students on the class list in last year's German classes, he realizes that more than two levels are represented in the class anyway. For speaking tasks, he decides to organize the students into groups of four or five for role playing and other activities. Following is the class list, with students' proficiency level, German class level, and German grade.

STUDENT NAME	PROFICIENCY LEVEL IN SPEAKING	GERMAN CLASS LEVEL	GERMAN GRADE LAST YEAR	GROUP
John	Novice low	German II	D+	Group A
Marie	Novice low	German II	B-	Group B
Kayla	Novice low	German II	A	Group C
Jihae	Novice low	German II	C+	Group D
Sabrina	Novice high	German II	B+	Group E
Sally	Novice high	German II	A-	Group E
Carola	Novice high	German II	A+	Group D
Andrey	Int. low	German II	A+	Group C
Flower	Int. low	German II	B+	Group B
Saleh	Int. low	German II	C+	Group A
Gary	Int. mid.	German II	C-	Group A
Constanza	Int. mid.	German II	C+	Group B
Jasmine	Int. mid.	German II	B	Group C
Kim	Int. mid.	German II	A-	Group D
Diego	Int. high	German II	B+	Group E
Yvonne	Int. low	German III	A-	Group E
Colette	Int. mid.	German III	B	Group D
Kitao	Int. mid.	German III	B	Group C
Chiang	Int. high	German III	A-	Group B
Lisbeth	Int. high	German III	A	Group A

Ask yourself these questions:

1. What reasons do you think the principal might have had for setting up the schedule this way?

2. What are some of the pedagogically sound arguments Mr. Klaus might have used to convince Mr. Henry that the two German classes should not have been combined?

3. How did Mr. Klaus define his groups?

4. What are some likely student reactions?

5. What reasons can you give for organizing groups in this fashion?

To prepare the case:

- Consult Slavin (1986), Slavin (1987), Sharan and Shaulov (1990), or Szostek (1994) for additional details about grouping students for cooperative learning tasks.
- Read Ur (1981) to find ways to build discussions in groups.
- Interview an experienced teacher in any discipline who regularly conducts cooperative learning activities. Find out how s/he groups students.
- Interview an experienced foreign language teacher who has a combined class with two different levels. Find out how s/he approaches language instruction in this situation.

To prepare for class discussion, think and write about these topics:

Mr. Klaus grouped his students on the basis of their previous grades in German and on their oral proficiency levels. Describe other variables you would take into consideration as you are placing your students into groups.

Now describe how you might deal with two different language levels in the same class (levels III and IV, for example). What types of oral activities might be particularly beneficial in this situation?

Case Study 2

Friday Is Culture Day

Mrs. Beecher has been teaching Spanish and social studies at Pelican High School for eight years. Her approach to teaching Spanish is essentially communicative in nature, as she involves her students in meaningful interaction with one another. She occasionally uses cooperative learning in her classes, although she is still experimenting with various techniques. Mrs. Beecher travels to Hispanic countries frequently and brings back materials, such as slides, posters, magazines, and realia that she can use in her classes.

Today is Friday and a rather chaotic day, because students are having their individual and club pictures taken for the yearbook. Because Mrs. Beecher realizes that she can accomplish very little today in terms of serious work, she decides to pull out her slides from Peru and show them to her classes. Since she visited the country, she has much that she can tell students about the scenes depicted on the slides.

After her first-period Spanish II class entered her classroom, Mrs. Beecher explained that she would be showing slides from Peru while describing them in Spanish. She asked students to take notes on the presentation, because afterward she would ask them questions. After her twenty-five minute slide presentation, Mrs. Beecher began asking questions. She was amazed and a little upset when she discovered that students had not taken notes as she had instructed and could not answer most of her questions.

Ask yourself these questions:

1. What was Mrs. Beecher's real objective in presenting the slide demonstration?

2. What might this lesson indicate about Mrs. Beecher's approach to teaching culture?

3. Mrs. Beecher thought that no serious work could be done today. What do you think she meant by *serious*? Was she justified in thinking this?

4. Why do you think the students failed to take notes during the slide presentation?

5. What are some possible students' reactions to Mrs. Beecher's activity?

To prepare the case:

- Read Schwartz and Kavanaugh (1997) and Haas and Reardon (1997) for information on approaches to integrating cultures and the other standards into language teaching.
- Read Chapter 8 of Curtain and Pesola (1994), which deals with experiencing culture in the classroom.
- Read Walz (1996) to find ways to incorporate information-gap activities with a cultural lesson.
- Interview an experienced social studies teacher to learn about strategies s/he uses for teaching students about other cultures.

To prepare for class discussion, think and write about these topics:

- If you were Mrs. Beecher, how might you (1) integrate this slide presentation into classroom work on a given unit; and (2) use cooperative learning as a strategy for helping students understand and discuss the information given in the presentation?
- What are some ways that Mrs. Beecher might use her skill in teaching social studies as a vehicle for integrating culture into her Spanish curriculum?
- What might you do with your classes on a day similar to Mrs. Beecher's chaotic Friday?
- Now choose a cultural concept and design one task that addresses the interpersonal mode and one task that addresses the presentational standard of the Communication Goal Area, using spoken language production.

References

Alatis, J. E., & Barnhardt, S. B. (1998). *Portfolio assessment in the foreign language classroom.* National Capital Language Resource Center. Washington, D.C.: Georgetown Univ./Center for Applied Linguistics.

Bassano, S., & Christison, M. A. (1987). Developing successful conversation groups. In M. H. Long & J. C. Richards (Eds.), *Methodology in TESOL: A book of readings* (pp. 201–207). New York: Newbury House/Harper.

Bonin, T., & Birckbichler, D. (1975). Real communication through conversation cards. *The Modern Language Journal, 59,* 22–25.

Bragger, J. (1985). The development of oral proficiency. In A. Omaggio, (Ed.), *Proficiency, curriculum, articulation: The ties that bind*, Northeast Conference Reports (pp. 41–75). Middlebury, VT: Northeast Conference on the Teaching of Foreign Languages.

Breiner-Sanders, K. E. (1991). Higher-level language abilities: The skills connection. In J. K. Phillips (Ed.), *Building Bridges and Making Connections*, Northeast Conference Reports (pp. 57–88). Middlebury, VT: Northeast Conference on the Teaching of Foreign Languages.

Brooks, F. B. (1990). Foreign language learning: A social interaction perspective. In B. VanPatten & J. F. Lee (Eds.), *Second language acquisition—Foreign language learning* (pp. 153–169). Clevedon, UK: Multilingual Matters.

Brooks, F. B. (1992). Can we talk? *Foreign Language Annals, 25,* 59–71.

Brooks, F. B., & Donato, R. (1994). Vygotskyan approaches to understanding foreign language learner discourse during communicative tasks. *Hispania, 77,* 262–274.

Brooks, F. B., Donato, R., McGlone, V. (1997). When are they going to say "it" right? Understanding learner talk during pair-work activity. *Foreign Language Annals, 30,* 524–541.

Cazden, C. B. (1992). Performing expository texts in the foreign language classroom. In C. Kramsch & S. McConnell-Ginet (Eds.), *Text and context—Cross disciplinary perspectives on language study* (pp. 67–78). Lexington, MA: Heath.

Cook, L. (1991). Cooperative learning: A successful college teaching strategy. *Innovative Higher Education, 16,* 27–38.

Crookall, D., & Oxford, R. L. (1990a). *Simulation, gaming, and language learning.* New York: Newbury House.

Crookall, D., & Oxford, R. L. (1990b). The island game. In D. Crookall & R. L. Oxford (Eds.), *Simulation, gaming, and language learning* (pp. 251–259). New York: Newbury House.

Crookes, G., & Gass, S. M. (Eds.). (1993a). *Tasks and language learning: Integrating theory and practice.* Clevedon, UK: Multilingual Matters.

Crookes, G., & Gass, S. M. (Eds.). (1993b). *Tasks in a pedagogical context: Integrating theory and practice.* Clevedon, UK: Multilingual Matters.

Curtain, H. A., & Pesola, C. A. (1994). *Languages and children: Making the match.* Reading, MA: Addison-Wesley.

DiPietro, R. J. (1987). *Strategic interaction: Learning languages through scenarios.* New York: Cambridge University Press.

Donato, R. (1992). Personal communication with the authors.

Donato, R., & Brooks, F. B. (1994). *Looking across collaborative tasks: Capturing L2 discourse development.* Paper presented at the annual meeting of the American Association for Applied Linguistics, March, Baltimore, MD.

Doughty, C., & Pica, T. (1986). Information gap tasks: Do they facilitate acquisition? *TESOL Quarterly, 20,* 315–326.

Dreke, M., & Lind, W. (1986). *Wechselspiel.* New York: Langenscheidt.

Ellis, R. (1990). *Instructed second language acquisition.* Cambridge, MA: Blackwell.

Fall, T. (1991). Personal communication.

Fleak, K. (1992). Moving toward accuracy: Using the student monitor sheet with communicative activities. *Foreign Language Annals, 25,* 173–178.

Fotos, S., & Ellis, R. (1991). Communicating about grammar: A task-based approach. *TESOL Quarterly 25,* 605–628.

Freed, B., & Bauer, B. W. (1989). *Contextos: Spanish for communication.* New York: Newbury House.

Freed, B., & Knutson, E. (1989). *Contextes: French for communication.* New York: Newbury House.

Fried-Booth, D. L. (1986). *Project work.* New York: Oxford University Press.

Gaier, S. J. (1985). *Peer involvement in language learning.* Orlando, FL: Harcourt Brace Jovanovich.

Galloway, V. (1992). Toward a cultural reading of authentic texts. In H. Byrnes (Ed.), *Languages for a multicultural world in transition,* Northeast Conference Reports (pp. 87–121). Lincolnwood, IL: NTC/Contemporary Publishing Group.

Gardner, R. C., & Lalonde, R. (1990). Social psychological considerations. In D. Crookall & R. L. Oxford (Eds.), *Simulation, gaming, and language learning* (pp. 215–221). New York: Newbury House.

Gass, S. M., & Magnan, S. S. (1993). Second-language production: SLA research in speaking and writing. In A. O. Hadley (Ed.), *Research in language learning* (pp. 156–197). Lincolnwood, IL: NTC/Contemporary Publishing Group.

Glisan, E. W., & Foltz, D. A. (1998). Assessing students' oral proficiency in an outcome-based curriculum: Student performance and teacher intuitions. *The Modern Language Journal, 82,* 1–18.

Goldenberg, C. (1991). *Instructional conversations and their classroom implication.* Washington, D. C.: The National Center for Research on Cultural Diversity and Second Language Learning.

Greenblat, C. S. (1988). *Designing games and simulations: An illustrated handbook.* Newbury Park, CA: Sage.

Haas, M., & Reardon, M. (1997). Communities of learners: From New York to Chile. In J. K. Phillips (Ed.), *Collaborations: Meeting new goals, new realities,* Northeast Conference Reports (pp. 213–241). Lincolnwood, IL: NTC/Contemporary Publishing Group.

Hadfield, J. (1984). *Elementary communication games. A collection of games and activities for elementary students of English.* Walton-on-Thames: Thomas Nelson.

Hadley, A. O. (1993). *Teaching language in context.* Boston, MA: Heinle & Heinle.

Hall, J. K. (1999). The communication standards. In J. K. Phillips & R. M. Terry (Eds.), *Foreign language standards: Linking research, theories, and practices,* ACTFL Foreign Language Education Series (pp. 15–56). Lincolnwood, IL: NTC/Contemporary Publishing Group.

Harper, S. N. (1985). Social psychological effects of simulation in foreign language learning. *System 13,* 219–224.

Hatch, E. (1978). Discourse analysis and second language acquisition. In E. Hatch (Ed.), *Second language acquisition* (pp. 401–435). Rowley, MA: Newbury House.

Honeycutt, C. A., & Vernon, N. D. (1985). Who should be asking the questions in the second language classroom? In P. Westphal (Ed.), *Meeting the call for excellence in the foreign language classroom* (pp. 38–42). Lincolnwood, IL: NTC/Contemporary Publishing Group.

Huebner, T., & Jensen, A. (1992). A study of foreign language proficiency-based testing in secondary schools. *Foreign Language Annals, 25,* 105–115.

Iandoli, L. J. (1991). Improving oral communications in an interactive literature course. *Foreign Language Annals, 24,* 479–486.

Johnson, D. D., & Johnson, R. T. (1987). *Learning together and alone: Cooperation, competition, and individualization.* Englewood Cliffs, NJ: Prentice Hall.

Johnson, D. D., Johnson, R. T., & Holubec, E. J. (1988). *Cooperation in the classroom.* Edina, MN: Interaction Book Company.

Johnson, K. (1979). Communicative approaches and communicative processes. In C. J. Brumfit & K. Johnson (Eds.), *The communicative approach to language teaching* (pp. 192–205). Oxford: Oxford University Press.

Kagan, S. (1989). *Cooperative learning: Resources for teachers.* San Juan Capistrano, CA: Resources for Teachers.

Keller, E., & Warner, S. T. (1979). *Gambits 1: Openers; Gambits 2: Links; Gambits 3: Responders, closers and inventory.* Hull, Canada: Public Service Commission of Canada.

Kinginger, C. (1990). *Task variation and classroom learner discourse.* Unpublished doctoral dissertation. University of Illinois: Urbana-Champaign.

Kinginger, C. (1994). Learner initiative in conversation management: An application of van Lier's pilot coding scheme. *The Modern Language Journal, 78,* 29–40.

Knop, C. K. (1986). Workshop handout. Concordia College. Moorhead, MN.

Kohn, A. (1987). It's hard to get out of a pair—Profile: David & Roger Johnson. *Psychology Today,* (October): 53–57.

Kramsch, C. (1987). Interactive discourse in small and large groups. In W. Rivers (Ed.), *Interactive language teaching* (pp. 17–30). Cambridge: Cambridge University Press.

Krashen, S. (1982). *Principles and practice in second language acquisition.* New York: Pergamon Press.

Lee, J. (1995). Using task-based instruction to restructure class discussions. *Foreign Language Annals, 28,* 437–446.

Lightbown, P. M., & Spada, N. (1990). Focus on form and corrective feedback in communicative language teaching. *Studies in Second Language Acquisition, 12,* 429–448.

Liskin-Gasparro, J. E. (1987). If you can't use a language, you don't know a language. *Middlebury Magazine,* (Winter): 26–27.

Liskin-Gasparro, J. E. (1996). Circumlocution, communication strategies, and the ACTFL proficiency guidelines: An analysis of student discourse. *Foreign Language Annals, 29,* 317–330.

Long, M. H. (1983). Native speaker/non-native speaker conversation in the second language classroom. In M. A. Clarke & J. Handscomb (Eds.), *On TESOL '82: Pacific perspectives on language learning and teaching* (pp. 207–205). Washington, D.C.: TESOL.

Long, M. H., & Crookes, G. (1986). Intervention points in second language classroom processes. Paper presented at RELC Seminar, Singapore.

Lyster, R., & Ranta, L. (1997). Corrective feedback and learner uptake. *Studies in Second Language Acquisition, 19,* 37–61.

Magnan, S. S. (1986). Assessing speaking proficiency in the undergraduate curriculum: Data from French. *Foreign Language Annals, 19,* 429–438.

Mings, R. C. (1993). Changing perspectives on the utility of error correction in second language acquisition. *Foreign Language Annals, 26,* 171–179.

National Standards in Foreign Language Education Project. (1996). *National standards for foreign language learning: Preparing for the 21st century.* Lawrence, KS: Allen Press.

Norman, U. (1996). Promoting spontaneous speech in the EFL class. *Foreign Language Annals, 29,* 597–604.

Oxford, R. L. (1992). Encouraging initiative and interest through the cooperative 'Heritage Project.' *Northeast Conference on the Teaching of Foreign Languages Newsletter, 32,* 13–16.

Pennsylvania Department of Education. (1993). *Pennsylvania Bulletin, 23,* 35–54.

Patthey-Chavez, G. G., Clare, L., & Gallimore, R. (1995). Creating a community of scholarship with instructional conversations in a transitional bilingual classroom. Washington, D.C.: The National Center for Research on Cultural Diversity and Second Language Learning.

Phillips, J. K. (Ed.). *Collaborations: Meeting new goals, new realities.* Northeast Conference Reports. Lincolnwood, IL: NTC/Contemporary Publishing Group.

Platt, E., & Brooks, F. B. (1994). The acquisition-rich environment revisited. *The Modern Language Journal, 78,* 497–511.

Porter, P. A. (1986). How learners talk to each other: Input and interaction in task-centered discussions. In R. Day (Ed.), *Talking to learn: Conversation in second language acquisition* (pp. 200–224). Rowley, MA: Newbury House.

Richard-Amato, P. A. (1988). *Making it happen—Interaction in the second language classroom.* New York: Longman.

Richards, J. (1985). *The context of language teaching.* Cambridge: Cambridge University Press.

Richards, J., Platt, J., & Weber, H. (1985). *Longman dictionary of applied linguistics.* New York: Longman.

Rollman, M. (1994). The communicative language teaching "revolution" tested: A comparison of two classroom studies: 1976 and 1993. *Foreign Language Annals, 27,* 221–233.

Rueda, R., Goldenberg, C. & Gallimore, R. (1992). *Rating instructional conversations: A guide.* Washington, D. C.: The National Center for Research on Cultural Diversity and Language Learning.

Sadow, S. A. (1982). *Idea bank: Creative activities for the language class.* Rowley, MA: Newbury House.

Sadow, S. A. (1987). Speaking and listening: Imaginative activities for the language class. In W. M. Rivers (Ed.), *Interactive language teaching* (pp. 33–43). Cambridge: Cambridge University Press.

Sadow, S. A. (1994). "Concoctions": Intrinsic motivation, creative thinking, frame theory, and structured interactions in the language class. *Foreign Language Annals, 27,* 241–251.

Saunders, D., & Crookall, D. (1985). Playing with a second language. *Simulation games for learning, 15*(4), 166–172 .

Scarcella, R. C., & Oxford, R. L. (1992). *The tapestry of language learning.* Boston, MA: Heinle & Heinle.

Schwartz, A. M., & Kavanaugh, M. S. (1997). Addressing the culture goal with authentic video. In J. K. Phillips (Ed.), *Collaborations: Meeting new goals, new realities,* Northeast Conference Reports (pp. 97–139). Lincolnwood, IL: NTC/Contemporary Publishing Group.

Sharan, S., & Shaulov, A. (1990). Cooperative learning, motivating to learn and academic achievement. In S. Sharan (Ed.), *Cooperative learning: Theory and research* (pp. 173–177). New York: Praeger.

Slavin, R. E. (1986). *Using student team learning.* Baltimore, MD: Johns Hopkins University Press.

Slavin, R. E. (1987). Cooperative learning and the cooperative school. *Educational Leadership, 45*(3), 7–13.

Swain, M. (1994). Large-scale communicative language testing: A case study. In S. Savignon & M. Berns (Eds.), *Initiatives in communicative language teaching: A book of readings* (pp. 185–201). Reading, MA: Addison-Wesley.

Swender, E. (1999). *ACTFL oral proficiency interview tester training manual.* Yonkers, NY: ACTFL.

Szostek, C. (1994). Assessing the effects of cooperative learning in an honors foreign language classroom. *Foreign Language Annals, 27,* 252–261.

Taylor, B. P. (1983). Teaching ESL: Incorporating a communicative, student-centered component. *TESOL Quarterly, 17,* 69–88.

Terrell, T. (1982). The natural approach to language teaching: An update. *The Modern Language Journal, 66,* 121–132.

Terrell, T. (1985). The natural approach to language teaching: An update. *The Canadian Modern Language Review, 41,* 461–479.

Tharp, R. G., & Gallimore, R. (1988). *Rousing minds to life: Teaching, learning, and schooling in social context.* New York: Cambridge University Press.

Thompson, I. (1996). Assessing foreign language skills: Data from Russian. *The Modern Language Journal, 80,* 47–65.

Tschirner, E. (1992). Oral proficiency base lines for first- and second-year college German. *Die Unterrichtspraxis, 25,* 10–14.

Ur, P. (1981). *Discussions that work: Task-centred fluency practice.* Cambridge: Cambridge University Press.

Vigil, N., & Oller, J. W. (1976). Rule fossilization: A tentative model. *Language Learning, 26,* 281–295.

Vygotsky, L. (1978). *Mind in society: The development of higher psychological processes.* Cambridge, MA: Harvard University Press.

Walz, J. (1996). The classroom dynamics of information-gap activities. *Foreign Language Annals, 29,* 481–494.

Wells, G. (1985). *Language development in the pre-school years.* Cambridge: Cambridge University Press.

thandbook.
heinle.com

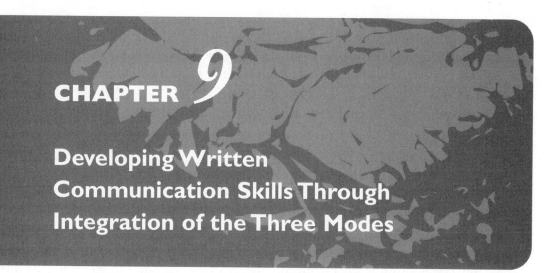

CHAPTER *9*

Developing Written Communication Skills Through Integration of the Three Modes

In this chapter you will learn about:

- writing as a tool for communicating and learning
- nature of the writing process
- relationship between writing and learning
- writing across the three modes of communication K–12 +
- proficiency-oriented writing

- task-oriented writing
- framework for teaching writing as a process
- the role of homework
- interactive homework
- responding to writing
- peer revision
- scoring methods for evaluating writing

Teach and Reflect: Designing an Interactive Homework Assignment for Elementary or Middle School Learners; Designing a Writing Activity for Secondary Levels or Beyond

- **Case Study 1: A Writing Assignment that Doesn't Work**
- **Case Study 2: Integrating Peer Revision into the Writing Process**

Conceptual Orientation

Rodby, in reviewing the influence of Chomsky, Vygotsky, Krashen, and others on our views of language and writing, affirms that "because language is thought, writing is a thinking process; because language acquisition unfolds in the individual, writing is also an individual process; because language is speech, writing is a secondary code, a representation of speech" (1992, p. 25). Since writing is often used as a tool for communication with others and is often created together with others, it can also be a social process (see discussion on mediation in Chapter 1). Traditionally writing in the foreign language curriculum has focused on the writing *product*, emphasizing the development of grammatical and syntactic accuracy (Kern & Schultz, 1992). Current research, however, supports more of a focus on the writing *process*,[1] that is, the steps involved in producing a written text, as well as the writing *product* which is the written text created by the writer (Barnett, 1989; Kern & Schultz, 1992; Scott, 1996). The present challenge for foreign language teachers is to integrate writing into language instruction right from the start, since students will benefit from the discovery that occurs as they compose using the target language (Scott, 1995). The *SFLL* provide a framework for teaching written communication skills through integration of the three modes of communication.

The Nature of Writing in the Foreign Language

❏ L1 and L2 Writing

Since the research in FL writing has been scant at best, much of what we know about it is based largely on research in L1 and ESL writing (Henry, 1996; Scott, 1996). In 1981, Flower and Hayes proposed a comprehensive problem-solving model of the L1 writing process, which has since been applied to L2 writing instruction. Their model attempts to explain the diverse set of thought processes in which writers engage while writing:

- *Planning:* Writers form an internal, abstract representation of the knowledge that will be used in writing. This involves subprocesses such as *generating ideas, organizing thoughts*, and *setting goals* for writing. Generating ideas includes retrieving information from long-term memory, grouping ideas, and forming new concepts. Organization of thoughts is often guided by the setting of goals. For example, a procedural goal such as "I'll start with a definition of the term . . ." will determine how the writer organizes his/her thoughts while composing (Lee & VanPatten, 1995). The nature of the goal is very important and affects the quality of the written product. If a writer's goal is to write a certain number of words rather than to appeal to the interest of the reader, for instance, the quality of the product might be different. Goal setting may account for some of the differences between more successful and less successful writers (Lee & VanPatten, 1995).
- *Translating:* Writers put ideas into language. They must decide to which aspects they will consciously attend, for example, grammar, spelling, organization.
- *Reviewing:* Writers *revise* and *evaluate* their writing by reading, examining, changing, and correcting the text. They make *surface changes* (changes that do not alter the meaning of the text such as spelling, punctuation, verb tenses) and *meaning or content changes* (changes that alter the meaning such as additions, deletions, substitutions). Inexperienced writers tend to make more surface changes and fewer global meaning changes than do more expert writers (Scott, 1996). Revising and evaluating may occur at any time during the writing process and are usually repeated many times.

In Flower and Hayes' model, the overall writing process is not viewed as a linear sequence of stages, but rather a set of optional actions that a writer may choose to use throughout the writing activity:

---

1. According to Scott, writing as a "process" means that "writing is a succession of actions undertaken to bring about some desired result" (1996, p. 31). She also notes that the term "process" has never been clearly defined in the literature.

Writing processes may be viewed as the writer's tool kit. In using the tools, the writer is not constrained to use them in a fixed order or in stages. And using any tool may create the need to use another. Generating ideas may require evaluation, as may writing sentences. And evaluation may force the writer to think up new ideas (1981, p. 376).

Within the complex process of writing, there are constraints facing the writer. Flower and Hayes (1981) acknowledge that these constraints include *knowledge, written speech,* and *the rhetorical problem.* The writer must retrieve knowledge from memory and clarify for herself/himself and for the audience the analysis of this knowledge by means of the written message. The writer must be aware of the linguistic and discourse conventions characteristic of written discourse (e.g., use of transitional words, not repeating words that appear in close proximity). The rhetorical problem consists of the writer's purpose and goals as well as the context of and audience for the written message. Good writers take into account the rhetorical problem while poor writers tend to focus on simply "completing the task." Flower and Hayes suggest that writers manage some of these constraints through strategies such as reducing the task to manageable segments, using a well-learned procedure in approaching the writing task, taking into account the real purpose of the task, and planning how to compose (e.g., doing free writing first, organzing ideas, putting it aside for a day, rewriting) (1981, p. 40).

> ⚷ **The writing process consists of a set of optional actions that a writer may choose to use throughout the writing activity.**

❏ Successful vs. Unsuccessful Writing

Research in ESL indicates that writing competence is not language-specific. The assumptions that students have about writing in their native language provide the foundation for making new hypotheses about writing in the foreign language (Edelsky, 1982). Similarly, both good and poor writing strategies transfer from L1 to L2 (Friedlander, 1990; Zamel, 1983). Successful writers spend time planning for writing, and they use a recursive, nonlinear approach, that is, they review and revise their written work as they compose. Good writers are also reader-centered because they keep the audience and the meaning of the message in focus. Furthermore, successful writers review what they write and use revisions to clarify meaning. Unsuccessful writers, on the other hand, are more likely to devote little time to planning and to use a linear approach to composing, that is, write in a step-by-step fashion without going back to review what was written. Poor writers focus more on their own goals for the task rather than on the audience, and they use revisions primarily to correct form errors and mechanics (Lapp, 1984; Magnan, 1985; Richards, 1990; Zamel, 1982).

❏ The Relationship Between Writing and Other Language Competencies

Studies have shown that knowledge of grammar does not guarantee writing competence. A student who is able to provide correct answers on a grammar test in the foreign language may not necessarily have effective writing skills (Schultz, 1991). Some research shows that writers' skill in using language structures to communicate successfully develops independently of their knowledge and use of grammatical rules (Coombs, 1986).

Some research proposes that reading may facilitate writing and that "a well-read person has more knowledge about the conventions and features of writing" (Scott, 1996). Reading can help learners to gain an understanding of patterns of discourse and connections between language and culture. Kern and Schultz (1992) found that composition instruction that is integrated with the reading of texts and that focuses on the writing process as well as on the final product helps learners improve in their writing performance. In their study, college French students enrolled in an intermediate-level composition course read and discussed a series of texts, analyzed the texts as models of good writing, received sequenced lessons on how to write essays based on the readings, and created in-class essays based on various essay topics. Over the course of a year, students made significant progress in their writing in terms of the syntactic complexity and overall quality of their writing (Kern & Schultz, 1992).

 A well-read person has more knowledge about the conventions and features of writing.

Integrating writing with other skill modalities relates to the concept of *writing to learn,* in which writing is not done as an end in and of itself but rather as a means of learning about content and/or culture. This concept fits well with the Vygotskyan (1978) framework presented in Chapter 1, in which the learner acquires knowledge and skills by interacting with language in social contexts. Language is a tool for building and shaping our thoughts rather than simply a means for conveying them. The writing-to-learn concept also supports the spirit of the *SFLL* and the integration of the three modes of communication, where language is used to learn new concepts and express ideas.

Research conducted by Koda (1993) indicates that there is a strong correlation between vocabulary knowledge and quality of a written text. Knowledge of vocabulary contributes to the learner's ability to produce effective compositions. Furthermore, Schultz (1994) found that syntactic complexity is also an indicator of the quality of writing. Hence, the more equipped students are to produce complex sentences (i.e., sentences with subordinate clauses and connector words), the better able they will be to write compositions of high quality. According to Schultz, "syntactic complexity serves not only as a tool for clear communication, but also as a tool for generating thought itself" (1994, p. 171).

❏ Implications of Writing Research for FL Teaching

The writing research summarized above points to the following suggestions for teachers as they incorporate writing into the foreign language classroom (adapted from Scott, 1996):

1. *Discuss the L1 writing process:* Make learners aware of the processes they use to write in L1 by having them identify their own L1 writing strategies and strategies that may be unique to the L2 writing process. Scott (1996) suggests a writing process

questionnaire such as the one that appears in Appendix 9.1 to help learners analyze what strategies they use as they write in their native languages.

2. *Teach about the FL writing process:* Ask learners to reflect on strategies that they use when they write in L2. Appendix 9.2 illustrates a FL writing process questionnaire that might be used to direct learners' attention to effective and ineffective strategies for writing in the target language (Scott, 1996).

Help learners generate ideas on a topic, organize their ideas, and revise and edit effectively. According to Scott (1992), generating ideas is the most challenging feature of the FL writing process because learners tend to use L1 idea generation strategies; that is, they try to transfer or translate their ideas from the NL to the TL. Since students may possess a limited amount of vocabulary and grammatical knowledge, their translated ideas often lack comprehensibility. Teachers can help students generate ideas in a FL by (a) providing topics that are familiar and personal to them; (b) encouraging them to recall words and expressions in the TL associated with the topic; and (c) providing enough direction to help them focus on the TL while generating ideas (Scott & Terry, 1992). Figure 9.1 illustrates a sample worksheet for helping learners to generate ideas in the FL (Scott, 1996). This type of worksheet might include, or be a springboard for, vocabulary exercises that provide a linguistic "scaffolding" for a given writing task (Koda, 1993). In this way, the writing process can be approached as an activity that stimulates new ideas and discovery instead of the tedious task of translating (Scott, 1996).

Since another challenging aspect of the FL writing process is reviewing, learners must be taught to reread frequently while writing. Raimes (1987) suggests that students read their texts aloud, either to themselves or to a classmate, as this will help them edit what is on the page and generate new ideas. Similarly, students need to be taught to revise throughout the writing process and to make content changes as well as surface changes. Students should reread their written text for content and organization as a separate activity from rereading for linguistic accuracy (Scott, 1996). Changes in content often require direct suggestions from the teacher and can be incorporated in later drafts (Scott, 1995, p. 119). When rereading for linguistic accuracy, students need explicit instructions on what types of errors to look for (e.g., subject-verb agreement, tense usage, noun-adjective agreement, etc.).

3. *Provide focused practice on syntax:* Since syntactic complexity is an important aspect of good writing, Schultz (1994) suggests that learners be engaged in *reformulation* activities, through which they (a) analyze a poorly written text consisting of only three or four sentences; (b) work individually or in groups to rewrite the text; and (c) compare their rewritten version to one rewritten by a native speaker. This technique enables learners to integrate their knowledge of grammar, vocabulary, and syntax and make interpretive choices about the content of the text in order to reformulate the passage (Schultz, 1994, p. 176).[2]

---

2. For a more detailed discussion of the use of stylistic reformulation to improve students' writing skills, see Schultz, 1994.

Figure 9.1   Sample Worksheet for Generating Ideas

SAMPLE WORKSHEET FOR GENERATING IDEAS
(Designed for use in the target language)

Topic: Describe your personality.

Underline the adjectives that describe you best:

intellectual	realistic	athletic	quiet
naïve	pessimistic	boring	loud
lazy	enthusiastic	anxious	active
serious	intelligent	calm	adventuresome
crazy	dull	depressed	loving
optimistic	hopeful	diligent	perfectionistic

Use the dictionary to find five more adjectives that describe you.

Use some of the following expressions as you describe yourself:

intellectual	realistic	athletic	quiet
always	rarely	often	when I'm tired
occasionally	never	regularly	when it's rainy
in the morning	during the day	at night	when it's sunny
with my friends	with my parents	on a date	at a party
on a trip	when I meet someone		

Source: Scott, 1996, 53.

4. *Distinguish between writing for communication and writing as an academic exercise:* Learners need to know the difference between using writing as a tool for communicating messages to others (e.g., notes, letters, e-mail messages) and using writing as an academic exercise in order to learn content (e.g., writing an essay about cultural comparisons). In writing to learn, students use critical thinking skills such as analyzing, synthesizing, and decision making (Scott, 1996).

5. *Combine reading and writing:* Give learners authentic models of written discourse by linking reading to writing, and thus supporting the "writing to learn" concept. The Interactive Model presented in Chapter 6 illustrates an effective way to lead students from interpreting a text to using the information learned as a basis for interpersonal activities and the creation of a product. Skimming, or reading for the gist, can help learners discover patterns of discourse, levels of register, and links between language and culture. Close analysis of the text can provide students with models to follow as they write (Scott, 1996).

6. *Redefine "creative" writing:* Teach learners that one goal of writing is to create personal meaning with the TL. According to Scott (1996), students sometimes have the mistaken idea that in order to use writing creatively, they must have the inspiration of a poet or novelist. When they don't feel inspired in this way, they often experience frustration with writing. Learners will be more likely to succeed if teachers can "remove the burden of creativity and teach the art of discovery" (Scott, 1996, p. 49). Various studies have shown the effectiveness of using journal writing in helping students create personal meaning and in increasing their motivation to write (Peyton, 1987, 1990; West & Donato, 1995). For example, in an interactive dialog journal, which is effective at all age levels, the teacher and the student carry on a written conversation. Learners write about topics of interest to them, and the teacher participates in the dialog by writing back with responses, comments, and observations. Since the learner and the teacher are focused on meaning, errors in language form are not corrected except by the teacher's use of correct modeling.

The following quote from Atwell (1985, p. 150) summarizes what teachers must keep in mind regarding the needs of writers:

> Writers need time—to think, write, confer, write, read, write, change our minds, and write some more. Writers need regular time that we can count on, so that even when we aren't writing we're anticipating the time we will be. And we need lots of time—to grow, to see what we think, to shape what we know, to get help where and when we need it . . . When we allow time, conferences, and responsibility, we create contexts in which writers write and get good at writing (cf. Kauffmann, 1996, p. 400).

 STANDARDS HIGHLIGHT: Developing Written Communication through Integration of the Three Modes

As you learned in Chapter 6, the three modes of the Communication Goal Area are interpersonal, interpretive, and presentational ways of using language. When working with text, learners can easily traverse all three modes. Study again the descriptions of the modes in Figure 6.1 (p. 122). In Chapter 6 you learned about the interpretive mode by exploring listening, reading, and viewing. In Chapter 7, you examined a strategy for teaching grammar that students will use in the interpersonal mode of communication. Chapter 8 presented ways to use the interpersonal and presentational modes to develop oral communication skills. This chapter focuses on development of written communication skills through integration of the three modes. Writing in the interpersonal mode is direct and requires that the writer know about the cultural perspectives that govern interactions between individuals of different ages, status, and backgrounds (NSFLEP, 1996); that is, writing a letter of inquiry to a school abroad requires knowledge of formal means of addressing individuals in positions of authority. The writer must also be familiar with the different practices used to communicate and the patterns of interaction; that is, the way in which envelopes are addressed, how soon a letter writer should expect a response. When a reader receives written communication, s/he applies knowledge of how cultural perspectives are embedded in the written piece, be it a phone message or a novel. To interpret the writing, the receiver must analyze content and compare it to prior knowledge s/he may have.

In writing in the presentational mode, the learner produces written language for an audience of readers (often called *writing for publication*). This involves the creation of texts through which the writer displays what s/he knows and explores what s/he does not know. The purposes for written presentational communication can be categorized into six major types: descriptive, persuasive, expository, narrative, expressive, and poetic (Bilash, 1998, p. 161, based on original work by Britton, Burgess, Martin, McLeod, & Rosen, 1975). In *descriptive writing*, the writer describes experiences, feelings, objects, places, people, or events (postcard, autobiography). The purpose of *persuasive writing* is to persuade an audience to take action or adopt a certain point of view (advertisements). Through *expository writing*, the writer informs the reader of facts (news, instructions). *Narratives* involve telling stories or relating events (stories, drama). In *expressive writing*, the author conveys thoughts and feelings, while in *poetic writing*, the writer expresses personal ideas and thoughts by means of poems, songs, and stories. Communication in this mode requires knowledge of how writers communicate with readers and audiences and an ability to present cross-cultural information based on the background of the audience. You will find examples of ways to integrate written communication within the three modes of communication of the *SFLL* in each of the following sections.

❏ Writing Across the Modes of Communication in Elementary School Instruction

In Chapter 4, you learned about how elementary school instruction makes the transition from oral to written skills through the use of the language experience chart approach. Students learn to read and write based on their experiences and oral communication. This strategy is based upon the developmental approach to writing described earlier in the chapter. The *SFLL* suggest a connection between the interpretive mode and the presentational mode that helps young learners make sense of what they read and experience. For instance, a sample progress indicator for grade four in the interpretive mode is: "Students comprehend the main themes and ideas and identify the principal characters of stories or children's literature" (NSFLEP, 1996, p. 40). Talking and writing about these topics via e-mail, sample postcards, or letters help students become aware of their own and other cultures. The reading of a fairy tale from the target culture containing information about dwellings and descriptions of characters can be planned into the lesson (interpretive mode). This could then lead to an activity in the presentational mode in which grade four "students prepare illustrated stories about activities or events in their environment and share these stories and events with an audience such as the class" (NSFLEP, 1996, p. 39). For young children, meaningful writing activities focus on their concrete worlds.

At the elementary school level, writing can be used for both *communication/personal expression* (interpersonal communication) and *publication* (presentational communication). Learners use writing to learn about language and to express personal messages. For young learners, Curtain and Pesola suggest a variety of copying/labeling activities: labeling items in a picture; completing graphs, charts, and maps; copying a language-experience story; making lists; and creating collages with visual representations of specific vocabulary (1994, p. 140). The interactive dialogue journal, mentioned in the previous section, is a particularly effective activity for engaging learners in personal expression at this level (Peyton, 1987, 1990). Activities that integrate reading and writing while emphasizing meaning and learners' experiences include reading and writing simple stories; reading and writing songs, rhymes, and poems that have been learned orally; writing weather reports with accompanying pictures; and writing simple captions for pictures in a class or personal album (Curtain & Pesola, 1994, p. 141).

Elementary school learners might also write "for publication" to a wider and public audience. Students might contribute to a class publication for use in the classroom or library, to a newsletter sent to parents or community members, or to an exchange of letters with students in another community. Learners might write books based on shared experiences and classroom writing tasks (Curtain & Pesola, 1994). Effective creative writing activities for beginning learners include simple forms of poetry such as *fixed-form poetry* and *diamantes*, through which learners can begin to play with language. Laidlaw (1989) suggests the use of fixed-form poetry to tap the creative processes of young learners while enabling them to synthesize information. A sample integrative activity, perhaps from a social studies lesson and resulting writing assignment, is the following fixed-form poem:

Monument Poem

Line 1: Name of the monument

Line 2: Four adjectives describing the monument

Line 3: Constructed in (date, century)

Line 4: Constructed by _____

Line 5: Which is (on the right bank, left bank, in Paris, . . .)

Line 6: Which is near (another monument or landmark)

Line 7: Don't miss (the monument name) because _____

(cf. Nerenz 1990, 120–121)

The following are directions for a *diamante* together with an example in English (Curtain & Pesola, 1994, p. 137):

1	WORD	noun	Cats
2	WORDS	adjective describing noun	soft, warm
3	WORDS	participle (or verbs)	playing, leaping, purring
4	WORDS	nouns related to subject	tails, tongues, paws, whiskers
3	WORDS	participles (or verbs)	biting, licking, teasing
2	WORDS	adjectives	elegant, rough
1	WORD	synonym for first word	Siamese

Writing can also be used successfully in activities that integrate interpretive, interpersonal, and presentational communication, culture, and other school subjects, such as those described in Chapter 4. Figure 9.2 illustrates a thematic web for a unit on trees, in which subject area activities (history, art, music, physical education, math) and reading/writing activities are highlighted (Peregoy & Boyle, 1997). The writing activities enable students to learn about various aspects of trees while practicing creative self-expression. Bilash (1998) suggests that teachers use a table such as the one illustrated in Figure 9.3 to help them monitor the writing functions and forms students produce in all subject areas, particularly for those in immersion settings. Figure 9.4 on page 230 shows the types of journal writing that might be used to foster student learning of content areas.

Figure 9.2   Thematic Web for Unit on Trees

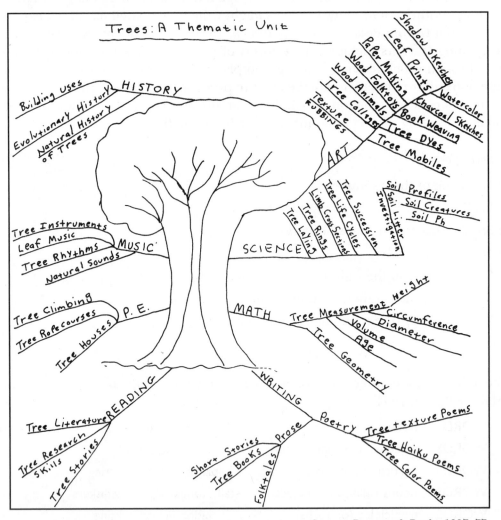

Source: Peregoy & Boyle, 1997, 77.

Figure 9.3 Table for Monitoring Writing Functions and Forms across Subject Areas

This table helps teachers monitor the writing functions and forms students produce in all subject areas over a month or term in bilingual or immersion second language settings, to better balance writing assignments.

	LANGUAGE ARTS	SCIENCE	SOCIAL STUDIES	OTHER
Descritive writing: autobiography, postcard, epitaphs				
Persuasive writing: advertisements, want ads, critiques, propaganda				
Expository writing: bulletin boards, agendas, instructions, interviews, headlines				
Narrative writing: cartoons, stories, drama, vignettes				
Expressive writing: diaries, greeting cards, graffiti				
Poetic writing: songs, rhymes, haiku, limericks, poems				

Source: Bilash, 1998, 165.

❏ Writing Across the Modes of Communication at the Secondary Level and Beyond

Writing as a Support Skill and as a Communicative Skill

Foreign language teachers at the secondary and post-secondary levels have traditionally used writing for two purposes: as a *support skill* and as a *communicative skill* (Magnan, 1985). When writing is used as a support skill, the focus is primarily on the mastery of the grammar, vocabulary, and syntax of the language (Hadley, 1993). Students learn a linguistic system by copying learned material; paying attention to grammatical features, vocabulary, and spelling; and by completing grammar practice exercises to reinforce their knowledge of structures (Hadley, 1993). In traditional writing activities of this nature, teachers tend to emphasize linguistic accuracy and provide models for students to follow in order to

Figure 9.4   Types of Journal Writing Used to Foster Learning of Content Areas

JOURNAL TYPE AND PURPOSE	SCIENCE	LANGUAGE ARTS	MATHE-MATICS	SOCIAL SCIENCE
Dialogue/Buddy: to share with another	Explain to teacher or to friend what is happening in class and what is understood	Share with another about a story or poem being read; share other aspects of class	Let teacher or friend know how class or assign-ments are going	"Discuss" informa-tion pertaining to topics in class
Notebook: to take notes to assist memory	Write down infor-mation pertaining to an experiment in class	Take down conver-sations overheard for use in a story to be written	Keep notes about math concepts	Write down key information dis-cussed in class
Learning logs: to discuss and process information from class	Write down notes about what one understands in the class and about what might seem unclear	Write down key concepts from class such as defini-tions of concepts: setting, theme, characterization	Try to explain math concepts for one-self or perhaps for another; clarify or try to apply a new concept	Take notes on causes of Civil War or other key ideas; ask self to identify and clarify ideas
Response journals: to respond openly and freely to any topic	Respond to feelings about scientific experimentation or use of animals as subjects of biogenetics	Make any com-ments on charac-ters or conflicts presented in a story being read	Respond to math in an interesting way, such as ask questions about why people who would never admit to being illiterate will seemingly brag about their math ignorance	Respond to politi-cians' handling of peace after World War I or about attitudes of pil-grims toward Native Americans

Source: Peregoy & Boyle, 1997, 320.

avoid making errors (Scarcella & Oxford, 1992). Activities in which writing is used as a sup-port skill include the following (Hadley, 1993):

- filling in forms
- writing a short description from questions
- completing a paragraph based on a visual
- writing a composition using a sentence-builder as a guide
- combining sentences
- elaborating on sentences within a paragraph

The second traditional use of writing is as a communicative skill, through which learn-ers communicate a message and/or express their own thoughts. In this type of writing, the focus is on the content of the message rather than on linguistic accuracy alone. According to Dvorak, "It is difficult for student and teacher to think of writing as a purposeful or communicative exercise if the goal of writing activity, whether stated or unstated, is grammatical accuracy" (1986, p. 157). In writing for communication, learners often base written interpersonal and presentational texts on what they have comprehended and interpreted of an oral or written message. Some typical communicative writing assignments include compositions, journal writing, descriptions and narrations, and note taking (Hadley, 1993). Learners benefit from being given purposes for writing; for example, instead of assigning students the task of asking classmates three questions about themselves, we might ask them to construct a class newspaper using reporters who write brief articles about their fellow students. In this case, they have a more authentic task, real reasons to ask questions, and an audience to address.

A look at the *SFLL* sample progress indicators for grade twelve illustrates the connection between interpretive and presentational modes for the secondary learner. In the interpretive mode, "students analyze the main plot, subplot, and characters, and their descriptions, roles, and significance in authentic literary texts" (NSFLEP, 1996, p. 40). These analyses can be mapped (see semantic maps in Chapter 4) and used as a pre-writing stage for an assignment in which learners summarize the text or create their own similar type of text. Working in small groups, learners might construct written texts for an audience (presentational mode), working toward the following sample progress indicator for grade twelve: "Students create stories and poems, short plays, or skits based on personal experiences and exposure to themes, ideas, and perspectives from the target culture" (NSFLEP, 1996, p. 42).

Proficiency-Oriented Writing

A proficiency-oriented approach to teaching writing involves designing activities that help students perform at a given level of proficiency as described in the *ACTFL Proficiency Guidelines* (see Appendix 2.2). Scott (1996) notes that proficiency-oriented approaches to teaching writing are quite eclectic since some teachers may focus on the development of grammar and syntax while others stress practice of language functions. Hadley (1993)

TASK LEVEL	EXAMPLE
Novice	paragraph completion, cloze passages,[3] filling out forms
Intermediate	slash sentences,[4] descriptions with visuals, dialog journals
Advanced	process-oriented compositions, journals
Superior	extensive note taking, full transcription, peer editing

---

3. A *cloze* exercise consists of a written passage with every "nth" word deleted. It can also be used as a global test of proficiency since it requires attention to longer stretches of linguistic contexts and often to inferences about extralinguistic context (Oller, 1979).

4. A *slash sentence* is a string of sentence elements to be used in constructing a complete sentence. Students combine the elements, conjugating the infinitives, adding necessary function words, and making other necessary agreement changes. Example: I / to go / swim / beach / Saturdays (I go swimming at the beach on Saturdays.)

presents a curricular guide for teaching writing based on the proficiency construct. She categorizes writing activities according to the levels as presented in the chart on page 231.

While proficiency-oriented activities may be useful in helping students to focus on writing functions at each level of proficiency, it is unclear to what extent the *ACTFL Proficiency Guidelines* capture the manner in which writing skills develop (Valdés, Haro, & Echevarriarza, 1992). Some researchers have argued that learners do not always begin FL writing at the novice level since they may transfer their writing competence from L1 to L2 (Henry, 1996; Valdés, Haro, & Echevarriarza, 1992). See Scott and Rodgers (1993) for a description of a proficiency-oriented Spanish Writing Contest designed for secondary and college level Spanish students. Appendix 9.3 illustrates the contest specifications and set of rubrics for each level of writing.

Figure 9.5 (Tussing, Lowe, & Clifford, 1998) shows ways to align task selection and assessment.

Figure 9.5A   The Writing Assignment Matrix

THE WRITING ASSIGNMENT MATRIX

Marjorie O. Tussing, Pardee Lowe, Jr., Ray T. Clifford

Real-world writing requires "knowing how, when, and why to write what to whom"* to accurately communicate facts, concepts, and feelings . . .

FUNCTION	CONTEXT	ACCURACY
About one or more real-life tasks, projects, or problems. [Such as setting up a meeting, disputing a grade, challenging a bill, coordinating a presentation, expressing condolences, applying for a job, requesting a raise, soliciting cooperation, etc.] **Through a suitable mode and format of written communication.** [The writer creates a note, memo, letter, e-mail message, press release, advertisement, bulletin, set of instructions, announcement, editorial, etc. to fit the task at hand.]	**To a specific audience.** [The writer considers the recipient's personality, education level, age, gender, culture, etc.] **Within known circumstances.** [The writer considers his/her relationship to the recipient, and knows whether the communication is to be student to student, student to teacher, teacher to student(s), employee to peer(s), employee to boss, boss to subordinate(s), parent to child, adult child to parent, customer to a store, intern to a business, individual to an agency, etc.]	**Using an appropriate communication strategy and language register.** [Matches the objective and communication task with an appropriate format and style for the audience.] **To accomplish the desired cognitive and affective results.** [Accurately communicates who is doing what, where, and when; explains how and why it is being done; and effectively creates the desired tone to motivate, correct without offending, cheer up, alienate, etc.]

*This phrase is from Standards for Foreign Language Learning: Preparing for the 21st Century. National Standards in Foreign Language Education Project, 1996.

Source: Tussing, Lowe, & Clifford, 1998.

Figure 9.5B   The Writing Assignment Matrix

EVALUATING WRITING ACTIVITIES

ACTFL, 22 Nov. 1998: Marjorie O. Tussing, Pardee Lowe, Jr., Ray T. Clifford

Assignment _____

Date _____ Reference _____ Page _____

Since real-world writing requires "knowing how, when, and why to write what to whom" to accurately communicate facts, concepts, and feelings . . .

FUNCTION	CONTEXT	ACCURACY
What are the real-life tasks, projects, or problems?	**Who is the audience or recipient?**	**What would be an appropriate communication strategy and language register?**
What is a suitable mode and format for the written communication?	**What special circumstances and relationships exist?**	**What are the desired cognitive and affective results?**

Source: Tussing, Lowe, & Clifford, 1998.

Task-Oriented Writing

Scott and Terry (1992) have suggested a task-oriented approach to teaching writing, which is based on the principle that learners need explicit guidelines in order to complete a writing assignment. They propose that the assignment include (1) a general situation and (2) a series of tasks that specify the language functions, vocabulary, and grammar structures necessary for completing the activity. Figure 9.6 illustrates a task-oriented writing activity. Using this task-based approach, Scott (1992) proposed a developmental writing program designed to begin writing practice from the earliest levels of language instruction. In each writing assignment, the situation might remain the same while the tasks are changed to progress from simple to more complex language structures and functions. Figure 9.7 on page 235 exemplifies a situation with tasks for first, second, and third year of study. Note that this particular activity also integrates the Communication, Cultures, and Comparisons goal areas of *SFLL*. It could also combine the three modes of communication if students were to read a text that pertains to the situation featured in the task (interpretive), discuss their findings and opinions with classmates (interpersonal), and complete the written task (presentational). Appendix 9.4 presents a checklist that might be used by teachers as they prepare the writing task.

Figure 9.5C   The Writing Assignment Matrix

PROFICIENCY LEVEL	FUNCTIONS/ TASK	CONTEXT/ TOPICS	ACCURACY
5 **Professional**	All expected of an educated NS	All subjects	Accepted as an educated NS
4	Tailor language, counsel, motivate, persuade, negotiate	A wide range of professional needs	Language is extensive, culturally accurate, precise, and appropriate in style and register
3 **Superior**	Support opinions, hypothesize, explain, deal with unfamiliar topics	Practical, abstract, and special interest subjects; professional topics at a general level	Cohesive, accurate, aware of audience; errors never interfere with communication and rarely disturb
2 **Advanced**	Describe, produce extended narration and sequenced instructions	Concrete, real-world, factual	Intelligible even to those not used to dealing with non-NS
1 **Intermediate**	Q & A, write short notes, create language at phrase and sentence level	Everyday survival	Intelligible with effort or practice
0 **Novice**	Make lists, fill in forms, write formulaic responses	Rehearsed, sporadic, random	Unintelligible to barely intelligible

Source: Tussing, Lowe, & Clifford, 1998.

Figure 9.6   Task-Oriented Writing Activity

Situation: You have been asked to write a complete description of yourself for the new student files.

Tasks:

1. Describe yourself physically.
   Function: Describing people
   Grammar: Adjective position and agreement
   Vocabulary: Hair color, body, face

2. Describe your personality, indicating positive as well as negative traits.
   Grammar: Negation
   Vocabulary: Personality

3. Conclude with a statement about how you feel about your school.
   Function: Expressing an opinion

Source: Modified from Scott and Terry, 1992, 25.

Figure 9.7 Task-Oriented Writing Activity

Situation: You have heard that American and French students are different. In order to promote cultural understanding, you are writing an article for a French magazine about American students.

First-year tasks:

1. Begin with a general remark about American students.
2. Describe the way a female student might look.
3. Describe the way a male student might look.
4. Indicate three things that some American students like to do.
5. Conclude with a personal opinion about American students.

Second-year tasks:

1. Begin with a general remark about American students.
2. Describe the way students, both male and female, might look.
3. Indicate at least five things that some American students like to do, and three things that they don't like to do.
4. Conclude with several personal opinions about the individuality or conformity of American students.

Third-year tasks:

1. You will argue either for or against the idea that all American students are alike. Begin with a thesis statement.
2. Describe American students.
3. Define the term "stereotype" as it relates to American students.
4. Conclude by showing how the argument supports the thesis statement.

Source: Modified from Scott, 1992, 7–8.

Teaching Writing as Process: Addressing the Rhetorical Problem

In both native and foreign language writing instruction, the last decade has brought a shift away from a focus on writing as *product* toward a focus on writing as *process;* that is, instruction has moved from emphasis on the final written text toward emphasis on the steps that learners complete in order to create a written product (Barnett, 1989; Dvorak, 1986; Silva, 1990). A process-oriented approach calls for a "positive, encouraging, and collaborative workshop environment within which students, with ample time and minimal intereference, can work through their composing processes" (Silva, 1990, p. 15). The teacher's role is to assist students in developing strategies for beginning to write (finding topics, generating ideas, focusing, planning, etc.), for drafting, for revising (adding, deleting, modifying), and for editing (attending to grammar, vocabulary, sentence structure, mechanics) (Silva, 1990).

Earlier in this chapter, you read about the *rhetorical problem*, that involves the writer's purposes for completing a writing task. According to Lee and VanPatten (1995), the nature of writing assignments in foreign language classrooms leads students to have only one purpose for doing them—"to complete the assignment." Since their writing goal in this case becomes meeting what they think is the teacher's desired outcome, the writing processes of planning and reviewing are minimized. Lee and VanPatten (1995) suggest an approach to engaging learners in writing that involves a series of "thoughtful processes" and that uses the basis of the Flower and Hayes (1981) model presented earlier in this chapter. Figure 9.8 illustrates this process writing approach, as adapted from Lee and VanPatten (1995).

Figure 9.8. A Process-Writing Model

FLOWER AND HAYES (1981) THOUGHT PROCESSES IN WRITING	LEE AND VAN-PATTEN (1995) WRITING PROCESS	LEARNER ACTIVITIES
Planning	Generating content Selecting audience and purpose Planning and Organizing	Learners brainstorm ideas related to topic. Learners select audience and discuss audience characteristics. Learners plan information to include and prepare outline to share with peer.
Translating	Composing	Using outline, learners write first draft and let it sit for a while.
Reviewing	Revising and Rewriting	Learners review first draft for quality of content and organization of ideas; they rewrite as necessary. Learners review draft for grammar, vocabulary, sentence structure, mechanics, and rewrite as necessary.

Source: Adapted from Lee and VanPatten, 1995.

You will notice that the activities in this model parallel closely the stages of writing suggested by Barnett (1989) in her process-writing approach model, which has been widely used in teaching foreign language writing: (1) pre-writing: brainstorming and organizing ideas; (2) writing: creating the first draft; and (3) rewriting: reviewing, editing, rewriting. However, the Lee and VanPatten (1995) model does not depict stages that must occur in a sequential manner. Rather, it describes possible thought processes, some of which might or might not occur, and all of which determine the direction a writer's composition will take. The following is an example of this process applied to a typical writing assignment given to a beginning foreign language class:

A. GENERATING CONTENT

Step 1. To each group of three or four students, the instructor will assign one of the following topics:

    a. family life at the turn of the century
    b. family life today

Each group will have ten minutes to make a list of as many ideas as possible relating its topic to each of the following:

    1. family size
    2. economic opportunities
    3. educational opportunities
    4. male and female roles
    5. society

Step 2. Report to the rest of the class the ideas your group has generated.

Step 3. Each member of the class should copy the lists from the board to use later in writing.

B. SELECTING AN AUDIENCE AND PURPOSE

Step 1. Keeping in mind the ideas the class generated in the Activity A, think about an audience for your writing. Select an audience from the following list or propose one yourself:

    a. high school students you are addressing as part of a college recruitment program
    b. the readers of the school newspaper
    c. the members of a businesswomen's organization
    d. the members of a church council
    e. the Panhellenic council that governs fraternities and sororities on campus
    f. other suggestions _____

Step 2. Select one of the two topics. Then form groups of three to work with the same topic, and list your audience's characteristics. Report your list to the rest of the class. Try to help other groups by proposing characteristics they may not have considered. Take down any suggestions your classmates offer you.

C. PLANNING AND ORGANIZING

Step 1. Now that you have an audience, what will you say to them? Working in the same groups as in Activity B, examine the lists of ideas you prepared for Activity A, and indicate what information you might include in your composition.

Step 2. Working individually, prepare an outline of the composition. Once each of you has an outline, present it to each other. Have your partners thought of some things you didn't?

Step 3. (Optional) Present your outline to someone who selected a different audience, and listen to her/his presentation. Can you offer any ideas or suggestions?

D. COMPOSING

Take your outline and list of ideas and keep them handy as you write a composition directed at the audience you selected. Suggestion: Write a draft of the work and let it sit for two days. Do not think about it or read it. At the end of the two days, pick it up and read it. As you do, answer the following questions:

    a. content: Are these still the ideas you want to include?

    b. organization: Does the order in which the ideas are presented help you get your message across to the audience?

If you answer "no" to either question, rewrite some of your composition.

E. REVISING AND REWRITING

Step 1. Once you think your composition is good enough to hand in, review the language you used.

    a. verbs: Are the forms, spelling, and accents correct?

    b. adjectives: What noun do they go with? Do the adjectives agree?

    c. *[other elements of the language on which you want learners to focus]*

Step 2. If necessary, rewrite your composition.

Source: Lee and VanPatten, 1995, 222–223.

 How does this model address the rhetorical problem?

Barnett (1989) gives her learners a direction sheet titled "Comment écrire une composition" (see Appendix 9.5) that summarizes the thinking and writing process and suggests how to organize ideas and prepare the final draft of the composition. The categories on this direction sheet can also be used by the teacher for assessment purposes (see Appendix 9.6 for scoring guide).

Teaching Writing as a Product

The previous sections of this chapter have explored ways to focus on the writing process in foreign language teaching. The writing process culminates in a final written product. An important consideration for the foreign language teacher is how to use the written product in order to help learners improve their written communication skills and heighten their motivation about using writing as a tool for self-expression and academic learning.

❏ Writing Homework

Students create written products for homework. Research indicates that student achievement rises when teachers regularly assign homework and students conscientiously do it (United States Department of Education, 1986). According to Antonek, Tucker, and Donato, homework functions on three interrelated levels:

1. Homework communicates to the parent what and how well the child is learning in the classroom.

2. Homework facilitates classroom learning if it is linked to what the child can realistically perform without the assistance of the teacher and other students.

3. Homework mediates the relationship of school and home by serving as a public awareness tool that informs parents about the curriculum and encourages their support for programs (1997, p. 65).

The principles of language in context for real communication found throughout this book apply to homework tasks as well. Specifically, *Teacher's Handbook* suggests that homework assignments

- consist of more than mechanical, decontextualized workbook exercises.
- be clear enough so that students can understand instructions at home.
- be related to activities done in class.
- provide the basis for activities to be done in class the next day (e.g., students might prepare interview questions that they will use the next day in a pair activity).
- be meaningful and interesting to students.
- evaluate the extent to which learners can use language independently (i.e., beyond the ZPD).
- if possible, engage students in interaction with others (peers, parents).
- enable students to self-assess their progress.
- provide the teacher with feedback regarding the effectiveness of instruction (e.g., if many students are experiencing difficulty with an assignment, it may point to specific work that needs to be done in class).

The professional literature (research articles and methodology textbooks) has failed to examine fully the role of homework. Recently, however, one study has appeared that suggests the concept of "interactive foreign language homework" as a way to involve parents/caretakers in schoolwork. Antonek, Tucker, and Donato (1997) based their work on that done by the Center on Families, Communities, Schools, and Children's Learning at the Johns Hopkins University, where interactive homework in various subject areas was piloted (Epstein, 1993). Through a process called "Teachers Involve Parents in Schoolwork" (TIPS), students talk about homework in the classroom, describe the types of homework they like best, explain how their parents help them with homework at home, and solicit parents' active involvement in completing assignments at home (Epstein, 1993).

 Interactive foreign language homework is a way to involve parents/caretakers in schoolwork.

In a study by Antonek, Tucker, and Donato (1997), interactive homework assignments were developed and piloted in a K–5 Japanese program in an effort to involve parents in helping students with Japanese vocabulary and cultural information. The majority of parents reported having enjoyed completing the assignments with their children and having the opportunity to learn more about the Japanese program. Figure 9.9 illustrates a sample interactive homework assignment, which consists of six parts:

1. title introducing the topic of the homework, a statement indicating the connection between the assignment and classwork, the date, and student signature;

2. a list of FL phrases with English translations;

3. instructions for students to carry out three to five language functions (e.g., expressing thanks and greeting someone);

4. instructions for students to teach their parents how to carry out language functions;

5. ways for students and parents to interact in the foreign language (e.g., exchange greetings and courtesy expressions); and

6. cultural information relevant to the lesson.

Space is also provided for parents to sign and give feedback on the child's performance (Antonek, Tucker, & Donato, 1997, pp. 67–68).

The researchers suggest that ten-minute assignments work best and that they be kept to one page and be reproduced on colored paper for easy identification by parent and child. Although the example in Figure 9.9 focuses on verbal language, the assignments could also guide students and parents in producing a short written product such as a note, letter, or creative paragraph. Appendix 9.7 contains a checklist for constructing an interactive homework assignment.

Whether the homework assignment is interactive or not, it can play an important role in helping the student to use language without assistance from the teacher and peers and to provide useful feedback about learner progress.

❒ Technologically Enhanced Writing

Technology has opened new ways of communication in all languages and offers learners many possibilities for creating written products that can be shared with others. E-mail communication with keypals in foreign countries and with businesses on the World Wide Web have opened the world to the language classroom. Computer-assisted learning can help learners in the creation of a written product. More information on the use of technology for writing appears in Chapter 12.

❒ Responding to Writing

Traditionally responding to writing simply meant that the teacher corrected students' errors in grammar, vocabulary, and mechanics. However, this narrow view of correction has been expanded in recent years as we consider the effect that various kinds of feedback have on improving the quality of students' written work. Specifically, the research in this area has sought to answer the following questions:

Figure 9.9 Interactive Homework Assignment

Japanese: Greetings

Dear Family,
In Japanese class we have learned how to greet people. This activity will let me show you how I do it. This assignment is due _____

Sincerely, _____
Student's signature

In Japanese I am able to say and respond greetings and courtesy expression properly.

O.high.yo!	"Good morning!"
Cone.knee.chi.wa!	"Hello, Good afternoon!"
Cone.ban.wa!	"Good evening!"
Sa.yo.(o).na.ra!	"Good bye!"
Are.lee.ga.toe!	"Thank you!"
Dough.e.ta.she.ma.she.tay.	"You are welcome."
ao.men.na.sigh.	"I am sorry."
Ee.des.yo!	"It's OK!"

To your parent, how do you...
greet him or her in the morning? afternoon? evening?
greet him or her when you go apart?
thank him or her? or respond when he or she says "thank you"?
apologize? or respond when he or she says "I'm sorry"?

Teach your parent how to greet in Japanese!

With your parent, exchange greetings and courtesy expressions.

1. A.M.   2. early P.M.   3. Evening   4. Gift   5. Oops!   6. Bye!

The tradition of bowing in Japan is a
common gesture used in introductions,
greetings, partings, apologizing, and thanking.

Student's name _____ Class _____ Date _____
How well do you think your child performed this skill?
1. ____ Child seems to perform this skill well.
2. ____ Please check work. Child needs some help on this.
3. ____ Please note (other comments below):

_____
Parent's signature

Source: Antonek, Tucker, and Donato, 1997.

- What type of teacher response to learner writing is more beneficial, that which focuses on form (e.g., grammar, vocabulary, and mechanics) or on content (e.g., organization and amount of detail)?
- What types of feedback do learners report being most helpful to them in helping them to improve their writing?
- What role should learners have in correcting their own writing and that of their peers?
- What are effective methods of scoring and assigning grades to written work?

Focus on Form vs. Focus on Content

In a 1993 review of the literature on error correction, Mings concludes that there is agreement among researchers on the following points:

- Different types of errors are made by learners.
- [Errors] do not all produce identical consequences.
- [Errors] originate from a variety of causes.
- [Errors] serve a very useful purpose in interlanguage development (1993, p. 176).

Much of the literature on correcting written errors supports the claim that learners' writing skills may improve with teacher responses that focus on content rather than on form (Donovan & McClelland, 1980; Kepner, 1991; Semke, 1984; Zamel, 1983). Semke's (1984) landmark study researched the effects of four types of feedback on students' freewriting journal assignments: (1) comments only, (2) corrections only, (3) corrections with comments, and (4) errors signaled with a correction code for students to self-correct. The results indicated that there was no significant difference among the groups in terms of writing accuracy, but that the group receiving comments wrote signficantly more than the other groups and made more progress in general language ability (Semke, 1984). Similarly, Kepner (1991) compared the effects of sentence-level error correction and message-related comments. She found that sentence-level correction did not help students avoid surface errors and that responding to the message was more effective in helping learners improve the quality of their written ideas and grammatical accuracy (Kepner, 1991).

Much of the research examining the effect of correction of form errors provides little support for overt correction (i.e., giving the correct forms) (Hendrickson, 1978). In a study examining the effect of no feedback, Graham (1983) found that students who received feedback on every assignment did not make fewer errors than those students who received feedback on every third assignment. However, some studies indicate that identifying errors or providing information about the kinds of errors made may be helpful to learners (Lalande, 1982, 1984; Robb, Ross, & Shortreed, 1986). Lalande found that learners were able to reduce the number of errors in their writing when the teacher marked all errors using the "Essay Correction Code" (ECCO), tracked error frequency with the "Error Awareness Sheet" (EASE), and required students to interpret the codes, correct their own mistakes, and rewrite their essays (1984, pp. 116–117). (See Appendix 9.8 for an adapted version of ECCO and Appendix 9.9 for an adapted version of EASE.) Similarly, Fathman and Whalley (1990) found that writing accuracy increases when teacher feedback gives the location of grammar errors and that grammar and content feedback, whether given alone or simultaneously, positively affect rewriting. However, of interest in their study is the fact that students significantly improved the content and wrote longer compositions when they did revisions in the absence of teacher feedback, which suggests that rewriting is valuable and teacher feedback may not always be necessary. Some evidence also points to the likelihood that those learners who appreciate grammatical information most may be those who are able to identify gaps in their own grammatical knowledge (Manley & Calk, 1997).

Student Responses to Teacher Feedback

The research indicates that learners want feedback on their writing, but they do not often find their teachers' comments useful because they are too short and uninformative

(Cohen, 1987; Cohen & Cavalcanti, 1990). Students typically handle teacher feedback by making a mental note or wanting additional teacher explanation (Cohen & Cavalcanti, 1990). In an extensive study of over two hundred college students learning foreign and second languages, Cohen (1987) found a difference between learners self-assessed as "good learners" and those self-assessed as "poor learners" with respect to their use of feedback. Learners who felt they were "good" at language learning paid greater attention to comments dealing with vocabulary, grammar, and mechanics than did those learners who reported being "poor language learners" (Cohen, 1987).

 Learners want feedback on their writing, but they do not often find their teachers' comments useful because they are too short and uninformative.

Hedgcock and Lefkowitz (1996) interviewed FL and ESL writers about the types of responses they would like to have in order to improve their writing. They gave the following suggestions for teachers:

- more practice in writing and more systematic opportunities to revise;
- more personalized and explicit written feedback from expert readers;
- grammatical and rhetorical feedback geared more specifically to writers' level of proficiency and degree of readiness;
- individualized writing conferences with instructors, other expert readers, or both;
- more peer interaction and response;
- more student control over the nature and extent of instructor/expert feedback;
- more extensive reading of L2 texts, particularly models that students are asked to imitate (p. 299).

According to Beach (1989), students can learn to describe, judge, and revise their written work on their own if they are first guided through this process during a student-teacher "conference." Teachers may want to conduct individual writing conferences with students several times throughout the year in order to teach students about the revision process, review individual writing needs, and report on writing progress.

Chastain (1990) found that there may be some relationship between the quality of learner compositions and whether or not a grade is being given by the teacher. His study showed that (1) periodic grades on compositions may motivate learners to work harder to increase the length of the written text and complexity of its sentences and (2) including ungraded written work in language classes enables learners to work on developing their writing skills without constant preoccupation with grades. The portfolio approach has been suggested as an alternative to grading every individual writing assignment. In this approach, a representative sample of the learner's best written work is assembled, and the entire portfolio can be evaluated for a grade (Leki, 1990; Moore, 1994; Tierney, Carter, & Desai, 1991). Figure 9.10 shows a diagram of the kinds of writing selections that might be included in a portfolio. See Chapter 11 for additional information about portfolio assessment.

Figure 9.10 Writing That Might Be Included in a Portfolio

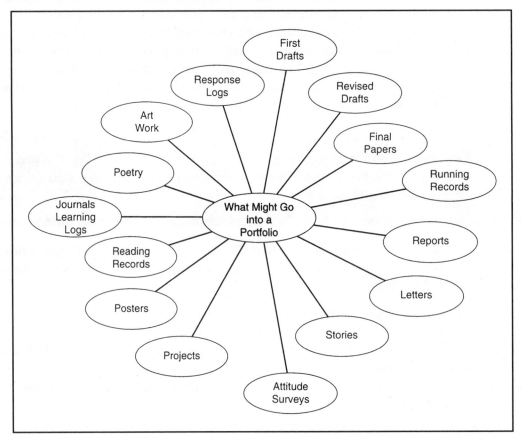

Source: Peregoy & Boyle, 1997, 334.

Peer Revision

Having students engage in peer revision can help them to edit and revise their written texts while providing them with an audience other than the teacher and encouraging them to work together during the writing process (Scott, 1996). Interactive peer revision supports the Vygotskyan framework presented in Chapter 1, since cognitive processes occur in collaboration and are then internalized for eventual independent problem solving. In a study of ESL students conducting peer reviews, De Guerrero and Villamil (1994) studied the socio-cognitive dimensions of interactive peer revision from a Vygotskyan perspective. In highlighting the complexity of student relationships during peer review sessions, this study illustrated the various ways in which students interact as they move from being controlled by their written drafts and not responding to directions from a peer, to being guided by a peer, to responding quickly and efficiently to suggestions from a peer (De Guerrero & Villamil, 1994).[5]

---

5. See De Guerrero and Villamil (1994) for detailed information about the cognitive stages of regulation and social relationships that occur during peer review sessions.

Mangelsdorf and Schlumberger (1992) analyzed peer review comments made by students as they read compositions and found that they adopted one of three perspectives as they reviewed: (1) prescriptive—focused on form and on a predetermined notion of what the text should be; (2) interpretive—imposed their own ideas about the topic onto the text; and (3) collaborative—viewed the text from the author's perspective, made suggestions, and did not focus exclusively on form. Nearly half of the peer reviewers adopted a prescriptive approach, which the researchers attribute to the fact that they received the same kind of feedback from teachers in the past (Mangelsdorf & Schlumberger, 1992).

What seems to be clear in the research is that peer revision can be successful if peer reviewers are given clear guidelines so that they know what to look for and what kinds of feedback will be most helpful (Amores, 1997; Birckbichler, 1985; Hedgcock & Lefkowitz, 1996; Stanley, 1992). In fact, peer assistance might be just as useful as feedback provided by the teacher (Hedgcock & Lefkowitz, 1996). Amores (1997) cautions, however, that students often seem to be more concerned with the personal, social, and emotional aspects of peer editing. She therefore recommends that teachers (1) structure peer editing sessions so that students review texts that were not written by members of the editing group; (2) clearly define both the role of the students and the role of the teacher during the peer revision process; and (3) group students carefully into peer revision groups so that they are able to collaborate effectively (Amores, 1997).

Hedgcock and Lefkowitz (1996) suggested the following guidelines for the peer revision process:

Stage 1: Student writer disributes photocopies of the composition to peer reviewers and then reads the text aloud while the others listen and note their reactions. Peer reviewers are directed to ignore the grammatical aspects of the text and to focus on the content and clarity of the message.

Stage 2: Student writer distributes photocopies of the revised composition to peer reviewers and the same process is repeated, followed by a final reading aloud by the student writer during which peer reviewers identify grammatical errors (cf. Scott, 1996, p. 111).

Appendix 9.10 illustrates a written guide that students could be given to help them evaluate the writing of others when they are doing peer editing in pairs.

Implications of Research on Writing Feedback in the FL Classroom

In summarizing the research on writing feedback given to learners, Gass and Magnan developed the following continuum of types of feedback:

- no feedback (Fathman & Whalley, 1990; Graham, 1983)
- no correction but comments and questions on content (Kepner, 1991; Semke, 1984)
- positive comments and suggestions for improving content (Fathman & Whalley, 1990)
- positive comments and suggestions for improving content and grammar (Fathman & Whalley, 1990)
- identification of form errors without help toward correction (Fathman & Whalley, 1990)

- indirect error marking using a coding system for learner self-correction (Lalande, 1982, 1984; Semke, 1984)
- direct correction of form errors and positive comments (Semke, 1984)
- direct correction of form errors (Kepner, 1991; Lalande, 1982; Semke, 1984; Gass & Magnan, 1993, pp. 181–182)

The following are implications of the research on feedback for responding to writing in the FL classroom:

1. Learners want and benefit from feedback on both form and content.

2. Feedback that focuses on form is most useful if errors are identified by the teacher and students are given the responsibility for correcting them.

3. Learners' writing improves most when they receive feedback dealing with the content of the message.

4. Peer revision can be successful if learners are given explicit guidelines for how to review others' writing.

 Learners' writing improves most when they receive feedback dealing with the content of the message.

Scoring Methods for Evaluating Writing

The following are three methods for scoring and assigning a grade to compositions. Throughout the year teachers will find it beneficial to use these types of scoring systems with different writing assignments, depending on the nature and purpose of each task:

1. Holistic (also called integrative or global): The rater gives one grade as an overall impression of the entire text; criteria may include clarity, effectiveness of message, control of language, and so forth. According to Terry (1989), the holistic scoring instrument used by the Educational Testing Service for evaluating the Advanced Placement Evaluation in foreign languages, as shown in Appendix 9.11, can be adapted to fit the level of students and the focus of instruction. This method is most reliable when raters are trained to establish common standards based on practice rating the types of writing samples they will be evaluating (Cooper, 1977).

2. Analytic: The rater scores various components of the composition separately and gives specific responses to the learner; components may include content, organization, vocabulary, language use, and mechanics (see Appendix 9.12 for an example of an analytic scoring tool [the ESL Composition Profile Scale]).

3. Primary trait: The rater assigns a holistic score to one particular feature of writing, such as organization or vocabulary usage, that has been identified in the writing assignment. Lloyd-Jones (1977) suggests using primary trait scoring to evaluate the quality of a particular mode of discourse such as explanatory, persuasive, or expressive (see Appendix 9.13).

Teach and Reflect

Episode One

Designing an Interactive Homework Assignment for Elementary or Middle School Learners

Using the information presented in this chapter, design an interactive homework activity suitable for either an elementary school or a middle school lesson. Describe how the assignment is linked to classroom work and how it might be used in class the next day. Follow the suggestions for interactive homework design in Appendix 9.7 and create the activity using the one in Figure 9.8 as a model.

Episode Two

Designing a Writing Activity for Secondary Levels or Beyond

For this activity, select a chapter in a textbook for the target language you teach, as approved by your instructor. Develop a process-oriented writing composition task that you might assign as part of your work on the chapter. Use the criteria provided in Appendix 9.4 as you prepare the task. Develop the assignment by using the process-oriented model presented in Figure 9.7. Choose a scoring method and explain how you will assign a grade to the final product.

Discuss and Reflect

Case Study 1

A Writing Assignment That Doesn't Work

Dr. Marie Flayer teaches French full-time at Flagston High School and part-time at Ardamore Community College. She has been teaching at the high school for eight years and recently started teaching a class each semester at the college after completing her Ph.D. Dr. Flayer is well respected in the school district and community as an instructor who knows her subject area and how to relate it to her learners. She brings the language to life in the classroom and involves learners in meaningful language use.

This year, Dr. Flayer was given a French IV class to teach at the high school for the first time. She was quite enthusiastic about the assignment because she wanted to try more advanced-level activities such as composition writing. In Levels One through Three at Flagston, the focus is on developing listening and speaking skills, and the creative writing skill is introduced in Level Four.

During the second week of classes, Dr. Flayer assigned her first composition. She asked learners to write three paragraphs about their summer vacations, and she gave them three days to complete the task. She reminded them about using the past tenses in French as they wrote. She was rather surprised to hear the many complaints by the learners and wondered why they thought this assignment was so difficult, given their extensive knowledge of French. The learners seemed not to be pleased with their work as they handed in their compositions to Dr. Flayer. Some of the best learners said that they had spent more than four hours writing their three paragraphs. Dr. Flayer collected the compositions on Friday and went home in a good mood, satisfied that she had made her learners create with the language and certain that the learners' complaints were exaggerated.

Dr. Flayer's happy mood soon changed to despair on Sunday as she painstakingly plowed through the stack of compositions that no competent user of French would ever understand. It was quite apparent that learners had done their assignments with their dictionaries in hand, for there were French words used that even Dr. Flayer had never before seen. There were so many grammatical errors that the message was practically incomprehensible. It was clear, Dr. Flayer thought, that her learners had not spent sufficient time on this task, or they would have been able to use the language more accurately. She spent eight hours correcting all the errors with her red pen, in the hope that learners would at least learn from their mistakes when she returned their compositions.

Ask yourself these questions:

1. What was Dr. Flayer's approach to integrating writing into her teaching?

2. How did she prepare learners to write the composition?

3. Did she use a process-oriented approach? Explain.

4. What was her rationale for correcting the errors found in the compositions?

To prepare the case:

- Review the process-oriented approach to writing presented in this chapter.
- Consult the following sources for more information about error correction: Kepner (1991), Chastain (1990), Lalande (1984), Semke (1984), Schultz (1996), and Manley and Calk (1997).
- Talk with high school or college learners about how they feel when a teacher returns their writing assignments covered with red ink. Ask other language teachers what color pens they use to correct papers. Think about the effect of using red to make corrections.

To prepare for class discussion, think and write about these topics:

- Appendix 9.4 contains a Checklist for Preparing the Writing Task (Jacobs, et al. 1981). Evaluate Dr. Flayer's writing task according to the criteria presented in the list.
- If you were Dr. Flayer, what would you have done differently in making this assignment?

Describe the various steps or processes through which you might have guided your learners.

- How would you have corrected and graded these compositions?

- This is what one of Dr. Flayer's learners told her about how he planned to work through revisions: "Noticing my mistakes helps improve my writing; I, I think that maybe writing them out . . . is what, is what I do most often, because I do . . . I sometimes correct one composition with one mistake and then do it again" (adapted from Hedgecock & Lefkowitz, 1996, p. 306). What implications are there for teachers when learners notice mistakes but make them again?
- Give three alternatives for what Dr. Flayer might now do with these compositions. Consider how each alternative will help learners learn to write.

Case Study 2

Integrating Peer Revision into the Writing Process

Ms. Reynolds has been teaching Spanish and German at Yuristown High School for three years. She has a heavy teaching schedule of seven classes, with one of the Spanish classes having Levels Three and Four together. Ms. Reynolds believes in teaching language for proficiency, and she provides many opportunities for her learners to use the language in meaningful contexts. Because of time constraints, and her own training and teaching experience, she tends to focus more on listening and speaking in her classroom.

Recently she spoke to Ms. Savage, who has been teaching English at Yuristown for seven years, about the issue of doing more writing activities in her language classes. Ms. Reynolds assigns periodic compositions and even used a process-oriented approach to some degree as she guided learners' writing. However, she was frustrated that learners did not seem to care much about correcting their errors, and she ended up practically rewriting their compositions for them. Ms. Savage suggested that Ms. Reynolds try peer revision, a technique that English teachers have been using for some time. She explained that learners work in pairs (usually with one weaker learner and one stronger) to help each other correct their mistakes. Ms. Savage also suggested the use of some type of correction code and the use of the Error Awareness Sheet to help learners keep track of their errors.

Ask yourself these questions:

1. At what stage of the writing process would the peer revision be done?

2. What difficulties could Ms. Reynolds anticipate when introducing the peer revision technique to her classes?

3. What type of guidance will Ms. Reynolds need to give her learners so that they can use peer revision successfully?

To prepare the case:

- Consult Appendix 9.10 for an example of how to teach learners to evaluate others' writing (Koch & Brazil, 1978).
- Consult Appendixes 9.8 and 9.9 for versions of ECCO and EASE scoring guides.

- Consult Chapter 8 of Scarcella and Oxford (1992) for sample peer review and writer response sheets.
- Interview an experienced English teacher to find out how s/he does peer editing in the classroom.

To prepare for class discussion, think and write about these topics:

- Imagine that you are Ms. Reynolds. Develop your own instruction sheet similar to the one found in Appendix 9.10 to help learners use peer editing.
- Remember that you have one class of Level Three and Four Spanish learners together. How might you use this situation to your advantage for the purposes of peer editing?

References

Amores, M. J. (1997). A new perspective on peer-editing. *Foreign Language Annals, 30,* 513–522.

Antonek, J. L., Tucker, G. R., & Donato, R. (1997). Interactive homework: Creating connections between home and school. In A. Mollica (Ed.), *Teaching languages—Selected readings from Mosaic* (pp. 63–79). Lewiston, NY: Soleil Publishing, Inc.

Atwell, N. (1985). Writing and reading from the inside out. In J. Hansen, T. Newkirt, & D. Graves (Eds.), *Breaking ground: Teachers relate reading and writing in the elementary school* (pp. 147–165). Portsmouth, NH: Heinemann.

Barnett, M. A. (1989). Writing as a process. *The French Review, 63,* 39–41.

Beach, R. (1989). Showing students how to assess: Demonstrating techniques for response in the writing conference. In C. Anson (Ed.), *Writing and Response* (pp. 127–148). Urbana, IL: National Council of Teachers of English.

Bilash, O. S. E. (1998). Planning for writing instruction in a middle-years immersion/partial immersion setting. *Foreign Language Annals, 31,* 159–168.

Britton, J., Burgess, T., Martin, N., McLeod, A., & Rosen, H. (1975). *The development of writing abilities.* Schools Council Research Studies. London: Macmillan Education.

Chastain, K. B. (1990). Characteristics of graded and ungraded compositions. *The Modern Language Journal, 74,* 10–14.

Cohen, A. D. (1987). Student processing of feedback on their compositions. In A. Wenden & J. Rubin (Eds.), *Learner strategies in language learning* (pp. 57–68). Englewood Cliffs, NJ: Prentice Hall.

Cohen, A. D., & Cavalcanti, M. C. (1990). Feedback on compositions: Teacher and student verbal reports. In B. Kroll (ed.), *Second language writing: research insights for the classroom* (pp. 155–177). Cambridge: Cambridge University Press.

Coombs, V. M. (1986). Syntax and communicative strategies in intermediate German composition. *The Modern Language Journal, 70,* 114–124.

Cooper, C. R. (1977). Holistic evaluation of writing. In C. R. Cooper & L. Odell (Eds.), *Evaluating writing* (pp. 3–31). Urbana, IL: National Council of Teachers of English.

Curtain, H., & Pesola, C. (1994). *Languages and children—Making the match.* Reading, MA: Addison-Wesley.

De Guerrero, M. C. M., & Villamil, O. S. (1994). Social-cognitive dimensions of interaction in L2 peer revision. *The Modern Language Journal, 78,* 484–496.

Donovan, T. R., & McClelland, B. W. (1980). *Eight approaches to teaching composition.* Urbana, IL: National Council of Teachers of English.

Dvorak, T. (1986). Writing in the foreign language. In B. H. Wing (Ed.), *Listening, reading, writing: Analysis and application* (pp. 145–167). Northeast Conference Reports. Middlebury, VT: Northeast Conference on the Teaching of Foreign Languages.

Edelsky, C. (1982). Writing in a bilingual program: The relation of L1 and L2 texts. *TESOL Quarterly, 16,* 211–228.

Epstein, J. (1993). School and family partnerships. *Instructor, 103 (2),* 73–76.

Fathman, A. K., & Whalley, E. (1990). Teacher response to student writing. In B. Kroll (Ed.), *Second language writing: Research insights for the classroom* (pp. 178–190). New York: Cambridge University Press.

Flower, L., & Hayes, J. R. (1981). A cognitive process theory of writing. *College composition and communication, 32,* 365–387.

Friedlander, A. (1990). Composing in English: Effects of a first language on writing in English as a second language. In B. Kroll (Ed.), *Second language writing: Research insights for the classroom* (pp. 109–125). New York: Cambridge University Press.

Gass, S. M., & Magnan, S. S. (1993). Second-language production: SLA research in speaking and writing. In A. O. Hadley (Ed.), *Research in language learning: Principles, processes, and prospects* (pp. 156–197), The ACTFL Foreign Language Education Series, Lincolnwood, IL: NTC/Contemporary Publishing Group.

Graham, M. F. (1983). The effect of teacher feedback on the reduction of usage errors in junior college freshmen's writing. Unpublished doctoral dissertation. University of Southern Mississippi: Hattiesburg.

Hadley, A. C. (1993). *Teaching language in context.* Boston, MA: Heinle & Heinle.

Hedgcock, J. & Lefkowitz, N. (1996). Some input on input: Two analyses of student response to expert feedback in L2 writing. *The Modern Language Journal, 80,* 287–308.

Hendrickson, J. M. (1978). Error correction in foreign language teaching: Recent theory, research, and practice. *The Modern Language Journal, 62,* 387–398.

Henry, K. (1996). Early L2 writing development: A study of autobiographical essays by university-level students of Russian. *The Modern Language Journal, 80,* 309–326.

Jacobs, H. L., Zingraf, S., Wormuth, D., Hartfield, V., & Hughey, J. (1981). *Testing ESL composition: A practical approach.* Rowley, MA: Newbury House.

Johnson, L. W. (1983). *Grading the advanced placement examination in French language.* Princeton, NJ: Advanced Placement Program of the College Board.

Kauffmann, R. A. (1996). Writing to read and reading to write: Teaching literature in the foreign language classroom. *Foreign Language Annals, 29,* 396–402.

Kepner, C. G. (1991). An experiment in the relationship of types of written feedback to the development of second-language writing skills. *The Modern Language Journal, 75,* 305–313.

Kern, R. G., & Schultz, J. M. (1992). The effects of composition instruction on intermediate level French students' writing performance: Some preliminary findings. *The Modern Language Journal, 76,* 1–13.

Koch, C., & Brazil, J. (1978). *Strategies for teaching the composition process.* Urbana, IL: National Council of Teachers of English.

Koda, K. (1993). Task-induced variability in foreign language composition: Language-specific perspectives. *Foreign Language Annals, 26,* 332–346.

Laidlaw, A. (1989). Formula poetry fun. A presentation to the Washtenaw/Livingston Academic Alliance of Foreign Language Teachers, Ypsilanti, MI.

Lalande, J. F., II. (1984). Reducing composition errors: An experiment. *Foreign Language Annals, 17,* 109–117.

Lapp, R. (1984). *The process approach to writing: Towards a curriculum for international students.* MA Thesis, University of Hawaii.

Lee, J. F., & VanPatten, B. (1995). *Making communicative language teaching happen.* New York: McGraw-Hill, Inc.

Leki, I. (1990). Coaching from the margins: Issues in written response. In B. Kroll, (Ed.). *Second language writing: Research insights for the classroom* (pp. 57–68). Cambridge, UK: Cambridge University Press, 57–68.

Lloyd-Jones, R. (1977). Primary trait scoring. In C. R. Cooper & L. Odell (Eds.), *Evaluating writing* (pp. 33–66). Urbana, IL: National Council of Teachers of English.

Magnan, S. (1985). Teaching and testing proficiency in writing: Skills to transcend the second-language classroom. In A. Omaggio (Ed.), *Proficiency, curriculum, articulation: The ties that bind* (pp. 109–136), Northeast Conference Reports. Middlebury, VT: Northeast Conference on the Teaching of Foreign Languages.

Mangelsdort, K., & Schlumberger, A. (1992). ESL student response stances in a peer-review task. *Journal of Second Language Writing, 1,* 235–254.

Manley, J. H., & Calk, L. (1997). Grammar instruction for writing skills: Do students perceive grammar as useful? *Foreign Language Annals, 30,* 73–83.

Mings, R. C. (1993). Changing perspectives on the utility of error correction in second language acquisition. *Foreign Language Annals, 26,* 171–179.

National Standards in Foreign Language Education Project. (1996). *Standards for foreign language learning: Preparing for the 21st century.* Lawrence, KS: Allen Press.

Nerenz, A. G. (1990). The exploratory years: Foreign languages in the middle-level curriculum. In S. Magnan (Ed.), *Shifting the Instructional Focus to the Learner* (pp. 93–126), Northeast Conference Reports. Middlebury, VT: Northeast Conference on the Teaching of Foreign Languages.

Moore, Z. (1994). The portfolio and testing culture. In C. Hancock (Ed.), *Teaching, testing, and assessment: Making the connection* (pp. 163–182), Northeast Conference Reports. Lincolnwood, IL: NTC/Contemporary Publishing Group.

Oller, J. (1979). *Language tests at school.* London, UK: Longman.

Peregoy, S. F., & Boyle, O. F. (1997). *Reading, writing and learning in ESL: A resource book for K–12 teachers.* New York: Addison Wesley Longman.

Peyton, J. K. (1987). Dialogue journal writing with limited English proficient students. In *Q and A.* Washington, D.C.: Center for Applied Linguistics.

Peyton, J. K. (1990). *Students and teachers writing together: Perspectives on journal writing.* Alexandria, VA: TESOL.

Raimes, A. (1987). Language proficiency, writing ability, and composing strategies: A study of ESL college student writers. *Language learning, 37,* 439–467.

Richards, J. (1990). *The language teaching matrix.* Cambridge: Cambridge University Press.

Robb, T., Ross, S., & Shortreed, I. (1986). Salience of feedback on error and its effect on EFL writing quality. *TESOL Quarterly, 20,* 83–93.

Rodby, J. (1992). *Appropriating literacy.* Portsmouth, NH: Boynton/Cook Publishers.

Scarcella, R., & Oxford, R. (1992). *The tapestry of language learning.* Boston, MA: Heinle & Heinle.

Schultz, J. M. (1991). Writing mode in the articulation of language and literature classes: Theory and practice. *The Modern Language Journal, 75,* 411–417.

Schultz, J. M. (1994). Stylistic reformulation: Theoretical premises and practical applications. *The Modern Language Journal, 78,* 169–178.

Schultz, R. A. (1996). Focus on form in the foreign language classroom: Students' and teachers' views on error correction and the role of grammar. *Foreign Language Annals, 29,* 343–364.

Scott, R. S., & Rodgers, B. C. (1993). Assessing communication in writing: The development of a Spanish writing contest. *Foreign Language Annals, 26,* 383–392.

Scott, V. M. (1992). Writing from the start: A task-oriented developmental writing program for foreign language students. In R. Terry (Ed.), *Dimension: Language '91* (pp. 1–15) Southern Conference on Language Teaching. Valdosta, GA: Valdosta State University.

Scott, V. M. (1995). Writing. In V. Galloway & C. Herron (Eds.), *Research within reach II* (pp. 115–127). Southern Conference on Language Teaching. Valdosta, GA: Valdosta State University.

Scott, V. M. (1996). *Rethinking foreign language writing.* Boston, MA: Heinle & Heinle.

Scott, V. M., & Terry, R. M. (1992). *Système-D Teacher's Guide.* Boston, MA: Heinle & Heinle.

Semke, H. D. (1984). Effects of the red pen. *Foreign Language Annals, 17,* 195–202.

Silva, T. (1990). Second language composition instruction: Developments, issues, and directions in ESL. In B. Kroll (Ed.), *Second language writing—Research insights for the classroom* (pp. 11–23). Cambridge: Cambridge University Press.

Stanley, J. (1992). Coaching student writers to be more effective peer evaluators. *Journal of Second Language Writing, 1,* 217–233.

Terry, R. M. (1989). Teaching and evaluating writing as a communicative skill. *Foreign Language Annals, 22,* 43–54.

Tierney, R. J., Carter, M. A., & Desai, L.E. (1991). *Portfolio assessment in the reading-writing classroom.* Norwood, MA: Christopher-Gordon.

Tussing, M., Lowe, P., Jr., & Clifford, R. (1998). The writing assignment matrix. Paper presented at the annual meeting of the American Council on the Teaching of Foreign Languages.

United States Department of Education. (1986). *What works: Research about teaching and learning.* Washington, D.C.: United States Department of Education.

Valdés, G., Haro, P., & Echevarriarza, M. P. (1992). The development of writing abilities in a foreign language: Contributions toward a general theory of L2 writing. *The Modern Language Journal, 76,* 333–352.

Vygotsky, L. S. (1978). *Mind in society: The development of higher psychological processes.* Cambridge, MA: Harvard University Press.

West, M. J., & Donato, R. D. (1995). Stories and stances: Cross-cultural encounters with African folk-tales. *Foreign Language Annals 28,* 392–406.

Zamel, V. (1982).Writing: The process of discovering meaning. *TESOL Quarterly, 16,* 195–209.

Zamel, V. (1983).The composing processes of advanced ESL students: Six case studies. *TESOL Quarterly, 17,* 165–187.

CHAPTER *10*

Addressing Student Diversity in the Language Classroom

In this chapter you will learn about:

- students of diverse cultural, ethnic, and racial backgrounds
- multiple intelligences
- learning styles
- learning strategies
- students with physical and learning disabilities

- "at-risk" students
- gifted learners
- heritage language learners
- the Communities Goal Area and Standards

Teach and Reflect: Designing a Lesson Appropriate for Diverse Learning Styles; Working within Communities

- **Case Study 1: Preparing to Teach Special Education Spanish I and II Classes**
- **Case Study 2: Cultural Diversity in a Small Rural Community**

As you prepare to read and discuss this chapter, you might want to take the following self-test as a way to examine your beliefs about the diversity of students whom you will teach:

Do I (or Will I). . .

- truly believe that *all* students can learn?
- have *high* expectations for all students?
- value and respect *all* students and cultures and model that respect in my classroom?
- go beyond school requirements for contacting parents?
- consult guidance counselors and ask why students have been taken out of my class or why a change in schedule has been made?
- share pertinent information with colleagues regarding learners with special needs and the strategies that promote student success?
- allow for differences in learning styles, amount of time needed to learn, and ways students most effectively demonstrate knowledge?

- try to teach to the strengths of each individual student?
- send home letters of commendation/appreciation?
- demand non-prejudicial conversations and/or comments in my classroom?

Fairfax County Public Schools, 1992, p. 12.

Conceptual Orientation

"I will try to be at the edge between my fear and outside, on the edge at my skin, listening, asking what new thing will I hear, will I see, will I let myself feel, beyond the fear. I try to say to myself: To acknowledge the complexity of another's existence is not to deny my own" (Pratt, 1984, p. 18).

These words by Ms. Pratt, a leading activist in the civil rights movement, show a commitment to blending the self with the community for the sake of what can be learned, in spite of the fear of the unknown. They are part of the thinking that leads scholars to affirm in the standards of foreign language learning that "ALL students are capable of learning other languages given opportunities for quality instruction" (NSFLEP, 1996, p. 19), regardless of the ways in which these learners may differ. The inclusivity of the standards implies that in any given language classroom there may be students who differ from each other in motivation, goals for learning, aptitude, zone of proximal development, ethnic or national origin, gender, socio-economic status, and linguistic or cultural heritage. Even in classes in which students appear to be relatively homogeneous in background and goals, they may differ along some other dimension. The challenge to the language teacher is to recognize and help learners appreciate these differences and similarities, and then to design differentiated instruction so that each learner has opportunities to enhance thinking skills and to learn how other cultures express ideas.

Diversity of gender, age, race, national origin, and ethnicity are often ways in which we think of diverse populations. According to Spinelli (1996), thirty percent of school children were students "of color," the term the U.S. Department of Education uses to refer to African American, Hispanic, Asian American, and Native American students (sometimes this grouping is called AHANA). Of the thirty percent, fifteen percent were African American, eleven percent Hispanic, three percent Asian American, and one percent Native American, while only thirteen percent of the nation's teachers were members of the AHANA group. By the year 2020, minority learners will constitute fifty percent of the public school population (*Digest of Educational Statistics*, 1991). Leaders in foreign language education call for mentoring and incentives to attract an increasing number of strong students who are members of minority groups into the field of foreign language teaching (Lange, 1991; Wilberschied & Dassier, 1995). When the term "diversity" is mentioned, we usually think of a certain ethnic and racial background. However, diversity also includes the range of academic, physical, and emotional abilities that students have. In addition, learners are unique in the ways in which they approach language learning.

The Diverse Ways in Which Learners Approach Language Learning

❒ Multiple Intelligences

Theories of multiple intelligences are often used to help explain how learners approach all types of learning, including language learning. Gardner's (1993) explanation of multiple intelligences captured the attention of researchers and practitioners. In his view, an "intelligence" is a set of brain functions that can be developed and expanded and that consists of skills for (1) resolving genuine problems or difficulties, and for (2) finding or creating problems (Gardner, 1993, p. 61). Gardner's (1993, 1995) theory suggests eight intelligences. Figure 10.1 categorizes these intelligences, together with the characteristics of each and sample foreign language classroom activities that help develop each.

These multiple intelligences can enable us to understand how a learner might more easily grasp a linguistic concept if it is presented in the form of a mathematical formula (logical/mathematical); how singing songs and doing TPR activities help learners who have trouble focusing attention on printed pages (musical/rhythmic, bodily/kinesthetic); how interacting in pairs helps learners acquire a new linguistic concept (interpersonal). Appendix 10.1 provides an extensive list of multiple intelligences activities, classroom environments, and assessments.

 Multiple intelligences help explain how learners approach language learning.

❒ Learning Styles

A *learning style* is a general approach a learner uses to learn a new language (Scarcella & Oxford, 1992, p. 61). Learning styles research has had particular influence in helping teachers identify ways in which learners differ in their approaches to language learning. Oxford (1990a) and Scarcella & Oxford (1992) have identified five key dimensions of language learning styles:

1. *Analytic-global:* This dimension illustrates the difference between a detail-oriented individual and a holistic one. Analytic students concentrate on grammatical details and often do not participate well in communicative activities. They would rather find the meanings of words in a dictionary than guess in context. Global students like interactive tasks in which they use main ideas. They have difficulty dealing with grammatical details and are content to use guessing strategies.

2. *Sensory preferences:* This dimension highlights the physical, perceptual avenues for learning, such as visual, auditory, and hands-on (kinesthetic or movement oriented and tactile or touch oriented). Visual students prefer to read and visualize information; they usually dislike having to process oral input in the absence of visual support. Auditory students enjoy conversations and other types of verbal interaction and often have difficulty with written work. Hands-on students do well with movement around the classroom and work easily with objects and realia.

Figure 10.1 Multiple Intelligences

CATEGORY OF INTELLIGENCE	CHARACTERISTICS	FL CLASSROOM ACTIVITIES
PERSONAL: Intrapersonal/Introspective	Self Smart: understanding oneself and taking responsibility for thinking on one's own	Goal setting; journals and personal reflection; problem-solving activities, independent assignments such as autobiographies and family heritage study; open-ended expression
Interpersonal/Social	People Smart: understanding others, getting along with others, interpreting individuals' moods, motivations, inhibitions	Cooperative tasks such as think-pair-share and jigsaws; creative group tasks such as collages and story books; interactive technology such as e-mail, CD-ROM, and Internet
ACADEMIC: Logical/Mathematical	Logic Smart: logical reasoning, categorizing facts, sequential thought	Graphic organizers that show patterns and relationships; problem-solving manipulatives; puzzles and games; challenge tasks
Verbal/Linguistic	Word Smart: communicating by listening, speaking, reading, and writing; using language to link new knowledge to prior experiences	Graphic organizers to promote brainstorming and generating ideas; list making; mnemonics; verbal games; speakers; interviews; peer teaching; personal expression (opinions, reactions); logs or journals
EXPRESSIVE: Bodily/Kinesthetic	Body Smart: skillfully controlling body motions; showing a keen sense of direction and timing in movement	TPR; creative dramatics and mime; creating things; role playing and interviews; projects, field trips, active learning
Visual/Spatial	Picture Smart: accurately comprehending the visual word; transforming mental images; seeing things in terms of pictures	Learning experiences using drawings, charts, props, posters, photographs; illustrations; demonstrations; use of overhead projector, chalkboard, video
Musical/Rhythmic	Music Smart: using pitch, rhythm, and so on, in enjoying and creating musical experiences; being attuned to rhythms, responding with actions	Songs, music, dance of the target culture; music mnemonics; jingles, raps, cheers; using movement or dance to illustrate ideas or concepts
EMERGING: Naturalist	Nature Smart: seeing deeply into the nature of living things; identifying and classifying things; problem solving	Data collection; demonstrations; research projects; logs; reports

Source: Compiled from Lange, 1999, (pp. 106–109) and Gahala & Lange, 1997, (pp. 30–32); adapted from Gardner, 1993, 1995.

3. *Intuitive/Random and Sensory/Sequential Learning:* This dimension deals with the type of organization students prefer in the presentation of material. Intuitive/Random students think in an abstract, nonsequential, or random manner, making sense of the global picture. Sensory/Sequential students prefer to learn new information by means of a step-by-step, ordered presentation. They perform tasks in a linear order and often have difficulty seeing the bigger picture.

4. *Orientation to closure:* This dimension refers to the degree to which students need to reach conclusions and can tolerate ambiguity. Students oriented toward closure want all rules spelled out for them and use metacognitive skills such as planning, organizing, and self-evaluating. However, they often tend to analyze prematurely and experience difficulty dealing with abstract or subtle issues. Ehrman and Oxford (1989) showed that the desire for closure might have a negative effect on a student's ability to participate in open-ended communication. "Open learners," or those who have less need for closure, learn by osmosis rather than by conscientious effort and appear to use more effective language learning strategies than students who require quick closure (Scarcella & Oxford, 1992, p. 62).

5. *Competition-cooperation:* This dimension illustrates the degree to which learners benefit from competing against or cooperating with others. Competitive learners are motivated by competition in which winning is of utmost importance. Cooperative individuals prefer working with others in a helpful, supportive situation. Studies show that the high degree of competitiveness in education may account for the fact that learners seldom report using cooperative, social strategies (Kohn, 1987; Reid, 1987). According to Bailey (1983), competition in language learning may result in feelings of anxiety, inadequacy, hostility, fear of failure, guilt, and too strong a desire for approval. As you learned in Chapter 8, cooperative learning provides an avenue for student interaction while increasing self-esteem, achievement, motivation, and the use of cognitive strategies (Kohn, 1987).

 What is your preferred learning style and why?

What implications do these learning styles have for teaching language in a classroom situation? Oxford and Lavine examine the mismatch between instructors' teaching styles and their students' learning styles. They claim that "students whose learning processes resemble the teacher's are more likely to achieve good grades (and want to continue studying the language) than are students with opposing styles, who may drop the course or even discontinue studying the language" (Oxford & Lavine, 1992, p. 38). They further assert that style wars between teachers and students are often disguised as "poor language aptitudes," "personality clashes," and "bad learner attitudes." (1992, p. 42). Oxford and Lavine (1992) suggest six ways in which these teacher-student style conflicts can be dealt with realistically:

1. Assess students' and teachers' styles and use this information to understand classroom dynamics. As teachers and students become aware of their major learning style

preferences, they may be able to help one another understand diverse views and make an effort to compensate for any style mismatches. Instruments for assessing learning styles can be used, such as the Learning Styles Inventory (Kolb, 1984), the Swassing-Barbe Modality Index (Barbe, Swassing, & Milone, 1979), and the Myers-Briggs Type Indicator (Myers & McCaulley, 1985), among others.

2. **Change your teaching behavior.** Teachers can orient their teaching styles to meet their students' needs by providing a variety of multisensory, abstract, and concrete learning activities that appeal to different learning styles. Learners who are analytic, sequential, or closure-oriented usually like questions and exercises requiring unambiguous information such as completions, definitions, true-false, slash sentences, cloze passages, and guided writing. Learners who are global, intuitive, or open often prefer open-ended activities, personalized questions, simulations and games, interviews, reading for the gist, and social conversation. Visual learners need visual stimuli such as transparencies, slides, video, charts, maps, magnetic or felt boards, posters, board games, and puppets. They benefit from written directions and from being shown, not told, what to do. Auditory learners prefer auditory input from radio, television, video, songs, interviews, oral reports, discussions, telephone conversations, and recordings. They need oral instructions and must be told, not shown, what to do. Hands-on learners require hands-on experiences such as making things, manipulating real cultural items, taking notes, doing TPR activities, and following directions. If these learners "do not receive enough sensory stimuli, they might create their own movement activities unrelated to the learning task (such as tapping pencils, drawing, doodling, wiggling, or bouncing)" (Oxford and Lavine, 1992, p. 43).

3. **Change learners' behavior.** Language learners use their style preferences to their own advantage. Learners can benefit when teachers realize this and when teachers provide opportunities for students to move beyond their "stylistic comfort zone" through the use of strategies with which they might not initially feel comfortable (Scarcella & Oxford, 1992). For example, an analytic learner can benefit from an activity that involves understanding global meaning, while a global student similarly can benefit from doing some linguistic analysis in order to improve accuracy.

4. **Change the way students work in groups in the classroom.** Teachers can use the principles of cooperative learning in grouping students for interactive work. In certain tasks, students with similar learning styles might be grouped together, while in other activities, students might be grouped in a heterogenous fashion so that members might practice stretching beyond their comfort zones.

5. **Change the curriculum.** Teachers might organize lessons as a series of activities or episodes, each with a different objective and style. New materials might be developed in learning-style modules. Multimedia materials could be integrated into the curriculum for classroom and individual use in order to guarantee the tapping of different sensory styles.

6. **Change the way style conflicts are viewed.** Teachers who encourage students to become aware of learning style preferences help promote flexibility and openness to the use of many styles.

A communicative teaching approach that provides for a variety of activities, individual guidance, and an emphasis on meaning can enable students to experience many learning styles.

☐ Language Learning Strategies

Scarcella and Oxford define language learning strategies as "specific actions, behaviors, steps, or techniques—such as seeking out conversation partners, or giving oneself encouragement to tackle a difficult language task—used by students to enhance their own learning" (1992, p. 63). According to MacIntyre and Noels, almost any tactic or plan that the learner believes will help in learning some part of the language or in managing the language learning process can be considered a strategy (1996, p. 373). Oxford's (1990b) Strategy Inventory for Language Learning (SILL) lists as many as eighty strategies. Research shows that strategies can be taught, although not all strategies are useful for all people in all situations. However, they are effective when used, particularly when learners create their own strategies. Donato and McCormick (1994), for example, developed a successful portfolio assessment project for a French conversation class, which helped students to identify and create their own learning strategies. Figure 10.2 depicts a list of language learning strategies categorized in terms of four stages in the learning process: (1) planning for learning, (2) regulating or facilitating one's learning, (3) problem solving, and (4) evaluating one's progress in learning (Alatis & Barnhardt, 1998).

 Language learning strategies are specific actions, behaviors, steps, or techniques used by students to enhance their own learning.

The use of appropriate learning strategies often results in increased language proficiency and greater self-confidence (Cohen, 1990; Oxford & Crookall, 1989). Research supports the idea that many learners are relatively unaware of the strategies they use and do not take advantage of the full range of available strategies (Oxford & Crookall, 1989). Oxford (1990a) suggests that instructors teach students how to use strategies in order to help them in the language learning process. Earlier chapters of *Teacher's Handbook* presented ways to teach students effective strategies for comprehending oral and written input and for communicating in oral and written form. Strategy training can be integrated with language learning activities and conducted through simulations, games, and other interactive tasks. Oxford developed the following eight-step model for integrating strategy training into classroom activities:

1. Identify students' needs to determine what strategies they are currently using, how effective the strategies are, and how they can be improved.

2. Choose relevant strategies to be taught.

3. Determine how best to integrate strategy training into regular classroom activities.

4. Consider students' motivations and attitudes about themselves as learners and about learning new ways to learn.

Figure 10.2 Learning Strategies Model

PLAN		
Strategy name	*Question student asks self*	*Definition*
Goal-setting	What is my personal objective? What strategies can help me?	Develop personal objectives, identify purpose of task, choose appropriate strategies
Directed attention	What distractions can I ignore? How can I focus my attention?	Decide in advance to focus on particular tasks and ignore distractions
Activate background knowledge	What do I already know about this topic/task?	Think about and use what you already know to help do the task
Predict/ Brainstorm	What kinds of information can I predict for this task? What might I need to do?	Anticipate information to prepare and give yourself direction for the task
REGULATE		
Self-Monitor	Do I understand this? Am I making sense?	Check your understanding to keep track of how you're doing and to identify problems
Selective attention	What should I pay most attention to? Is the information important?	Focus on specific aspects of language or situational details
Deduction	Which rules can I apply to help complete the task?	Apply known rules
Visualize	Can I imagine a picture or situation that will help me understand?	Create an image to represent information to help you remember and check your understanding
Contextualize/ Personalize	How does this fit into the real world?	Think about how to use material in real life, relate information to background knowledge
Cooperate	How can I work with others to do this?	Work with others to help build confidence and to give and receive feedback
Self-talk	I can do this! What strategies can I use to help me?	Reduce anxiety by reminding self of progress, resources available, and goals
PROBLEM-SOLVE		
Inference/ Substitute	Can I guess what this means? Is there another way to say/do this?	Make guesses based on previous knowledge
Question for clarification	What help do I need? Who/Where can I ask?	Ask for explanation and examples
Resource	What information do I need? Where can I find more information about this?	Use reference materials
EVALUATE		
Verify	Were my predictions and guesses right? Why or why not?	Check whether your predictions/guesses were right
Summarize	What is the gist/main idea of this?	Create a mental, oral, written summary

Source: Alatis & Barnhardt, 1998, 82.

5. Prepare materials and activities.

6. Conduct "completely informed training," in which students learn and practice new strategies, learn why the strategies are important, learn to evaluate their use of the strategies, and learn how to apply them in new situations (see Appendix 10.2 for an example of this training model in action).

7. Evaluate the strategy training.

8. Revise the strategy training procedure for the next set of strategies to be taught.

Oxford 1990a, pp. 48–49.

MacIntyre and Noels further add that strategy training should encourage the actual use of the strategy by building assurance in learners that they know the strategies well, that the strategies will work, and that they are not difficult to use (1996, p. 383).

 Knowing strategies and using them help learners succeed.

Addressing Diverse Learner Needs

☐ Teaching Foreign Language to Students with Disabilities

Teaching foreign languages to all students, as specified in the SFLL, requires special attention to the needs of students with disabilities. A "disability" is a mental or physical impairment that limits a major life activity, for example, caring for oneself, performing a manual task, hearing, walking, speaking, thinking, and so forth. Disabilities include autism, deafness, deaf-blindness, hearing impairment, mental retardation, multiple disabilities, orthopedic impairment, other health impairments (such as limited strength due to asthma, heart condition, leukemia, etc.), serious emotional disturbance, specific learning disability, speech or language impairment, traumatic brain injury, and visual impairment including blindness. Prior to 1975, students with these types of disabilities were placed together in classes often labeled "Special Education." In 1975, Public Law 94-142 (Education for All Handicapped Children Act of 1975) directed public schools "to search out and enroll all handicapped children and to educate these children in the least restrictive environment in which they are able to function and still have their special needs met" (Good & Brophy, 1991, p. 389). In addition, Public Law 101-476 (Individuals with Disabilities Act, sometimes called IDEA, of 1990) and Public Law 105-17 (Amendments to IDEA of 1997) ensure that persons with disabilities are not denied participation in or benefits from educational programs or activities, and that these persons do not face negative bias or stereotyping associated with a disability. Through a provision called "inclusion" or "mainstreaming," students who have physical, intellectual, or emotional impairments are part of regular classrooms and receive special accommodations in those classrooms (Good & Brophy, 1991). In 1995–1996 more than five million children ages birth to twenty-one in the United States received special support services to address their disabilities (*Implementation of the Individuals with Disabilities Act, Sec. 618*, 1997). School personnel work with families and learners to outline individualized education programs (IEPs) or individualized family service plans (IFSPs) to provide accommodations that must be offered to learners with disabilities.

Teaching Foreign Language to Learners with Special Physical Needs

Language teachers who work with students who are physically disabled must make arrangements to ensure that these students have access to various areas in the classroom and that their special physical needs are met. The teacher needs to be aware of how students' physical limitations will affect participation in certain types of hands-on activities, such as TPR, and how s/he will need to provide alternative activities. Students who have physical disabilites will require space for a wheelchair, crutches, or a walker. They also need extra time to move through the halls to the next class and thus might require early dismissal or a companion to help negotiate the hallways or carry books. Spinelli (1996) suggests many ways for teachers to accommodate students with visual or auditory impairments in the language classroom.

Teachers should keep in mind that for deaf students whose home background is a community of hearing impaired persons, American Sign Language or another form of hand language is often the first and primary language; learning English in school is the second language. In a foreign language class, these students could be learning a third or subsequent language (Strong, 1988). Spinelli (1989) describes an approach to language instruction for deaf students in which they are taught to use sign language in the foreign language through the use of videotapes showing target-culture signing. Using the TL signing system is a more effective system for communication than finger spelling the foreign language. Foreign language teachers of deaf students must think "visually" about their teaching. Students might be given the scripts that often accompany audiocassette programs, and they should be permitted to refer to their textbooks or to other written material during oral presentations. The teacher may need to prepare written scripts of oral activities to assist students with comprehension, and a note taker may be required for discussions. The visual and written modalities might be stressed in combination with study of the deaf culture as opposed to that of the hearing culture. Students who have hearing impairments may also require preferred seating arrangements, face-to-face talk if they read lips, and perhaps interpreters. Students who are hearing impaired can often tell the teacher how they learn most effectively and can suggest ways for the teacher to aid their learning. Teachers should keep in mind that reading can be difficult and frustrating for a deaf person, depending on the degree of hearing loss. Since a great deal of reading ability is associated with phonological awareness, and profoundly deaf children cannot make letter-sound correspondences, reading is a tedious process for most deaf children.

In the case of students with visual impairments, large-type, braille, or auditory texts are needed; oral examinations, reading services, preferred seating in the classroom, and perhaps space for a guide dog are other accommodations. Teachers can capitalize on oral skills and the use of discussion. In addition, students need extra class time to process material that they read in braille. Partnerships between class members can be arranged for TPR activities that involve manipulatives, which may result in greater use of the target language. For example, in practicing vocabulary dealing with clothing, a student with visual impairment tells a sighted student where to place specific items of clothing on a laminated paper doll (Kraft, 1992). In exam situations, special considerations can be made, such as giving only oral exams for these students or having each student dictate her/his answers to another student who writes them down (Phillips de Herrera, 1984).

Teaching Foreign Language to Learners with Special Learning Needs

Among the types of learners with special cognitive needs are (1) average or non-gifted students with special needs and (2) learning disabled (LD) students (Fairfax County Public Schools, 1992). It is paramount that the foreign language teacher understand the characteristics of these groups in order to use specific teaching strategies that will enable them to experience success in the language classroom.

Average or non-gifted students with special needs are able to perform at expected levels, but they may perform at a lower level of expectation or ability because of emotional, motivational, cultural, or social difficulties. These students may also have poor study skills. Specific strategies for the foreign language teacher include the following:

- Communicate specific expectations and monitor student progress constantly.
- Give specific explanations and instructions orally and visually, step by step.
- Provide a variety of activities, some of which require physical movement.
- Get students on task immediately and provide frequent changes of pace.
- Display student work as a form of reinforcement for work well done.
- Choose reading selections, writing assignments, and presentation topics related to student interests.
- Provide choices of activities and higher-level thinking activities as students seem ready.
- Have students repeat the homework assignment instructions and, if time allows, begin the assignment. This provides time to work with students needing assistance.

Fairfax County Public Schools, 1992, p. 5.

A second group of special needs students are *learning disabled students*. Public Law 94-142 cites the legal definition of a *learning disability*:

> A disorder in one or more of the basic psychological processes involved in understanding or in using language, spoken or written, which may manifest itself in an imperfect ability to listen, speak, read, write, spell, or do mathematical calculations. The term does not include children who have learning problems which are primarily the result of visual, hearing, or motor handicaps, or mental retardation, emotional disturbance, or environmental, cultural, or economic disadvantage (Federal Register, 1975; cf. Sparks, Ganschow, & Javorsky, 1995, p. 480).

Learning disorders are intrinsic to the individual (child or adult), are presumed to be due to central nervous system dysfunction, and may occur across the life span. Problems in self-regulatory behaviors, social perception, and social interaction may exist with learning disorders but do not by themselves constitute a learning disorder. Although learning disorders may occur concomitantly with other handicapping conditions (for example, sensory impairment, mental retardation, or serious emotional disturbance) or with extrinsic influences (such as cultural differences and insufficient or inappropriate instruction), they are not the result of those conditions or influences. (Brinckerhoff, Shaw, & McGuire, 1993, p. 71). A learning disorder interferes with someone's ability to store, process, or produce information. The impairment can be quite subtle and may go undetected throughout life.

Nevertheless, learning disorders create a gap between a person's true capacity and day-to-day productivity and performance (Levine, 1984, p. 3).

However, the category of students labeled as learning disabled (LD) continues to pose a challenge for teachers of all disciplines partially because there continues to be a lack of agreement among cognition experts concerning the specific criteria that should be used to determine whether or not a student has a learning disability. State and local agencies have the responsibility of testing and diagnosing learners as having a learning disability. However, Lyon and Moats (1993) point out that these agencies use different testing measures and criteria in classifying LD learners, and they are often influenced by the political/social agendas of community groups. For example, one of the criteria often used in diagnosing a learning disability is the discrepancy between the IQ score and the score on a measure of academic achievement. In some states, a fifteen-point discrepancy would classify a student as being LD while in other states the discrepancy must be twenty-two points (Sparks & Javorsky, 1998). Unfortunately, many learners are incorrectly classified as LD and carry that label with them throughout their educational experience, while other learners who may require special assistance are never diagnosed with a learning disability.

Although LD students may vary widely in their specific learning problems, Levine (1984) cites the following types of difficulties often exhibited by them:

- difficulties in keeping attention focused: tuning in and out, inconsistent performance, impulsive behavior, and a negative self-image
- language difficulties: oral, aural, and written
- spatial orientation problems: words look different, and reversals in letters and in placement of letters and words are common
- poor memory
- fine motor control problems: a breakdown between head and paper, handwriting difficulties
- difficulty in organizing work
- sequencing problems: difficulty in putting a series of items in correct order, difficulty in following instructions, difficulty in organizing work (cf. Spinelli, 1996, pp. 74–75).

Research examining the success and difficulties that LD learners experience with foreign language study indicates that there is no such distinct entity as a foreign language learning disability (Sparks & Ganschow, 1995). Over the past decade, Sparks, Ganschow, and colleagues (all in the field of Special Education) have published a number of studies that claim that students who experience FL learning difficulties are likely to have phonological/syntactic problems in their native language (Sparks, Ganschow & Pohlman, 1989; Javorsky, Sparks & Ganschow, 1992; Sparks, Ganschow, Javorsky, Pohlman, & Patton, 1992). They initially called this position the Linguistic Coding Deficit Hypothesis and later renamed it the Linguistic Coding Differences Hypothesis (LCDH) in an attempt to explain that successful FL learners exhibit subtle but significant differences in their oral/written native language skills and FL aptitude when compared to unsuccessful FL learners (Sparks & Ganschow, 1995, 1996). They further state that skill in one's native language and aptitude for learning a foreign language may affect the learner's anxiety level (Sparks & Ganschow, 1996). However, the claims of these researchers have not gone unchallenged. The LCDH has been criticized for not recognizing the ways in which the social context can influence cognitive processes and language learning and the potential effects of affective variables when considering the relation between aptitude and achievement (Mabbott, 1995; MacIntyre, 1995). Mabbott's (1994) study indicated that students with L1 difficulties were able to successfully acquire a second language. The LCDH would undoubtedly make a stronger case if terms such as "language difficulties" and "proficiency" were more clearly defined in the research and if these claims were examined in light of sociocultural theories of language learning.

At the postsecondary level, an issue regarding LD-labeled students is under what circumstances, if ever, they should be given waivers for foreign language course requirements. Recent studies completed by Sparks and Javorsky (1998) and Sparks, Artzer, Javorsky, Patton, Ganschow, Miller, and Hordubay (1998) revealed that (1) students classified/not classified LD who experience FL difficulties do not show significant differences in cognitive, achievement, FL aptitude, or FL grades; and (2) the majority of students receiving FL course substitutions failed to meet any LD legal/research criteria. According to a 1998 legal ruling in the Guckenberg vs. Trustees of Boston University, "universities must provide accommodations, but are not legally required to provide course substitutions for the FL requirement, . . . if the university deems foreign language as an essential part of the curriculum" (cf. Sparks & Javorsky, 1998, p. 11). The implication of this ruling is that everyone can learn a language if appropriate accommodations are made.

There are several implications from the LD foreign language research for the language teacher who has students manifesting learning difficulties:

1. Given the lack of consensus regarding the classification of a learner as LD, the language teacher should not assume that the LD-labeled students really do have learning disabilities nor should s/he assume that other students in the class do not have learning disabilities.

2. The language teacher should not assume that LD-labeled students cannot experience success in foreign language learning. Students are often categorized as learning disabled as a result of the type of instruction they receive and not necessarily because of verified learning disorders. For example, Bruck (1978) discovered that students with learning disabilities who learned French by means of a traditional approach actually acquired little knowledge of the language, because the method exploited the areas in which they had the most difficulties: memory work, learning language out of context, understanding abstract rules. Learning disabilities, particularly in cases of students labeled "mildly disabled," may be exacerbated by traditional classrooms that emphasize rules and bottom-up processing. Curtain (1986), Spinelli (1996), and Mabbott (1994) suggest that immersion programs may provide the best environment in which LD students can learn a foreign language, since students are involved in meaningful interaction and hands-on experiences. When immersion experiences are unavailable, content-based and story-based approaches (see Chapter 7) can provide the same type of instructional support.

3. The language teacher should carefully assess why an individual is having a problem in the class. The teacher should be familiar with and use a variety of strategies for helping students with specific kinds of difficulties in learning the foreign language.

The following are some general strategies for helping students with learning disabilities in the foreign language classroom:

- Use a well-organized daily classroom routine, with frequent praise and repetition of ideas (McCabe, 1985).
- Develop a communicative-oriented rather than a grammar-oriented class, with as much personal interaction as possible (Mabbott, 1994).
- Use frequent review and repetition, and presentation of small amounts of material at one time (Sparks, Ganschow, Javorsky, Pohlman, & Patton, 1992).
- When conducting listening and reading activities, give fewer instructions at one time, provide pre-listening/pre-reading discussion, and give comprehension questions prior to and again after the reading selection, focusing on a literal rather than a figurative level (Barnett, 1985).
- Provide opportunities for students to learn through more than one modality, particularly through the tactile (touching, manipulating objects) or kinesthetic (use of movement, gestures) modalities (Spinelli, 1989). The Orton-Gillingham approach emphasizes the use of the tactile and kinesthetic modalities in teaching reading to dyslexic/learning disabled students (Gillingham & Stillman, 1960; Sparks, Ganschow, Kenneweg & Miller, 1991). Kennewig (1986) uses an adaptation of this method in her Spanish class for learning disabled students. Sparks and Ganschow (1993) showed significant gains in teaching Spanish to learning disabled students using a multisensory, structured language approach for teaching phonological and syntactic elements of a foreign language.
- Have realistic expectations of what LD students can do, and measure their progress in terms of their own abilities rather than in terms of what the entire class can attain.
- Provide ample opportunities for LD students to interact with other students in the class by means of cooperative learning activities. Emphasize how important it is for all students to understand, respect, and help one another in the learning process.
- Allow extra time, if needed, for LD students to complete assignments and tests.
- Make special provisions for testing: Allow students to take a test orally if they have trouble reading; allow students to take a test a second time if they did not do well the first time; give students additional time to complete tests; allow students to use grammar charts and dictionaries during tests. Realize that LD students may not perform well on certain test formats such as spelling, memorizing dialogs, reading aloud, and taking notes (Mabbott, 1994).
- Provide time for more individualized work with special education students and offer continued feedback on their progress. During this time, work with them on developing effective learning strategies.

The Fairfax County Public Schools suggest that language teachers use the following strategies with students who are predominantly visual learners and who may have difficulty processing information auditorily:

- Use visuals with lectures: maps, slides, transparencies, pictures, and charts.
- Summarize key points in an introduction.
- Provide a typed outline for students.

- Provide written directions for all assignments using a handout or a specific place on the blackboard.
- Reduce directions to a few key words.
- Repeat instructions on a one-to-one basis or have a responsible student do this for you.
- Help with spelling of key words in directions.
- Do not give instructions while students are copying from the board. Also, it is best to wait until copying is finished before explaining material on board.
- Require students to keep daily assignment sheets (1992, p. 25).

The following are sample strategies for students who are predominantly auditory learners and who may have difficulty processing information visually (e.g., difficulty reading):

- Limit the length of written assignments and copy work.
- Give students a brief and simple outline of material before reading an assignment.
- Give aural/oral tests if possible.
- Allow students to make oral responses to homework or test items that involve a lot of writing.
- Let students make models or give demonstrations instead of doing written projects.
- Combine taped instruction and questions with short-answer worksheets.
- Have a skilled student make a copy of his/her class notes for any student absent during key lectures.
- Allow students to tape lectures, discussions, or directions when feasible.
- Seat students near front of room.
- Allow students to copy from another student's notes instead of from the board.
- Use a typewriter or large, clear script for assignment sheets and tests.
- Allow students to type homework.
- Require students to keep a daily assignment sheet and verify its corrections.

Fairfax County Public Schools, 1992, p. 26.

As you read through the lists of strategies listed here, you may have recognized that many of these approaches have already been suggested throughout the *Teacher's Handbook* for use with all students. Research suggests that the instructional methods that are effective with LD students tend to be the same as those that are effective with other students, except that LD students may need closer supervision (Larrivee, 1985). Students with physical or learning disabilities may need more individualized instruction and more one-to-one instruction from the teacher (Madden & Slavin, 1983), while students with behavior disorders may require closer supervision (Thompson, White, & Morgan, 1982).

❏ Providing Effective Learning Experiences for At-Risk Students

As foreign language teachers face the challenge of teaching special needs students who have been mainstreamed into regular classes, they are also encountering more and more children labeled "at-risk" or "high risk." "At-risk" students are those who "are likely to fail—either in school or in life" (Frymier & Gansneder, 1989, p. 142) due to circumstances beyond their control (Spinelli, 1996, p. 72). These students have a high likelihood of dropping out of school, being low achievers, or even committing suicide. They are at risk because of a wide variety of circumstances they face outside of school: poverty, dysfunctional family life, neglect, abuse, or cultural/ethnic/racial background. The "three strongest social correlates of suicidal behavior in youth are family breakdown, a youth's unemployment, and decreasing religious observance among the young" (Garfinkel, interviewed by Frymier, 1989, p. 290). "At-riskness" has been described as "a function of what bad things happen to a child, how severe they are, how often they happen, and what else happens in the child's immediate environment" (Frymier & Gansneder, 1989, p. 142). At-risk students often display emotional and/or psychological symptoms such as depression, anxiety, difficulty in concentrating, and excessive anger, as well as physical symptoms such as respiratory problems, headaches, and muscle tension (Vanucci, 1991).

> **"At-risk" students are those who are likely to fail due to circumstances beyond their control.**

A majority of at-risk students are from AHANA heritage groups, who often are also from low socio-economic environments and single-parent families. They frequently experience problems in school because of their loss of identity or ethnic roots, difficulty in integrating themselves into the majority culture, and other students' incorrect perceptions of them. In many cases, the difficulties that minority students face seem insurmountable when the students are placed in classrooms that stress total conformity to the majority culture. Heining-Boynton (1994) points out that frequent assessment and adaptation of instruction to learners' needs are beneficial for these learners, along with techniques that foreign language teachers have praised for years as good instruction.

Educators have come a long way in the past twenty years in learning to address the needs of at-risk and minority students. In 1998, the U.S. Department of Education Statistics showed that educational attainment of Hispanic and Black students and their parents has increased in recent years, although it is still lower than that for non-Black and non-Hispanic students. Furthermore, parental involvement has also increased (Sable, 1998; Sable & Stennett, 1998).

The Gender/Ethnic Expectations and Student Achievement (GESA) Program was developed in Los Angeles in 1970 for the purpose of helping teachers confront and overcome their own gender and ethnic biases within the classroom. Grayson and Martin (1988) identified five areas in which teachers tend not to treat all students equally: (1) instructional contact: opportunities for students to respond and acknowledgment or feedback from the teacher; (2) grouping/organization: includes wait-time for responses and physical closeness of teacher and students; (3) discipline: touching and reproof; (4) developing students' self-esteem: includes listening and probing, and guiding students through the thought process; and (5) evaluation: high-level questioning and analytical feedback.

Much of the research in multicultural education and teaching at-risk students has clear implications for classroom instruction. The following list illustrates possible strategies that foreign language teachers might use as they attempt to provide successful language learning for all students:

1. Engage students in activities that encourage social interaction and promote the use of higher-order thinking skills to challenge students' creativity (Kuykendall, 1989) (see Appendix 10.2 for a chart of strategies to extend student thinking).

2. Relate learning about another language and culture to students' own life experiences (Kuykendall, 1989).

3. Offer descriptive instead of evaluative feedback in an effort to encourage progress rather than to cause frustration. Also, display each student's work at some time during the academic year (Kuykendall, 1989).

4. Maintain direct, sincere eye contact when communicating with individual students (Kuykendall, 1989).

5. Make every effort to give all students equal opportunities to participate (Grayson & Martin, 1988).

6. Use heterogenous and cooperative groupings for interactive tasks, as described in Chapter 8 (Kuykendall, 1989).

7. Make the language curriculum reflect the individual cultures of the students by including study of key historical/political figures from various cultures, inviting guest speakers from various cultures, engaging students in discussion in the target language about their own cultures, and discussing in the target language current events that involve the students' own cultures (Kuykendall, 1989).

8. If there are native speakers of the target language who are students in the language class, encourage their ethnic pride by engaging them in activities such as providing oral input in the target language, helping other students undertake culture projects, offering classmates additional cultural information, and sharing family photographs.

9. When presenting the cultures of the people who speak the target language, include people of different age groups, both male and female, and from as many geographical regions as possible.

10. When sharing opinions or discussing abstract topics, encourage students to express their own ideas concerning values, morals, and religious views, as shaped by their own cultures and religious convictions.

11. Use visuals that portray males and females of diverse racial and ethnic origins.

12. Hold the same achievement expectations for all students in the class, except in cases of physical or intellectual disabilities (Kuykendall, 1989).

13. Provide opportunities for students to help one another. Sullivan and McDonald (1990) found that cross-age peer tutoring is an effective strategy that enables students to exercise autonomy, gain self-esteem, achieve at a higher level than normal, and learn more about students who are different from themselves. In Sullivan and McDonald's (1990) study, high school Spanish III students in an urban school district taught Spanish to elementary school children.

14. Maintain positive teacher-parent relationships by inviting parents to see students' work in the foreign language, such as special projects, exhibits, or drama presentations. Talk to parents about their children's individual talents and progress (Kuykendall, 1989).

❑ Teaching Gifted Learners

Johnson and Johnson point out that a "concern of all educators is how to challenge the academic capabilities of all students and maximize their intellectual development" (1991, p. 24). *Gifted learners* make up another category of special needs students. Challenging the academic capabilities of gifted learners is neither a more nor a less important charge than challenging the academic capabilities of slow learners. A specific definition of the term "gifted" was provided by Congress in P.L. 97-35 (1981), the Omnibus Education Reconciliation Act:

> Children who give evidence of high performance capability in areas such as intellectual, creative, artistic, leadership capacity, or specific academic fields, and who require services or activities not ordinarily provided by the school in order to fully develop such capabilities. (Sec. 582[3][A])

In their presentation of the work of twenty-nine researchers, Sternberg and Davidson (1986) conclude that giftedness is viewed most often in terms of cognitive processing capacities. Although identification of gifted learners has been a major focus of much of the literature in the area of gifted education, most measures are unsatisfactory. Researchers agree that multiple measures are preferred over any single achievement test and that efforts should be made to specify alternate types of giftedness (Feldhusen, 1989). The National Council of State Supervisors of Foreign Languages describes linguistically gifted students as those who have an IQ, based on a standardized intelligence test, in the top three to five percent of the student population and scores of five to six hundred on the SAT exam (Bartz, 1982). Although functional definitions generally refer to the upper two percent of the population as the highly gifted and the top five percent of the population as the gifted, to date there are no data to show what portion of the general population and what portion of the gifted population are linguistically gifted. Nor is there conclusive evidence to explain why certain students are gifted learners. Treffinger and Feldhusen (1996) recently proposed identification and nurturing the talents of all students rather than identifying and serving a small percentage of the population as the gifted few. While practices in the past have been to identify a percentage of the population as gifted, current practice is to identify the giftedness within each learner.

> 🔑 **Try to identify the giftedness in each learner.**

The research in giftedness as it relates specifically to foreign and second-language learning is scant at best. Shrum (1989) suggested that linguistically gifted students may be able to process language more rapidly. Program models for gifted learners traditionally involved acceleration, which is instruction provided at a level and pace appropriate to the student's level of achievement or readiness (Feldhusen, 1989), and enrichment, which is in-depth study on broad topics involving higher-level thinking processes. Curriculum compacting and differentiated instruction for gifted learners allow for modification of programming and instruction according to the learner's needs and abilities, often within, but not limited to, the regular classroom setting. While there is no list of best practices for teaching the gifted learner, a variety of techniques and programs nearly always includes challenging real-world tasks and instruction targeted to the learner's strengths. There is concern among researchers and practitioners of gifted learners that cultural, racial, and linguistic minorities are underrepresented or underachieve. Ford and Thomas (1997) cite studies that show that, on average, fifty percent of the gifted minority students underachieve. Ogbu (1997) points out that neither the core curriculum movement nor the multicultural movement addresses the problem of minority groups who could be gifted but do not do well in school. For the classroom teacher, specific challenges arise when attempting to help such learners. Ford and Thomas (1997) outline useful techniques (Figure 10.3) to enhance the achievement of gifted minority students.

The language teacher's task is to organize instruction so that the linguistically gifted can benefit while the other learners also benefit (Fenstermacher, 1982). Gifted learners need opportunities to use all of their abilities and to acquire new knowledge and skills. The following are strategies that might be used by the language teacher to teach gifted learners:

- Provide opportunities for students to study and research certain cultural topics in greater depth, for example, through projects in which they investigate the living patterns of the target language group.
- Present taped segments and readings that are appropriately challenging.
- Provide opportunities for students to use their critical thinking skills through debate of controversial societal issues and interpretation of literary works.
- Allow gifted students to choose the topic of their taped segments or readings from time to time, thereby encouraging work in areas of interest.
- Build in some time for gifted students to work with one another on assignments or projects, with the teacher serving as facilitator.
- Allow some opportunities for gifted students to assume leadership roles through activities such as serving as group leaders/facilitators and providing peer help to students who missed class or need extra assistance.
- Involve gifted learners in interaction with other students in the class through cooperative learning tasks, such as those presented in Chapter 8. Research shows that cooperative learning for gifted students may result in (1) higher mastery and retention of material than that achieved in competitive or individual learning; (2) increased opportunities to use critical thinking and higher-level reasoning strategies; (3) acquisition of cognitive restructuring, along with practice gained by explaining tasks and solutions to peers—in other words, learning through teaching; and (4) enhancement of social interaction and self-esteem (Fulghum, 1992; Johnson & Johnson, 1991).

Differentiated instruction for gifted learners will require that teachers deepen and widen fields of study, allow for accelerated progress through assigned material, minimize the extent of drill and practice activities, provide for in-depth study and use of critical-thinking skills, and employ every possible strategy to ensure that instruction and practice are contextualized and meaningful.

❑ Heritage Language Learners

Another growing group of students requiring specific types of attention in the classroom is the heritage language learner group. *Heritage language learners*, sometimes also called

Figure 10.3 Strategies to Enhance Achievement among Gifted Minority Students

Goal/Objective

To affirm the self-worth of students and convey the promise of greater potential and success

To provide social and emotional support

Recommended Strategies: Supportive

Provide opportunities for students to discuss concerns with teachers and counselors

Address issues of motivation, self-perception, and self-efficacy

Accommodate learning styles

Modify teaching styles (e.g., abstract, concrete, visual, auditory)

Use mastery learning

Decrease competitive, norm-referenced environments

Use cooperative learning and group work

Use positive reinforcement and praise

Seek affective and student-centered classroom

Set high expectations of students

Use multicultural education and counseling techniques and strategies

Involve mentors and role models

Involve family members in substantive ways

Goal/Objective

To help students develop internal motivation

To increase academic engagement and self-efficacy

Recommended Strategies: Intrinsic

Provide constructive and consistent feedback

Give choices, focus on interests

Vary teaching styles to accommodate learning styles

Provide for active and experiential learning (e.g., role plays, simulations, case studies, projects, internships)

Use bibliotherapy and biographies

Use mentorships and role models

Adopt an education that is multicultural—culturally relevant and personally meaningful, an education that provides insight and self-understanding

Have nurturing, affirming classrooms

Goal/Objective

To improve students' academic performance in the specific area(s) of difficulty

Recommended Strategies: Remedial

Implement academic counseling (e.g., tutoring, study skills, test-taking skills)

Teach time management and organization

Use individual and small group instruction

Use learning contracts, learning journals

Source: Ford & Thomas, 1997.

home background learners, learned languages other than English at home in the United States as a result of their cultural or ethnic backgrounds. The *SFLL* classified students into four categories, depending on their home background: (1) those who have no home background other than English; (2) those who are second- and third-generation "bilinguals" schooled exclusively in English in the United States; (3) first-generation immigrant students schooled primarily in the United States; and (4) newly arrived immigrant students. The issue of the heritage language learner is worldwide. In the United States, home background learners speak many languages, including Chinese, Spanish, Korean, Hmong, Greek, Armenian; while in Canada the languages include Chinese, French, Italian, Japanese, Vietnamese; and in Australia fourteen languages ranging from Arabic to Vietnamese are listed as national priority languages (Gutiérrez, 1997; Valdés, 1995; Ingram, 1994).

 Heritage or home background learners learned languages other than English at home in the United States, as a result of their cultural or ethnic backgrounds.

The United States Constitution does not specify a national language (Thomas, 1996). In fact, documents written by the founding leaders of the Continental Congress as they were shaping the new country were circulated in French, German, and English. Researchers studying language changes among the multiethnic waves of immigrants who came to the United States found that the mother tongue was displaced. However, ethnic bilingualism is a mid-stage in the transition from the mother tongue to English monolingualism in the United States. Researchers show that the mother tongue is displaced with monolingual English by the second, third, or fourth generation (Fishman, 1964, 1994; Veltman, 1983). While it is clear that learning to use English will result in greater access to education and employment opportunities (Valdés, 1999), preservation of the heritage language and culture helps foster understanding and diversity. Valdés (1999) issues a strong challenge to language teachers, calling for awareness that the "language maintenance efforts are as important a part of our profession as is the teaching of language to monolingual speakers of English." In the 1990s, a group called "U.S. English" attempted to establish English as the national language and later as the language of individual states. Fearing that English in the United States was threatened by immigrant populations, these groups ignored the facts of the United States 1990 census in which the pattern of assimilation of immigrant groups outlined by Fishman in 1964 was affirmed (Valdés, 1999). Schools have recently recognized, with the support of the National Association of Secondary School Principals, the American Association of Applied Linguistics, and other professional groups, that maintaining the heritage language while learning a new language enriches the academic and cultural experience of the learner and the society. Figure 10.4 shows the needs of each home background learner group in terms of the development in English and the heritage language. In further describing the language maintenance needs of home background or heritage learners, Valdés (1999) shows that these students already have highly developed interpersonal communicative abilities and will perhaps need only to be able to learn communicative ways to establish respect, distance, or friendliness and how to talk with adult strangers and in professional contexts. Heritage learners will require further assistance in developing interpretive skills and will need to read a wide variety of authentic materials. Perhaps their greatest need is in the presentational mode as the registers (i.e., formal contexts) of language use appropriate for a presentation to a formal audience are often unfamiliar to heritage speakers.[1]

Figure 10.4 Characteristics of Home Background Students

STUDENT CHARACTERISTICS	ENGLISH LANGUAGE DEVELOPMENT NEEDS	HERITAGE/HOME LANGUAGE DEVELOPMENT NEEDS
Second- and third-generation "bilinguals" schooled exclusively in English in the United States	Continued development of age-appropriate English language competencies	Maintenance, retrieval, and/or acquisition of language competencies (e.g., oral productive abilities) Transfer of literacy skills developed in English to the home language Continued development of age-appropriate competencies in both oral and written modes
First-generation immigrant students schooled primarily in the United States	Continued development of age-appropriate English language competencies	Development of literacy skills in first language Continued development of age-appropriate language competencies in oral mode
Newly arrived immigrant students	Acquisition of oral and written English	Continued development of age-appropriate competencies in both oral and written modes

Source: SFLL, 1996, 19.

❏ Goals and Strategies for Teaching Heritage Language Learners

Addressing Spanish in particular, Valdés outlined four goals for instruction to heritage speakers:

1. Spanish language maintenance: enabling learners to maintain their understanding and use of Spanish.

2. Acquisition of the prestige variety of Spanish: helping speakers of nonprestige varieties of Spanish to acquire the prestige or "standard" variety so that they are able to function in professional, more formal contexts.

---

1. For a thorough treatment of issues and pedagogical implications for teaching Spanish to native speakers of Spanish, consult Sandstedt, L. (Project Director), *AATSP Professional Development Handbook Series for Teachers: Spanish for Native Speakers*, Vol. 1 (1999), in press at this writing.

3. Expansion of the bilingual range: helping speakers to expand the range of linguistic abilities and communicative strategies in both languages.

4. Transfer of literacy skills: enabling learners to carry over skills such as reading and writing efficiently and effectively into the other language (Valdés, 1995, pp. 309–317).

 Preservation of the heritage language and culture enriches the academic and cultural experience of the learner and the society.

Knowing that these needs exist in their heritage language development, heritage speakers sometimes enroll in language classes. An example of the diversity even among heritage speakers of Chinese at Portland State University includes a diverse mix of Chinese American students, young native English speakers, older native English speakers, native Japanese speakers, native Korean speakers, ethnic Chinese from Vietnam, ethnic Vietnamese, ethnic Chinese from Indonesia, and students from Hong Kong (Pease, 1996). Research is needed to identify the role of instruction in classes with such a wide range of home background learners in order to find out what the role of instruction is in prevention of heritage language loss, in identifying the ranges of linguistic capabilities held by heritage speakers in a variety of languages, and in development of instructional materials. Valdés (1995) acknowledges that few theoretical advances have been made in teaching heritage language learners and no attempts have been made to analyze the theories underlying existing instruction. However, instructors have reported success in using certain types of teaching strategies. Figure 10.5 depicts sample instructional strategies that have been used at both the secondary and post-secondary levels as they address the four goals listed earlier (Valdés, 1995). As illustrated, more research is needed in the area of how to teach the sociolinguistic aspects of language use and how to connect effectively with multilingual communities.

Rodríguez Pino suggests that home background language learners be engaged in the following types of classroom activities:

- ethnographic study of the community, such as tracing the genealogy of a family;
- vocabulary expansion activities to identify standardized synonyms and regional words beyond their current usage level;
- interactive diaries in which they write to each other and share ideas about subthemes such as the future, their culture, society, literature, vices and virtues, values, social relationships, and the arts: A typical assignment appears in Figure 10.6;
- sociolinguistic surveys: An example is one in which students might collect photos of six examples of flowers (or animals or tools or professions, etc.) all representing a specific category. Students place them on a card and conduct a survey in their community asking native speakers to speak the words for the photographed items into a tape recorder. Then they tabulate their results to make a linguistic map of their neighborhood;

Figure 10.5 Heritage Language Learners: Instructional Goals and Frequently Used Pedagogies

INSTRUCTIONAL GOAL	FREQUENTLY USED PEDAGOGY	LESS FREQUENTLY USED PEDAGOGY
Transfer of literacy skills	Instruction in reading and writing Teaching of traditional grammar	
Acquisition of prestige variety	Teaching of prestige variety Teaching of traditional grammar Teaching of strategies helpful in monitoring use of contact features Teaching of strategies designed to monitor use of stigmatized features	Introduction to sociolinguistic principles of language variation and language use
Expansion of bilingual range	Teaching of vocabulary Reading of different types and kinds of texts	Structuring of classwork to provide participation in activities designed to expand linguistic, sociolinguistic, and pragmatic competence
Language maintenance	Instruction in reading and writing Teaching of vocabulary	Consciousness raising around issues of identity and language Reading of texts focusing on issues of race, class, gender, and other sociopolitical topics Carrying out ethnographic projects in language community

Source: Valdés, 1995, p. 309.

- reading of the literature of the home background student, especially if it is not yet an integral part of the literary canon: For example, native speakers of Spanish in the southwestern United States might read Ricardo Aguilar's *Madreselvas en flor*, listen to the tape of the author reading aloud from his work, and complete the following sentences in Spanish:

1. When the author read about _____, I felt _____.

2. I like the way in which the author _____.

3. I didn't like _____.

4. I didn't understand _____.

5. The experiences of this author remind me of _____.

(Adapted from Rodríguez Pino, 1997, pp. 70–75.)

Figure 10.6 Sample Assignment for Journal Writing for Home Background Students

EXPERIENCIAS ESCOLARES	SCHOOL EXPERIENCES
Instrucciones: Hable con dos o tres parientes (preferiblemente, su/s abuelos/as, si es posible) y pregúnteles sobre sus experiencias en la escuela. Pregunte sobre las materias, los maestros, la descripción de la escuela y de la sala de clase, los juegos de recreo, sus experiencias con la primera y segunda lengua, las aventuras después de clase, etcétera. **Escritura:** En su diario compare sus propias experiencias con las de sus parientes. ¿En qué se parecen o difieren? ¿Cómo han cambiado las cosas/situaciones escolares? Mencione una o dos cosas del pasado que le hubiera gustado experimentar en la escuela.	**Instructions:** Talk with two or three of your relatives (preferably your grandparents, if possible) and ask them about their experiences in school. Ask about subjects, teachers, the description of the school and the classroom, games during recess, their experiences with the first and second language, adventures after school, etc. **Writing:** In your journal, compare your own experiences with those of your relatives. How are they similar or how are they different? How have things and circumstances in school changed? Mention one or two aspects of the past that you would have liked to experience in your schooling.

Source: Rodríguez Pino, 1997, 72.

In addition, development of program models for heritage speakers is vital in order to find data that will help teachers to determine whether heritage speakers maximize their potential when included in the regular language sequence, or whether special courses or even lines of study should be developed for them, or how helpful self-instructional models are (see Mazzocco,1996, for an example).

 STANDARDS HIGHLIGHT: Bringing Diverse Student Groups Together through Participation in Multilingual Communities

☐ The Communities Goal Area

The Communities goal area of *SFLL* (NFLSEP, 1996) can be a vehicle for engaging diverse groups of learners in using the language both within and beyond the school setting. The Communities standards, which combine elements from each of the other goal areas, require careful language use, application of cultural practices, products, and perspectives, connections to other discipline areas, and development of insights into one's own language and culture. The two Communities standards are the following:

- Students use the language both within and beyond the school setting.
- Students show evidence of becoming life-long learners by using the language for personal enjoyment and enrichment (NSFLEP, 1996, pp. 60, 62).

The first standard focuses on language as a tool for communication with speakers in a variety of "communities": the community within the classroom, the school, the local community, target language communities within the United States, and target language communities abroad (NSFLEP, 1996). The second standard relates to the use of the target language for continued learning and for personal entertainment and enjoyment. As students gain confidence in the second language, they might use the language to access various entertainment and information sources, read a novel, or travel abroad.

 The Communities goal area focuses on language use within and beyond the school setting and for personal enrichment and enjoyment.

❑ Linking Language Learning Experiences to Communities

Having read about diverse kinds of students who may be in your foreign language class, you may begin to see that developing communities among learners in the classroom can complement learners' work within the larger school community and in communities beyond the school. Over the past decade, colleges and universities have incorporated "community-based learning" (CBL) into their curricula in an attempt to engage students in responsible and challenging projects both inside and outside the classroom. Kolb's (1984) Model of CBL, shown in Figure 10.7, is a useful way to think about making learning real in communities. It is a student-centered model that uses learners' experiences as a basis for learning. Using concrete experiences with members of a community, the learner participates in guided reflection (e.g., class journal or group discussion), thinks about the hypotheses s/he formed prior to the experience, and formulates abstract concepts which are then put into practice in communicative situations outside the classroom (Overfield, 1997, p. 486). Overfield describes an example in which students use language to connect with a community by responding to a call from a local agency to help refugees and recent immigrants learn about their new community (1997, pp. 488–489). Spanish I students socialized with Cuban refugees through various activities such as visiting an art gallery together. The two groups learned about each other by asking and answering questions and comparing their cultures. Language learning was mediated through classroom reflection, written journal entries and portfolio documents, and generating comments like the following about the value of the learning experience: "As an African American, I didn't think I'd have anything in common with these Cuban refugees. My Spanish isn't very good, and what do they know about my culture? When one asked me what I like to eat, I told her she wouldn't understand. She told me to tell her. So I tried to tell her what I eat, and I told her about Sunday dinners with my family. She said she does the same things with her family! We talked for an hour. On Saturday we [another student and herself] are going to the mall with her and her mother" (Overfield, 1997, p. 489). This type of mediated learning is the result of "building bridges between classrooms and communities" (Cone & Harris, 1996, p. 39). As seen in Kolb's (1984) model, the abstract conceptualization of not having anything in common with the refugees was changed by active experimentation and concrete experiences, leading to reflective observation and more concrete experiences.

Figure 10.7   Kolb's Model of Community-Based Learning

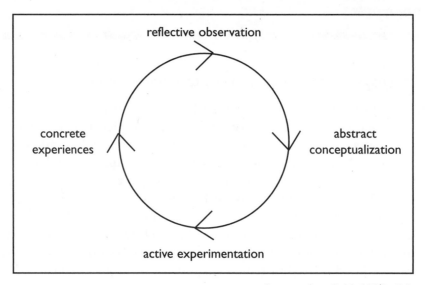

Source: Overfield, 1997, 486.

An interesting example of multiple-community-based experiences is seen in the collaborative project implemented by Haas, a teacher-educator and folk art author, and Reardon, a seventh-grade Spanish teacher, (1997). Although the project culminated in a trip to a local Chilean bakery, the other aspects of it show that the Communities goal area does not imply that students have to be transported physically to other countries or neighborhoods (Phillips, 1997). Spanish students living in a town near New York City engaged in e-mail correspondence with their peers in a Chilean village, conducted research about Chile, presented oral reports with illustrations, and interviewed guest informants from Chile (Haas & Reardon, 1997). Community-based experiences might also lead students to use the language for enjoyment and enrichment. For example, students on Long Island, in New York, interviewed Canadian-born, French-speaking hockey players in French asking about professional hockey and the players' lives (NSFLEP, 1996, p. 80). In this process of establishing meaningful interaction with a community of native speakers, it is important to set the structure of the interaction around vocabulary and linguistic functions that students know.

For instance, Beebe and Leonard (1994) suggest that both students and native speakers of the target language need to prepare before meeting to interact in the target language. Students might brainstorm topics of interest, prepare questions in advance, anticipate necessary vocabulary, and review strategies for negotiating meaning. Native informants might anticipate ways in which they might simplify their speech and help students convey their messages in meaningful ways. The two groups might explore topics such as family, interests, hobbies, native speakers' reasons for coming to the United States, their first impressions of the United States, and their hometowns compared with their current place of residence. The native informants might also describe their experiences learning English as a second language and offer suggestions to students about improving their target language speaking skills (Beebe & Leonard, 1994).

Teach and Reflect

Episode One

Designing a Language Lesson Appropriate for Diverse Learning Styles

For this activity, you might either use a lesson you created during earlier chapters of the *Teacher's Handbook* or design a new one. Your lesson could focus on any of the elements previously discussed—for example, a presentation of grammar with a whole language approach or work with an authentic listening or a reading appropriate for students at the elementary school, middle school, or high school level and beyond. Within your lesson, design at least three activities that appeal to different learning styles. Refer to the elements of learning styles described earlier in this chapter (Scarcella & Oxford, 1992; Oxford, 1990a), and keep in mind the following suggestions (Gahala, 1993) to differentiate instruction:

1. Provide basic instruction of vocabulary and structures by appealing to as many senses as possible.

2. Proceed through carefully sequenced in-class practice.

3. In interactive classroom activities, such as question-answer practice, allow sufficient wait time for students to process the questions, think of possible responses, formulate a response, and make the response.

4. Give clear instructions on all assignments and model process or desired outcomes with students before they begin the task. Use a more able student to assist in modeling the activity.

5. Regularly give a choice among two or three homework assignments. Instead of grading solely on correctness, consider grading on any two of the following criteria: completion of task, comprehensibility, quality or appropriateness of information generated, individual improvement. Be sure to let students know the criteria in advance.

6. Base evaluation on a variety of procedures: taking short quizzes, participating in role plays, writing scenarios of oral activities, labeling pictures or visuals, creating personal flashcards or study devices, creating posters or cultural projects, actively participating in classroom interaction, describing a picture, creating a drawing from a description in the target language, writing a new study exercise, writing comprehension check questions for a reading or listening selection.

In order to differentiate instruction, you need to know some of the basic elements about the diversity of learners in your classroom.

Episode Two

Working within Communities

Identify a community near your school where a language other than English is spoken at home or at work. Interview a selection of community members about how they learned the language and what it means to them. Identify a way in which students in your school can interact with members of the community in a focused project, perhaps reading some poems, writing a play, helping with child care, or helping teach literacy. Design the project so that it addresses the Communities Goal Area of the Standards for Foreign Language Learning. Read Overfield (1997) for greater insights into how she combined a model of communicative competence with Kolb's (1984) model of community-based learning, and incorporate some of the aspects of her work into your project.

Discuss and Reflect

Case Study 1

Preparing to Teach Special Education Spanish I and II Classes

Ms. Vella is a first-year Spanish teacher at Westtown High School, part of a small rural district in a farming community. She has been taught the latest research in language learning and teaching and is thoroughly prepared to teach Spanish for real communication. Ms. Vella developed a repertoire of strategies for involving students in active language use, and she successfully used whole-language tasks and cooperative learning in her student teaching. She believes in using the target language as much as possible, integrating culture with her teaching, and providing opportunities for students to succeed with the language.

The principal at Westtown High School told Ms. Vella that one of the classes she would be teaching is conversational Spanish and that the class would consist of twelve special education students: eight in Spanish Level I and four in Spanish Level II. The principal told her that "the goal for the class is to make students aware of different cultures through the use of Spanish." Ms. Vella was a little perplexed by this assignment since these students would be in a separate class, rather than included with other students, and Levels I and II would be combined.

Ask yourself these questions:

1. What expectations should Ms. Vella have for these students?

2. What difficulties/successes might these students have in a language class?

3. What additional information will Ms. Vella need about these students as she plans for the class?

4. According to the principal, the goal for this class is "to make students aware of different cultures through the use of Spanish." What do you think is the philosophy or attitude that motivates this goal? What other goals could there be?

5. What techniques might work well in teaching these students Spanish?

To prepare the case:

Read Spinelli (1989, 1996) for more information on how to teach slow learners; interview an experienced special education teacher to discuss potential difficulties students might experience as well as how a language teacher might plan for these difficulties; talk to an experienced language teacher who has worked with mainstreamed and/or special education students to gain additional insights about implications for language teaching.

To prepare for class discussion, think and write about these topics:

- How would you approach Ms. Vella's conversational Spanish class? Describe your expectations and the types of classroom activities you would provide.
- How would you include opportunities to work with learners with special needs on an individual basis?

Case Study 2

Cultural Diversity in a Small Rural Community

Mr. Davensmith was excited about starting his second teaching job, which was in Johnson County, a small, rural school system in the southeastern United States. Mr. Davensmith moved to Johnson County because his wife secured a position at a state university in a neighboring county. During his interview, Mr. Davensmith learned from the principal that the primary source of income in the community was raising beef cattle, growing cabbage and other vegetables, and doing piecework in the local textile factory. Many of the citizens had grown up in the county and shared similar religious and social values. Mr. Davensmith expected that the students in his French class would be mostly farmers' children. In actuality, however, he found that these were some of the students in his French II class:

- Betty, whose parents cooperatively owned and operated a dairy farm having 100 milk cows, spent extra time after school helping her French I teacher last year. She also completed an in-depth study of French culture and hopes to earn enough money to go to France next summer to improve her oral and listening skills. She prefers to read and write French, but her former French teacher told her she would have to improve her listening and speaking abilities if she wanted to continue to study the language.

- Calvin, who is Betty's neighbor, works on his parents' farm helping to raise alfalfa hay for local horse farms. Calvin has been in enrolled in learning disability classes since the fifth grade and knows he is dyslexic, but he compensates for it by watching for the letters *d, b,* and *c.* His parents note that he tracks grain and hay prices in three local marketplaces and keeps track of his father's financial records.

- Bentley spends his summers, part of the spring, and most of the fall helping trim and harvest white pines for landscaping companies and Christmas tree distributors. He is in the eleventh grade but is two years younger than his grade-level peers because he was promoted through two grade levels, one in elementary school and one in middle school. He wears a hearing aid in each ear, sits near the center of the semicircle Mr. Davensmith arranged for the class, but sometimes does not hear what other students say. Bentley likes to check frequently with Mr. Davensmith to be sure he "has it right." He does best if he can put his work in writing. Bentley likes Mr. Davensmith and confided in him that he is worried about the stability of his home life since his parents argue all the time. Because Bentley is small, he is often the target of jokes. He is on the wrestling team and has grown in stoutness, if not in height, since he began to work on the Christmas tree farms.

- Susan had been enrolled in a gifted student program that focused on creative writing. Susan's mother, a single parent, moved from a large urban area so that she could raise horses and write a book about her experiences as an investigative reporter. Susan feels somewhat isolated in this community because she was used to going to a major national museum for her Saturday entertainment. In Johnson County, there is an ample library which she uses, but most people use the bookmobile instead. Susan seldom feels challenged in her French class.

- Miguel is from Mexico. His parents were hired at a local cabbage farm to help with the harvest. Miguel prefers not to speak Spanish at school, is enrolled in an advanced ESL program, and earned As in French I. He would like to play football on the school team, but he cannot stay after school for practice because he often helps his family on the cabbage farm. Miguel is a kinesthetic learner, and in his spare time he likes to play the guitar and carve wood. He especially likes to be with long-term residents of the mountains when they are playing banjos and fiddles or whittling.

- Carlos is from Colombia. His father recently purchased a large cabbage farm and hired Miguel's family. Carlos speaks English without a trace of accent, although he often has difficulty understanding regional expressions that some of his school friends use. For example, one of his friends gave him directions to his home, saying "Cross the branch, and turn left." Carlos thought the branch referred to the road, not to the creek.

- Navid is an Iranian girl whose father is a professor of electrical engineering at the nearby university. Navid likes details and is always straightening up the stacks of papers on Mr. Davensmith's desk. She is shy and interacts with her peers very little. She earns very good grades in French and hopes to major in that language in college.

- Bela and Aggrey are the twin sons of Akinseye Sindabu, who is attending the university as a doctoral student in agricultural economics. Mr. Sindabu will return to his native Kenya next year as Director of Agricultural Development. Bela and Aggrey learned three languages before leaving Kenya, and they earned all As in their French I class. Their pronunciation is perfect, and their written work is sufficiently accurate to keep Mr. Davensmith very happy.

Ask yourself these questions:

1. In what ways do these students differ? What do they have in common?

2. What learning strategies from those outlined by Scarcella and Oxford (1992) do you think each student might use most frequently?

3. Make a list of the various ways in which these students represent a multicultural group. Be sure to include those aspects that are as obvious as national origin, but do not neglect more subtle cultural differences and similarities, such as "hometown youngster" vs. "transplant."

4. A colleague was overheard stating "Teach through the strengths to turn the weaknesses into strengths." Discuss this statement and its relationship to the benefits and disadvantages in matching learning styles.

To prepare the case:

Read Chapter 5 of Richard-Amato (1988) to identify three classroom activities that relate to the affective environment of a foreign language classroom; determine which of the activities would best engage Mr. Davensmith's students; read McCarthy (1987) for an explanation of the 4-MAT system for teaching to student learning styles; interview an experienced foreign language teacher to find out what s/he does to encourage cooperative attitudes among students who are different and similar along the lines you identified; read Rodríguez Pino (1997) to develop some exercises you could use with native speakers of Spanish in your classroom.

To prepare for class discussion, think and write about these topics:

- Imagine that you are Mr. Davensmith and are planning to teach a segment about French bread. You want to be sure that students understand that the bread is purchased daily, has a hard outer shell and chewy white center, is not wrapped in plastic, and is shaped like a long, thin torpedo, ranging from twelve to about twenty-four inches long. You also want them to understand that, in France, bread is the staple food, often served with cheese and a beverage as a full meal, especially for people working in fields or traveling. How will you make this lesson relevant?
- Imagine that you are Mr. Davensmith's principal. How could you help him work with this group of students so that learners can realize their greatest potential?

References

Alatis, J., & Barnhardt, S. (Eds.). (1998). *Portfolio assessment in the foreign language classroom.* Washington, D.C.: National Capital Language Resource Center.

Bailey, K. M. (1983). Competitiveness and anxiety in adult second language learning: Looking at and through the diary studies. In H. W. Seliger & M. H. Long (Eds.), *Classroom-oriented research in second language acquisition* (pp. 67–103). Rowley, MA: Newbury House.

Barbe, W. B., Swassing, R. H., & Milone, M. N. (1979). *The Swassing-Barbe modality index in the Zaner-Bloser modality kit.* Columbus, OH: Zaner-Bloser.

Barnett, H. (1985). Foreign languages for the learning disabled: A reading teacher's perspective. *New York State Association of Foreign Language Teachers Bulletin, 36,* 7–9.

Bartz, W. (1982). The role of foreign language education for gifted and talented students. *Foreign Language Annals, 15,* 329–334.

Beebe, R. M., & Leonard, K. (1994). *Second language learning in a social context.* Report No. OERI-RR93002010. Washington, D.C.: U.S. Department of Education. (ERIC Document Reproduction Service No. ED367143).

Brinckerhoff, L. C., Shaw, S. F., & McGuire, J. M. (1993). *Promoting postsecondary education for students with learning disabilities: A handbook for practitioners.* Austin, TX: Pro-ed.

Bruck, M. (1978). The suitability of early French immersion programs for the language disabled child. *Canadian Modern Language Review, 34,* 884–887.

Cohen, A. D. (1990). *Language learning: Insights for learners, teachers, and researchers.* New York: Newbury House/Harper.

Cone, D., & Harris, S. (1996). Service-learning practice: Developing a theoretical framework. *Michigan Journal of Community Service Learning, 3,* 31–43.

Curtain, H. A. (1986). The immersion approach: Principle and practice. In B. Snyder (Ed.), *Second language acquisition: Preparing for tomorrow* (pp. 1–14). Central States Conference Proceedings. Lincolnwood, IL: NTC/Contemporary Publishing Group.

Digest of Educational Statistics. (1991). Washington, D.C.: U.S. Government Printing Office.

Donato, R., & McCormick, D. (1994). A sociocultural perspective on learning strategies: The role of mediation. *The Modern Language Journal, 78,* 453–464.

Ehrman, M. E., & Oxford, R. L. (1989). Effects of sex differences, career choice, and psychological type on adults' language learning strategies. *The Modern Language Journal, 73,* 1–13.

Fairfax County Public Schools. (1992). *Strategies for learners with special needs in the foreign language classroom—A teacher's guide.* Fairfax, VA: Fairfax County School Board.

Feldhusen, J. F. (1989). Synthesis of research on gifted youth. *Educational Leadership, 46*(6), 6–11.

Fenstermacher, G. (1982). To be or not to be gifted: What is the question? *Elementary School Journal, 82,* 299–303.

Fishman, J. (1964). Language maintenance and language shift as a field of inquiry. *Linguistics, 9,* 32–70.

Fishman, J. (1994). Critiques of language planning: A minority languages perspective. *Journal of Multilingual and Multicultural Development, 15,* 91–99.

Ford, D. Y., & Thomas, A. (1997). *Underachievement among gifted minority students: Problems and promises.* Available: http://www.cec.sped.org/digests/e544.htm (1998, October 29).

Frymier, J. (1989). Understanding and preventing teen suicide. *Phi Delta Kappan, 70,* 290–293.

Frymier, J., & Gansneder, B. (1989). The Phi Delta Kappa study of students at risk. *Phi Delta Kappan, 70,* 142–146.

Fulghum, R. (1992). A bag of possibles and other matters of the mind. *Newsweek, 88,* 90, 92.

Gahala, E. (1993). Differentiating instruction: Teaching all your students. *Foreign Language News/Notes, 9,* 1–3. Glenview, IL: Scott Foresman.

Gahala, E., & Lange, D. L. (1997). Multiple intelligences: Multiple ways to help students learn foreign languages. *Northeast Conference Newsletter, 41,* 29–34.

Gardner, H. (1993). *Frames of mind: The theory of multiple intelligences.* New York: Basic Books.

Gardner, H. (1995). Reflections on multiple intelligences: Myths and messages. *Phi Delta Kappan, 77,* 200–202, 206–209.

Gillingham, A., & Stillman, B. W. (1960). *Remedial training for children with specific disability in reading, spelling, and penmanship.* Cambridge, MA: Educators Publishing Service.

Good, T., & Brophy, J. (1991). *Looking in classrooms.* New York: Harper Collins.

Grayson, D. A., & Martin, M. D. (1988). *Gender/Ethnic expectations and student achievement—The GESA facilitator.* Earlham, IA: Gray Mill Foundation.

Gutiérrez, J. R. (1997). Teaching Spanish as a heritage language: A case for language awareness. *ADFL Bulletin, 29,* 33–36.

Haas, M., & Reardon, M. (1997). Communities of learners: From New York to Chile. In J. Phillips (Ed.), *Collaborations: Meeting new goals, new realities,* Northeast Conference Reports (pp. 213–241). Lincolnwood, IL: NTC/Contemporary Publishing Group.

Heining-Boynton, A. (1994). The at-risk student in the foreign language classoom. In B. Wing (Ed.), *Meeting new challenges in the foreign language classroom,* Northeast Conference Reports (pp. 21–38) Lincolnwood, IL: NTC/Contemporary Publishing Group.

Implementation of the Individuals with Disabilities Act: Sec 618. (1997). Nineteenth Annual Report to Congress. Washington, D.C.: U.S. Department of Education. (ERIC Document Reproduction Service No. ED 412 721).

Ingram, D. E. (1994). Language policy in Australia in the 1990s. In R. D. Lambert (Ed.), *Language planning around the world: Contexts and systemic change* (pp. 69–109). Washington, D.C.: National Foreign Language Center.

Javorsky, J., Sparks, R. L., & Ganschow, L. (1992). Perceptions of college students with and without learning disabilities about foreign language courses. *Learning Disabilities: Research and Practice, 7,* 31–44.

Johnson, D. W., & Johnson, R. T. (1991). What cooperative learning has to offer the gifted. *Cooperative Learning, 11,* 24–27.

Kennewig, S. (1986). Language disability students: Spanish is for you. Paper presented at the Fifth Conference on the Teaching of Spanish, Miami University, OH.

Kohn, A. (1987). It's hard to get out of a pair—Profile: David and Roger Johnson. *Psychology Today,* 53–57.

Kolb, D. A. (1984). *Experiential learning: Experience as the source of learning and development.* Englewood Cliffs, NJ: Prentice Hall.

Kraft, B. (1992). Personal communication with the authors.

Kuykendall, C. (1989). *Improving Black student achievement by enhancing students' self-image.* Washington, D.C.: Mid-Atlantic Equity Center.

Lange, D. (1991). Implications of recent reports on teacher education reform for departments of foreign languages and literatures. *ADFL Bulletin, 23,* 28–34.

Lange, D. (1999). Planning for and using the new national culture standards. In J. K. Phillips & R. M. Terry (Eds.), *Foreign language standards: Linking research, theories, and practices.* The ACTFL Foreign Language Education Series (pp. 57–135). Lincolnwood, IL: NTC/Contemporary Publishing Group.

Larrivee, B. (1985). *Effective teaching for successful mainstreaming.* New York: Longman.

Levine, M. (1984). Learning abilities and disabilities. *The Harvard Medical School Health Letter: Medical Forum 9,* 1–3.

Lyon, R., & Moats, L. C. (1993). An examination of research in learning disabilities: Past practices and future directions. In G. R. Lyon, D. Gray, J. Kavanagh, & N. Krasnegor (Eds.), *Better understanding learning disabilities: New views from research and their implications for education and public policies,* pp. 1–15. Baltimore, MD: Brookes Publishing Co.

Mabbott, A. S. (1994). An exploration of reading comprehension, oral reading errors, and written errors by subjects labeled learning disabled. *Foreign Language Annals, 27,* 293–324.

Mabbott, A. S. (1995). Arguing for multiple perspectives on the issue of learning disabilities and foreign language acquistion: A response to Sparks, Ganschow, and Javorsky. *Foreign Language Annals, 28,* 488–494.

MacIntyre, P. (1995). How does anxiety affect second language learning? A reply to Sparks and Ganschow. *The Modern Language Journal, 79,* 90–99.

MacIntyre, P., & Noels, K. A. (1996). Using social-psychological variables to predict the use of language learning strategies. *Foreign Language Annals, 29,* 373–386.

Madden, N., & Slavin, R. (1983). Mainstreaming students with mild handicaps: Academic and social outcomes. *Review of Educational Research, 53,* 519–569.

Mazzocco, E. H. D. (1996). The heritage versus the nonheritage language learner: The Five- College Self-Instructional Language Program's solutions to the problem of separation or unification. *ADFL Bulletin, 28,* 20–23.

McCabe, L. (1985). Teaching the slower student. *New York State Association of Foreign Language Teachers Bulletin,* 36, 5–6.

McCarthy, B. (1987). *The 4 MAT System.* Barrington, IL: Excel, Inc.

Myers, I. B., & McCaulley, M. H. (1985). *A guide to the development and use of the Myers- Briggs Type Indicator.* Palo Alto: Consulting Psychologists Press.

National Standards in Foreign Language Education Project (NSFLEP). (1996). *National standards for foreign language learning: Preparing for the 21st century.* Lawrence, KS: Allen Press.

Ogbu, J. U. (1997). Understanding cultural diversity and learning. *Journal for the Education of the Gifted* 17, 355–83.

Omnibus Budget Reconciliation Act of 1981, P.L. 97–35, §582. (Congressional Information Services, 1981).

Overfield, D. M. (1997). From the margins to the mainstream: Foreign language education and community-based learning. *Foreign Language Annals, 30,* 485–491.

Oxford, R. L. (1990a). Language learning strategies and beyond: A look at strategies in the context of styles. In S. Magnan (Ed.), *Shifting the instructional focus to the learner,* Northeast Conference Reports, (pp. 35–55). Lincolnwood, IL: NTC/Contemporary Publishing Group.

Oxford, R. L. (1990b). *Language learning strategies: What every teacher should know.* Boston, MA: Heinle & Heinle.

Oxford, R. L., & Crookall, D. (1989). Research on language learning strategies: Methods, findings, and instructional issues. *The Modern Language Journal, 73,* 404–419.

Oxford, R. L., & Lavine, R. Z. (1992). Teacher-student style wars in the language classroom: Research insights and suggestions. *ADFL Bulletin, 23,* 38–45.

Pease, J. (1996). Teaching Chinese at an urban university. *ADFL Bulletin, 27*(2), 9–13.

Phillips, J. (1997). Introduction. In J. Phillips (Ed.), *Collaborations: Meeting new goals, new realities,* Northeast Conference Reports (pp. xii–xviii). Lincolnwood, IL: NTC/Contemporary Publishing Group.

Phillips de Herrera, B. (1984). Teaching English as a foreign language to the visually handicapped. Paper presented at the Annual Convention of Teachers of English to Speakers of Other Languages, Houston, TX.

Pratt, M. B. (1984). Identity: Skin, blood, heart. In E. Bulkin, M. B. Pratt, & B. Smith (Eds.), *Yours in struggle* (pp. 11–63). Ithaca, NY: Firebrand Books.

Reid, J. M. (1987). The learning style preferences of ESL students. *TESOL Quarterly, 21,* 87–111.

Richard-Amato, P. A. (1988). *Making it happen—Interaction in the second language classroom.* New York: Longman.

Rodríguez Pino, C. (1997). La reconceptualización del programa español para hispanohablantes: Estrategias que reflejan la realidad sociolingüística de la clase. In M. C. Colombi & F. X. Alarcón (Eds.), *La enseñanza del español a hispanohablantes: Praxis y teoría* (pp. 65–82). Boston: Houghton Mifflin.

Sable, J. (1998). The educational progress of Black students. *The condition of education.* Available: http://nces.ed.gov/pubs98/condition98/index.html [1998, October 29].

Sable, J., & Stennett, J. (1998). The educational progress of Hispanic students. *The condition of education.* Available: http://nces.ed.gov/pubs98/condition98/index.html [1998, October 29].

Scarcella, R. C., & Oxford, R. L. (1992). *The tapestry of language learning.* Boston, MA: Heinle & Heinle.

Shrum, J. L. (1989). Challenging linguistically gifted students in the regular foreign language classroom. In R. M. Milgram (Ed.), *Teaching gifted and talented learners in the regular classroom* (pp. 269–294). New York: Charles R. Thomas.

Sparks, R. L., Artzer, M. L., Javorsky, J., Patton, J., Ganschow, L., Miller, K., & Hordubay, D. (1998). Students classified as learning disabled and non-learning disabled: Two comparison studies of native language skill, foreign language aptitude, and foreign language proficiency. *Foreign Language Annals, 31,* 535–551.

Sparks, R. L., & Ganschow, L. (1993). The effects of a multisensory, structured language approach to teaching Spanish on the native language and foreign language aptitude skills of at-risk learners: A follow-up and replication study. *Annals of Dyslexia, 43,* 194–216.

Sparks, R. L., & Ganschow, L. (1995). A strong inference approach to causal factors in foreign language learning: A response to MacIntyre. *The Modern Language Journal, 79,* 235–244.

Sparks, R. L., & Ganshow, L. (1996). Anxiety about foreign language learning among high school women. *The Modern Language Journal, 80,* 199–212.

Sparks, R. L., Ganschow, L., & Javorsky, J. (1995). I know one when I see one (Or I know one because I am one): A response to Mabbott. *Foreign Language Annals, 28,* 479–487.

Sparks, R. L., Ganschow, L., Javorsky, J., Pohlman, J., & Patton, J. (1992). Test comparisons among students identified as high-risk, low-risk, and learning disabled in high school foreign language courses. *The Modern Language Journal, 76,* 42–159.

Sparks, R. L., Ganschow, L., Kenneweg, S., & Miller, K. (1991). Use of an Orton-Gillingham approach to teach a foreign language to dyslexic/learning disabled students: Explicit teaching of phonology in a second language. *Annals of Dyslexia, 41,* 96–118.

Sparks, R. L., Ganschow, L., & Pohlman, J. (1989). Linguistic coding deficits in foreign language learners. *Annals of Dyslexia, 39,* 179–195.

Sparks, R. L., & Javorsky, J. (1998). Learning disabilities, foreign language learning, and the foreign language requirement. Paper presented at the American Council on the Teaching of Foreign Languages Annual Conference, Chicago, IL.

Spinelli, E. L. (1989). Beyond the traditional classroom. In H. S. Lepke (Ed.), *Shaping the future: Challenges and opportunities,* Northeast Conference Reports (pp. 139–158). Burlington, VT: Northeast Conference on the Teaching of Foreign Languages.

Spinelli, E. L. (1996). Meeting the challenges of the diverse secondary school population. In B. Wing (Ed.), *Foreign languages for all: Challenges and choices,* Northeast Conference Reports, pp. 57–90. Lincolnwood, IL: NTC/Contemporary Publishing Group.

Sternberg, R., & Davidson, J. (Eds.). (1986). *Conceptions of giftedness.* New York: Cambridge University Press.

Strength through Wisdom: A Critique of U.S. Capability. A Report to the President from the President's Commision on Foreign Languages and International Studies. Washington, D.C.: Government Printing Office, 1979. Report in *The Modern Language Journal, 64,* 1980, 9–57.

Strong, M. (1988). *Language learning and deafness.* Cambridge: Cambridge University Press.

Sullivan, V. J., & McDonald, W. E. (1990). Cross-age tutoring in Spanish: One motivating method. *The Pennsylvania State Modern Language Association Bulletin, 63*(2), 13–17.

Thomas, L. (1996). Language as power: A linguistic critique of U.S. English. *The Modern Language Journal, 80,* 129–140.

Thompson, R. H., White, K. R., & Morgan, D. P. (1982). Teacher-student interaction patterns in classrooms with mainstreamed mildly handicapped students. *American Educational Research Journal, 19,* 220–236.

Treffinger, D. J., & Feldhusen, J. F. (1996). Talent recognition and development: Successor to gifted education. *Journal for the Education of the Gifted, 19*(2), 181–193.

Vanucci, S. R. (1991). Understanding dysfunctional systems. Unpublished manuscript.

Valdés, G. (1995). The teaching of minority languages as academic subjects: Pedagogical and theoretical challenges. *The Modern Language Journal, 79,* 299–328.

Valdés, G. (1999). Introduction. In L. A. Sandstedt (Project Director), *The AATSP professional development handbook series for teachers: Spanish for native speakers,* Vol. 1. Greeley, CO: American Association of Teachers of Spanish and Portuguese.

Veltman, C. (1983). *Language shift in the United States.* Berlin, Germany: Mouton de Gruyter.

Wilberschied, L., & Dassier, J. L. P. (1995). Increasing the number of minority FL educators: Local action to meet a national imperative. *The Modern Language Journal, 79,* 1–14.

CHAPTER *11*

Assessing Language Performance in Context

In this chapter you will learn about:

- a theoretical and practical framework for assessing learners' abilities to use language meaningfully
- assessment types according to purpose, format, and audience

- authentic assessment, scoring rubrics, and portfolios
- contextualized classroom tests
- performance-based assessment
- alternatives to paper-and-pencil tests

Teach and Reflect: Analyzing and Adapting a Traditional Test; Adding An Authentic Dimension to a Performance-Based Assessment Task

Case Study 1: Developing Authentic Assessment Tasks and Rubrics

Case Study 2: Using Audio Tapes for Oral Assessment

Conceptual Orientation

Test: a means of examination, trial or proof; a series of questions or problems designed to determine knowledge or intelligence; a criterion; a standard.

Assess: to evaluate, appraise.

Evaluate: to ascertain or fix the value or worth of; to examine and judge standard (American Heritage Dictionary, 1973).

All of the terms defined above are related to gathering information, interpreting it, and making decisions in a systematic way (Genessee & Upshur, 1996). The reason why we test, evaluate, or assess is to make an informed decision. Sometimes we want to determine what the learner knows already, sometimes we want to sample a learner's knowledge about something that was taught, sometimes we want to determine how to structure a lesson for a learner. Testing refers to the performance of the task, whether it is written or oral. In assessment, the results of the performance are reported to provide information; in evaluation, those results are given some selective judgment by the interpreters of the results (Hammadou, 1998, p. 290). Although the definition of *assessment* and *evaluation* includes judgments, educators most often assign the value judgment feature to *evaluation,* while *assessment* consists of describing and reporting performance. The people who will make informed decisions are the "audience" for the test: Sometimes they are within the school, close to the instruction, such as teachers and learners. Sometimes they are parents, school board members, or administrative personnel. Sometimes the audience is outside the school and consists of legislators, college admissions officials, scholarship agencies, accreditation or funding agencies. The types of decisions that can be made are as varied as the types of audiences. From the perspective of the learner and the teacher, the primary purpose of testing is to provide feedback to the learners and to assess instruction.[1] At one time, learners viewed the feedback as grades (Oller, 1991a). Many teachers, about to introduce a topic they consider particularly significant for the learners' progress, hear the comment from learners who ask, "Will this be on the test?" while digging for pencil and paper to take notes. As teachers help learners take responsibility for their own learning and engage them in the structuring of classroom tasks, grades become a weak motivating factor for classroom performance (Hahn, Stassen, & Reschke, 1989; Moeller & Reschke, 1993). These researchers state: "If the activity is hands-on, interactive, and relevant, the students will perform the task to the best of their ability regardless of 'grading'" (Moeller & Reschke, 1993, p.169). Thus teachers should structure hands-on classroom activities and testing tasks that provide relevance and interaction.

Current research in testing argues for a more direct connection between teaching and testing. The same kinds of activities designed for classroom interaction can serve as valid testing formats, with instruction and evaluation more closely integrated. As Oller points out, "Perhaps the essential insight of a quarter of a century of language testing (both research and practice) is that good teaching and good testing are, or ought to be, nearly indistinguishable" (1991a, p. 38). Indeed, "teaching to the test" is no longer viewed with disdain, but rather as a logical procedure that connects goal setting with goal accomplishment (Wiggins, 1989; Oller, 1991a). Terry points out that "any material or technique that is effective for teaching a foreign language can also be used for testing" (1998, p. 277). Thus as teachers and learners work toward standards-driven goals using authentic materials from real world contexts, testing also takes a more realistic form.

Four basic principles foreign language teachers follow in the development of classroom tests are: (1) test *what* was taught; (2) test it in a manner that reflects the *way* in which it was taught; (3) focus the test on what students *can* do rather than what they cannot do; and (4) capture creative use of language by learners (Donato, Antonek, & Tucker, 1996). For example, if learners spend their class time developing oral skills, then the test should include assessment of oral language output. Similarly, students who learn in class how to narrate in the past by writing paragraphs about events that occurred during their childhood should be tested on their learning by being asked to write paragraphs about past events in their lives. Since a large portion of classroom time is spent in learning language for communication in real-life contexts, testing should also reflect language used for communication within realistic contexts (Adair-Hauck, 1996; Shrum, 1991; Harper, Lively, & Williams, 1998).

---

1. Thanks to Rick Donato for his insights in this definition.

Purposes of Tests

Oller categorized several types of tests according to the purposes they serve (Oller, 1991a, p. 36):

TYPE OF TEST	PURPOSE	EXAMPLE
Instructional	enables learners to improve their proficiency in the target language	two learners negotiate plans for the weekend
Managerial	helps teachers and learners manage instruction and study practices—for instance, by providing a sensible basis for grading	a quiz on a set of related vocabulary items before beginning another set, such as daily activities before foods
Motivational	serves as a reward or as a goal, urging learners and teachers toward higher achievement relative to well-defined goals	Oral Proficiency Interview to assign a level on the ACTFL Oral Proficiency Scale
Diagnostic	helps teachers and learners identify specific instructional problems	paragraph describing themselves, asked of learners entering an intermediate-level course
Curricular	defines the curriculum as a whole	International Baccalaureate or Advanced Placement test

❏ Summative vs. Formative Tests

All tests have some characteristics in common, related to what learners can expect from them. Learners have the reasonable right to expect that their scores should be the same regardless of who is doing the scoring; that is, learners can expect that scorers will view the responses objectively. Learners should also be able to expect that the test measures what it is supposed to measure and that this measurement is appropriate for this group of learners. This is referred to as *validity*. Furthermore, learners can expect that the test consistently measures whatever it measures. This is called *reliability* (Gay, 1987).

Described in broad categories, testing can be classified as either summative or formative. Summative testing often occurs at the end of a course and is designed to determine what the learner can do with the language at that point. Opportunities for further input or performance after the test is administered usually occur in the next language learning experience or course. The most common summative test is a final exam. Formative tests are designed to help form or shape the learners' ongoing understanding or skills while the teacher and learners still have opportunities to interact for the purposes of repair and improvement within a given course or setting. Shohamy (1990) suggests that language teachers make extensive use of formative testing that is integrated into the teaching and learning process. Examples include quizzes (five to fifteen minutes), class interaction activities such as paired interviews, and chapter or unit tests. The act of entering a grade into the gradebook, to be averaged at the end of a term, changes formative tests, such as quizzes, into summative instruments. A sufficient amount of formative testing must be done in the classroom in order to enable learners to revisit and review the material in a variety of ways, and formative feedback must enable the learner to improve without penalty. In this regard, teachers find it helpful to distinguish between ungraded assessment, which gives objective and formative information to the learner, and graded assessment or evaluation, which places value judgments on performance.

 Formative testing provides interpretation and feedback to learners so they can modify and improve their performance.

❒ Bipolar Terms for Testing

Natural-situational	Unnatural-contrived
Direct	Indirect
Integrative/Global	Discrete point

"Most language tests can be viewed as lying somewhere on a continuum from natural-situational to unnatural-contrived" (Henning, 1987). With this statement, Henning framed the continuum that contains several similar sets of bipolar terms. Regarding direct and indirect tests, Ke and Reed point out that indirect tests try to find out how well someone could possibly speak or write a target language by sampling that person's knowledge of forms and structures, usually through multiple-choice formats. Direct tests, on the other hand, sample language proficiency by asking the person to actually perform a communicative task (Ke & Reed, 1995, p. 209). These distinctions are described historically in two different testing formats: discrete-point tests and integrative or global tests (Carroll, 1961). The contrast between these two formats often reflects different teaching philosophies. A discrete-point test focuses on one linguistic component at a time: grammar, vocabulary, syntax, or phonology. It assesses one skill at a time, such as listening, reading, or writing. Test items include a variety of formats, such as multiple-choice, true-false, matching, and completion. Discrete-point tests require responses to single items, usually in unconnected linguistic contexts; or they may focus on one aspect of a linguistic element within a more complex language context. Discrete-point items are useful when teachers want to determine whether specific linguistic forms have been learned. An example is a quiz on verb endings.

Unlike discrete-point tests, integrative or global tests assess the learner's ability to use various components of the language at the same time, and often multiple skills as well. For example, an integrative test might ask learners to listen to a taped segment, identify main ideas, and then use the information as the topic for discussion, as the theme of a composition, or to compare the segment to a reading on the same topic.

Range of Test Types

Figure 11.1 describes the range of test types. *Standardized tests* measure learners' progress against that of others, while *proficiency tests* measure performance against a criterion. For example, the College Board prepares comparisons of all the scores earned on the SAT and

Figure 11.1 Range of Test Types

TEST TYPE	ASSESSMENT PROCEDURE	DECISION	AUDIENCE	EXAMPLE
Standardized test: the learner's performance is measured against that of others in a large population, norm-referenced.	Tally of number correct less number wrong is sometimes corrected by a formula to account for guessing: maximum score for SAT, for example, is 800.	Should the learner be promoted to the next grade? Should the learner be admitted to "X" college? Compared to others who took this test, where is this learner?	Governmental funding agency, scholarship-granting organizations, colleges and universities	Iowa test of Basic Skills, Literacy Passport tests, Advanced Placement Exams, SAT, TOEFL, GRE
Proficiency exams: the learner's performance is measured against a criterion, the educated native speaker.	Descriptive terms delineate progress along a scale toward the same level as that of the criterion speaker, e.g., Intermediate-Mid.	Where is the learner at this time in the progression toward becoming like the educated native speaker?	Employers, schools, colleges and universities, learner	Interagency Language Round-table (ILR) Oral Proficiency Interview, ACTFL Oral Proficiency Interview
Commercially-prepared achievement tests: the learner's mastery of an instructed body of knowledge is measured.	Score reflects weighted values for certain topics studied, usually 1–100 points.	How much has the student learned about "X" material presented from "Y" set of instructional materials?	Teacher, learner, employers, school and governmental administrators	Publisher's test for Chapters 6 and 7; SAT exams
Teacher-made classroom tests, quizzes: learner's performance on instructed body of knowledge is measured, usually an assessment of oral and written classrooms skills; may be *prochievement* and/or *performance-based* and/or *interactive*.	Score reflects weighted values, often percentage of number correct; sometimes converted to letter grades; simple descriptions of performance; collection and description of artifacts; narration of progress by learner.	Does the learner know what was taught? Can s/he perform the tasks that were practiced in class? How should the teacher design instruction based on the results?	Teacher, learner, parents, school personnel	Mrs. Chin's ESL midterm exam; Mr. Frey's essay test on "La joya del Inca"; Ms. Broderick's vocabulary quiz; oral plays and interviews
Authentic assessment: learner performs real-world tasks with actual audience.	Success is determined by the response of the real-world audience.	Can the learner address challenge faced by individuals in real-world situations? Can s/he integrate knowledge and skills to solve complex problems and situations?	Consumer, peer, learner, teacher	Multifaceted situations; problems; projects that require integration of knowledge, content, skills

Source: Shrum & Glisan, 1999; original compilation.

creates a chart so that any one score can be compared to the normed grouping of all the other scores. An example of a proficiency test scored against a criterion is the ACTFL Oral Proficiency Interview in which examinees can see the point at which their score falls in relation to an educated native speaker, which is the criterion. *Commercially prepared achievement tests*, such as textbook publishers' tests, examine the extent to which learners have learned a body of material taught. Teachers use a repertoire of *teacher-made instruments* to assess both achievement of course objectives and development of overall language performance. A test or shorter quiz may consist of one of the following formats or may be a blending of the two:

- *prochievement format*: a blending of achievement and proficiency testing that incorporates linguistic (i.e., structural, syntactic, lexical) items from the course content/objectives to test achievement but also elicits language performance to assess ability to function along a proficiency-based continuum (Harper, Lively, & Williams, 1998) (see Figure 11.2 for a sample prochievement test item).

Figure 11.2 Prochievement Test Item for Grammar/Vocabulary

Une description ennuyeuse. *(A boring description.)* Spice up this description a learner wrote in French about an evening on the town. Do so by adding at least one adjective to each underlined word. ATTENTION: Watch word order and agreement.

Nous partons à six personnes dans une <u>voiture</u>. Nous arrivons à un <u>restaurant</u>. Les <u>serveurs</u> qui y travaillent ont tous une <u>moustache</u>. A une table à côté, deux hommes bavardent. Ce sont le <u>propriétaire</u> et son <u>fils</u>. Un homme se plaint du restaurant à cause de ses <u>chaises</u> et son <u>service</u>. Lui et le propriétaire se disputent. Les <u>clients</u> quittent le restaurant. Nous, nous terminons cette <u>soirée</u> dans un bar où on a du Karioka.

N.B. You may use adjectives from this list or substitute those of your choice.

ancien	inconfortable	noir
dynamique	inefficace	nouveau
européen	jeune	petit
excellent	long	vrai
français	mémorable	???
gros	mécontent	

We leave, six people in one car. We arrive at a restaurant. The waiters who work there all have mustaches. At a nearby table, two men chat. They are the owner and his son. A man complains about the seating and the service. He and the owner argue. The customers leave the restaurant. As for us, we finish this evening in a Karioke bar.

old	uncomfortable	black
dynamic	inefficient	new
European	young	small
excellent	long	true
French	memorable	???
fat	mischievous	

Source: Adapted from Phillips, 1996; original material.

- *performance-based format*: requires learners to demonstrate their level of competence and knowledge by creating a product or a response (Koda, 1998). This format includes the use of *prompts*, which are complex questions or situations requiring the learner to make connections among concepts and develop a strategy for addressing the question. There can be more than one right answer (Wiggins, 1998) (see Figure 11.3 for a sample performance-based test item).

Figure 11.3   Performance-Based Test Item

Cruceros Marítimos Skorpios. Read the following advertisement. Give your reactions to the ad by talking for two minutes, during which time you explain:

- the type of vacation being advertised;
- four things this trip offers;
- whether or not you will go on this trip;
- if you are going on this trip, what preparation you will have to make before you leave;
- if you are not going on this trip, what type of trip you might take instead.

Source: Glisan & Shrum, 1996, p. 142.

❒ An Interactive Model for Testing

Another type of teacher-made test is the interactive format proposed by Swaffar, Arens, and Byrnes. Their interactive model for testing reading parallels their approach to teaching reading. Their test design, which can also be applied to the testing of other skills, features three components to verify whether the learner can:

1. understand both linguistic and extralinguistic pragmatic aspects of the text;

2. connect comprehension of the text to production or self-expression;

3. express meaning in one's own words (Swaffar, Arens, & Byrnes, 1991, pp. 157–159).

The principles underlying this type of model might be used to design tests that are (1) interactive—learner interacts with an assigned text; (2) pragmatic—learner uses both linguistic and extralinguistic information; and (3) integrative—learner uses more than one skill at a time. For example, earlier chapters presented ideas for contextualizing language teaching by using an initial oral or written text. In a testing format, learners might go through similar steps. Hence, the test would include a series of questions that enable the teacher to evaluate the learners' ability to summarize in the native language what a text is about, interact with the text to isolate significant details, use the target language to write about ideas in the text, and use the target language to express their opinions about the text. This is far different from the simple plot summaries or single factual questions that often appear on tests. The design illustrated below is an adaptation of a five-step model proposed by Swaffar, Byrnes, and Arens (1991). Sample items from their text are included to exemplify each step.

1. Students listen to or read an authentic segment.

2. Students identify main ideas by focusing on content or text schema.

> Instructions: Identify and write down key words from the text that provide the following information about the main idea of the text:
> Who: _____   What: _____
> When: _____   Where: _____
> Using these words, write a sentence expressing the main idea of the text.

3. Students identify details (vocabulary development).

> Instructions: Find synonyms or references from the text for the following words:

4. Students use the grammatical structures in the text to further explore text ideas.

> Instructions: In the story, events and their timing are of major importance. Write two sentences about major events in the story. Use past tenses.

5. Students develop their points of view.

> Instructions: What do you think would have happened if the story had continued? Write a three-to-five sentence description of another ending to the story. (This section could also engage learners' attention to particular cultural points.)

This model tests learners on their listening and/or reading skills; grammatical, lexical, and cultural knowledge; ability to interact with the text; and productive skills, all within the framework of a real context (see Appendix 11.1 for an example of a German reading used as a test within this framework).

Authentic tasks (see next section) reflect a range of communication behaviors commonly observed in the target language communities and workplaces (Koda, 1998). These tasks require learners to address a meaningful audience and mirror challenges faced by real individuals in real-world settings (Wiggins, 1998).

Prochievement test items evaluate achievement of course content and assess performance along a proficiency continuum.

Performance-based tests elicit an open-ended response or a product.

Authentic tasks require learners to address an actual audience and mirror challenges faced by real individuals in real-world settings (Wiggins, 1998).

❑ Assessment

We have seen earlier that test results are often used by various groups of individuals in order to make decisions about instruction and about learners. Wiggins proposes that assessment also be *educative* in two ways: (1) It should be designed to teach by improving the performance of both teacher and learner; and (2) it should evoke exemplary pedagogy (1998, p. 12). Educative tests must include credible tasks from which performance is assessed, reflecting a performance-based classroom and challenges learners will face in the real world. Recently the term *authentic* has been used to describe the type of assessment that mirrors the tasks and challenges faced by individuals in the real world (Wiggins, 1998). An assessment task, problem, or project is authentic if it

- is realistic in that it tests the learner's knowledge and abilities in real-world situations.
- requires judgment and innovation.
- asks the student to "do" the [academic] subject rather than reciting information so that the student carries out a task using the language in a meaningful way.

- replicates or simulates the contexts in which adults are "tested" in the workplace, in civic life, and in personal life so that students address an actual audience, not just their teacher.
- assesses the student's ability to use a repertoire of knowledge and skill efficiently and effectively to negotiate a complex task.
- allows appropriate opportunities to rehearse, practice, consult resources, and get feedback and refine performances and products (Wiggins, 1998, pp. 22–23).

According to Koda (1998), authentic tests are based on activities representing a full range of communication behaviors commonly observed in the target language communities and workplaces, or "real world" use of language. Authentic assessments enable teachers to "assess what we value so that we value what we assess" (CLASS, 1998). Often learners are engaged in proficiency-based or standards-driven activities in the classroom, but they are still tested on their knowledge of linguistic details by means of paper-and-pencil, discrete-point formats; in this scenario, there is a gap between the communication we value and the linguistic forms we assess. Authentic tests provide a way to reduce the gap between what we value and what we assess. Figure 11.4 depicts the key differences between typical tests and authentic tests (Liskin-Gasparro, 1997). Authentic tests share the characteristics of performance-based tests except that they add the dimension of a *meaningful audience*. For example, compare the performance-based task in Figure 11.3 with the authentic task shown in Figure 11.5. In Figure 11.3, the learner is performing with the language in a meaningful task, but the only audience is the classroom teacher. In Figure 11.5, the learner is also performing, but the audience is now a consumer who needs a particular service, which the learner will provide. The task described in Figure 11.5 will require multistaged research and interaction on the part of the learner, but the end result is meaningful use of language for real audiences. In Case Study One of the **Discuss and Reflect** section of this chapter, you will find a Performance Task Template (CLASS, 1998) that includes the steps that might be followed in designing an authentic assessment task.

> **Authentic tasks mirror the challenges faced by individuals in the real world.**

> **The teacher is not the only audience in authentic tests.**

❑ Grading Authentic and Performance-Based Tasks: Scoring Rubrics

Authentic and performance-based tasks can be assigned a grade with the use of a *rubric*,[2] a

---

2. The word "rubric" comes from the Latin word *ruber* meaning "red." In medieval times, a rubric was a set of instructions or a commentary attached to a law or liturgical service and was usually written in red. "Rubric" came to mean a guideline or something that instructs people (Wiggins, 1998, p. 154).

Figure 11.4 Key Differences Between Typical Tests and Authentic Tests

AUTHENTIC ASSESSMENT	TRADITIONAL STANDARDIZED TESTING
Direct examination of student performance on "worthy intellectual tasks."	Indirect examination of student performance and knowledge through test items that "represent competence."
Authentic tasks involve **challenges** and roles that help students rehearse for the complex ambiguities of the "game" of adult and professional life.	Traditional tests are more like **drills,** assessing discrete and often simplistic versions of the activities in authentic assessments.
Students are required to be effective performers with their acquired knowledge.	Students are required to recognize, recall, or "plug in" their acquired knowledge.
Modes of assessment are designed to mirror the priorities and challenges found in the best instructional activities, for example, conduct research; write, revise, and discuss papers; provide oral analysis of an event or reading.	Modes of assessment are usually limited to paper-and-pencil, one-answer questions.
Focus is on whether student can craft polished, thorough, and justifiable responses, performances, or products. Authentic assessment asks for **rationales.**	Focus is on whether students can select or provide the one correct answer allowed for each question. Traditional assessment asks for **right answers.**
Aims to **improve** performance.	Aims to **monitor** performance.
Implies teacher involvement and investment in the form and content of assessment.	Tests are often external and "secure," which promotes distance between teacher and assessment.
Scores, often criticized as "subjective," are based on informed and trained judgments.	Tests, often labeled "objective," have many subjective aspects, for example, choice of items, manner in which norms and cut-off scores are established.
Test validity and reliability are established by emphasizing and standardizing appropriate **criteria** for scoring.	Test validity and reliability are established by having standardized discrete-point items and one accepted right response for each.

Source: Liskin-Gasparro, 1997, adapted from Wiggins, 1990.

set of scoring guidelines for evaluating student work (Wiggins, 1998, p. 154). Rubrics answer the following questions:

- By what criteria should performance be judged?
- Where and for what should we look to judge performance success?
- What does the range in the quality of performance look like?
- How do we determine validly, reliably, and fairly what score should be given and what that score means?
- How should the different levels of quality be described and distinguished from one another? (Wiggins, 1998, p. 154)

Rubrics provide the means for teachers to provide feedback to learners about their progress as well as to assign grades. However, perhaps of more importance, they show learners what good performance "looks like" even before they perform an assessment task.

Rubrics contain a scale of possible points with four, five, or six points for the best performance and provide descriptors for each level of performance. They can be holistic (one general rubric) or analytic (multiple rubrics, one for each dimension of the performance being analyzed). If analytic, rubrics provide guidelines for feasibility and aptness for each dimension of performance (Wiggins, 1998). The *ACTFL Guidelines* are rubrics because each level contains descriptive language that defines the unique performance that is characteristic of that level; that is, what the language user can and cannot do. To create a rubric for an authentic task, keep in mind that the audience is another individual in a real-world or simulated setting. What would an excellent performance look like if that person were the judge? Create a response that such a person would judge as excellent. Then list the elements contained in that excellent performance and assign a range of points to each element. Then describe what unacceptable task completion would look like and develop the levels in between. Figure 11.6 illustrates a set of rubrics that might be used to assess the authentic task in Figure 11.5.

Figure 11.5   Authentic Assessment Task

Un viaje por España *(A Trip through Spain)*

You and your partner are Spanish travel agents who have decided to market your services to American school groups. You know there is intensive competition for this business. You have received a memo from Señorita Surprenant, one of New England's most traveled Spanish language teachers. She is heading back to Spain this spring with a group of her students. She is not committed to any specific regions, cities, or sights. She is looking for the following: a good price, great art museums, famous settings in literature, rare cultural opportunities (e.g., dance, sport, food), and all within a 7–10-day time frame.

   You know Spain and its opportunities, but you are not really sure what will please Señorita Surprenant. You draw up a list of options that could be included in a trip and then call Señorita Surprenant. You talk with her about the options and use this chance to decide what will be the kinds of things that will most convince her that you are the agency to handle the trip.

   Using your knowledge and your impression of what Señorita Surprenant is looking for in the trip, you submit a written proposal, including an itinerary and your rationale for the itinerary, a map setting out the route to be followed, and a price list for students and chaperones.

Source: Adapted from CLASS, 1998; contributed by J. Surprenant, teacher

❏ Other Characteristics of Contextualized Tests

In our discussion of performance-based and authentic tests, the contexts in which learners are asked to perform linguistic tasks are implied or stipulated. These tests are considered *pragmatic* tests (Oller, 1991a), in which the learner has the opportunity to process authentic language within normal contextual constraints and link that language to her/his personal experience. Pragmatic and authentic tests share many similar features. They involve the use of linguistic content—grammar, syntax, and vocabulary; extralinguistic content—gestures and tone of voice in speaking, subtle, indirect implications in writing;

Figure 11.6 Sample Scoring Rubrics for the Authentic Task in Figure 11.5

	EXCELLENT 4 POINTS	GOOD 3 POINTS	MINIMAL 2 POINTS	INADEQUATE I POINT
Quality of Research	Evidence of thorough research in preparation for proposal design; main facts and wealth of details about site, museums, culture	Evidence of effective research in preparation for proposal design; main facts with a few details about site, museums, culture	Evidence of some research; main facts with few or no details about sites, museums, culture	Little evidence of research; incomplete facts and details
Quality of Written Proposal	Well-written, clear, easy to understand; uses own words; few errors in grammar, vocabulary, spelling	Well-written, mostly clear with a few unclear parts or easy to understand except for a few places; uses primarily own words and some language from sources; some patterns of errors in grammar and/or vocabulary and/or spelling	Approximately half of writing is clear; quality of writing interferes with understanding in places; uses much language directly from sources; when using own language, patterns of errors in grammar, and/or vocabulary, and/or spelling	Poorly written; hard to understand; uses primarily language directly from sources; or if using own language, many patterns of errors in grammar, vocabulary, and spelling
Degree to Which Proposal Is Convincing	Very persuasive; addresses the requested information of client; convinces client to take the trip	Gives some reasons that are convincing; addresses most of the requested information of client; seriously persuades client to consider the trip	Gives only a partial rationale for taking the trip; addresses many though not all of the requested details and/or is not very convincing	Not persuasive; fails to address most of the client's requested information; language used does not convince client to take trip[3]
Justification of Prices of Trip	Includes complete breakdown of prices with clear justification for costs	Includes some breakdown of prices and/or some justification for costs, although more clarity required	Either price breakdown or cost justification is incomplete; client still has questions	Incomplete breakdown of prices and incomplete justification of costs

Source: Glisan, 1998, based on CLASS, 1998.

and the learner's extralinguistic background knowledge and experience. These tests are *integrative* in nature as they require attention to many linguistic elements at once and the use of more than one skill at a time. However, integrative tests are not necessarily pragmatic in nature; only those tests that draw on learners' extralinguistic or world knowledge

---

3. If the client does not take the trip because of a sudden death in the family, the travel agent's language is not at fault. Authentic assessment enables learners and teachers to engage in elaborated role-play situations that resemble and prepare the learner for real-life circumstances.

are truly pragmatic. *Interactive* tests engage learners in listening to or reading an authentic text and using that knowledge to communicate their opinions or to perform a related task (Swaffar, Arens, & Byrnes, 1991). Authentic tests are performance-based, pragmatic, integrative, and often interactive. Formats for pragmatic and authentic tests can include essay writing, narration, oral interviews, and role plays. Bachman (1990) calls such tests *communicative*, since the tasks and content are integrated within communicative interaction.

❒ Portfolio Assessment: Selection and Reflection

A portfolio is a "collection of evidence used by the teacher and learner to monitor the growth of the learner's knowledge of content, use of strategies, and attitudes toward the accomplishment of goals in an organized and systematic way" (Tierney, Carter, & Desai, 1991, p. 41). A portfolio describes and evaluates learner performance across various language skills; it is a rich description of a learner's work and offers additional perspectives that tests do not provide. In a portfolio, learners have an opportunity to select evidence of their learning, reflect on it, and make it part of the assessment of their learning.[4] The form of a portfolio is negotiated between the teacher and the learner, who usually confer about the development of the portfolio. Scoring is flexible and constructive. Portfolios have also been used for assessment of teachers' performance.

There are generally two principal players in the creation of a portfolio. First is the person who designs the portfolio or who sets the guidelines for what it should contain. This person is either the audience for the portfolio, or knows what the audience will expect to see. The portfolio developer is the person whose work is featured in the portfolio. Usually this person selects items to be included as documents based on her/his judgment and the stipulations of the portfolio designer. The developer also provides the narrative reflection justifying why each piece of work was selected and what it means in his/her personal growth as a language learner. A sample reflection/goal setting statement that includes content and linguistic structure information follows.

> Writing this essay helped me understand why some people might join a group like "sendero luminoso" to protest what happens to their families. I fixed my mistakes in using the conditional and imperfect subjunctive, and now I can use *si* [if-clauses] a little better. On the next essay I will try to use it right on the first draft.[5]

The size and format of the portfolio are determined by decisions the designer or developer of the portfolio makes about the purpose of the portfolio, the selection of type and number of documents, and the narration to highlight importance of the documents. For example, within a classroom unit on housing, learners may have participated in a variety

---

4. The Center on Learning, Assessment, and School Structure (1998) has coined the term "anthology" to describe the "assessment portfolio" that contains a valid sample of student work including performance on authentic performance tasks, traditional classroom test results, and scores from standardized testing. The anthology can be used "to base important decisions about student competence, promotion, and graduation on a collection of credible work . . ." (Wiggins, 1998, p. 197).

5. This comment is from a student whose identity must remain anonymous, in Spanish 3106, spring 1996, Virginia Tech.

of activities such as TPR for learning the rooms of the house and furniture; listening to radio commercials that advertise furniture sales; reading newspaper classified ads for apartments for rent; exploring the products, practices, and perspectives associated with housing in the target culture and comparing them to the native culture; designing their own housing floor plans; searching the Internet for housing information in the target countries; interviewing a native speaker about her/his housing preferences. From those activities, learners might carefully select the following to demonstrate what they know and are able to do within each goal area as it pertains to this unit: an audio or video taped recording of an interview conducted with a native speaker in which the learner elicited information about housing in the target cultures; a rough draft and subsequent rewrites of a brief paper on comparisons between housing in the native and target cultures in terms of products, practices, and perspectives; an e-mail letter to a keypal in which correspondents share information about their dwellings; written results of an Internet search dealing with apartments for rent in a target country region. In the selection process, learners can see and document their progress and set goals for the next steps. Setting goals and self-assessment are key elements in helping learners take responsibility for their learning.

> **Portfolios offer learners opportunities to showcase and reflect on growth or improvement.**

Another use of portfolios has been for assessment of teachers, offering them an opportunity to demonstrate accountability to their students, parents, school administrators, and governmental agencies by showcasing their abilities and the performance of their students. Such a portfolio might include a teacher's certificate of rating on the Oral Proficiency Interview, a Statement of Philosophy about Teaching, an audiotape of a preferred classroom activity, a sample lesson plan addressing national standards, statewide frameworks and systemwide goals, and samples of student work. Hammadou (1998) identified several types of portfolios, showcase, documentation, evaluation, and process. Some of their characteristics are shown in Figure 11.7.

When teachers and learners score classroom portfolios or professional career portfolios, the experience should be constructive and positive. In some cases, portfolio designers may want simply to stimulate and reward goal-directed reflection, or they may want to use specific criteria such as (1) evidence of learner growth in the five goal areas; (2) diversity of entries; (3) organization and presentation; and (4) quality of self-reflection. Appendix 11.2 presents a Sample Portfolio Template; Appendix 11.3 presents a Portfolio Evaluation Sheet for use by the teacher; Appendix 11.4 presents a Portfolio Feedback Sheet for teachers and learners to use as the portfolio develops; and Appendix 11.5 is a Table of Contents Portfolio Sheet to assist teachers and learners in mapping out the work of portfolio development. Padilla, Aninao, and Sung offer the following suggestions for successful implementation of portfolio assessment, among others already elaborated and based on a research study of over one thousand students in fourteen language programs for less commonly taught languages:

- provide a brief annotation for each item in the portfolio
- date and number each item chronologically

Figure 11.7 Types of Portfolios

PORTFOLIO TYPE	DESIGNER/ DEVELOPER	TYPE OF ASSESSMENT	NUMBER OF ENTRIES; FREQUENCY	AUDIENCE
Show-case or best-works	Teacher designs according to a set of established goals; teacher selects documentation of own performance	Self-evaluation	Few, over a career	Hiring bodies, parents, school administrators, legislators
Documentation	Teacher or supervisor designs; teacher or students compile it	Student self-evaluation as well as teacher evaluation	Many, over time	Parents at parent conferences, student
Evaluation	Outside agency or statewide group of teachers; students and teachers create a set of tasks	Everyone completes the same tasks; standardization of evaluation	Specified and limited number and format	Legislators, parents, educational agencies
Process	Student selects goals; student selects and narrates value of documents	Self-reflection of the learning process, usually not graded	Rough drafts, peer reviews; usually shortened intensive period of time or single task	Primarily the student for self-reflection; also teachers and parents

Source: Adapted from Hammadou, 1998.

- if purpose is to document student growth, establish a baseline of performance first
- artifacts for the portfolio may include writing samples, speech samples, evidence of listening and reading comprehension
- spontaneous samples of student use of target language are viable for inclusion in a portfolio (1996, pp. 436-438).[6]

Alternatives to Paper-and-Pencil Testing

We have seen earlier in this chapter that teachers need to test what they teach. With a greater emphasis placed on oral performance, assessment should include ample opportunities for learners to demonstrate their communicative skills in ways other than paper-and-pencil formats. Assessing learners' oral progress does not have to be a time-consuming activity. Listening and speaking skills lend themselves to testing without written means. Among the many possible formats for testing listening and speaking without paper and pencil are the following ideas that can be adapted for use with elementary school, middle school/junior high school, high school, and postsecondary learners:

---

6. For additional information about portfolio assessments and worksheets to guide in planning, compiling, and evaluating a portfolio, see *Portfolio Assessment in the Foreign Language Classroom,* by Alatis and Barnhardt (1998) available from the National Capital Language Resource Center at (202) 739-0607.

Listening Formats:

- Students respond to TPR commands.
- Students verify in writing or speaking a description of a picture.
- Students listen to a narrative and number pictures or put them in order.

Listening and Speaking Formats:

- Students respond to oral questions in an interview procedure.
- Students recreate an oral story with the teacher.
- Students discuss an audio or video segment.
- Students invent a different ending for a story.

Speaking Formats:

- Students describe a picture.
- Students invent a story about a picture.
- Students present a spontaneous conversation or role play.
- Students respond to a given situation in a culturally appropriate way.
- Students present a narration/description or monologue.
- Students conduct a debate.

The Oral Proficiency Interview and Its Implications for Classroom Testing

As you learned in earlier chapters, the ACTFL Oral Proficiency Interview (OPI) is a standardized procedure for the global assessment of oral proficiency. It measures language production holistically by identifying patterns of strength and weakness within the assessment criteria of functions, contexts, and accuracy. An official OPI is a face-to-face, tape-recorded interview lasting from five to thirty minutes and conducted by a certified proficiency tester. Following is a brief description of how the interview is conducted. As pointed out in Chapter 8, an understanding of the scale and/or the interview procedure does not imply an ability to rate oral speech samples. Furthermore, the OPI is not designed to be used as a classroom test. See the ACTFL web site at **http://www.actfl.org** for procedures to schedule an Oral Proficiency Interview.

The interview begins with a brief *warm-up* in order to help the interviewee feel comfortable and confident. Next, the interviewer moves the conversation forward through one or more *level checks* to establish the floor of performance or to determine at what level the interviewee can consistently perform the tasks for a given level. This phase demonstrates the tasks/contexts that the interviewee can perform with confidence and accuracy. Once the interviewer has determined that the speaker can handle the tasks and topics of a particular level, he or she raises the interview to the next major level by means of *probes* to establish the ceiling of the performance. The interaction in this phase illustrates the limitations of the interviewee's proficiency. The level check and probe phases may need to be repeated as each level is verified and the next level is examined. After the level checks and probes have been conducted and the interviewer believes that the evidence points to a particular level, the interviewee is asked to participate in a role play, which serves as a final level check or probe. The role play checks functions that cannot easily be elicited by means of the conversation itself. Finally, the interview is brought to a close in the *wind-down*, at which time the discussion returns to a comfortable linguistic level for the interviewee and ends on a positive note (Swender, 1999).

The design of the OPI has provided many ideas for classroom testing of oral skills:

- interviews between teacher and learner
- interviews between learners
- spontaneous role plays with two to three learners
- oral monologues
- conversation and situation cards (Bonin & Birchbickler, 1975; Glisan & Shrum, 1996)
- narration/description: One or more learners narrate and/or describe an event in present, past, or future time frame.

A modified version of the OPI, called the simulated oral proficiency interview (SOPI), uses taped responses as a cost-effective alternative to the face-to-face interview. Interviewees are given open-ended questions and linguistic tasks to complete with the aid of visuals such as drawings to describe places, a sequence of pictures to narrate events, and maps to give directions. Their oral responses are recorded individually and evaluated by a tester. Stansfield and Kenyon (1992) report high correlations between the proficiency ratings given in the OPI and those given in the SOPI.

Conducting oral testing in the classroom poses two challenges: (1) how to manage the procedure with large classes and (2) how to evaluate speaking. In planning for testing, the teacher might consider the following alternatives: (1) test pairs of learners using audiotape; (2) test groups of four or five learners using videotapes; (3) manipulate the scheduling of the testing, for example, test only part of the class orally on each chapter or unit, making sure that at the end of the grading period every learner has the same number of oral test grades, or conduct oral testing over the course of several days so that part of the class is tested each day; or (4) while a group of learners is being tested orally, engage the rest of the class in an interesting reading or writing task. See Appendix 8.2 for a description of Donato's (1992) "Talk Scores," a technique for monitoring and evaluating group speaking activities.

The grade assigned to a speaking test should reflect various components of the speech sample. A scale like the following one can be used in a variety of settings to produce a fairly specific assessment of the linguistic functions used to communicate. As shown in Figure 11.8, this format can be used to design a twenty-five-point assessment. The system presumes that teachers delineate for learners the purpose of the testing situation, describe what the learners are expected to do with the target language, and designate linguistic tasks that will be evaluated. A teacher may decide to limit the testing situation to only one linguistic task, such as describing a family member, or the task may include several more simple linguistic tasks, such as greeting or asking for information. In this scoring system, a learner can earn one to five points for completing linguistic tasks. Five of the points are allocated to the category of "other," in which the teacher may reward better-than-usual performance, judging the learner's performance in comparison to the learner's previous performances, or the teacher may indicate to the learner that performance did not reflect adequate preparation or did not meet expectations described in the task. Space for an explanation or justification of this use of points is provided. Finally, fifteen of the points are allocated to describe the way in which the learner used the target language to complete the tasks: grammar, use of vocabulary, and pronunciation.

Figure 11.8 Oral Scoring Form

Learner task	Points assigned
Completion of linguistic tasks	I (inadequate) 2 3 4 5 (thorough)
Grammatical correctness	I (many errors, low use of targeted structures) 2 3 4 5 (few errors, use of targeted structures)
Use of vocabulary	I (inappropriate vocabulary) 2 3 4 5 (appropriate, newly acquired vocabulary)
Accurate pronunciation	I (many inaccuracies) 2 3 4 5 (accurate pronunciation)

Other: points assigned relative to the way the learner performed the task: I–5 points

Explanation: _____ Total score: _____

Source: Shrum & Glisan, 1999.

The scale may be applied to conversations among learners as they work in small groups or as they interact with the teacher in communicative tasks. Scoring may be done by the teacher as learners speak or from audiotapes prepared by the learners outside of class. One way to evaluate nonspontaneous speech is through the use of audiotapes made by the learner in a nonthreatening environment, perhaps at home or in a learning center corner of the classroom. Audiotapes provide learners with the opportunity to replay, hear themselves, and refine their work. Thus they can present their best work to the teacher. These tapes, combined with a global rating system like that shown, are also easy to evaluate.

Planning for Classroom Testing

To decide what kind of test to use, a teacher first identifies what kind of decision is to be made, what kind of information is needed to help make it, and finally who is the audience for the results. The following are general guidelines to help you design a performance-based chapter or unit test:

- Review your objectives for the chapter/unit. (Tip: Write a sample test item on your lesson plan when you first design the lesson.)
- Think of the contexts in which the language was used in this unit or chapter (e.g., in a bus station).
- Think of the linguistic functions that learners have learned to perform (e.g., asking for information).
- Think of the ways in which learners have learned to interact with one another (e.g., as passengers waiting in line; as travelers looking for schedules).

As you design the test, keep in mind the following principles:

- Test what was taught in the same way learners practiced it.
- Use authentic materials as test stimuli.
- Prepare an integrative test that reflects the types of activities done in class—what students learned to do orally should be tested orally, not with paper and pencil.
- Provide opportunities for learners to use global language skills in a naturalistic authentic context.
- Provide a model whenever possible to illustrate what learners are to do.
- Provide instructions in the native language until you are certain that learners' ability to perform the task is not limited by a misunderstanding of the instructions.
- Take the test yourself and multiply by three to find out how long it will take learners to complete the test.
- Develop a grading system that rewards both linguistic accuracy and creativity.
- Return graded tests promptly to show learners their progress.

Finally, as you prepare the learners for the test, keep in mind that they are entitled to know how they will be evaluated. This does *not* mean, however, that some version of the actual test should necessarily be provided to learners prior to the actual test session. One way to help ease learners' anxiety about test situations is to ask them what they think the test will contain, assuming of course that they have been informed about the objectives of each unit, chapter, and daily lesson. Asking learners to reflect on what they have spent their time doing in class helps them to reaffirm their progress and feel secure about what will be on the test. See Ballman's (1996) communicative five-day lesson plan with associated evaluative procedures.

Teach and Reflect

Episode One

Analyzing and Adapting a Traditional Test

Task One: Analyze the following traditional test given to a French I class. Why is it considered "traditional"? Explain, using the following questions as a guide:

1. Is there a context? If there is none, what context could be applied?

2. What knowledge and/or skills are being evaluated?

3. How is the learner asked to use the target language?

4. Does the test address standards-based competencies? Explain.

5. Why is this test not considered performance-based, authentic, integrative, or interactive?

6. What might this test reflect concerning the classroom practices of the test designer?

7. Do you think this is a quiz or a test? What characteristics do they share? How are they different?

```
┌─────────────────────────────────────────────────────────────────────┐
│ Chapter 6 Test: French I                                              │
│ Name _____ │
│                                                                       │
│ I. Write the French equivalents for the following numbers:            │
│                                                                       │
│ 1. 23 _____ │
│ 2. 46 _____ │
│ 3. 69 _____ │
│ 4. 72 _____ │
│ 5. 95 _____ │
│                                                                       │
│ II. Complete the following sentences with the present tense of the    │
│     infinitives:                                                      │
│                                                                       │
│ 1. (descendre) Nous _____ en ville.                 │
│ 2. (attendre) La famille _____ un autobus.          │
│ 3. (vendre) Un homme _____ des sandwiches.          │
│                                                                       │
│ III. Change the present-tense sentences below to the near future      │
│      using aller + infinitive.                                        │
│                                                                       │
│ 1. Nous arrivons de France. _____ │
│ 2. Il va de Paris à Chicago. _____ │
│                                                                       │
│ IV. Give the French translations for the words and expressions below. │
│                                                                       │
│ 1. tomorrow      _____    3. next week   _____    │
│ 2. next Wednesday _____   4. tonight     _____    │
└─────────────────────────────────────────────────────────────────────┘
```

Task Two: Now, on a separate sheet of paper, adapt this test to make it contextualized and performance-based. Explain how each section will be scored.

Episode Two

Adding an Authentic Dimension to a Performance-Based Assessment Task

Analyze the following oral performance-based assessment task in which learners are asked to use the language in order to communicate meaningful information. Make a list of the linguistic functions, information, vocabulary, and grammatical points learners would have to use to complete the following task:

> Describe your daily routine for a typical day during the week. Tell what you do throughout the day and at what times. Include details such as with whom and where you do these activities.

Now adapt this task to make it authentic according to the criteria for task authenticity presented earlier in the chapter (Wiggins, 1998). Think of which elements you need to add to the task in order to make it reflect a real-world situation. You might start by asking yourself, "In what settings do people find themselves having to elaborate their daily schedules?"

Discuss and Reflect

Case Study I

Developing Authentic Assessment Tasks and Rubrics

Mr. Alma teaches Spanish at Bustamante High School in La Plata City Schools, and this year he has three Spanish II classes and two Spanish III classes. A teacher for eight years, he has kept abreast of innovations in teaching foreign languages by reading journal articles and attending workshops and conferences. He is active in his local foreign language collaborative and the state foreign language association. Mr. Alma uses the principles of proficiency-oriented instruction in his planning and designing of activities, and recently he has experimented with standards-based learning scenarios. For the past year he has been trying to develop more effective means of assessing learners' functional use of the language. Last week, he attended a full-day workshop on authentic assessment sponsored by the state foreign language association. Mr. Alma had been integrating performance-based testing into his assessment plan by designing situations in which learners would use the language orally in order to complete a communicative task successfully. However, as he learned at the workshop, while his performance-based tasks were effective in eliciting oral performance, they tended to measure speaking alone with no integration of other skills, they were seldom designed to include more than two learners, and they did not address standards-based goals. With his new knowledge of and motivation for authentic assessment, Mr. Alma attempts the design of an authentic assessment task to evaluate learner performance in Unit 4 for Spanish II. He uses the following Authentic Performance Task Template presented at the workshop (ACTFL, 1998) in his task design. Here is the task he designs:

Task:

You are a writer for your school newspaper, and the editorial team is planning an issue of the paper for the Hispanic community nearest your school. You have been assigned a feature story dealing with a popular Hispanic singer, actor/actress, or sports figure. Your end product will be a magazine story describing the life of the person, together with a transcript of an interview with her/him, and some photographs.

You need to do the following:

1. Working with two cowriters (classmates), investigate other popular magazines to find out who some popular Hispanic singers, actors/actresses, or sports figures are. Use the Internet to access this information quickly. Choose a Hispanic figure of interest to you and your cowriters.

2. Find out everything you can about the Hispanic figure through research using the Internet and other sources. Decide what information each cowriter will be responsible for finding.

3. Using the information you found, design five to six questions that you will ask the person in the interview. Make the questions engaging so that the information you get will be interesting to your readers. Young people will undoubtedly want to know how the person got started in her/his career and became so famous.

4. Conduct the interview,* tape recording it so that you will be able to transcribe it for the article.

5. Together with your cowriters, write the newspaper story. Make it exciting enough to attract the attention of youth who will want to buy the issue just to read your article!

[*Note: A Hispanic student from the nearby community might be interviewed as the famous person. S/He will need to do in-depth research about herself/himself in order to answer your questions properly.]

Mr. Alma's task is a multistage one that requires various subtasks and opportunities for students to engage in discussion, research, and work together. Here is the template distributed during the workshop Mr. Alma attended. He plans to build his scoring rubrics from it.

AUTHENTIC PERFORMANCE TASK TEMPLATE

Spanish II: Unit 4 (The World of Work), Grade 10

Achievement Target(s):

Performance Competencies: Discuss work and career; narrate and describe in the past; obtain information.
Content Standards: Communication (1.1, 1.2, 1.3); Cultures (2.1); Connections (3.2); Communities (5.1)

Criteria To Be Used in Assessing Performance:

Impact of Performance: Is the article informative and engaging?
Work Quality and Craftsmanship: Is the article well-designed, effectively written, clear?
Adequacy of Methods and Behavior: Was the student methodological in the process of producing the product? Did s/he conduct appropriate research and keep in mind the audience?
Validity of Content: Is the article accurate? Does it reflect correct information?

Mode(s) and Genre(s) of Performance:

Modes: oral, written, displayed (presentational)
Genres: oral interview, discussion; written interview questions, article; displayed article with photographs

---

Source: Adapted from CLASS, 1998.

Ask yourself these questions:

1. What makes this an authentic task according to the criteria set forth by Wiggins (1998)?

2. Were opportunities provided for students to practice carrying out a range of tasks likely to be necessary in the real world? Explain.

3. Was there concern for the development of linguistic accuracy? Explain.

4. How does this task address standards-based goals?

To prepare the case:

Read Wiggins (1989, 1998) for additional information about authentic tests; read Genesee and Upshur (1996) for additional ideas about classroom testing; read Liskin-Gasparro (1996) for additional examples of multistage projects that include multiple goals and standards.

To prepare for discussion, think and write about these topics:

- Design a timeline for this task in order to project how much class time will be needed, which parts will be completed out of class, and which aspects will be done individually and collaboratively. What will students submit to Mr. Alma in addition to the final magazine article?
- Develop a scoring rubric to assess learner performance on this task. Remember to use the criteria on the template. Begin by developing the description of what exemplary task completion would look like for each criterion. Then describe what unacceptable or poor task completion would look like, and then develop the levels in between. Refer to the rubric presented in Figure 11.6 as an example.
- Use the same textbook chapter for which you designed objectives in Episode One of **Teach and Reflect** for Chapter 3. Refer to the objectives you wrote in Chapter 3 as you create an authentic assessment task for the chapter that requires learners to integrate knowledge and skills. Be sure that the task reflects a real-world activity and has a real audience. You may find it helpful to examine the authentic task presented in Figure 11.5 and the one given in this case study. You may also wish to use the Authentic Performance Task Template presented in this case study. Design a scoring rubric similar to the one presented in Figure 11.6.

Case Study Two

Using Audio Tapes for Oral Assessment

Among her teaching duties, Ms. Zerkle has three classes of Spanish III at Riverside High School in Niagara City Schools. This year she has a student teacher, Mr. Rafferty, from Cedar State College. Mr. Rafferty had heard about Ms. Zerkle's success in using oral testing with her learners and was very excited about learning to use these techniques. Mr. Rafferty has been student teaching now for three months, and he has seen Ms. Zerkle give several oral tests. She told him yesterday that she would like his help in conducting and scoring the oral tests for an exam on Unit 4, "Once Upon a Time:

Narrating and Describing in the Past." She gave him the following two oral tasks to be used in assessing the linguistic functions for this unit (Glisan & Shrum, 1996), together with a list of tips to ensure his successful implementation of this test.

Speaking Test: Unit 4

Option 1 Monologue: A Memorable Past Event

Describe a past event that you remember vividly. It should be something memorable because it was particularly funny, unusual, or sad. Talk for at least two minutes, describing the event using past tenses. Be as descriptive as possible so that the listener can picture the event.

You will be evaluated on your ability to

- talk for at least two minutes;
- narrate and describe in the past;
- give details;
- use appropriate grammar, vocabulary, pronunciation, and fluency in completing the task.

Option 2 Role Play

To the teacher: Give pairs of students the role play that follows. Designate which student is Student A and which is Student B.

You (Student A) and a friend (Student B) are studying abroad in Mexico. You have both been invited to give a talk about how North American families celebrate holidays. In preparation for the presentation, you and your friend get together at a local café and reminisce. Select a holiday and talk about how you and your family and friends usually celebrated that holiday during your childhood. To set the stage for your reminiscence, talk briefly about what you were like as a child and what your favorite childhood activities were.

You both will be evaluated on your ability to

- describe how your families celebrated a holiday during your childhood;
- describe what you were like as a child;
- describe your favorite childhood activities;
- describe in the past;
- use appropriate grammar, vocabulary, pronunciation, and fluency in completing the task.

Source: Glisan & Shrum, 1996, p. 140

Tips for Mr. Rafferty for oral testing:

1. Working in pairs, students should prepare an audiotape of one of the oral situations outlined on the handout. Use the native language on your handout so that you don't give away key vocabulary that students should know.

2. Allow the students at least three days to prepare their audiotapes outside of class.

3. Students should write the names of all participants on their tape and rewind the tape to the place where you (the instructor) will start to listen to their conversation.

4. When they get their graded tape back, students should listen to themselves again and read the instructor's written comments on the evaluation sheet. They should also listen to the spoken comments you left on the tape.

5. When you grade the tapes, be sure you have each student's evaluation sheet and a pen or pencil and a tape recorder. Grade the tapes in a quiet place so that you can listen carefully to the students' comments. Let your spoken and written comments contain positive statements about what the students have done. In your comments, respond to content and linguistic accuracy. It should take you about thirty to fifty minutes to grade the tapes for one class of twenty-five students.

Ask yourself these questions:

1. What makes the two speaking situations performance-based tasks?

2. Were opportunities provided for learners to practice carrying out real-world tasks? Explain.

3. Was there concern for the development of linguistic accuracy? Explain.

4. What do you think about Ms. Zerkle's tips for Mr. Rafferty?

To prepare the case:

- Read Robison's (1992) article on using a small-group approach to test speaking skills; read Harper, Lively, and Williams (1998) for additional ideas on cooperative oral testing.
- Study Ms. Zerkle's tips, and prepare your thoughts on these questions:
  - What reasons would Ms. Zerkle have for asking learners to perform these tasks in pairs?
  - If this is an oral test, what reasons do you think Ms. Zerkle has for giving learners so many days to prepare their tapes?
  - What purpose will Mr. Rafferty's oral comments on the learners' tapes serve?
  - How might Mr. Rafferty assess learners' spontaneous oral skills instead of asking them to prepare a tape in advance?
  - How would Mr. Rafferty handle this assessment if learners report that they do not have tape recorders at home?
- Imagine that you are Mr. Rafferty and that Ms. Zerkle gave you the following scoring form for Option 1 of the speaking test. How might you improve upon this form and make it easier for you to assign ratings?
- Design a similar scoring form for the role play in Option 2.

EVALUATION FORM: SPEAKING TEST UNIT 4

Option I Monologue: A Memorable Past Event (25 points)

Student _____

Fluency / Ability to talk for at least two minutes		4	3	2	I
Ability to narrate and describe in the past	5	4	3	2	I
Ability to provide details		4	3	2	I
Comprehensibility to instructor		4	3	2	I
Grammatical accuracy		4	3	2	I
Appropriateness of vocabulary		4	3	2	I

Comments:

References

ACTFL. (1998). The Standards assessment design project. Draft of performance assessment unit. Yonkers, NY: ACTFL.

Adair-Hauck, B. (1996). Authentic assessment in second language learning. *Pennsylvania Language Forum, 68*(1), 10–30.

Alatis, J., & Barnhardt, S. (Eds.) (1998). *Portfolio assessment in the foreign language classroom.* Washington, D.C.: National Capital Language Resource Center.

Bachman, L. F. (1990). *Fundamental considerations in language testing.* Oxford: Oxford University Press.

Ballman, T. L. (1996). Integrating vocabulary, grammar and culture: A model five-day communicative lesson plan. *Foreign Language Annals, 29*, 37–44.

Bonin, T., & Birckbichler, D. (1975). Real communication through conversation cards. *The Modern Language Journal, 59*, 22–25.

Carroll, J. (1961). Fundamental considerations in testing for English proficiency of foreign students. *Testing the English proficiency of foreign students.* Washington, D.C.: Center for Applied Linguistics.

CLASS (The Center on Learning, Assessment, and School Structure). (1998, June). *Developing authentic performance assessments.* Paper presented at the meeting of the ACTFL Beyond the OPI Assessment Group, Yonkers, NY: ACTFL.

Donato, R. (1995). Original unpublished material.

Donato, R., Antonek, J. L., & Tucker, G. R. (1996). Documenting a Japanese FLES Program: Ambiance and achievement. *Language Learning, 46*, 497–528.

Gay, L. R. (1987). *Educational research: Competencies for analysis and application.* Columbus, OH: Merrill Publishing Co.

Genesee, F., & Upshur, J. A. (1996). *Classroom-based evaluation in second language education.* Cambridge: Cambridge University Press.

Glisan, E. W., & Shrum, J. L. (1996). *Enlaces testing program.* Boston: Heinle & Heinle.

Hahn, S. L., Stassen, T., & Reschke, C. (1989). Grading classroom oral activities: Effects on motivation and proficiency. *Foreign Language Annals, 22*, 241–252.

Hammadou, J. A. (1998). A blueprint for teacher portfolios. In J. Harper, M. G. Lively, & M. K. Williams (Eds.), *The coming of age of the profession: Issues and emerging ideas for the teaching of foreign languages* (pp. 291–305). Boston: Heinle & Heinle.

Harper, J., Lively, M. G., & Williams, M. K. (1998). Testing the way we teach. In J. Harper, M. G. Lively, & M. K. Williams (Eds.), *The coming of age of the profession: Issues and emerging ideas for the teaching of foreign languages* (pp. 263–276). Boston: Heinle & Heinle.

Henning, G. (1987). *A guide to language testing.* Rowley, MA: Newbury House Publishers.

Ke, C., & Reed, D. J. (1995). An analysis of results from the ACTFL Oral Proficiency Interview and the Chinese Proficiency Test before and after intensive instruction in Chinese as a foreign language. *Foreign Language Annals, 28,* 208–222.

Koda, K. (1998, June). Authentic performance assessment. In CLASS (The Center on Learning, Assessment, & School Structure). *Developing authentic performance assessments* (n.p.). Presentation made to ACTFL Beyond the OPI Assessment Group, Yonkers, NY.

Liskin-Gasparro, J. E. (1996). Assessment: From content standards to student performance. In R. C. Lafayette (Ed.), *National standards: A catalyst for reform.* The ACTFL Foreign Language Education Series (pp. 169–196). Lincolnwood, IL: NTC/Contemporary Publishing Group.

Liskin-Gasparro, J. E. (1997, August). *Authentic assessment: Promises, possibilities and processes* (p. 1–15). Presentation made at University of Wisconsin-Eau Claire.

Moeller, A. J., & Reschke, C. (1993). A second look at grading and classroom performance: Report of a research study. *The Modern Language Journal, 77,* 163–169.

Morris, W. (Ed.) (1973).The American heritage dictionary. Boston: American Heritage Publishing Co., Inc. and Houghton Mifflin Co.

Oller, J. (1991a). Foreign language testing: Its breadth (Part 1). *ADFL Bulletin, 22(3),* 33–38.

Oller, J. (1991b). Foreign language testing: Its depth (Part 2). *ADFL Bulletin, 23(1),* 5–13.

Padilla, A. M., Aninao, J. C., & Sung, H. (1996). Development and implementation of student portfolios in foreign language programs. *Foreign Language Annals, 29,* 429–438.

Padilla, A. M., Silva, D. M., & Nomachi, T. (1996, November). *Portfolio assessment for secondary school foreign language classes.* Paper presented at the meeting of the American Council on the Teaching of Foreign Languages, Philadelphia, PA.

Phillips, J. K. (1996). Original material.

Robison, R. E. (1992). Developing practical speaking tests for the foreign language classroom: A small group approach. *Foreign Language Annals, 25,* 487–496.

Shohamy, E. (1990). Language testing priorities: A different perspective. *Foreign Language Annals, 23,* 385–394.

Shrum, J. L. (1991). Testing in context: A lesson from foreign language learning. *Vision,* 1, 3, 7–8.

Stansfield, C. W., & Kenyon, D. M. (1992). The development and validation of a simulated oral proficiency interview. *The Modern Language Journal, 76,* 129–41.

Surprenant, J. (1998). *Un viaje por España.* Test item developed for a workshop with CLASS. Nantucket, MA.

Swaffar, J., Arens, K., & Byrnes, H. (1991). *Reading for meaning.* Englewood Cliffs, NJ: Prentice Hall.

Swender, E. (1999). *The ACTFL oral proficiency interview tester training manual.* Yonkers, NY: ACTFL.

Terry, R. M. (1998). Authentic tasks and materials for testing in the foreign language classroom. In J. Harper, M. G. Lively, & M. K. Williams (Eds.), *The coming of age of the profession: Issues and emerging ideas for the teaching of foreign languages* (pp. 277–290). Boston: Heinle & Heinle.

Tierney, R. J., Carter, M. A., & Desai, L. E. (1991). *Portfolio assessment in the reading-writing classroom.* Norwood, MA: Christopher-Gordon.

Wiggins, G. (1989). Teaching to the (authentic) test. *Educational Leadership, 46(7),* 41–47.

Wiggins, G. (1990). The case for authentic assessment. *ERIC Digest,* Washington, D.C.: ERIC Clearinghouse on Tests, Measurement, and Evaluation.

Wiggins, G. (1998). *Educative assessment.* San Francisco: Jossey-Bass.

thandbook.
heinle.com

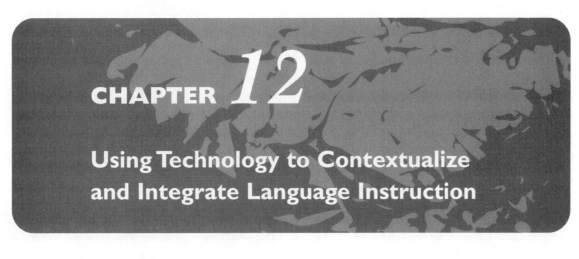

CHAPTER *12*

Using Technology to Contextualize and Integrate Language Instruction

In this chapter you will learn about:

- a definition of technology and technology-enhanced language learning (TELL)
- reasons for using TELL
- traditional technologies used in new ways: overhead projectors, language labs, software and courseware

- new technologies: e-mail, listservs, UserNets and News Groups, chatrooms, computer-assisted instruction (CAI), the Internet, and distance education
- future technological advances

Teach and Reflect: Selecting Video Materials; Examining the Potential Use of a TELL Exercise

Case Study 1: Incorporating Video in Language Instruction

Case Study 2: Creating a Template for Web-enhanced Materials

Conceptual Orientation

What Is Technology-Enhanced Language Learning?

According to Gendron, *technology* is "any systematized practical knowledge, based on experimentation and/or scientific theory, which enhances the capacity of society to produce goods and services, and which is embodied in productive skills, organization, or machinery" (1977; cf. Saettler, 1990, p. 23). The inclusive term "Technology-Enhanced Language Learning" (TELL) refers to the use of some means of technology to improve the flow or quality of the message between foreign/second language teachers, learners, and users.[1] In this chapter you will learn about some of the technologies that are available to teachers, how to make judgments and selections of technological tools and materials, and how to

---

1. Subsumed within TELL are computer-mediated communication (CMC), computer assisted language learning (CALL), and computer assisted language instruction (CALI).

integrate them into contextualized instruction.[2]

 Technology is "any systematized practical knowledge, based on experimentation and/or scientific theory, which enhances the capacity of society to produce goods and services, and which is embodied in productive skills, organization, or machinery."

 TELL is Technology-Enhanced Language Learning.

Technology Connects the Standards

In the *Teacher's Handbook,* you learned about the primary goal of language learning, which is to know how, when , and why to say what to whom; the motivation that students may have for reaching this goal; how the five Cs represent the content goal areas in broad terms; and how sample performance indicators can measure learners' progress in what they know and are able to do with the target language. Learning scenarios that accompany the standards show how teachers might address the standards in their instruction. The learning scenarios contain a broad richness of circumstances specific to each instructional setting that goes beyond the standards, and, indeed, forms a backdrop, or a fabric, on which the standards may operate. This fabric has been called the "weave" of curricular elements, and appears in Figure 2.3 (NSFLEP, 1996, p. 29). The elements of this weave are unique to each instructional setting, yet each setting contains all of them: the language system, cultural knowledge, communication strategies, critical-thinking skills, learning strategies, other subject areas, and technology. You saw that each language offers specific challenges to learners as they grapple with the forms of the language. Also, learners have a set of cultural understandings that they bring to the language learning experience, and they will take away new understandings of the target culture and their own culture as a result of language study. You saw that learners develop communication strategies, such as circumlocution or intelligent contextualized guessing, making inferences, and setting hypotheses as they study language. They use critical-thinking skills as they select information from what they already know and apply it to new situations or reflect on and evaluate their communication. They develop learning strategies like previewing, skimming, and reading for the main idea to enable them to build ways of approaching any new learning task. All of these elements of the weave can be brought together through the use of technology. Technology can thread rich curricular experiences through the language learning process. One of the challenges of teaching foreign languages is to present students with living, vibrant people who use the target language for daily communication. Cultural elements, from daily table manners to world-famous paintings and literature, constitute the multidimensional environment in which the language is used that can be represented in the textbook and on the

---

2. For definitions of technological terms, consult Heinich, Molenda, Russell, & Smaldino (1996, pp. 199; 260–261).

World Wide Web in authentic visual and print dimensions. Authentic audio to accompany the visual images can be delivered in person by the teacher, by classroom guests, or via technology in video/audio tape recordings or laserdiscs, CD-ROMS, and the Internet. Through the judicious use of technology, teachers can connect all five of the goal areas for productive language learning experiences.

Reasons for using TELL

In 1998, President Clinton's Educational Technology Initiative outlined the Technology Literacy Challenge, setting it up with four pillars:

1. Modern computers and learning devices will be accessible to every student.

2. Classrooms will be connected to one another and to the world.

3. Educational software will be an integral part of the curriculum and as engaging as the best video game.

4. Teachers will be ready to use and teach with technology (USDOE, 1998).

While most teachers hold a "healthy dose of skepticism" (Cubillos, 1998), you will see in this chapter that TELL can be used effectively to:

- facilitate the acquisition of vocabulary (Davis & Lyman-Hager, 1997; Chun & Plass, 1996; Grace, 1998);
- support input-rich activities such as reading assistant software, integrated video, and the Internet (Garza, 1991; Cononelos & Oliva, 1993);
- facilitate writing improvement in output activities through use of writing assistant software, e-mail, and chatrooms, for instance (Oliva & Pollastrini, 1995), and through intelligent computer-mediated feedback (Nagata, 1993; Nagata & Swisher, 1995);
- facilitate exploration of authentic language use through e-mail or the Internet (Oliva & Pollastrini, 1995); and
- enhance student motivation (Masters-Wicks, Postelwate, & Lewental, 1996; Borrás & Lafayette, 1994).

The decision regarding how to engage students with instructional processes rests with the teacher. Thus, in the case of technology, the teacher determines to what extent technological devices will be used to enhance language learning.[3] Figure 12.1 shows various kinds of technology and their uses.

In overall terms, technology can facilitate the transfer from teacher-centered to learner-centered environments. It can also enhance the authenticity of the learning process and can make language learning more available (Maxwell, 1998). There are strong indications of more and better language production when computer-mediated instruction is used for writing, grammar, and vocabulary acquisition (Cononelos & Oliva, 1993; Kern, 1995; Pennington, 1996; Beauvois, 1997). We also have indications of benefits of TELL in reading and listening comprehension. For instance, Davis and Lyman-Hager (1997) reported benefits in hearing portions of the text read aloud. Furthermore, Adair-Hauck, Youngs,

---

3. See Bush & Terry (1997) for a well-informed set of articles about TELL; and Otto & Pusack (1996) for a discussion about technological choices and challenges.

Figure 12.1 Selection of Teaching and Communication Technology

Medium	Function								
	Reading	Listening	Writing	Speaking	Culture	Student/Student interaction	Student/Instructor interaction	Ease of access by student	Cost to institution
Courseware									
Print	✓		✓		✓			1*	1**
Audio cassette		✓			✓			1	1
Video cassette	✓	✓			✓			2	2
Software	✓		✓	✓	✓			2	2
CD-ROM	✓	✓	✓		✓			2	2 or 3***
WWW		✓	✓		✓			3	2 or 3
Communication									
Telephone tutoring		✓		✓	✓		✓	1	2
Audio conferencing		✓		✓	✓	✓	✓	2	2
Video conferencing		✓	✓	✓	✓	✓	✓	3	3
E-mail / Internet	✓		✓		✓	✓	✓	2	2
Computer conferencing	✓			✓	✓	✓	✓	3	3

* 1 = openly accessible re: cost, time, place 2 = reduced flexibility 3 = limited flexibility
** 1 = relatively low cost to set up and run 2 = moderate cost 3 = high cost
*** Cost depends on whether product is purchased or custom produced

Source: Aplevich & Willment, 1998.

and Willingham-McLain (1998) reported the results of a study in which college-level French students in a control group met with the instructor four days per week, but the treatment group met with the instructor three days per week and spent the class period on the fourth day working on TELL activities. Textbook, instructor, and ancillary materials were the same for both groups. Results showed that the TELL group performed equally as well as the control group in listening and speaking and better on measures of reading and writing achievement. The TELL group also perceived improvement in reading, writing tests, and homework writing. Furthermore, because they could collaborate with a peer and could control the number of times they experienced the TELL activities, the students reported that their speaking skills also improved.

Using Technology to Support Standards-Oriented Instruction

A teacher's decision to use a tape recorder, overhead, video, or computer-related technology is similar to the decision to use a particular practice exercise or workbook handout. The technological device, like the practice exercise, is a tool that helps the learner interact with the body of content knowledge and processes. Teachers opt to design instructional tasks that are consistent with their philosophy of how students learn language. The excitement of using a new technology is often accompanied by anxiety on the part of the teacher and learners. While technology may seem both exciting and intimidating, teachers should use the knowledge they have about the five Cs and about the weave of other curricular elements particular to their circumstances in order to select suitable technological products and techniques. Certainly, an increased expenditure of time to design meaningful instruction and maintain enthusiasm will be needed. As you, the teacher, decide how to deliver instruction with the assistance of a technological tool, consider the following guidelines for selection:

1. What can my students presently do with the language in each of the five goal areas of the Standards?

2. What Standards within the goal areas will this tool help my students accomplish?

3. How will it help my students use language in response to those Standards?

4. What process will learners experience in using the technology and associated materials? What elements of the "weave" will be included?

5. What will it cost in terms of time, planning, supplies, and equipment? List costs.

6. What are the alternatives? Check to see if there is a high school, college, university, library, or other agency in your area that could help by providing services or resources.

7. Is this the best way to accomplish the objectives of instruction and to meet the needs of my students?

The technological device, like the practice exercise, is a tool that helps the learner interact with the body of content knowledge and processes throughout.

Traditional Technologies with New Uses for Foreign Language Instruction

Language learners develop several kinds of literacy: auditory literacy through listening and using tapes; visual literacy through pictures; and verbal literacy through words. The language lab or lab station of today and tomorrow can assist in the development of these literacies, as well as the development of computer literacy. Technologies operate hand in hand with prevailing views of learning and literacy, as you will see in the tracing of the historical development of language labs.

❒ Language Labs Convert to Multimedia Centers

Language teachers of the 1950s used the emerging technology of the language lab in order to offer the target language in ways that were authentic and useful. The prevailing behaviorist view of how learning happens influenced the design of instructional materials resulting in delivery of audiotaped dialogues from a teacher-controlled main console through earphones to students who sat in three-sided booths or carrels. Student tasks were limited to listening to and repeating after native speakers who modeled drill sentences. Some labs offered student recording and playback. These audio labs were interactive only in the sense that the teacher could monitor and speak with students from the main console and students could reply or record their responses on a separate recording track of an audiotape. Time in the lab was assigned to each teacher and group of students on a per-week or biweekly basis. In some schools, generally at the postsecondary level, students completed lab work as out-of-class assignments, sometimes helped by a teaching assistant.

Modern labs now incorporate important changes in their physical appearance and in the instructional tasks that students and teachers can perform. Today, labs might involve wireless transmission of taped authentic speech recorded live in the target country, with follow-up tasks in which students engage in contextualized two- or three-way communication with other students, the teacher, or native speakers. Labs may be mobile, and headsets can be incorporated into any lesson since they often drop from the ceiling or can be retrieved by students from a central console in the regular classroom. Sophisticated laboratory systems offer students the opportunity to view video, graphic, or Internet programs focused around workstation groupings of four to six multimedia computers at which four to eight students can work together to complete tasks. This sample scenario shows how learners function in contemporary language labs:

> There are no carrels and the student is "seated in front of a multimedia system. It looks pretty much like a computer system, perhaps with a few additional pieces of equipment connected to it via cables. The student reads the directions on the computer screen and clicks the mouse to get started. The lesson begins with a video clip,

originating from a videodisc [or a CD-ROM], which depicts a conversation between two native speakers of Spanish. The video not only allows the student to see and hear two native speakers, but it also provides a cultural backdrop, as it was shot on location overseas. As the lesson progresses, the student makes use of a Spanish dictionary that is stored on a CD-ROM. This provides definitions and translations, as well as the actual aural [*sic*] pronunciation of each word and phrase. The computer facilitates the student's access to all of this information and provides periodic review questions and feedback about the student's progress." (Newby, Stepich, Lehman, & Russell, 1996, p. 79–80)

To see a multimedia lab in operation, see the Web Site that accompanies *Teacher's Handbook* at **http://thandbook.heinle.com.**

When multimedia labs also incorporate the Internet and when students can access the learning center lab via a laptop, it is clear that technology creates a new dimension for language learning and teaching, as well as an additional literacy. In this kind of lab, it is the computer that brings together various pieces of equipment (hardware), which use many kinds of programs (software), or computer-mediated materials, designed for a specific course (courseware), which produce on the screen or via headsets several kinds of texts (audio, visual, or written). This is called computer-mediated instruction, since the computer serves in the channel of communication between the learner and the authentic materials contained on tape, disc, or the Internet.

As an alternative to a lab, many teachers use one or more small cassette tape or CD players in their classrooms. One can be used for listening as a whole class, or several can be placed around the classroom as listening stations with individualized directions for singles, pairs, or small groups of learners. Students often have their own CD or portable tape players and can practice at home. Many publishers package tapes and CD-ROMS with each textbook for use at home. Furthermore evidence of the mobility of the language lab is the laptop computer with Internet access. See Chapters 6 and 7 for ways to use authentic taped materials to enhance listening practice for students, and Chapters 8 and 9 for ideas about using these materials for written and spoken homework.

☐ Overhead Projector

Teachers frequently use the overhead projector to supplement or replace the chalkboard because it allows them to face the class. Teachers can prepare the transparency in advance and manipulate the order and arrangement of the presentation by using masks made of opaque paper or overlays containing additional coordinated material. Teachers or student scribes can write directly onto the transparency with a permanent or water-soluble marker to add information or student input generated during class discussion. For example, a set of interview questions can be printed onto the transparency in permanent ink, and then answers offered by the class in whole-class or small groups can be added during the lesson and washed off between class periods, allowing the original interview transparency to be used again during the next class. (See the web site at **http://thandbook.heinle.com** for additional tips on using the overhead projector.)

The next generation of overhead projectors is called "whiteboards" and can be used in this traditional way, but they can also be connected to a computer that projects materials from its hard drive or from a disk onto a screen or a television monitor, or they can be broadcast as part of a distance-learning class. Whether computer mediated or not, the overhead projector continues to be a tool with wide utility for teachers.

 Computer-mediated instruction is when the computer serves to facilitate or enhance communication between the learner and the source of authentic material, or between learners, or between machines.

❏ Video

Contemporary technologies using video include film, videotapes, and laserdiscs. Perhaps our understanding of video as an instructional medium can be enhanced if we think of a video or a contextualized segment of video as a *videotext*. It is a text in the sense that it presents an authentic piece of language that could be presented in written form as well. It may contain elements of language use and cultural authenticity so that we may access all five Cs of language learning through videotext. As we elect to use videotext, we should apply the same criteria and careful judgment in selection and use as we apply to reading or listening texts.

❏ Selecting the Video Material

The best video segments are those that are long enough to present a realistic context but short enough so as not to thwart students' ability to comprehend by using contextual cues and language knowledge. In Figure 12.2, Joiner (1990) offers guidelines to assist teachers as they select videotexts. Once the text is selected, the teacher will find it beneficial to intervene again to provide an advance organizer to enable learners to approach the video segment. Advance organizers, whether in statement or question form, work because they help learners "navigate the Zone of Proximal Development and progress from an actual developmental level toward a potential one" (Herron, 1994; Hanley, Herron, & Cole, 1995; Herron, Cole, York, & Linden, 1998). Herron (1994) offers this advance organizer for Video 26 of *French in Action:*

C'est dimanche. Robert se promène. Il parle avec la vendeuse dans une pâtisserie. Il entre dans un restaurant. Un jeune couple mystérieux dîne au restaurant. Le garçon au restaurant discute avec ses clients (1994, p. 195).	[It's Sunday. Robert is taking a walk. He speaks with the woman who works in a bakery. He goes into a restaurant. A young mysterious couple is dining in the restaurant. The waiter has a discussion with his customers.] (1994, p. 196)

 Advance organizers work because they help learners "navigate the Zone of Proximal Development and progress from an actual developmental level toward a potential one."

Figure 12.2 Choosing Videotexts

I. BASIC DATA

Title:

Subject:

Length (of broadcast or of sequence):

Circle the words below that apply:

Format/Standard: VHS   BETAMAX   UMATIC/PAL   SECAM   NTSC

Aids: Transcription   Study Guide   Suggested   Segmetation   Test

Other (specify) _____

II. GENERAL CHARACTERISTICS OF VIDEOTEXT

Circle the words/check the phrases that apply:

Category:

    Literature   Civilization   Oral communication   Contemporary culture

Purpose of text:

    To inform   To instruct   To entertain   To persuade

Audience for which text is intended:

    General
    Limited (specify) _____

Linguistic assumptions with respect to viewers/listeners:

    Assumes native/near-native ability to comprehend the language in question
    Assumes less than native ability to comprehend the language in question

Cultural assumptions with respect to viewers/listeners:

    Assumes familiarity with the culture portrayed
    Assumes lack of, or limited, familiarity with the culture portrayed
    Culture not an important consideration

III. TECHNICAL CHARACTERISTICS OF VIDEOTEXT

Check the point along the line that best represents your opinion.

Quality of images

    fuzzy, blurred _____: _____: _____: _____: _____ very clear

Quality of Sound Track

    inaudible _____: _____: _____: _____: _____ very clear

Editing of Video

    amateurish _____: _____: _____: _____: _____ very clear

Figure 12.2   Choosing Videotexts (continued)

IV. LINGUISTIC/PARALINGUISTIC CHARACTERISTICS OF VIDEOTEXT

A. Image

In the space provided, note the following elements:

View of society represented in text (historical, outmoded, up-to-date)

Gestures/body language/dress (handshake, proximity of speakers, types of clothing)

Socio-cultural groups represented in text (levels of society, age groups, professions/occupations, rural/urban/small town)

Printed text/graphics

B. Soundtrack/Script

Check the point along the line that corresponds to your opinion:

Rate of delivery:

    slow _____: _____: _____: _____: _____ very rapid

Quality of articulation:

    incomprehensible _____: _____: _____: _____: _____ very clear

Voiceover (off-screen) narration:

    none _____: _____: _____: _____: _____ extensive

Check all choices that apply:

On screen speakers:	One (monologue) Two (dialogue, interview) More than two (conversation, discussion)
Accents of speakers:	Metropolitan, nonregional French Regionally accented European French Canadian French African French Carribean French
Types of spoken language:	Spontaneous free speech (conversation) Deliberate free speech (inverviews, discussions) Oral presentation of a written text (newscasts, lectures, commentaries) Oral presentation of a fixed, rehearsed script (films, plays)
Levels of language:	Familiar Informal conversational Formal conversational Formal nonconversational Archaic
Vocabulary:	Limited, primarily concrete, high-frequency words Extensive, but nontechnical Technical

Figure 12.2 Choosing Videotexts (continued)

Music/sound effect: Distracting (may hinder comprehension)
Helpful (may aid comprehension)

C. Relationship of Image to Sound

Message received primarily through image
Message received primarily through sound
Verbal message and visual message redundant
Verbal message and visual message complementary

D. Language in Context

List below the functions and contexts illustrated in the text:

Content/context (making a telephone call from a phone booth, getting a hotel room, ordering a meal in a restaurant)

Functions (narrating, describing, giving commands, asking directions)

V. POTENTIAL USEFULNESS

For attaining course goals:

Of little use _____: _____: _____: _____: _____ very useful

For motivating students

Of little use _____: _____: _____: _____: _____ very useful

Source: Joiner, 1990.

Altman points out the golden rule of video pedagogy: *"Don't expect—or even seek—full comprehension"* (1989, p. 42). As we become tolerant of incomplete comprehension, we begin to appreciate the greatest value of authentic materials in general and of video in particular. The use of video teaches students to "hear, to break down the spoken chain into appropriate chunks and gives students practice in understanding. *At the same time, it does not ask them to understand what they are not yet prepared to understand"* (Altman, 1989, p. 42). Since video is a familiar medium, students relate easily to it. When they find that they understand portions of the video, their confidence improves. As teachers, we need to remain aware of the level of our students' comprehension by checking it through recognition questions, discussion, or short in-class quizzes. Altman compares the strategies students use in comprehending a video to "finding hidden objects in drawings of trees" (1989, p. 43). Strategies such as asking students to make direct transcriptions of the video soundtrack are counterproductive to the type of strategy building this medium makes possible. Video provides the context for a wide variety of communicative and interactive activities in the classroom. As you select video materials, keep these points in mind:

- Remember the function you expect the program to perform.
- Select short segments.
- View the program repeatedly and completely before assigning it.
- Manipulate the video in order to make it more comprehensible (Altman, 1989).

❐ Integrating Video into Language Instruction

Video can provide the authentic input, both visual and auditory, necessary for language acquisition and development of cultural awareness. Teachers can help students develop strategies for understanding linguistic and paralinguistic aspects of language in video segments by using the interactive model for listening and reading presented in Chapter 6. This model is organized in a fashion similar to the list of activities in Figure 12.3 that can be used as students are guided through pre- and postviewing of the videotext (Joiner, 1990). The activities proceed from previewing, to identifying important information, to postviewing activities using the information for real communication; tasks include attention to cultural elements and the language of the text itself; extension activities are suggested.

Samples of viewing guides for use prior to and following the viewing of the videotext offer students clues on how to benefit from the experience. Figure 12.4 is an example of a viewing guide that could be used prior to viewing as an advance organizer, in order to encourage students to visualize the spoken and performed messages they will see. Listening for verbal clues could also be conducted in groups of three. In Figure 12.5, learners are directed to watch and listen for language functions, paralinguistic information, and emotional states that are expressed with language. Figure 12.6 is an example of a pre- or postviewing guide that uses pictures and drawings to build viewing and listening skills. To see a teacher using a laserdisc program with learners, see the web site that accompanies *Teacher's Handbook* at **http://thandbook.heinle.com.**

Figure 12.3   Using Videotexts

I. GENERAL POSSIBILITIES FOR EXPLOITING VIDEOTEXTS

Replay sequences (or entire video) for more detailed viewing

Use pause/still frame

Interrupt viewing to check comprehension

Cut off sound to focus on image

Replace soundtrack with own narration or ask students to narrate

Select certain sequences for intensive viewing, pass over others

Assign certain sequences for out-of-class viewing

View with or without script

II. PREPARATION OF STUDENTS FOR LISTENING/VIEWING

Supply essential cultural information

Review/Introduce essential vocabulary/structures

Preview (overview of content, text characteristics)

Motivate, arouse interest

Provide listening/viewing tasks

Figure 12.3   Using Videotexts (continued)

III. LISTENING/VIEWING TASKS

A. Skills-Oriented Tasks

Comprehension (listening, reading)

> yes-no questions, true-false, multiple choice, physical response, checklist, fill-ins

Comprehension plus production (listening, reading, speaking, writing)

> open-ended questions, role play, brainstorming, debate, discussion, note taking, summaries, continuations

B. Culture-Oriented tasks

Awareness: notice, identify

Understanding: compare, contrast, contrast with other cultures

Integration: imitate, role play

C. Script-Oriented Tasks

Find examples of redundancy

Underline certain structures/vocabulary items

Identify words/phrases used to express emotion, to persuade, etc.

Read aloud portions of the script

Rewrite portions of the script

Cross out extra words in "doctored" version of script

Fill-in words omitted from script

IV. EXPANSION ACTIVITIES

Play game, work puzzle

Build or make something

Read related material

Learn song or dance and perform

Create own audio or video broadcast

Source: Joiner, 1990.

Information-gap activities can be created using a technique called *video split* (Lavery, 1981), in which half of a class views, with the sound turned off, a videotext that has five or six speaking actors. The other half of the class hears only the sound and does not see the visual aspects of the videotext. The teacher then pairs the students, one viewer with one listener, and assigns each pair the task of recreating the conversation(s) in the videotext. Students verify the accuracy of their recreation by watching the videotext with sound.

Swaffar and Vlatten (1997) offer a systematic way to integrate video by manipulating the viewing and sound first to identify value systems in the video and then to connect verbal systems to the visual systems of the video. They suggest the following:

Figure 12.4 Viewing Guide

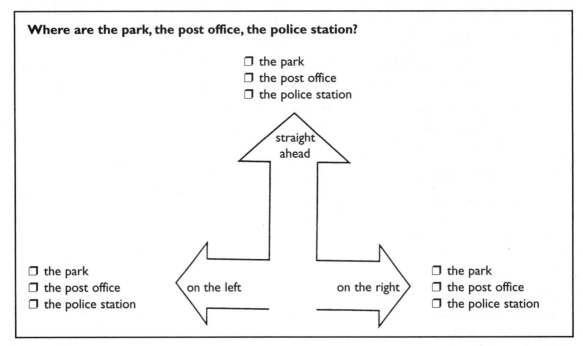

Where are the park, the post office, the police station?

❏ the park
❏ the post office
❏ the police station

straight
ahead

on the left   on the right

❏ the park
❏ the post office
❏ the police station

❏ the park
❏ the post office
❏ the police station

Source: Lonergan, 1984.

Figure 12.5 Video Guide: Watching and Listening for Clues

LEARNER A	**LEARNER B**	**LEARNER C**
As you watch the sequence, note examples of	As you watch the sequence, note examples of	As you watch the sequence, note examples of
• displeasure • disappointment • optimism	• agreement • disagreement • pessimism	• direct commands • indirect commands • resignation

Source: Lonergan, 1984.

I. Identifying value systems in visual sequences

Stage 1: How genres tell stories in initial silent viewing. In this stage, learners and teacher view the selection together in silent mode in order to establish suppositions about the setting and the culture in which the scenes occur so that learners can more easily absorb the meaning of the scenes. An example would be establishing the who, what, when, and where of different camera angles, or figuring out whether the selection is an interview or a report. Swaffar and Vlatten suggest that comprehension checks for this stage might ask students to rearrange the following scrambled items in the order in which they were viewed in a weather report segment the students watched: a series of dated temperature charts with ranges from -2 to 4 degrees; a man

Figure 12.6 Pre- or Post-Viewing Guide

Mettez, selon le cas, des croix dans les boîtes:

Françoise demande   avec

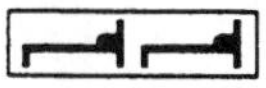

Françoise doit payer
- ☐ plus que 100Ff
- ☐ 100Ff
- ☐ moins que 100Ff

Elle prend la chambre
- ☐ 47
- ☐ 107
- ☐ 407

Elle part le demain
- ☐ vers 8 h.
- ☐ vers 7 h.
- ☐ vers 9 h.

Source: Lonergan, 1984.

in a red jacket standing in front of a weather map showing cloud movement; a map of France with temperatures; a map of Europe with temperatures (p. 178).

Stage 2: Identifying cultural differences in visual relationships. To focus on the Cultures, Connections, or Comparisons goal areas, teachers can cue students to look for lifestyle similarities and differences. Swaffar and Vlatten suggest that students can view silently portions of the video and answer questions such as: What do Viennese [people] at coffee houses and museums consider casual summer wear? What geological or architectural features of a regional landscape suggest the economic and symbolic status of that locale? (1997, p. 179)

II. Linking visual systems to verbal systems

Stage 3: Verbalizing visual themes. At this point students hear the sound of the video, and the task given them is only to recognize repeated or emphasized words or phrases. Beginning learners can match eye movements with phrases heard often such as "no," "rarely," and "seldom." More advanced learners can identify sound and music associated with upbeat talk, weak applause, or complaints.

Stage 4: Identifying minimal linguistic differences as differences in meaning. In this microlistening task, students practice fine tuning by identifying, with the teacher's help, what they heard in German, for example, *Sie fahren später* [They leave later] or *Sie fährt später* [She leaves later] (Swaffar & Vlatten, 1997, p. 181).

Stage 5: Information as the basis for student perspectives. In this stage the students view the video again, using the redundancy of viewing, listening to draw conclusions, and then using that language to communicate their perspectives on the video.

At this stage, teachers can incorporate the communication standards by designing learning tasks in each of the three modes. To use language in an interpretive mode, learners might read an e-mail complaint about the circumstances portrayed in the video; in the interpersonal mode learners might exchange views with a classmate about the value systems portrayed in the video; in the presentational mode, they might prepare a student-produced video as a commercial or public service announcement about the circumstances seen in the video. Another teacher might choose to address the culture standard by having students identify and discuss the relationships seen in the video between products, perspectives, and practices. For more specific examples of how this model works in German, see Appendix 12.1. For a video segment in Spanish that includes authentic communication, see the Web site that accompanies *Teacher's Handbook* at **http://thandbook.heinle.com.**

One of the concerns sometimes expressed about the use of video, especially if a feature-length film is the videotext, relates to the ability of learners to process captioned target language reading material, or subtexts, while listening to acoustically rich, authentic video segments. In his work with advanced students, Garza (1991) found that captioning is beneficial because it allows students to use their skills in reading comprehension to develop aural comprehension, increase the accessibility and memorability of authentic language in the selected materials, and enable other language-processing strategies that accommodate varied modes of input. Most important, captioning leads students to use new vocabulary in appropriate contexts.

❏ Computer-Assisted Instruction (CAI)

Research indicates that students have positive attitudes about using computers (Kulik & Kulik, 1986, 1987; Phinney, 1991). The individualization possibilities presented by computers also make this medium an attractive one for teachers. They imagine a bank of questions that can be purposefully or randomly accessed to create class tests, individualized tests, and make-up tests, with weighting of certain parts to suit learners' needs. Teachers also dream of practice exercises that can be accessed to offer students additional individualized practice on troublesome points, especially if only one or two students require the extra work. Teachers wish for feedback systems that offer students meaningful comments on their input in response to computerized stimuli, and limitless branching possibilities, depending on their interests, needs, and abilities. They expect easy access to dictionary and thesaurus support and to other reference materials. Some such materials have been developed and researched. Grace (1998) studied word and sentence-level translations in software, and Nagata (1993) and Nagata and Swisher (1995) showed that traditional computer drill feedback can be beneficial at the word level. More important, they showed that computer-mediated feedback that recognizes and offers meaningful language practice is beneficial to learners at the sentence level. Research examining CAI suggests that the design of programming can encourage the development of language learning skills and result in more learning (Johansen & Tennyson, 1983; Robinson, 1989; Masters-Wicks, Postelwate, & Lewental, 1996). Other studies have claimed that learner differences can affect learner strategies, attitudes, and the kinds of learning gains students make by using TELL programs (Chapelle & Jamieson, 1986; Pederson, 1986, 1987).

Figure 12.7 Criteria for Communicative CALL

1. Communicative CALL will aim at acquisition practice rather than learning practice. There will be no drill.

2. In a Communicative CALL lesson or activity, grammar will always be implicit rather than explicit. Grammar will be built into the lesson.

3. Communicative CALL will allow and encourage the student to generate original utterances.

4. Communicative CALL will not try to judge and evaluate everything the student does.

5. Communicative CALL will avoid telling students they are "wrong."

6. Communicative CALL will not try to "reward" students with congratulatory messages, lights, bells, whistles, or other such nonsense.

7. Communicative CALL will not try to be "cute".

8. Communicative CALL will use the target language exclusively.

9. Communicative CALL will be flexible.

10. Communicative CALL will allow the student to explore the subject matter. Exploratory CALL can offer the student an environment in which to play with language or manipulate it to see how things go together.

11. Communicative CALL will create an environement in which using the target language feels natural, both on screen and off. An important source of comprehensible input that is often overlooked in the discussion of computer materials is the communication that usually takes place, not between computer and user, but between users.

12. Communicative CALL will never try to do anything that a book could do just as well. (This rule should apply to any use of the computer.)

13. Above all, Communicative CALL will be fun.

Source: Underwood, 1984; cf Beauvois, 1992.

Although the basic questions of how much and when to implement CAI have yet to be answered, at some time in your career you are likely to have to select computer hardware or software. Since computer software is generally designed by technicians who are not foreign language teachers, you may find the guidelines offered by Underwood in Figure 12.7 very helpful. For a description of the types of computerized programs, see Figure 12.8 (Kassen & Higgins, 1997).

Thus, as you look at examples of usage of CAI, you will find aspects of behaviorist exercises or fill-in-the-blank, mechanistic, habit-formation drills for vocabulary and verb conjugations that computers can perform well. You will also find examples of TELL that will help learners interact with software in a cognitive or memory-based way, repeating or filling in the blanks. TELL also includes software that helps recall vocabulary by using visual images or storage systems like a dictionary or a thesaurus. In recent years, TELL has developed in ways to help learners communicate with each other via electronic means such as chatrooms, to do information-based research on the Web, or to use photos on the Web from museums in the target country. Otto and Pusack (1997) predict that in the future there will be "few instances where courseware would engage solely in cognitively oriented presentation of linguistic content without significant opportunities for meaningful and contextualized practice (p. 29). For a set of instructions and evaluative procedures for a

Figure 12.8   Some Types of Programs Used in CALL

Types of Software

- **Generic:** supplemental software not based on a text *(Triple Play Plus)*.
- **Text-based:** textbook-specific software easily integrated into curriculum.
- **Course-based:** software that serves as the basis of a course *(Éxito)*.
- **Course-adapted:** software adapted from various sources to serve a specific course (authoring: i.e., *Libra* lessons).

Types of Programs

- **Drill and Practice**   use word level exercises like fill-in-the-blank and multiple-choice to focus on discrete grammar skills.
- **Simulations**   make the users' responses have specific consequences to the character or story line of the program.
- **Tutorials**   offer users pre- and posttests, exercises, and explanations for improving linguistic skills.
- **Games**   utilize the elements of competition, challenge, and problem solving to teach and/or reinforce learning.
- **Writing Assistants**   are word-processing programs that provide learners with on-line aids for writing.
- **Authoring Programs**   provide the teacher with the ability to alter or create lessons for specific classes or commerical use.
- **Information Resources**   are collections of information such as dictionaries, atlases, galleries, and encyclopedias.
- **Information Management**   are database and spreadsheet software packages used to track student grades, progress, and more.

Source: Kassen & Higgins, 1997.

chatroom, see the web site that accompanies *Teacher's Handbook* at **http://thandbook. heinle.com.**

❏ Using Software and Courseware to Assist with Language Learning Processes

Software and courseware program types include tutorials, drill and practice, holistic practice, and many games programs in which learners respond to stimuli along predetermined user-selected learning paths (Wyatt, 1987). By contrast, in modeling, discovery, and simulation programs, students are initiators; they work *with* the computer, and they take more responsibility for their learning. There are no predetermined learning paths (Wyatt, 1987). Word and idea processing programs, spell checkers, on-line thesauruses, and text analysis programs are considered helpful for students who are completely responsible for their own learning. Students are initiators and use the computer as a tool to reduce labor. Learning objectives or paths are not specified or embodied in the computer program (Wyatt, 1987).

It is generally assumed that TELL serves as a supplement or enrichment rather than as a substitute for regular classroom learning. A recent summary of studies (Warschauer & Healey, 1998) shows that software requiring minimal verbal interaction among students generates very little and poor quality talk among them, while software asking students to write a joint report or to produce a collaborative project results in substantial interaction that can involve negotiation of meaning and self-correction of error. When students are in groups around a computer to use software designed for cooperative learning tasks introducing new material or practicing newly learned material, research has shown no negative effects on learning (Chang & Smith, 1991). Furthermore, other research showed improved results in kinds and numbers of language functions used and in topics discussed in CALL groups (Abraham & Liou, 1991; Johnson, Johnson, & Stanne, 1986).

As more communicative TELL software and courseware develops, teachers should look for products that include numerous communicative-gap exercises in which participants in the conversational arrangement have certain pieces of information but are required to talk with each other to find the pieces they do not have. An example is presented in the Teach and Reflect section of this chapter, as illustrated in Figure 12.9 (Chun and Brandl, 1992).

Writing assistant software is an example of TELL that goes beyond the mechanical drill formats typical of early programs and provides opportunities for students to practice meaningful language use and self-expression. The unique *Système-D* package developed by Noblitt, Pet, and Solá (1998)[4] enables students to develop their creative writing skills in French. Also available in Spanish and German, this package differs from other CALL programs in that it offers students the opportunity to express themselves by accessing a 4,400-word dictionary, a verb conjugator, a grammar index, a vocabulary index, and a phrase index. Students can use the English/French dictionary, the French/English dictionary, and the verb conjugator for reference aids as they compose written texts. The dictionary includes most verbs used by elementary, intermediate, and advanced students. The program features a complete conjugation screen for each verb in all tenses in the affirmative, negative, and reflexive forms. In addition, the grammar index provides a relatively complete list of grammatical structures with brief but clear explanations and model sentences. In the vocabulary index, many commonly used words are arranged in sixty-five categories by context/theme. The phrase index includes a wealth of idiomatic expressions organized by language functions. Finally, the program features a tracking device that records keystrokes that can inform the teacher about how long the learner spent in formulating each phrase, and which resources were consulted so that teachers can assist learners in the writing process.

The challenging nature of creative writing opportunities offered by *Système-D* was confirmed in Scott's study (1990, 1992). However, her study points out that the feature of this program students use most is the dictionary. She suggests that teachers create a series of interesting real-life situations with tasks that students need to do in order to respond to each situation in writing. The tasks direct students to consult the grammar, vocabulary, and phrase indexes in *Système-D*. According to Scott, "students who are encouraged to access the unique linguistic features of the software should, over time, increase their general competence in preparation for autonomous written expression without depending upon the software" (1990, p. 64). Although further research is needed to confirm the long-term benefits of using *Système-D*, the program provides an exciting and challenging tool for teaching creative writing in French. Scott (1990) includes a detailed description of *Système-D* and her proposed framework for including task-oriented writing activities that engage

---

4. This software (Noblitt, Pet, & Solá, 1998, version 3.0) is a writing assistant, also available from Heinle & Heinle publishers as *Quelle* (Kossuth, Noblitt, & Pet, 1998, version 3.0) in German and *Atajo* (Domínguez, Noblitt, & Pet, 1998, version 3.0) in Spanish.

Figure 12.9 "Room": Example of a Meaning-Enhancing Communicative Information-Gap Exercise

This exercise called "Room" is designed to simulate a typical conversation between, for example, roommates or housemates. The functional goal of this situation is to locate objects in a room and to differentiate between stationary physical location and the action of motion involved in placing an object somewhere. In German this entails comprehending the grammatical difference between the accusative and the dative cases when using the so-called " two-way" prepositions. In addition, the use of pronouns can be practiced once their referents have been established. Consider, for example, typical everyday questions and answers:

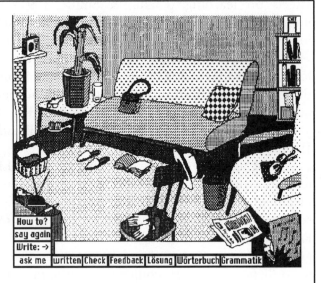

A: "Honey, where did you put the keys?"

B: "I put them on the table."

A: " Where are my glasses?"

B: "They're next to the lamp."

In order to simulate an authentic situation the program displays the picture of a messy room including many different objects which are located in various places (see illustration).

In the program, the user is asked to imagine the following situation:

You are living in the year 2101 with a robot for a roommate. Unfortunately you are not a very orderly person, but you usually know where all your things in your living room are. Your roommate, who is programmed to be very orderly, wants to clean up your room, but it/he/she cannot find anything. You know where all the objects are and help your roommate find these things when it/he/she asks you.

As stated above, the goal of this exercise is to establish a brief, meaningful dialogue between the user and the computer. At the student's command, the computer in its function as a robot asks a question about the location of an object in the room. The user responds to the question by typing in the location of the particular object. In response to correct grammatical input from the user, the object that was sought flashes on the screen and the computer concludes each miniconference conversation by telling the user that it found the object.

For each question generated by the computer, an object on the screen is chosen at random, and a question is asked using one of two different syntactic structures, e.g.:

A: "Wo ist mein Füller?" (Where is my fountain pen?) **or**

B: "Wohin hast du meinen Füller gelegt?" (Where did you put my fountain pen?)

Accordingly the student answers:

A: "Er liegt auf dem Fernseher." (It is on [top of] the TV.) **or**

B: "Ich habe ihn auf den Fernseher gelegt." (I put it on [top of] the TV.)

Figure 12.9 "ROOM": Example of a Meaning-Enhancing Communicative Information-Gap Exercise (continued)

The computer concludes the minidialogue by reinforcing the student's answer:

A: "Ich habe ihn gefunden. Er liegt auf dem Fernseher." (I found it. It's on top of the TV.) **or**

B: "Ich habe ihn gefunden. Du hast ihn auf den Fernseher gelegt." (I found it. You put it on top of the TV.)

Note that this concluding response from the computer reinforces not only the two-way prepositions but also the pragmatically necessary shifts in pronominal reference, which make the discourse natural and coherent.

The program incorporates a number of built-in features to help learners during the communication process. For example, students can retrieve any of the oral questions or statements of the computer in written format by simply clicking on a button on the screen. They can listen to the computer's questions or responses as many times as they want, also at the touch of a button. An on-line dictionary allows users to look up any of the vocabulary words used in the program. Furthermore, the software also provides a detailed grammatical review of the two-way prepositions in German, so that students are reminded about the formal requirements of the situation.

Unlike most programs which require users to input single words and thus need only to check single words, this program has an error-checking device which checks the grammaticality of entire sentences. The error-checking program goes through students' answers word by word from left to right and highlights the first word which either is in the wrong place or contains a spelling or morphological mistake. When users see a word highlighted, they then have several options: They may choose to get feedback with grammatical information or hints or see the correct answer.

If they choose grammatical feedback, the program anticipates many of the most common students' mistakes and provides, based on the mistakes, either a general feedback message, e.g., "A pronoun should be in this position of the sentence," or, in a case in which the student used a pronoun with the wrong case or gender, more detailed grammatical information, "The gender of your pronoun is wrong." While many other programs provide these same options, e.g., to get hints, grammatical explanations, or the correct answer, most do so only for single words rather than for entire sentences.

Source: Chun & Brandl, 1992.

students in the use of various writing strategies. See the Case Study on the web site at **http://thandbook.heinle.com** for ways to use this software.

Reading assistant software has also been developed, using HTML (Hyper Text Markup Language), which enables the creator of materials to organize them in nonlinear, layered formats using a complex system of cross-referencing. Most word processing programs now have the capability to convert any word processing document into HTML for use on the Internet so that teachers can make these materials available to any student with Internet access. These programs are often integrated with audio, video, and graphic materials. Garrett (1991) gives an example of a reading comprehension presentation via Hyper Text, in which the student can select certain words with a mouse or cursor and be directly referenced to a synonym, paraphrase, translation, grammatical analysis, map, picture, audio rendition, or cultural note. Students reading literary texts can call up the author's biographical information or explanations of historical or political background, interpretations of the works, and so on. Davis and Lyman-Hager (1997) report successful use of a reading assistant to accompany an authentic francophone novel, *Une vie de boy,* by Oyono (1956). Intermediate-level readers reported more satisfying experiences with authentic reading of the novel through the reading assistant software. They had access to definitions in English, definitions in French, audio pronunciation by a native speaker, grammatical explanations, relationships between grammatical elements, and cultural references. Using a query log to track the look-up behavior of the readers, the researchers found that eighty-five percent of the look-ups were definitions in English. Interestingly, the case studies in this research revealed that three subsequent look-ups sometimes still resulted in misuse of the word in a composition for some students, while only one look-up was necessary for others. Individual needs for redundancy of exposure and practice were underscored. The authors predicted, as did Scott with the writing assistant programs (1990), that learners will make more thorough use of the more complex elements of reading and writing assistant programs if their teachers show them how to use them and benefit from them.

Yet another application of computer software is in the development of computerized language learning simulations. Jones (1982) identifies the necessary elements of a simulation as (1) a simulated environment or a representation of the real world; (2) structure, created by rules of conversational interaction; and (3) reality of function or the learner's "reality" perspective of the event. A simulated environment is provided by the computer, which presents an image on the display screen. The structure of a simulation is created by rules concerning the learner task. In simulations, the computer appears to understand language and produces it meaningfully, thus supporting the learner's "reality" perspective of the exchange (Crookall & Oxford, 1990). Following early examples of simulations (Coleman, 1985; Cook & Fass, 1986), several programs have been developed that respond to selections and choices that students make as they solve daily problems (*A la rencontre de Philippe* [Furstenberg & Malone, 1993] and *Dans un quartier de Paris* [Furstenberg, 1999]) and move about situations on site in foreign countries (*Montevidisco* [Larson & Bush, 1992] and *Ciberteca: Una carta a Dios* [Chun & Plass, 1999]).

Some simulation software packages integrate use of a CD-ROM containing the program with the Internet and e-mail to enable students to practice a variety of language uses as they solve mysteries (*Un Muerte à Cinet* [Oliver & Nelson, 1997b] and *Un Misterio en Toluca* [Oliver & Nelson, 1997a]) through the technology media. Discussion "rooms" are also available through the publishers of the materials, in which possible theories about the murder mystery can be developed with students from schools worldwide who are using the program. Other programs are complete courses in language that include simulations among their many techniques (Hughes, 1993): *Khorosho!* is a laserdisc program of language study equivalent to 100 hours of classroom study in Russian, developed by the Federal Language Training Laboratory. It incorporates TPR and the Natural Approach to enable learners to reach a level of 1 on the FSI scale. *Éxito* is a similar program developed by the Central Intelligence Agency (Hughes, 1989).

New Technologies

❏ E-mail

E-mail is perhaps the mode of electronic communication that has most rapidly been turned to use in teaching foreign languages. Foreign and second language teachers find that the use of this medium immediately breaks the isolation in which they may work in their schools and puts them in touch with teachers around the globe to share the exhilaration of success and to find solutions to challenges. For instance, connecting students to international students who speak and write the target language is now within reach (Fischer, 1996). E-mail penpals, called "keypals," are suggested throughout the standards for foreign language learning as a way to relate the curricular weave elements through technology with standards and goal areas. A sample progress indicator for grade four regarding presentational communication is: "Students give short oral notes and messages or write reports about people and things in their school environment and exchange the information with another language class either locally or via e-mail." (NSFLEP, 1996, p. 41)

Although e-mail is a written mode of communication, the tone and register used is nevertheless like that of spoken language, with the added advantage reported by students that they have time to look at their messages, to think about how they will be received, and to make corrections. The rapid-fire turn taking of speaking face-to-face that intimidates slow or timid learners can be modified with a "window" on the screen in which learners can type their comments and make them as correct as they can.

Another use of e-mail can be designed around tasks teachers design for learners: For example, to practice realistic communication, a student could write the instructor an e-mail message explaining an absence from school, justifying the seriousness of the excuse, requesting information about the assignment for the next class day, and apologizing for being absent. Many teachers report that the students who are quiet in class find this mode of communication a more accessible means of gaining the floor and making conversational gambits, thus creating their opportunities to practice the target language.

The possibility of connecting students with keypals who reside in the target country is exciting and rewarding. Teachers and learners working together on a standards-based cultural project, for instance, might ask keypals for information about birthday celebrations, how birthdays are celebrated (practices), whether invitations are sent (products), and whether there are alternative celebrations, for instance saints' days (practices). Warschauer (1995) reports effective ways to use e-mail for teaching ESL.

❑ Listservs

An outgrowth of e-mail is the use of a list of student e-mail addresses that the teacher controls through an electronic address book contained in most e-mail software. This enables the teacher to contact all students via a single e-mail address. In order to enable students to communicate with each other and the teacher via a single address, the teacher can have the class e-mail address list placed on another computer which has been designated a "server," allowing only authorized students to join the "listserv." Teachers can also use e-mail for communication with students about assignments, for writing and correcting drafts of compositions or short writing tasks, or for communicating with parents about student progress.

Teachers can also join listservs available to them as professionals. Two international listservs that teachers find helpful are FLTEACH, administered by LeLoup and Ponterio at SUNY Cortland and LLTI (Language Learners and Teachers International). On these listservs, teachers exchange information about texts, materials, teaching techniques, learner difficulties and successes, and sources of new information. Some listservs allow members to receive a compilation of e-mail messages, called a "digest," instead of receiving each message singly.

❒ UserNets and News Groups

News groups or usernets are extensions of listservs that operate on the Internet and thus are open to any Internet user. Caution should be exercised in accessing news groups because of their unmonitored use. Teacher-monitored use of these resources can be effective, as reported by Cononelos and Oliva (1993) who successfully used e-mail and Italian usernet groups to enable learners to access Italian news broadcasts and write to each other via e-mail about the weather and news in their areas.

❒ Networked products

An exciting use of the computer's capacity for increasing learner communication is in products such as *Daedalus InterChange,* which is basically a chatroom used on a local area network, such as a computer lab. *Daedalus InterChange,* which is part of a product called *Daedalus Interactive Writing Environment,* is one example of a writing environment that shows remarkable success. Kern (1995) supplemented work by L2 researchers (Kreeft Peyton, 1986; Kreeft Peyton & Mackinson-Smyth, 1989; Esling, 1991; Beauvois, 1992) when he reported increased written language production by learners who used *Daedalus InterChange* for on-line discussion. Furthermore, learners' language was more sophisticated in terms of its morphosyntactic features and in terms of its discourse features. Student-to-student interaction occurred more frequently, with students taking a personal interest in each other through the on-line conversations. Chávez (1997) affirmed the benefits of this writing environment. This work reinforces Johnson's assertion that "computers can be a way to bring students together to interact, to negotiate meaning, to think and to negotiate strategies related to the social and academic tasks at hand (1991, p. 79). Johnson goes on to point out the essential nature of the teacher's role as paramount in the selection and design of materials. Kern's work affirmed that even the minute-to-minute teacher talk is different and more productive for communication as reported in the two exchanges from Kern's (1995) second-semester French class, on page 343. You can easily see that more language was used in the networked classroom. In addition, the quality of the interaction is substantially more communicative in the networked classroom. For instance, in the traditional classroom, the interaction is student-to-teacher, and no individual is called by name until the end when the teacher concludes the first student's comments and calls on Kelly in order to move the class along in limited time. In the networked classroom, on the other hand, the interaction is between students who capture each other's attention by using their names, and time is not a concern. Even the student's interaction with the teacher is qualitatively different in length and in the detail contained in the narrative past response as illustrated exactly as it was produced by the students and teacher.

❒ The World Wide Web and the Internet

The Internet is a collection of local and wide area networks linked together (Scinicariello, 1998), and the World Wide Web (WWW) is perhaps its most famous and user-friendly component. The WWW brings the world to the fingertips of each learner quickly and inexpensively through a variety of "browsers," which are software that enable the user to search for information. By means of Hyper Text Markup Language (HTML), words and information can be linked much in the same ways as they are linked in human thought.

TRADITIONAL CLASSROOM, TEACHER FRONT AND CENTER IN THE ROOM:		INTERCHANGE CLASSROOM, TEACHER NETWORKED WITH STUDENTS:	
STUDENT:	La pilule termine...? [The pill terminates . . . ?]	ALDA:	Je pense que je suis comme mes parents en un sens, nous sommes toujours heureux. Mais en general, nous sommes tres differents. Peut-etre c-est parce que je deviens adulte aux Etats-Unis, et ils habitaient aux autre pays la plus grande partie de temps. Ils aiment les traditions chinois, mais je n'en aime pas trop. [I think I'm like my parents in one sense; we're always happy. But in general, we are very different. Maybe it's because I grew up in the United States, and they lived in another country for the majority of their lives. They love the Chinese traditions, but I don't love them so much.]
INSTRUCTOR:	Comment? [Pardon?]		
STUDENT:	La pilule termine, termine... [The pill terminates, terminates . . .]		
INSTRUCTOR:	Termine ou finit, oui... [Terminates or finishes, yes . . .]		
STUDENT:	La... [The . . .]		
INSTRUCTOR:	La grossesse. [Pregnancy.]		
STUDENT:	La... pregnancy... [The . . . pregnancy . . .]	RICK (PROFESSOR):	Alda, est-ce que vous participez aux fêtes chinoises, même si vous ne les aimez pas? [Alda, do you participate in Chinese festivals, even if you don't like them?]
INSTRUCTOR:	La grossesse. [Pregnancy.]		
STUDENT:	La grossesse avant qu'il y a les jambes, le coeur,... La pilule termine la grossesse... ? [The pill terminates the pregnancy before there are legs, the heart . . . The pill terminates the . . . pregnancy?]	ALDA:	Professeur Kern, hier c'etait le premier d'annee au calendrier chinoises. Je suis retourne chex mes parents, et nous avons celebre. Les premieres trois jours de la nouvel annee sont tres important. Il me faut celebrer. Je n'en aime pas la tradition trop, mais je (et peute-etre tous les enfants chinoises) aime le premier d'annee. C'est parce que les adultes donnent des poches rouges. Et il y a beaucoup d'argent. [Professor Kern, yesterday was the first day of the Chinese new year. I went home to my parents', and we celebrated. The first three days of the new year are very important. I had to celebrate. I don't like tradition very much but I (and maybe all Chinese young people) love the first of the new year. It's because the adults give red pouches. And there is a lot of money.]
INSTRUCTOR:	La grossesse. [The pregnancy.]		
STUDENT:	Un jour, deux jours, après la conception. [One day, two days, after conception.]		
INSTRUCTOR:	D'accord...Vous, Kelly, vous vouliez dire quelque chose? [OK . . . You, Kelly, you wanted to say something?]	KANG:	Alda, est-ce que tes parents parle à toi en chinois et tu parle aux parents en anglais? [Alda, do your parents speak to you in Chinese, and do you speak to them in English?]
		BILLY:	Alda, Est-ce que vous etes chinoise? [Alda, are you Chinese?]

Student comments are unaltered and may contain errors.

Source: Kern, 1995.

The WWW can be used to promote active learning (Brooks, 1997), to find information, to conduct standards-driven research projects about communities or comparisons of cultures. According to Walz, the WWW can be related to the Standards in at least five ways: "Competence in more than one language and culture enables people to gain access to additional bodies of knowledge; ... all students learn in a variety of ways and settings; . . . language and culture education incorporate effective technologies (1998, p. 104). "Web activities also help students discover content knowledge, they are consistent with learning theories about learning to read authentic materials, and they stress varied use of language" (Walz, 1998, p. 104).

Information on the WWW is located at specific addresses, called web sites. Web addresses are similar to e-mail addresses but they rather consistently start with "http://www. . . . " In using web-based information, teachers can apply the principles outlined in the *Teacher's Handbook* to the text-based and graphic information available from the World Wide Web. An example of using the interactive listening and reading chart presented in Chapter 6 applied to a web-enhanced activity is presented in Case Study 2. Since web sites change or are temporarily unavailable, teachers should check them before assigning learners tasks that require use of the sites. Some web sites have been specifically designed for use by educators. Those that are especially useful are available at the web sites for museums that offer guided tours of the Louvre or the Prado, for example. Less famous museums offer sites that contain the works of well-known artists, and restaurants or resorts provide visual images of their locations so that learners feel like they are almost in the buildings they see. For instance, Walz (1998) suggests that teachers might address the Connections Standard for grade four by visiting the web site for the *Musée des enfants* (Children's Museum) in Hull, Québec, at **http://www.cmcc.muse.digital.ca/cmc/cmcfra/cmfra.html.** At this site, one of the activities students can do is tour the anthropological section of the museum, viewing pictures of cultures around the world, with short captions in French for four-year-old native speakers of French. See Walz (1998) for useful web sites and model descriptions of standards-related web activities that will still be useful if web sites disappear.

In using the Web, teachers should apply the same techniques they would to the development of any authentic material for use in the classroom. The model for interactive reading and listening, presented in Chapter 6, provides a structured way to engage students with visual and auditory material from authentic sources such as the Web (see the module in Case Study 2 that presents a module developed using the interactive model and a web site for Frida Kahlo).[5] Teachers and students can create modules, or single activities, simply by typing in a word such as *voiture* in the "search" box of a search engine like Yahoo! or Excite or Snap.com, and then developing an exercise or a series of exercises around the web site that is found (Donato, 1999).

❏ Chatrooms

A chatroom is a protected space where teachers can give assignments for students to interact or write about topics they will later discuss in class, or to practice short compositions. Chatrooms can be on a local area network or on a wider linked network or on the Internet. Although they are written, the tone, vocabulary, and style of communication are informal, like those of spoken speech. Rankin (1997) and Jenlink and Carr (1996) report benefits of the kinds of dialogic conversations that are appropriate to the goals of foreign language instruction. Chatrooms provide learners with opportunities to practice what they might

---

5. This project, funded by the Center for Innovation in Learning at Virginia Polytechnic Institute and State University, is a proposal written by Judith Shrum; project leader, Elizabeth Calvera; technology consultants, Theresa Swann, Eddie Watson, Sharon Robinson. Early versions of the template and additional modules created by project participants: Sharon Robinson, Heide Witthoeft, Elizabeth Calvera, Theresa Swann, Kris Lubbs, Iris Myers, June Stubbs, Yumiko Younos, Shoshanna Slawny-Levitan, Sue Farquhar, Laura Gorfkle, Fumiko Yamagami-Snidow.

later say in class or in face-to-face communication. Chatrooms are advantageous because learners can gain access to the conversation simply by typing at their computers and sending the message; they can see their work before they send it and make corrections; their keyboarding skills are not critical to communication. As reported by Rankin, the affective filter is lowered, learners can communicate beyond the boundaries of their institutions, teachers can track the syntactic structures and common errors, and a classwide discourse can be built (1997, p. 543).

Chatrooms can be conducted in "real-time," that is, when all the learners are on line at once. This is a "synchronous" chatroom. Depending on the design the teacher gives the assignment, chatrooms can be used in a synchronous way, or the students can go to the chatroom to complete their assigned tasks at their own convenience, in an "asynchronous" way. This gives maximum flexibility to the learner who may or may not find other users on line at the same time.

An example of an advanced-level activity relating to the culture and the communication standards is the creation of dialogue between a professional school in France and an American university in which students from each group selected images that they felt were representative of their cultures. Each group then commented on the images and commented on the comments via a chatroom, in their native language and in their target language. Besides improving their grammatical skills, practicing more frequent writing, and learning how to view and defend their own and others' cultures, the students learned how to manage language in order to sustain meaningful communication. They learned what words prompt negative responses, and how to select alternatives, how to manage writing in order to elicit information, how to select where the "hot-spots" of intercultural communication lie.[6]

Other extensions of chatrooms are MOOs (Multiple-User Object Oriented) and MUDs (Multiple User Domain). These are electronic spaces accessible through the Internet, often password protected, at which users can communicate around settings or tasks that are often incorporated with a CD-ROM. The complexity of these spaces is such that most teachers will purchase products that incorporate them, such as *MundoHispano,* a MOO maintained by Lonnie Turbee at **http://www.umsl.edu/~moosproj/mundo.html.** For example, *MundoHispano* is a community of native speakers of Spanish from around the world, teachers and learners of Spanish, and computer programmers who volunteer to create a virtual world in which learners can enter at a visual representation of the Puerto del Sol in the center of Madrid and have *tapas* (snacks) and web conversation in the Café Ojalá. According to Warschauer and Healey (1998), sentences produced in these spaces are generally shorter and simpler than those produced with *Daedalus InterChange.* Some such technologies are available on CD-ROM with Internet connections and combine text-based communication with instructions and sometimes with graphics and video interface. These technologies break the requirement for simultaneous time and space contact between teacher and learners and are useful for out-of-class assignments for additional time-on-task.

---

6. Thanks to Sharon P. Johnson (Virginia Polytechnic Institute and State University) and Catherine English (Institute des Télécomunications) for insights into their Transatlantic Project. See Appendix 12.2 for a link to their students' chatroom.

❐ Distance Education and Videoconferencing

Distance education is "an organized instructional program in which the teacher and learners are physically separated by time or by geography" (Newby, Stepich, Lehman, & Russell, 1996, p. 347). By this definition, asynchronous chatrooms are a form of distance learning, but distance education most often applies to the broadcasting of instruction between two (point-to-point) or more (multiple) sites. Videoconferencing is a distance education technology that currently uses telephone lines to send video and audio between originating and receiving sites (Newby, Stepich, Lehman, & Russell, 1996, p. 352). Development of this technology using wireless communication is within reach. Recent technical advances such as compressed video have enabled two-way video and two-way audio that provide the benefits of delivery of instruction where it could not otherwise be delivered, particularly in the case of less commonly taught languages where instructors are not readily available in all regions, or where learners are physically distant from the instructor in rural settings. Other benefits are opportunities to connect learners with native speakers around the world and cost-effective delivery. Warriner-Burke (1990) warned that often administrators and technology specialists decide to use this form of technology without consulting language specialists. According to Aplevich and Willment (1998), distance education calls for a change in the teaching process, or delivery, not in teaching philosophy. In recent years, this technology has been used in the service of sound principles of communicative language instruction, including person-to-person interaction via two-way video and audio, so that class members at each of the sites can see and hear each other. Other elements of a well-designed distance learning origination site include computers, CD-ROMS, whiteboards to project overhead transparencies and to write on during class, video or laserdisc machines, and document cameras to photograph and send images. Users report that the delay in transmission is less than two seconds, and once users are accustomed to the technology, the face-to-face personal interaction assumes preeminence in the learning process. Despite reports of high costs (Kinginger, 1998), this technology has become cost-effective (Moore & Thompson, 1997; Sussex, 1991; Otto & Pusack, 1996) compared to the expense of providing an instructor in each of the areas served, or compared to the undesirable alternative of not providing instruction at all.

Kinginger (1998) reported on a videoconference exchange between American and French students, in which it was hoped that the two peer groups would assist each other in French and English throughout the hour-long conversation. The researcher/instructor theorized that the American students would use their background knowledge of French and would be assisted by their French peers as their comprehension improved, thus illustrating the Vygotskian Zone of Proximal Development. Results were at first disappointing because the colloquial nature of the spoken French language was so unique to the American students that they were unable to benefit from their French peers' use of language as extensively as their instructors had hoped. However, in later sessions after the call, the ZPD did become relevant as the American learners analyzed the conversations and identified language variations.

As they experiment with new technologies, language educators are learning how to manage them for maximal benefit. Research shows that distance learning effectiveness is most enhanced when learners are motivated, assume responsibility for learning, and have a classroom facilitator at the site where they receive the broadcasts (Glisan, Dudt, & Howe, 1998; Nielsen & Hoffman, 1996; Oxford, Park-Oh, Ito, & Sumrall, 1993; Yi & Majima,

1993). This facilitator provides technical support in terms of connecting machines and setting up the technology, and most significantly, provides support for learning, either as a co-learner in the broadcast course, or as a provider of additional information or review sessions about the course material.

Success of distance education projects in foreign language learning is reported by numerous researchers (Glisan, Dudt, & Howe, 1998; Yi & Majima, 1993; Nielsen & Hoffman, 1996; Oxford, Park-Oh, Ito, & Sumrall, 1993), although most of the projects are grant-supported or have a vested interest in demonstrating success. The full benefits of program delivery via this technology remains to be seen as its implementation grows and as research is conducted on its benefits.

What the Future of Technology Holds for Language Learning

The future of technology in language learning is becoming the present more rapidly than the profession can assimilate the currently available materials. Video, whether from the Internet or in VHS or laserdisc format, offers the opportunity to present language in its cultural context, underscoring the most important contribution technology can make in language teaching, which is the integration of teaching language and culture. The addition of computer-mediated technology allows for further integration of language, literature, and culture (Garrett, 1991).

Among future technological environments are "virtual realities" in which a learner wears headgear or a body-suit with sensors that present visual and auditory texts and stimuli to the student with each turn of the head or touch of the finger. For instance, a learner could prelive a study abroad experience, relive the painting of a famous portrait, or participate in a Chinese New Year celebration. A student learning how to pronounce sounds might enter a virtual representation of the mouth in order to see which structures are used when sounds are made (Jenkins, 1999). It is anticipated that virtual realities will be accompanied by increased use of the Internet and increased use of technology for assessment of language gain.

The services and information available on the WWW today will form part of what technologist visionaries call the "Information Superhighway," and the ways in which we use it now have been compared to the way people traveled to the West Coast on the Oregon Trail in the nineteenth century. What it will bring us in educational opportunities in the twenty-first century has been compared to the smooth and fast highways that enable comfortable travel (Gates, 1995). The growth of this elaborate network has facilitated an exponential increase in demands and opportunities for the rapid transfer of knowledge and information on a global scale, but the United States does not yet have the linguistic or cultural competency to take full advantage of all that the technology has to offer (Maxwell, 1998).

While the future is bright, there are yet some discouraging concerns about access to technologies, as pointed out by Gates: "Preschoolers familiar with cellular telephones, pagers, and personal computers enter kindergartens where chalkboards and overhead projectors represent the state of the art" (1995, p. 186). According to Hundt, Chairman of the U.S. Federal Communications Commission, "There are thousands of buildings in this country with millions of people in them who have no telephones, no cable television and no reasonable prospect of broadband service. They are called schools" (cf. Gates, 1995, p. 186).

In addition to problems of access and availability, much research specific to the field of language learning and technology has yet to be done. Despite the proven effectiveness of TELL, additional research is needed to investigate specific issues such as "What kind of software, integrated how into what kind of syllabus, at what level of language learning, for what kind of language learners, is likely to be effective for what specific learning purposes?" (Garrett, 1991, p. 75). We do not know whether students at certain levels of proficiency or with certain learning styles benefit from using computers more than do students at other levels or with other styles. We do not have replicated studies on what kind of immediate feedback or tutorial help is most beneficial for learners, nor do we know whether the program, the learner, or a combination of both best facilitates learning.

The challenge is to make the technology work to enhance learning for students, to ensure faculty support and enrichment, and to ensure careful investment by schools in technology that enables meaningful language learning for that locality. As educators and technologists work together with the support of the private sector and federal projects, the use of technology has the potential to change learning and the lives of all involved in it in profound ways.

Teach and Reflect

Episode One

Selecting Video Materials

Randomly select three videos from a collection in a school's library or media center. Rentals from a private company or purchases from video or computer catalogues may also be used. Apply to them the guidelines presented in this chapter for the selection of videotexts (Joiner, 1990). View and critique the videos by using the criteria listed in the guidelines, and select a two-minute segment of the video to use in your class. Outline a step-by-step process you will follow that incorporates the five stages suggested on pages 332–333 by Swaffar and Vlatten (1997) of identifying value systems in visual sequences and linking visual systems to verbal systems, as described in this chapter. Be sure to include a justification using this particular segment. Your instructor may ask you to present your segment to the class.

Episode Two

Examining the Potential Use of a TELL Exercise

Figure 12.9 is an example of a TELL meaning-enhancing communicative information-gap exercise presented by Chun and Brandl (1992, pp. 260–262). Using what you learned about information-gap activities in earlier chapters, analyze this activity for its communicative potential. Then answer the following questions:

1. How do you think students will communicate with the computer in this exercise?

2. What do you think students will be able to do, as a result of using this exercise, when they communicate with peers?

Figure 12.10 Continuum of Learning Activities

FORM RESTRICTED	MEANING ENHANCING	MEANINGFUL COMMUNICATION
Grammar-based	**Guided communication**	**Free (human) communication**
Not contextualized; single, isolated words or sentences	Contextualized, interrelated sentences; but somewhat restricted grammatically, semantically, pragmatically	Fully contextualized grammatically, semantically, pragmatically; interrelated sentences
CALL exercises: fill-in-the-blank; multiple choice; cloze	CALL exercises: communicative-gap exercises	CALL exercises: artificial intelligence with parsing, speech recognition
User's input: single words, single letters	User's input: whole sentences, but limited syntax and semantics	User's input: unrestricted, complete, original sentences

Source: Chun & Brandl, 1992.

3. What kind of grouping circumstances do you envision when using this kind of exercise with a class?

4. At what point in a lesson would this exercise be used?

How would you revise this activity for your language? Consult Figure 12.7 (Underwood 1984; cf. Beauvois 1992, p. 457) and Figure 12.10 (Chun & Brandl, 1992) for guidance.

Discuss and Reflect

Case Study 1

Incorporating Video in Language Instruction

Ms. Silver has taught German at Ridge Runner High School in Beaverton for three years. She began her teaching career in Austria, teaching elementary school, but she changed to teaching high school German when her children grew up and left for college. She is a dynamic, energetic, and enthusiastic teacher who expects as much from her students as she gives in preparation and presentation. In class, Ms. Silver speaks German almost entirely and uses a wide variety of communicative activities. She spends several hours each day planning her lessons.

Over the past several months, Ms. Silver has been reading about the use of video in language teaching, and she attended a workshop on listening comprehension that offered some ideas about integrating video. She soon became interested in experimenting with video in her German classes. She used her many connections in her Austrian hometown to her advantage and asked a relative who was working in a television station to seek permission for her to obtain a videotape of various television segments. The station sent Ms. Silver a video containing several segments from a television drama, some news broadcasts, a variety of commercials, and a talk show segment. The station granted her permission to use the video for educational purposes. Ms. Silver received the video in the mail today and set about planning how to integrate it into her teaching.

Ask yourself these questions:

1. What will Ms. Silver have to consider as she decides how to integrate the video segments into her teaching?

2. What functions, contexts, and standards goal areas might be addressed with the types of segments included in her video?

3. How might she use Joiner's (1990) guide to using videotexts as she plans her lessons?

4. How might she address the fact that the video contains authentic speech and has not been produced for use in teaching?

To prepare the case:

Read the article by Swaffar and Vlatten (1997) and by Joiner (1990) on how to select and use videotexts; read Maxim's (1998) article on implementation of the Swaffar system if you are a German teacher; read Ito's (1996) article if you teach Japanese; read Herron's (1994) article for secondary/college teachers or Herron and Hanley's (1992) article for FLES teachers about effectiveness of using video; read the section of Garrett's (1991) article that deals with using video in the classroom; interview a language teacher who has had some experience with video in language teaching; obtain some practical suggestions.

To prepare for class discussion, think and write about this topic:

How you would use the interactive model for teaching listening and reading that is presented in Chapter 6 to engage students as they watch the talk show segment?

Case Study 2

Creating a Template for Web-Enhanced Materials[7]

A group of teachers from Garfield High School met with a group of college instructors from State University to try to figure out some ways to use new technologies in their classrooms. They discussed their students' abilities and interests and their lesson materials, and they discovered that the high school teachers and the college teachers had interest in the work of Frida Kahlo, had some text materials in their textbooks that they could use, but they wanted to give their students more. When they talked about their students' proficiency in Spanish, they realized that their students were mostly somewhere in the intermediate mid range, regardless of whether they were in Spanish III and IV of high school or 201 or 202 in college. They wanted to use authentic materials, and they wanted to engage their students in a process approach to

---

7. Thanks to the students of SPAN 2984 (2114) Accelerated Intermediate Spanish, fall 1998, for their commentary on this chatroom.

TECHNOLOGY-ENHANCED FOREIGN LANGUAGE MODULE ON FRIDA KAHLO

For the Teacher's Information:

Standard goal area(s) addressed: Communication, Cultures

Description of what a student can do with language:

Communication: Students exchange opinions in chatroom conversations later also conducted in discussion groups in class (interpersonal mode); students interpret written language about Kahlo's paintings from the *pasillos* at the web site (interpretive mode); students present information (presentational mode) that can be used in the next edition of the author's textbook.

Cultures: Students use products of the culture (Kahlo's paintings) to demonstrate relationship between perspectives of the culture regarding roles of men and women as artists.

Linguistic Function(s): The students will be able to describe, narrate in the past, and give opinions/interpretations.

ACTFL Level: Intermediate mid

Authentic Material: Frida Kahlo web site at **http://www.telesat.com.co/Telesat/home2/ galeria/kahlo/index.html;** chatroom for the instructor which is at ___ (instructor inserts personal homepage here); additional follow-up on a famous poet, José Martí, at **http://www.josemarti.org/ Default.htm.**

Supporting Technology: Web Browser, chatroom at **http://www._____** (instructor inserts chatroom web site here).

What the Student Receives:

(A Spanish version appears at **http://thandbook.heinle.com.**)

UN MÓDULO SOBRE FRIDA KAHLO

Student's name: _____

Interpretive mode: Preparation

Write three things you already know about Frida Kahlo:

_____; _____; _____

Interpretive and Interpersonal modes: Identify the main ideas

Using your Web explorer, visit the following site about Frida Kahlo:
   http://www.telesat.com.co/Telesat/home2/galeria/kahlo/index.html

Now, answer the following questions:
   Look at the photo of Frida, taken around 1938–1939, by her lover Nickolas Muray. (This photo is the front page of the Frida Kahlo homepage, which also contains the buttons, called *pasillos,* that you will use to access the other parts of this page. It is in Appendix 12.3 of this *Teacher's Handbook.*)

What impression does her face/expression give you? _____

What do you think her personality was like? Why? _____

Write three adjectives that describe her clothing: _____

Describe her hair. What does her pose suggest to you? _____

Identify details

Now, select three of the buttons, and read the descriptions of the paintings you see at each. Write the Spanish for these words:

monkey _____   spider web _____
obsessive love _____   matriarchal _____
domination _____   self-portrait _____
overcome _____   abortion _____
married people _____   spinal column _____
developed _____

Now, write two uses of the true passive voice you found in the descriptions you read. (to be + past participle; ejemplo: they were exposed)

_____; _____

Now, write two uses of the use of *se* to express the passive that you found in the descriptions (example: *se reveló*).

_____; _____

Organize main ideas

Now, imagine that you have to explain to a student in another class the life and work of Frida Kahlo. Write five sentences about these aspects of her life and work.

   Personal life: where she's from, her body, her marriage, her lovers
   Art: reflection of her personality as a Mexican woman, as a European woman
   Symbols: animals, hair, blood
   Events in her life: abortion, marriage, separation

_____
_____
_____
_____

Presentational mode: Recreate the text

Now, write a brief summary about Frida Kahlo that the authors of your textbook might add to the text. You must include the use of new vocabulary you have learned in this module, the use of the true passive voice, and the use of *se* in the passive.

_____
_____
_____

Interpersonal and Interpretive modes: React to the text, explore other similar texts

Now, in the chatroom (which you can find at your instructor's homepage, _____; write five opinions of six lines each about what you have read and seen in the work of Frida Kahlo. You may have to visit some additional *pasillos* to have enough to say or to respond to the commentary of your group members.

If you liked the art and poetry you found in Chapter 8 of your textbook, *Enlaces,* you might visit the homepage of José Martí, at **http://www.josemarti.org/Default.htm**.

language learning. They hoped that what they devised could be used as a template for other modules they might devise or for other teachers in other languages. Knowing that they would have to check the web sites regularly since they can change and disappear, they created a technology-enhanced foreign language module on Frida Kahlo.

Evaluation:

1. Students will be evaluated on the accuracy of their completion of the module pages, that is, how well they completed the process of prereading, identifying main ideas, identifying details of vocabulary and grammar, organizing main ideas, recreating the text, reacting to the text, and exploring other texts. Since this will be done outside of class as homework, only a completion grade will be assigned.

2. Students will be evaluated on the paragraph they write in the section for recreation of the text using this grid (numbers of points may be manipulated according to the instructor's and learners' goals):

RECREATION OF TEXT EVALUATION

Student's name: _____

Module Name: Frida Kahlo

Content: Summary of Frido Kahlo's life and work

Main ideas about her life	2 4 6 8 10
Main ideas about her work	2 4 6 8 10
Details about her life	2 4 6 8 10
Details about her work	2 4 6 8 10
Interpreting products of the culture	2 4 6 8 10
Interpreting perspectives on roles of women and men as artists	2 4 6 8 10
Interpreting perspectives on roles of women and men in Mexican society	2 4 6 8 10

Structure of the paragraph:

Use of *new vocabulary*	2 4 6 8 10
Use of grammar: *passive voice with se*	2 4 6 8 10
Use of grammar: *true passive voice*	2 4 6 8 10

Total: _____ /100

---

3. Students will be evaluated on the quality, length, and frequency of their comments in the chatroom using this grid (points may be manipulated according to the instructor's and learners' goals):

CHATROOM EVALUATION

Student name: _____

Module name: Frida Kahlo

Frequency of entries: 5 opinions required (5 points each entry)   5   10   15   20   25

Length of entries: 6 lines each (5 points for each entry that is six lines long)   5   10   15   20   25

Quality of entries: must be opinions about the work and life of Frida Kahlo

    Are the entries opinions about the life and work of Kahlo?   **Yes = 5 points   No = 0 points**

    Do the entries reflect an understanding about the role of men and women as artists as revealed in Kahlo's work?   **Yes = 5 points   No = 0 points**

    Do the entries reflect an understanding of the relationships between men and women in Mexican society in the first half of the twentieth century?   **Yes = 5 points   No = 0 points**

Form of entries:

    Does the student present information in the past and present?
      Yes = 5 points   No = 0 points

    Does the student ask for the opinions of others?   **Yes = 5 points   No = 0 points**

    Does the student respond to the opinions of others?   **Yes = 5 points   No = 0 points**

Use of *new vocabulary*	1 2 3 4 5
Use of grammar: *passive voice with se*	1 2 3 4 5
Use of grammar: *true passive voice*	1 2 3 4 5
Use of subjunctive to state opinions/hypotheses	1 2 3 4 5

Total: _____/100

Ask yourself these questions:

1. What principles of language learning have you learned in this *Teacher's Handbook* that you also see embodied in this module?

2. What elements of the module appear especially workable to you? What elements appear to need more development?

To prepare the case:

Read Blyth (1999) for a description of other approaches to web-based learning; read Kern (1995) for summaries of student-to-student interactions in chatrooms.

1. What elements of the curricular weave do you see in this module?

2. Here are some selections from the chatroom-written "conversations" learners had after completing the module. These comments were written in Spanish, over several days, according to the learners' schedules. Identify the the five Cs, and the elements

of the curricular weave in these comments. Identify discourse about the topic, about the computer mediation, about personal opinions, and about extended learning. Ultimately, determine whether you think this tool has been useful for the learners.

Ana: Fine. I've just finished the module on Frida Kahlo, and I'm happy about that because I had not seen her work before doing this homework. Some things I remember about Kahlo are that her works contain many symbols from literature, poetry, and religion. Maybe members of the group can discuss the monkey or the hair in her works. Or, tell me, which painting by Kahlo do you like?

Katia: Hi! I like to study Kahlo. I like the work in which she has a monkey on her shoulder. I noticed that she painted her own facial hair like a mustache. And, above her eyes, she painted her eyebrows as if they were only one brow. Her hair is long and black, and she used it to express emotion. What do you notice about her work?

Martín: I think that the art of Frida Kahlo is a study in brilliant art that sometimes results from a tragic life. She used mythological Mexican themes, and I like that a lot. Also, the symbolism of the hair and the animals augments the forcefulness of her paintings. In the self-portraits, her masculine face adds a lot of strength too. Above all, I'm interested in the paintings with surrealist themes in her work. My favorite painting is *The Love Embrace of the Universe, Earth, Myself, Diego and Xólotl*.

Susana: I think Frida Kahlo had a sad life. She had to overcome an abortion. Her husband, Diego Rivera, did not support her very well. He dominated her. Then, they got divorced. The public realized that she had two personalities.

Ana: Greetings! The monkey is probably a familiar symbol in traditional Mexican tales. The web site for Frida Kahlo says that the monkey is a symbol of lasciviousness, but I'd like to know more about the history of the Mexican people. I like the surreal paintings more than her other paintings. Even the paintings that have her two personalities are very interesting and passionate. What other ideas do you have about the work of Kahlo?

Martín: Well, I like the symbolism of the different clothing to represent her different personalities with love for Diego. The European personality is fresh with love and aristocratic, but the Mexican one has more passion for life and love with Diego. It's important to remember that the heart of the European personality does not have its own blood but is using the blood of the Mexican Frida. The heart of the true Frida is the one that has blood in it. I think that Frida was saying that sometimes she had doubts, but her true personality was filled with love for Diego. Do you all agree?

Ana: Yes, I agree with Martín's comments. The paintings of Kahlo unfold the broad variety of feelings she had for Diego. On another web page, at another site for Kahlo she says: They say I was a surrealist, but I wasn't. I never painted dreams. I painted my reality." (I don't know how to do a *tilde* on the computer.) I think this quote says a lot about the world and personality of Kahlo. It's possible that I might go to the National Museum of Women in the Arts in Washington to see some of Kahlo's paintings during our next break. They have a self-portrait of Kahlo that shows her love relationship with Leon Trotsky. What else do you notice about her works?

Martín: I really liked the sentence by Frida about her surrealist paintings. It shows more and more the power of obsessive love in her work. I didn't know that she knew Trotsky, but I think it's not so strange because Diego Rivera, her husband, was communist. Diego also could not travel to the United States for art exhibits because the governments did not approve of his communist ideology. Do you know if Trotsky was a lover of Frida, or did she simply like his ideas?

José: Salvador Dalí was a surrealist, right? The painting *What I Saw in the Water* reminded me of him. Ana wrote in her quote by Kahlo "They say I was . . . " In her paintings there are symbols of the events of her life. She was very surrealistic! She was a realist, but in this painting I don't see it. In the title she says "What I saw . . . " It could be a dream, but . . . I don't know. I'm not sure.

To prepare for class discussion, think and write about these topics:

Apply the questions on p. 354 of this chapter to use in this or a similar module to see if this is useful for you. Using a lesson you have prepared or a topic in the textbook from which you teach, find a web site that uses authentic language and create a short module of your own, using the process for interactive reading and listening described in Chapter 6. The module template appears in Appendix 12.4.

To get started using recent technologies, try the following (Scinicariello, 1998, p. 37):

- FLTEACH at http://www.cortland.edu/www_root/flteach/flteach.html
- Lixi-Purcell, Andreas. Internet Foreign Language Studies Workshops. Web document URL: http://www.uncg.edu:80/~lixpurc/publications/Internet_Workshops.html
- On-line journals have now been established. Try this one for starters: *Language Learning and Technology* at http://polyglot.cal.msu.edu/llt.
- For German teachers wishing to use e-mail, the Transatlantic Classroom (TAC) has been established between schools in Chicago and Hamburg and is moderated by the Goethe Institute of Chicago and the Körber Stiftung of Hamburg (see Fischer, 1996).
- Also, consult the National K–12 Foreign Language Resource Center at N131 Lagomarcino Hall, Iowa State University, Ames, Iowa 50011, (515) 294-6699 or http://www.educ.iastate.edu/nflrc.
- The Spanish Embassy prepared *Materiales 26: Los recursos de Internet,* August–September 1998, which includes several step-wise modules for students and teachers to experience on the Web.
- ACTFL's site is http://www.actfl.org.
- For excellent graphically illustrated assistance for teaching with the Web, consult Brooks (1997) or Williams (1995)
- See Warschauer and Healey (1998) for a listing of web sites and addresses of journals, professional organizations, and other resources for TELL.

References

Abraham, R. G., & Liou, H. C. (1991). Interaction generated by three computer programs. In P. Dunkel (Ed.), *Computer-assisted language learning and testing* (pp. 85–109). New York: Newbury House.

Adair-Hauck, B., Youngs, B. E., & Willingham-McLain, L. (1998). *Assessing the integration of technology and second language learning.* Paper presented at the meeting of the American Council on the Teaching of Foreign Languages, Chicago, IL.

Altman, R. 1989. *The video connection.* Boston: Houghton Mifflin.

Aplevich, P. A., & Willment, J. A. (1998). Teaching and learning language through distance education: The challenges, expectations, and outcomes. In J. Harper, M. G. Lively, & M. K. Williams (Eds.), *The coming of age of the profession: Issues and emerging ideas for the teaching of foreign languages* (pp. 53–77). Boston: Heinle & Heinle.

Beauvois, M. H. (1992). Computer-assisted classroom discussion in the foreign language classroom: Conversation in slow motion. *Foreign Language Annals, 25,* 455–464.

Beauvois, M. H. (1997). Computer-mediated communication (CMC): Technology for improving speaking and writing. In Bush, M. D., & Terry, R. M. (Eds.). *Technology-enhanced language learning* (pp. 165–184). American Council on the Teaching of Foreign Languages. Lincolnwood, IL: NTC/Contemporary Publishing Group.

Bloom, M. E. (1995). Using early silent film to teach French: The language of *cinéma muet*. *ADFL Bulletin, 2,* 25–37.

Blyth, C. (1999). *Untangling the web.* New York: Nonce Publishing Consultants, Ltd.

Borrás, I., & Lafayette, R. C. (1994). Effects of multimedia courseware subtitling on the speaking performance of college students of French. *The Modern Language Journal, 78,* 61–75.

Brooks, D. W. (1997). *Web-teaching: A guide to designing interactive teaching for the world-wide web.* New York: Plenum Press.

Bush, M. D., & Terry, R. M. (1997). *Technology-enhanced language learning.* American Council on the Teaching of Foreign Languages. Lincolnwood, IL: NTC/Contemporary Publishing Group.

Chang, K. R., & Smith, W. F. (1991). Cooperative learning and CALL/IVD in beginning Spanish: An experiment. *The Modern Language Journal, 75,* 205–211.

Chapelle, C., & Jamieson, J. (1986). Computer-assisted language learning as a predictor of success in acquiring English as a second language. *TESOL Quarterly, 20,* 27–46.

Chávez, C. L. (1997). Students take flight with *Daedalus:* Learning Spanish in a networked classroom. *Foreign Language Annals, 30,* 26–37.

Chun, D. M., & Brandl, K. K. (1992). Beyond form-based drill and practice: Meaning-enhanced CALL on the Macintosh. *Foreign Language Annals, 25,* 255–267.

Chun, D., & Plass, J. (1996). Effects of multimedia annotations on vocabulary acquisition. *The Modern Language Journal, 80,* 183–98.

Chun, D., & Plass, J. (1999). *Ciberteca: Una carta a Dios.* New York: Nonce Publishing Consultants, Ltd.

Coleman, D. W. (1985). *Terri:* A CALL lesson simulating conversational interaction. In D. Crookall, (Ed.), *Simulation applications in L2 education and research.* Oxford: Pergamon Press.

Cononelos, T., & Oliva, M. (1993). Using computer networks to enhance foreign language/culture education. *Foreign Language Annals, 26,* 527–534.

Cook, V. J., & Fass, D. (1986). Natural language processing in EFL. In J. Higgins (Ed.), *How real is a computer simulation? ELT documents* 113. London: British Council.

Crookall, D., & Oxford, R. L. (1990). *Simulation, gaming, and language learning.* New York: Newbury House.

Cubillos, J. (1998). Technology: A step forward in the teaching of foreign languages. In J. Harper, M. G. Lively, & M. K. Williams, (Eds.), *The coming of age of the profession* (pp. 37–52). Boston, MA: Heinle & Heinle.

Davis, J. N., & Lyman-Hager, M. A. (1997). Computers and L2 reading: Student performance, student attitudes. *Foreign Language Annals, 30,* 58–72.

Domínguez, F., Noblitt, J., & Pet, W. (1998). *Atajo.* Boston: MA: Heinle & Heinle.

Donato, R. (1999, February 9). Personal communication.

Esling, J. H. (1991). Researching the effects of networking. In P. Dunkel (Ed.), *Computer-assisted language learning and testing* (pp. 111–131). New York: Newbury House.

Fischer, G. (1996). Tourist or explorer? Reflection in the foreign language classroom. *Foreign Language Annals, 29,* 73–81.

Furstenberg, G. (1999). *Dans un quartier de Paris.* New Haven: Yale University Press.

Furstenberg, G., & Malone, S. A. (1993). *A la rencontre de Philippe.* New Haven: Yale University Press.

Garrett, N. (1991). Technology in the service of language learning: Trends and issues. *The Modern Language Journal, 75,* 74–101.

Garza, T. J. (1991). Evaluating the use of captioned video material in advanced foreign language learning. *Foreign Language Annals, 24,* 239–258.

Gates, W. (1995). *The road ahead.* Allentown, PA: Viking.

Gendron, B. (1977). *Technology and the human condition.* New York: St. Martin's.

Glisan, E. W., Dudt, K. P., & Howe, M. S. (1998). Teaching Spanish through distance education: Implications of a pilot study. *Foreign Language Annals, 31,* 48–66.

Grace, C. A. (1998). Retention of word meanings inferred from context and sentence-level translations: Implications for the design of beginning-level CALL software. *The Modern Language Journal, 82,* 533–544.

Hanley, J. E. B., Herron, C. A., & Cole, S. P. (1995). Using video as an advance organizer to a written passage in the FLES classroom. *The Modern Language Journal, 70,* 99–106.

Heinich, R., Molenda, M., Russell, J. D., & Smaldino, S. E. (1996). *Instructional media and technologies for learning.* Englewood Cliffs, NJ: Prentice Hall.

Herron, C. (1994). An investigation of the effectiveness of using an advance organizer to introduce video in the foreign language classroom. *The Modern Language Journal, 78,* 190–198.

Herron, C., Cole, S. P., York, H., & Linden, P. (1998). A comparison study of student retention of foreign language video: Declarative versus interrogative advance organizer. *The Modern Language Journal, 82,* 237–247.

Herron, C. A., & Hanley, J. E. B., (1992). Using video to introduce children to culture. *Foreign Languge Annals, 25,* 419–426.

Herron, C. A., Hanley, J. E. B., Cole, S. P. (1995). A comparison study of two advance organizers for introducing beginning foreign language students to video. *The Modern Language Journal, 79,* 387–395.

Herron, C., & Tomasello, M. (1992). Acquiring grammatical structures by guided induction. *French Review, 65,* 708–718.

Hughes, H. E. (1989). Conversion of a teacher delivered course into an interactive videodisc delivered program. *Foreign Language Annals, 26,* 392–398.

Hughes, H. E. (1993). *Khorosho!* An interactive videodisc survival Russian Program. *Foreign Language Annals, 26,* 392–398.

Ito, Y. (1996). Communication between high school and college Japanese language education: Implications from a survey on the use of video materials in the United States. *Foreign Language Annals, 29,* 463–479.

Jenkins, D. (1999, January 26). Personal communication.

Jenlink, P., & Carr, A. (1996). Conversation as a medium for change in education. *Educational Technology, 36*(1), 31–38.

Johansen, K., & Tennyson, R. (1983). Effects of adaptive advisement perception in learner-controlled, computer-based instruction using a rule-learning task. *Educational Communication and Technology, 31,* 226–236.

Johnson, D. M. (1991) Second language and content learning with computers: Research in the role of social factors. In P. Dunkel (Ed.), *Computer-assisted language learning and testing: Research issues and practice* (pp. 61–83). New York: Newbury House.

Johnson, D. W., & Johnson, R. T. (1986). Computer-assisted cooperative learning. *Educational Technology, 26,* 12–18.

Johnson, R. T., Johnson, D. W., & Stanne, M. B. (1986). Comparison of computer-assisted cooperative, competitive and individualistic learning. *American Educational Research Journal, 23,* 382–392.

Joiner, E. G. (1990). Choosing and using videotext. *Foreign Language Annals, 23,* 53–64.

Jones, K. (1982). *Simulations in language teaching.* Cambridge: Cambridge University Press.

Kassen, M. A., & Higgins, C. J. (1997). Meeting the technology challenge: Introducing teachers to language-learning technology. In M. D. Bush, & R. M. Terry, (Eds.). *Technology-enhanced language learning* (pp. 165–184). American Council on the Teaching of Foreign Languages. Lincolnwood, IL: NTC/Contemporary Publishing Group.

Kern. R. G. (1995). Restructuring classroom interaction with networked computers: Effects on quantity and characteristics of language production. *The Modern Language Journal, 79,* 457–476.

Kinginger, C. (1998). Videoconferencing as access to spoken French. *The Modern Language Journal, 82,* 502–513.

Kossuth, K. C., Noblitt, J., & Pet, W. (1998). *Quelle*. Boston, MA: Heinle & Heinle.

Kreeft Peyton, J. K. (1986). Computer networking: Making connections between speech and writing. *ERIC/CLL News Bulletin, 10*, 5–7.

Kreeft Peyton, J. K., & Mackinson-Smyth, J. (1989). Writing and talking about writing: Computer networking with elementary students. In D. M. Johnson (Ed.), *Richness in writing: Empowering ESL students*. New York: Longman.

Kulik, C. C., & Kulik, J. A. (1986). Effectiveness of computer-based education in colleges. *AEDS Journal, 2*, 267–276.

Kulik, J. A., & Kulik, C.C. (1987). Review of recent research literature on computer-based instruction. *Contemporary Educational Psychology, 12*, 222–230.

Larson, J., & Bush, C. (1992). *Montevidisco*. Provo, UT: Brigham Young University.

Lavery, M. (1981). *Active viewing*. Canterbury, MA: Pilgrim's Publications.

Lonergan, J. (1984). *Using video in language teaching*. Cambridge: Cambridge University Press.

Masters-Wicks, K., Postlewate, L., & Lewental, M. (1996). Developing interactive instructional software for language acquisition. *Foreign Language Annals, 29*, 217–22.

Maxim, H. H. (1998). Authorizing the foreign language student. *Foreign Language Annals, 31*, 407–430.

Maxwell, D. (1998). Technology and foreign language learning. A report to the Charles E. Culpeper Foundation. Washington, D.C.: National Foreign Language Center.

Moore, M., & Thompson, M. (1997). *The effects of distance learning 15*. ACSDE Research Monograph. State College, PA: The Pennsylvania State University.

Nagata, N. (1993). Intelligent computer feedback for second language instruction. *The Modern Language Journal, 77*, 330–339.

Nagata, N., & Swisher, M. V. (1995) A study of consciousness-raising by computer: The effect of metalinguistic feedback on second language learning. *Foreign Language Annals, 28*, 337–347.

National Standards in Foreign Language Education Project. (1996). *National standards for foreign language learning: Preparing for the 21st century*. Lawrence, KS: Allen Press.

Newby, T. J., Stepich, D. A., Lehman, J. D., & Russell, J. D. (1996). *Instructional technology for teaching and learning*. Englewood Cliffs, NJ: Prentice Hall.

Nielsen, M. & Hoffman, E. (1996). Technology, reform and foreign language standards: A vision for change. In R. Lafayette (Ed.), *National standards: A catalyst for reform* (pp. 119–137). Lincolnwood, IL: NTC/Contemporary Publishing Group.

Noblitt, J. S., Pet, W. J. A., & Solá, D. (1991). *Système-D 2.0*. Boston, MA: Heinle & Heinle.

Oliva, M., & Pollastrini, Y. (1995). Internet resources and second language acquisition: An evaluation of virtual immersion. *Foreign Language Annals, 28*, 551–563.

Oliver, W., & Nelson, T. (1997a). *Un Misterio en Toluca*. Boston: Heinle & Heinle.

Oliver, W., & Nelson, T. (1997b). *Un Muertre à Cinet*. Boston: Heinle & Heinle.

Otto, S. K., & Pusack, J. P. (1996). Technological choices to meet the challenges. In Wing, B. (Ed.), *Foreign languages for all* (pp. 141–186), Northeast Conference on the Teaching of Foreign Languages. Lincolnwood, IL: NTC/Contemporary Publishing Group.

Otto, S. K., & Pusack, J. P. (1997). Taking control of multimedia. In M. D. Bush, & R. M. Terry, (Eds.), *Technology-enhanced language learning* (pp. 1–48), American Council on the Teaching of Foreign Languages, Lincolnwood, IL: NTC/Contemporary Publishing Group.

Oxford, R., Park-Oh, Y., Ito, S., & Sumrall, M. (1993). Factors affecting achievement in a satellite-delivered Japanese language program. *The American Journal of Distance Education, 7(1)* 11–25.

Oyono, F. (1956). *Une vie de boy*. Paris: Julliard.

Pederson, K. M., (1986). An experiment in computer-assisted second-language reading. *The Modern Language Journal, 70*, 36–41.

Pederson, K. M., (1987). Research on CALL. In W. F. Smith (Ed.), *Modern media in foreign language education: Theory and implementation* (pp. 99–131). Lincolnwood, IL: NTC/Contemporary Publishing Group.

Pennington, M., (1996). *The computer and the non-native writer: An natural partnership.* Cresskill, NJ: Hampton Press.

Phinney, M., (1991). Computer-assisted writing and writing apprehension in ESL students. In P. Dunkel (Ed.), *Computer-assisted language learning and testing,* (pp. 189–204). Rowley, MA: Newbury House.

Piper, A. (1986). Conversation and the computer: A study of conversational spin-off generated among learners of English as a foreign language working in groups. *System, 14,* 187–198.

Rankin, W. (1997). Increasing the communicative competence of foreign language students through the FL chatroom. *Foreign Language Annals, 30,* 542–546.

Robinson, G. (1989). The CLCCS CALL study: Methods, error feedback, attitudes, and achievement. In W. F. Smith (Ed.), *Modern technology in foreign language education: Applications and projects* (pp. 119–134). Lincolnwood, IL: NTC/Contemporary Publishing Group.

Robinson, S. D. (1998) *Viaje virtual.* Unpublished manuscript. Blacksburg, VA: Department of Foreign Languages and Literatures, Virginia Tech.

Saettler, P. (1990). *The evolution of American educational technology.* Englewood, CO: Libraries Unlimited.

Scinicariello, S. (1998). Getting started in networked computing: Basic resources for foreign language teachers. *Northeast Conference Newsletter, 43,* 33–36.

Scott, V. (1990). Task-oriented creative writing with *Système-D. CALICO Journal,* 7(2), 58–67.

Scott, V. (1992). Writing from the start: A task-oriented developmental writing program for foreign language students. In R. M. Terry (Ed.) *Dimension: Language '91, making a world of difference* (pp. 1–15). Valdosta, GA: Southern Conference on Language Teaching.

Secules, T., Herron, C., & Tomasello, M. (1992). The effect of video context on foreign language learning. *Foreign Language Annals, 28,* 527–535.

Stempleski, S., & Tomalin, B. (1990). *Video in action.* New York: Prentice Hall.

Sussex, R. (1991). Current issues in distance language education and open learning: An overview and an Australian perspective. In Ervin, G. L. (Ed.), *International perspectives on foreign language teaching.* (pp. 177–193), American Council on the Teaching of Foreign Languages. Lincolnwood, IL: NTC/Contemporary Publishing Group.

Swaffar, J., & Vlatten, A. (1997). A sequential model for video viewing in the foreign language curriculum. *The Modern Language Journal, 81,* 175–188.

Underwood, J. (1984). *Linguistics, computers and the language teacher: A communicative approach.* Rowley, MA: Newbury House.

United States Department of Education. (August 3, 1998). The Technology Literacy Challenge. Office of Educational Technology. Available: http://www.ed.gov/Technology [1998, November 19].

Walz, J. (1998). Meeting the standards for foreign language learning with world wide web activities. *Foreign Language Annals, 31,* 103–104.

Warriner-Burke, H. (1990) Distance learning: What we don't know can hurt us. *Foreign Language Annals, 23,* 129–133.

Warschauer, M., & Healey, D. (1998). *Language Learning, 31*(2), 57–71.

Warschauer, M. (1995). *E-mail for English teaching.* Alexandria, VA: TESOL Publications.

Williams, B. (1995). *The Internet for teachers.* Foster City, CA: IDG Books.

Wyatt, D. H. (1987). Applying pedagogical principles to CALL software development. In W. F. Smith, (Ed.), *Modern media in foreign language education: Theory and implementation* (pp. 85–89). Lincolnwood, IL: NTC/Contemporary Publishing Group.

Yi, H., & Majima, J. (1993). The teacher-learner relationship and classroom interaction in distance learning: A case study of the Japanese language classes at an American high school. *Foreign Language Annals, 26,* 211–30.

INDEX

A

ACTFL (American Council on the Teaching of Foreign Languages)
  guidelines, 63
  rating scale, levels of, 173
Activities
  cooperative learning, 182; 199–203
  imaginative, 203–204
  information gap, 195
  interactive, 180–181
  jigsaw, 183–185
  simulation, 204–205
  task-oriented, 234–235
Affect and motivation, role of, 13–14
American Council on the Teaching of Foreign Languages. *See* ACTFL
Anxiety level
  activities arranged by, 116
  ranking of, 115
Assessing language performance, 291 ff.
At-risk students, 268–270
Audiolingual Method (ALM), 26
Authentic materials, 57–58;
  texts, 57–58
  use, 130–132
Authentic performance task template, 313
Authentic tasks, 300–304

B

Bottom-up approach, 33

C

Communication, 146–148
  three modes of, 134–136
    elementary school, 226–227
  written, 225 ff.
Communicative CALL, 335–336
Communicative competence
  Canale and Swain, 2
  Chomsky, 2

Communicative gap exercise
  Example, 338–339
Communicative modes, 120–121; 122
  framework for, 122
Communities goal area, 278–279
Community-based learning
  Kolb's model, 280
Community Language Learning (Curran), 27
Comparisons goal area, 107–111
Comprehension and interpretation, 125–128
  text-based factors, 128–130
  variables, 125–128
Connections goal area, 91
Content-based instruction (CBI), 58–60; 86
Content-compatible objectives, 86
Content-obligatory objectives, 86
Contextualized tests, 303–304
Cooperative learning, 88–89
  Activities, 182–199
    examples, 183–194; 196–197
  Interactive activities, 180–181
  Strategies, 88–89
Culture
  Learning through, 89–90
  Practices, products, perspectives, 107

D

Daily lesson planning, 62–65
  Designing, 63–65
  Objectives, 62–63
Direct method, 26

E

Elementary school level, 78–84; 85
  Children's developmental characteristics, 80
  FLES programs, 84–85
  Foreign language program goals, 82–83
  Program models, 79–84
  Strategies, 85
  Writing, 226–227
Episode Hypothesis (Oller), 51–52

F

FLES (Foreign Language in the Elementary School), 76–78; 79–86
FLEX (Foreign Language Exploratory or Experience); 76; 79–84
Foreign Language Exploratory or Experience. *See* FLEX
Foreign Language in the Elementary School. *See* FLES
Foreign language learning
defined, 2
Five Cs of, 29–30
Standards, 30

G

Gifted students, 271–272
Strategies, 273
Global units, 90
Grammar instruction, 148–148; 149–150
approaches, 150; 158
explicit/implicit controversy, 148–149
reformulation of, 149–150
Group
activities, 201–203
structuring tasks, 200–201
teaching interaction skills, 199–200

H

Heritage language learners, 272–274
goals and strategies, 275–276, 277
Home background students, 275
journal writing for, 278
strategies, 276–278

I

Imaginative activities, 203–204
Immersion instruction, 81–82
Information gap activities, 195
Examples, 183–194; 196–197
Input, 55–57
I-R-E (Input-Response-Evaluation) 55–57; 177
I-R-F (Input-Response-Feedback), 57; 177
Input Hypothesis (Krashen), 3
Instructional conversation (IC), 177–178

Instructional planning, 50–51
Interactional competence, 12–13
Interaction Hypothesis (Long), 5–6
Interactive listening, 127
strategies, 127
Interlanguage, defined, 6
Interlanguage theory, 6
Interpretive communication, 121–124
reading skills, 121; 133–134; 134–136
listening skills, 121
viewing process, 124–125

J

Jigsaw activities, 183–185
Journal writing, 230
for home background students, 278

K

Kluckhohn Model, 109
Kolb's model of community-based learning, 280

L

Language lab, 324–325
Language learning
approaches, 256–262
defined, 2
input, role of, 2–3
methods, 256
model, 261–262
strategies, 260–262
technology enhanced, 319–323
Language play, 11–12
Learner needs, 262–281
Learning center, 89
Learning-disabled students, 262–268
Learning styles, 256–260
Listening, 87
characteristics, 126–127
skills, 121
Long-term instructional planning, 60–61
unit planning, 61

M

N

O

P

R

S

T

NOTES

NOTES